THE ALLIANCE OF Pirates

Ireland and Atlantic piracy in the early seventeenth century

Penar
Don Hog
Croock haven
Mesan hed
80

THE ALLIANCE OF Pirates

Ireland and Atlantic piracy in the early seventeenth century

Connie Kelleher

CORK UNIVERSITY PRESS

First published in 2020 by
Cork University Press
Boole Library
University College Cork
Cork T12 ND89
Ireland

Reprinted 2023

Library of Congress Control Number: 2019955525

Distribution in the USA Longleaf Services, Chapel Hill,
NC, USA.

British Library Cataloguing in Publication Data
A CIP catalogue record for this book is available from the British Library.

ISBN 978-1-78205-365-1
Printed by Gutenberg in Malta
Typeset by Alison Burns at Studio 10 Design, Cork

Cover image credits –

FRONT COVER AND SPINE: The 1612 chart of southwest Munster and the area of Roaringwater Bay drafted by English cartographer John Hunt. Commissioned by Dutch hydrographer Hessel Gerritszoon on behalf of the States-General, the chart is one of four found within a leeskaart written to inform on the harbours of Ireland in an effort to rid them of pirates.
SUB GÖTTINGEN, 4 H BRIT P III, 6 RARA, UNIVERSITÄTSBIBLIOTHEK, GÖTTINGEN, GERMANY

FLAPS: The province of Munster, Ireland, dated c. 1595, artist unknown. The chart shows Munster with lands targeted for resettlement under the plantation following the failed Irish rebellion and fall of the Gaelic order.
E9078, P/49(27), NATIONAL MARITIME MUSEUM, GREENWICH, LONDON

To Rob, for everything.

In memory of Lee Snodgrass –
a true pirate queen

CONTENTS

ACKNOWLEDGEMENTS

I first went to Baltimore in the mid-1990s to study the O'Driscoll lordship. Very quickly, however, I encountered pirates. While the O'Driscolls were at times accused of piracy, it became clear that there had been a separate and distinct piratical power in place in southwest Munster during the early part of the seventeenth century. The idea that pirates had walked the foreshore and sailed the waters of Roaringwater Bay intrigued me and I wondered if they had left any physical trace of their existence – above or below the water. So began my fascination with the Alliance of Pirates.

This book has been a long time in the writing due in no small part to distractions from other work projects and the intervention of life in general. It could not have happened, however, without the support and assistance of certain institutions and individuals. The Department of Culture, Heritage and the Gaeltacht funded my initial doctoral thesis and the support of senior staff in the National Monuments Service (NMS) was always forthcoming: former Acting Chief Archaeologist Dr Ann Lynch, who also graciously supplied information and images from her excavations on Sherkin Island; former Senior Archaeologist Con Manning, who sourced images for me, and the NMS Photographic Unit, in particular Con Brogan, John Lalor and Tony Roche, who supplied images of national monument sites for use in the book. My two colleagues in the Underwater Archaeology Unit (UAU), Senior Archaeologist Fionnbarr Moore and Karl Brady, have been constant advocates and allies.

In Trinity College Dublin, Prof. Jane Ohlmeyer encouraged, supervised and guided my research throughout my time there, while her colleagues Prof. Micheál Ó Siochrú, Dr Paul Ferguson, Dr Kevin Costello and Dr David Brown graciously shared their wisdom and knowledge. In the Berkeley Library, Mark Brennan remains my faceless cohort, and his assistance has been invaluable – thank you, Mark. Dr John Appleby of Liverpool Hope University was a fountain of knowledge and advice and his work over the years on the pirates of Munster and piracy in general continues to be a source of inspiration.

Dr Elaine Murphy of Plymouth University was and remains a constant co-conspirator in all things 'piraty'. I would like to thank her for tirelessly transcribing many, many manuscripts for me and for her continued scholarly engagement. Other colleagues too deserve due acknowledgement: Prof. Audrey Horning of the College of William and Mary, Virginia and Queen's

University Belfast, who has supported me to the very end; Dr Colin Breen, University of Ulster, Coleraine; Dr James Lyttleton of AECOM, Bristol, and freelance senior archaeological consultant Eamon Cotter; Prof. Richard Pennell of Melbourne University whose expert understanding of the history of the Islamic world of North Africa was fundamental, along with his supplying of source information and images; Dr Wendy Duivenbord of Flinders University, Australia, who helped with details on Dutch ship typology; Dr David Heffernan of Queen's University Belfast, who freely shared information on his and Dr David Edwards' work in University College Cork on the Richard Boyle Colonial Landscapes Project.

I would like to thank the following institutions and their staff for providing access to their collections and granting permission to reproduce material from their holdings: Trinity College Dublin; University College Cork; Royal Irish Academy, Dublin; London Metropolitan Archives and City of London Corporation; Fr Tim Hanley and Garlickhythe Church and Cemetery, London; The National Archives, London; Greenwich Maritime Museum (Royal Museums, Greenwich), London; Museum of London Archives; Sheffield City Library Archives; Birmingham University Archives; National Portrait Gallery, Scotland; The Huntingham Library, San Marino, California, USA; Georg-August-Universität, Göttingen, Germany, particularly Dr Helmut Rohlfing and Bärbel Mund, for their assistance over the years when accessing the Hessel Gerritszoon document and for granting permission to reproduce it. Aisling Collins Archaeological Services (ACAS), Dublin and Mizen Archaeology, Cork both provided access to their material and gave permission to publish images of artefacts from their excavations. RM Diving Services, Cork provided sponsorship towards the colour reproductions in the book, for which I am very grateful. Professional photographer and friend, Cathal Twomey, deserves due thanks for giving graciously of his time for certain imagery in the book.

Throughout the process of research and writing on pirates, I had the pleasure of engaging with many residents of west Cork, who were always willing to help with their time, local knowledge and locations of new sites. They all deserve due credit: Thomas and Jane Somerville of Drishane House, Castlehaven; Terri Kearney of Skibbereen Heritage Centre; Brian, Corrine and Jenny Marten, Ringaroige Island, Baltimore; Tom and Aidan Bushe of Bushe's Bar, Baltimore; Bernie and Pat McCarthy of Dún na Séad Castle, Baltimore; Rabbi Baroness Julia Neuberger and her husband Prof. Anthony

Neuberger, of Leamcon House, Schull; Diarmuid and Nora O'Donovan of Leamcon; Niall Hyde of Leamcon Castle, Castlepoint, Schull. Special thanks are owing to Nigel Towes of Sherkin Island, Baltimore, in whose beautiful Heir Island lobster boat *Hanora* we sailed among the islands in Roaringwater and Baltimore Bays, where we re-traced the routes of the pirates.

Dr Peter Murray, former curator of the Crawford Municipal Art Gallery, Cork and accomplished maritime artist, freely supplied copies of two of his paintings for reproduction in this book; Nick Hogan of University College Cork (UCC) undertook the mapping imagery, and is ever so gracious with his time and expertise; Prof. William O'Brien, head of the Archaeology Department, UCC, has always provided academic support and indispensable advice. I am very grateful to Cork University Press (CUP), and particularly Mike Collins and Maria O'Donovan, for commissioning the book, patience while I finished it and for their high standards in publication. For CUP, I am very grateful to Aonghus Meaney for his copy editing skills, and to Studio 10 Design, Cork for their excellent design and layout. The anonymous reviewers are also due acknowledgement for their welcome comments and suggestions.

Fieldwork formed a large part of my research, and I did not go it alone. On many a trip fellow wenches Mary Jordan, Julianna O'Donoghue, Áine Brosnan and Lee Snodgrass were by my side. I will remember those trips forever.

Friend and colleague Madeline O'Brien went beyond the call of duty and friendship with her professional editorial skills and advice on drafts of this book: her expert eye and guiding hand are embedded within these pages. I will never be able to repay those hours. A book like this inevitably takes up the time that should be spent with family and loved ones. The support of my brothers Nigel and Conor, sisters-in-law Marian and Ger, nieces Irene, Andrea and Tara and their partners, Adrian, Jack and Yuhei, has always been unwavering and for that I am truly grateful.

My husband Rob has lived with this book as long as he has lived with me. He has been my promoter, my staunch supporter, my greatest constructive critic and my most patient partner. I could not have done it without him.

CONNIE KELLEHER
Ballyvourney, Macroom, County Cork
January 2020

CONVENTIONS

DATE: The start of the year is taken as 1 January. Unless indicated otherwise, dates relating to primary sources consulted are entered according to the Julian calendar. Where primary sources are referred to from secondary source material, the date given is as used in the secondary source.

MONEY CONVERSIONS: The National Archives' (London) Currency Converter: 1270–2017(http://www.nationalarchives.gov.uk/currency-converter) has been used to obtain an approximate value for both contemporary and modern periods. XE Currency Converter: Live Rates (https://www.xe.com/currencyconverter) has been used to convert sterling values to their euro equivalent. The conversions are not a categorical fact but a general guide to historical values in modern equivalent terms.

PLACENAMES: Contemporary names of places are retained where they appear frequently within the sources, a case in point being 'Villafranca'. Its modern name is that of Villefranche-sur-Mer but could be variously written 'Villafranca', 'Villefranca' or 'Villafrancha' in contemporary sources. 'Villafranca' has been used throughout this publication.

LIST OF ILLUSTRATIONS

ABBREVIATIONS

APC	Acts of the Privy Council
ASI	Archaeological Survey of Ireland
BL	British Library, London
Cal. Carew MSS	*Calendar of Carew Manuscript, Lambeth Palace Library, London*
Cal. Salisbury MSS	*Calendar of the Manuscripts of the Most Hon. the Marquis of Salisbury, 1612–1668*
Cal. S.P. Col.	*Calendar of State Papers, Colonial, America and West Indies 1720–1721*
Cal. S.P. Dom. Jas. I	*Calendar of State Papers, Domestic, James I, 1603–1640*
Cal. S.P. Eliz. I Add	*Calendar of State Papers, Elizabeth I, 1566–1579*
Cal. S.P. Ire.	*Calendar of State Papers, Ireland, 1558–1782*
Cal. S.P. Ven.	*Calendar of State Papers, Venetian, 1603–1623*
Cal. S.P. Wm. III	*Calendar of State Papers, Domestic, William III, 1697*
Carte MSS	*Carte Manuscript, Bodleian Library, Oxford*
Cottonian MSS	*Cottonian Manuscript, British Museum*
DCHG	Department of Culture, Heritage and the Gaeltacht
EEBO	Early English Books Online
Hardwick MSS	*Hardwick Manuscript, Chatsworth House, Derbyshire*
Harlaein MSS	*Harlaein Manuscript, British Library*
HCA	High Court of Admiralty Papers, TNA, London
HMC	Historical Manuscripts Commission
Lansd. MSS	*Lansdowne Manuscript, British Museum*
MSS	Manuscript
NLI	National Library of Ireland
RAC	Royal African Company Papers, TNA, London
RMP	Register of Monuments and Places
SP	State Papers, TNA, London
TNA	The National Archives, Kew Gardens, London
UAU	Underwater Archaeology Unit, DCHG
WWM	Wentworth Woodhouse Muniments, Sheffield City Library Archives

GLOSSARY

Alehouse: Place where drink (i.e. 'ale') was sold, usually licensed.

Algerine: Contemporary word used to denote a native or inhabitant of Algeria, or something relating to Algeria, like the Ottoman pirates. The modern term would be 'Algerian', but the contemporary word is used within this book.

Alliance: An association of people formed to advance common interests or causes; a connection between parties or individuals to co-operate for specific purposes; a merging of efforts for the advancement of a common cause.

Argosy: A merchant ship, or a fleet of merchant ships operating together.

Bagnio: In antiquity, it refers to a prison or slave quarters (particularly galley slaves) in North Africa during the late-historic and early modern period; can also refer to a brothel or bath house, but it is in the context of a prison that it is used here.

Barbary: Generally refers to the part of the continent now known as North Africa, including Morocco, Algeria, Tunisia and Libya.

Barbary Corsair: Historical term generally referring to North African pirates operating out of Barbary. See **Corsair**.

Bedticks/Bedsticks: Flat bags of straw that acted as mattresses.

Benefit of Clergy: An exemption in English law from trial in the civil courts – which could result in punishment of death – if the accused could show they could read the Bible or another ecclesiastical source, whereupon they came under the auspices of ecclesiastical law for adjudication.

Boatswain (Bo'sun/bosun): A warrant or petty officer on board a ship and in charge of deck duties, with responsibility for the ship's hull, anchors, cordage, sails, rigging, etc.

Bolt: A roll of material; generally a unit of measurement used as an industry standard for materials, lengths of which varied.

Booty: In antiquity, and for the period covered in this book, it refers to plundered or pirated goods.

Bower: Main anchor (formerly called a sheet anchor) on a ship and normally carried at the bow of a vessel.

Buckler: The round lid used as part of the pressing mechanism for extracting train oil from fish; placed at the top of the barrels, press beams slowly moved the buckler downwards inside the barrel to depress the fish inside, with the oil being drained out of the bottom and then collected.

Bulged: A nautical term, to founder or to sink, to fill with water and sink; to founder or sink to the bilges to the point of semi-submergence.

Bullion: Gold or silver, in quantity, usually uncoined; precious metals valued by weight.

Cable: An anchor rope.

Carbuncle: A precious stone, usually almandine, that has a deep scarlet colour and appears to glow when held up to the light.

Careen: To clean the bottom/outer hull of a vessel by means of turning it on its side or listing it to one side or the other.

Carrack: Type of ship, generally dating to the fifteenth century, though variations lasted into the sixteenth century; developed in Western Europe by the Portuguese and further developed by the Spanish; also referred to as a *nau*; three- or four-masted.

Coastal Access Points: The term is applied here to refer to various types of sites, generally rock-cut, that have been identified during the course of this study and that allow access to or from the coastal edge to the sea; examples include rock-cut steps, rock-cut platforms, rock-cut slipways.

Confederacy: An alliance or an association of individuals into a loose community; a league or alliance formed for an unlawful purpose.

Confederate: A member of a confederacy; one who assists in a plot; an accomplice; someone united in a league, alliance, conspiracy or confederacy.

Corsair: An individual pirate or a privately operated vessel usually associated with the Barbary States or the southern coast of the Mediterranean and active during the sixteenth and seventeenth centuries; from the Arabic word *qursan* and the Turkish word *corsar*, which entered the English language through Christian merchants; also has origins in the French word corsaire, from the Latin *cursarius* meaning 'raid' or 'plunder'.

Diapers: Cloths with repeated patterns forming a napkin for general use; in later periods they were to be used for babies, and the English word 'nappy' stems from the original 'napkin'; http://dirtydiaperlaundry.com/the-history-of-cloth-diapers

Doubloon: Generic name from the Spanish world *doblón* meaning 'double' indicating that it was a 2-escudo or 32-real gold coin. It was usually hand minted in Spain and the New World and had a long use period, from the sixteenth to the nineteenth centuries. It superseded the ducat for trade in the New World. See also **Escudo** and **Ducat.**

Ducat: Could be gold or silver and was traded extensively throughout Europe from the Middle Ages and became the currency of choice from the sixteenth century. The name comes from the Latin *ducalis*, with the coins initially associated with a dukedom.

East Indies: Generally taken to represent South and Southeast Asia and the area now comprising the islands of Indonesia and the Philippines.

Entrenchment: A defensive mound of earth placed around a particular location to give protection during military bombardment.

Entrepôt: From the French *entreposer* – to put in; a port where merchandise could be imported and exported without paying import duties, thus providing scope for greater profits.

Escudo: A Spanish gold currency minted from the sixteenth century, it had various values depending on the size and weight of the coin (e.g. originally worth 16 reales); most were minted in Spain, and often bore the Royal Coat of Arms on one side and the mint master's initials on the other; see **Reales** and **Doubloon**.

Fluyt: A Dutch-built vessel for carrying cargo, it was first constructed in the sixteenth century for the transatlantic trade. A speedy vessel, easily managed by crew.

Flyboat (also Flyboate, Vlieboot, Flemish Bottom): Derived from the Dutch word *vlieboot*, these were fast and easily handled vessels primarily of the sixteenth and seventeenth centuries. They were 60–200 tons in size and had shallow draft, hence the ship of choice for pirates.

Follower: See **Seine Fishing**.

Fowling Piece: Earliest smooth-bore hand gun that was filled with lead shot; appeared in Europe in the sixteenth century but in the seventeenth century the barrels were made longer and could be up to six feet long; used generally for game hunting – hence the name.

Frigate: A swift-sailing, fully rigged warship, built for speed and manoeuvrability; it mounted a selection of guns and usually had one or two decks. Designs changed over the centuries, with different deck numbers and rigging configurations.

Golden Age of Piracy: A term used to describe the piracy of the early eighteenth century, generally 1716–26, and focused on the Caribbean, West Indies and African coast.

Grosgrain: A tightly woven fabric that is strong and durable.

Harlot: A Middle English term derived from the French word for a vagabond or beggar; more commonly used in a derogatory sense, suggesting a woman was promiscuous or engaged in prostitution.

Hewer: See **Seine Fishing**.

Historical Archaeology: The study of material culture from the period after *c*. AD 1550, it utilises written sources and/or oral traditions. See **Post-medieval**.

Holland Cloth: Plain-woven, unbleached or dull-finish linen, traded from Europe but primarily from the Netherlands (reflecting the growth in the linen industry there), from the seventeenth century onwards.

Inn: A place where drink, food and accommodation was provided. Earlier usage: place of refuge.

Interloper: A ship that followed established trade routes without sanction, and in direct contravention of a state's or merchant shipping company's monopoly rights on trade to specific places. A ship that did not hold a specific commission to attack other ships but was licensed to trade.

Jolly Roger (also Black Flag; Red Flag): Traditional name applied to a pirate flag. There are various suggested origins, including from the French *jolie rouge*, in which a red flag was used to strike terror into those being attacked. Became popular in the eighteenth century during the Golden Age of Piracy in the Caribbean, and individual pirates personalised their own flags.

Kedge: Secondary, smaller anchor on a ship; usually stored aft, it could be deployed quickly if needed.

Letter of Marque: A government or state commission/licence authorising an individual (a privately owned ship) to attack and capture enemy ships and bring them before the admiralty court. These were usually issued during times of peace to allow shipowners, merchants or travellers to recoup losses.

Mark: A unit of currency in certain countries (e.g. Germany and Poland) but a unit of account in England; the latter was equivalent to 160 pence (or 13 shillings and 4 pence).

Massy: Antiquated term for massive or enormous, indicating something large or substantial; large amounts; example of contemporary usage: 'massy gold' referring to ingots, bars or lumps of gold.

Narrow Seas Fleet: Comparable to the Channel Fleet of modern times.

'On the Account'/ 'On Account': Generally referring to men who have signed a pirate code or articles and therefore are tied into a code of conduct when serving on board a particular pirate ship or under a specific pirate captain.

Ordnance: Cannon or large guns, including those carried on board a ship.

Ottoman: Refers historically to the Turkish Empire or 'Ottoman Turks' (European corruption of the word 'Osman', the founder of the dynasty in the thirteenth century); the Ottoman Empire ruled for over 600 years. An 'Ottoman' in the context of literature from the period refers to an individual 'Turk' or Turkish pirate.

Packet Ship/boat: A vessel that regularly engaged in the mail trade, transporting cargo that included letters, dispatches or correspondences.

Pancheon: A large, shallow, utilitarian dish usually made of earthenware.

Perforst: From the French *par force*, meaning 'by force' and more frequently used in regard to the English Navy and later Royal Navy (after 1660) when 'perforce men' were engaged to walk the boards of the dockyards and press-gang individuals to serve on board their ships.

Pieces of Eight: See **Reales**.

Pinnace: A small- to medium-sized vessel; can refer to either a fully rigged ship or a small tender vessel to larger ships.

Plunder: To rob goods, generally through attack and usually used in the context of pirates.

Post-medieval: Archaeological term referring to the period after *c*. AD 1550 and relating to archaeology, history and material culture up to modern times.

Privateer: A person or ship privately owned or hired, operating under commission/letter of marque from a government or state to attack and capture enemy shipping. Generally operating during wartime. An official/licensed pirate, with the term coming into main use in the mid-seventeenth century.

Prize: Term used in admiralty law to refer to vessels, goods or equipment captured at sea either by an official privateer (under a letter of marque) or by pirates. The Admiralty held a prize court, which oversaw the equitable distribution of goods captured, with the Admiralty taking a percentage of the overall value of the goods.

Quartermaster: A military or naval term, denoting a petty or relatively senior officer with responsibility for supplies, stores, provisions and distribution of goods.

Reales: Also written 'reals' and 'realls'. Commonly known as 'pieces of eight' or 'Spanish dollars', these were silver coins in use since 1497; the 'pieces of eight' moniker was due to the fact that a reale could be cut into eight pieces and used as international currency.

Rutter: From the French *routier*, and originally from the Portuguese *roteiro*, a route or road, it is an early name for a book of sailing directions and was usually illustrated with views of ports and coastline seen from seaward.

Sea-rover: From the old Dutch word *zeeroover*, referring to robbers at sea or pirates.

Seine Fishing: Method of fishing that uses a drag net; either deployed from the land (fixed engine seining) and anchored across a watercourse or deployed from two boats (open seining), one boat deploying the net and the other hauling (known as the hewer and follower). The net encircles the fish and is then hauled in.

Shipworm: Generic term that refers to marine infestation of ship timbers. Not worms, but saltwater molluscs that infest wood. They were a constant problem for wooden sailing ships as they would bore into the hull timbers. Most common are teredo (tunnel), navalis (naval) or bivalve molluscs.

Síbín/Shebeen: An illicit inn or tavern that sold alcohol without a licence. Originated in Ireland but is now internationally known. Similar meaning/

establishment as a 'speakeasy' in places like the USA, when they became underground establishments during the prohibition era of the 1920s.

Sloop: Medium to small sailing ship with a single mast and rigged fore and aft; there were various types of sloops, including sloops of war, river sloops, Bermuda sloops and cutters.

Spice Islands: Small group of islands to the northeast of Indonesia between Celebes and New Guinea. So called as they were the largest producers of mace, nutmeg, cloves and pepper.

Strumpet: Similar in meaning to 'harlot', an antiquated derogatory term for a promiscuous woman or a prostitute.

Sucket: A dried sweetmeat or sugarplum; an historic term for a sweet food item or sugary dessert.

Tavern: A place, usually licensed, where drink and often food was served. Also associated with places where drink was provided and business carried out.

Teredo Navalis: See *Shipworm*.

Train Oil: See **Buckler**.

Uisce Beatha: Irish word generally used for alcohol (the equivalent in Latin is aqua vita). The modern term refers to whiskey but in the seventeenth century would have referred to any distilled alcoholic drink.

Villafranca: This was the contemporary spelling for Villefranche-sur-Mer, which is now a territory within the Côte d'Azur region of southern France, on the French-Italian border near the Principality of Monaco. In the early part of the seventeenth century it was part of the Duchy of Savoy in Italy.

Vlieboot: See **Flyboat**.

West Indies: Generally refers to the Greater Antilles and Lesser Antilles (the latter formed part of the Caribbean islands of Barbados, Bahamas, and the Turks and Caicos Islands at the time of the pirate confederacy and was the base for much of the eighteenth-century piracy in the region).

Introduction

... since your Highness' reign there have been more Pirates by ten for one than were in the whole reign of the last Queen.[1]

Pirate! The very name summons up images of swashbuckling brigands at the helm of prowling ships about to board a captured vessel and attack its terrified crew. A roar of terror, the Black Flag flying, and cutlass-wielding cut-throats in a state of frenzy and intent on pillage, plunder and booty. Such depiction conjures up the archetypal figure of a pirate, and whether reading Captain Charles Johnson's rather unreliable eighteenth-century account of the *History of the Robberies & Murders of the Most Notorious Pirates* or Robert Louis Stevenson's classic nineteenth-century *Treasure Island*, the typical image of pirates as half-crazed sea rovers, but with a hint of romanticism, has become the norm. Indeed, Hollywood's portrayals of pirates in their heyday in the Caribbean continue to promote such imagery, and it is one that we have come to love or to hate.

This juxtaposition has been made easier because the general opinion about the main protagonists is that they were 'desperate rogues' or unrefined heroes, with reality clouded by misrepresentation, the latter often deliberate. Without doubt they operated outside the established law, but there was a degree of acceptance of their lifestyle and behaviour because the laws of the day, particularly as applicable in remote coastal areas, could be interpreted rather broadly, depending on who was doing the interpreting.[2] There was even greater difficulty in distinguishing between what constituted lawful and unlawful maritime marauding during a time when such actions were part and parcel of emerging modern states and of maritime affairs generally.[3] Such a view is supported by the 'Robin Hood' factor – or comedic portrayal of fictional pirate Jack Sparrow by Johnny Depp – that while plundering others' property, their intentions were essentially honourable, and though operating beyond the bounds of 'civilised' culture, they did so for the greater good of lesser members of society. The reality, of course, was – and still is, when considering modern-day piracy in places such as Somalia – somewhat different: piracy was and is a business centred on private economic warfare at sea with commercial motivations at its root.[4]

Recent scholarly works have challenged the stereotypical, one-dimensional image of the pirate. Published works such as those of John Appleby and Daphne Palmer Geanacopoulos, or Edward Fox's interesting doctoral study, look more broadly at the character, functionality and social diversity of pirates. These authors have shown how, in many cases, these pirates had strong family ties and were guided by an agreed code of ship-board practice – underscored by economic incentives – while striving to better themselves and the lives of their families and love ones.[5] Eric Hobsbawm, in his study of banditry, considered the concept of living as an outcast and beyond 'ordinary' social norms; he argued that this lifestyle was intrinsically linked with the history and exercise of power that flourished best in remote areas and within peasant/poorer societies, during periods of ongoing social change and attempts at colonisation. Here, too, capitalism would be taking root, controlled by locally based groups through coercion and negotiation with resident government officials, to the mutual benefit of all involved. In a sense, this explains why such criminal-based commerce can be so successful and so hard to combat.[6]

Marcus Rediker, in turn, wrote, that 'pirates perceived themselves and their social relations through a collectivistic ethos that had been forged in their struggle for survival, first as seamen, then as outlaws'.[7] The evolution of this thought process and its practical application to piracy is traced in Peter Lehr's most recent publication, looking at how piracy evolved or indeed 'devolved' over the centuries, and how it continues to menace the seas today.[8] Many men who later became pirates began their sea careers in legitimate employment, but changing circumstances compelled them to turn to piracy. Others chose their piratical lifestyles. Those active during the heyday of piracy in southwest Ireland comprised men of both types – those who had no choice and those who had.

THE PIRATE ALLIANCE IN IRELAND

In the early years of the seventeenth century in Munster, along the southwest coast of Ireland, an Alliance of Pirates that comprised primarily, though not exclusively, of Englishmen dominated, with a central base located in the wilds of west Cork. This stretch of the Irish coast is rugged and remote, but wholly conducive to activities that needed to take place beyond the watchful eye of government, in Dublin and London. The numerous bays, harbours, ports and havens enabled shipping, trade and communication to take place beyond the official area earmarked under the plantation scheme. Local traditions continued more or less unchanged in these littoral places, though they adapted to new influences arriving by sea, including trade in a greater diversity of goods. New people arrived and settled, interchanging with the coastal communities, utilising the landscape and carrying on coastal business, both legal and illegal.

The piratical activity that emerged and grew at this stage occurred within the context of the plantation policy in Munster played out among politicians and government officials, old English élites, new English aristocrats, entrepreneurs, merchant venturers and regular settlers. Most were looking to enhance their standing and their wealth, to extend their landholdings, and to find new homes.[9] The majority of those engaged in piracy had relocated from the south coast of England to the southwestern harbours of Ireland following the outlawing of privately commissioned vessels from 1603 (and by formal proclamation of 1604) the new king of England, James I (who was also James VI of Scotland)[10] and his enquiry into corruption among admiralty officers and landed gentry in the ports and harbours of southwest England in 1608–9. Many of these men would have considered the move westward, across the English Channel and Celtic Sea, as an extension of their sphere of operations rather than a necessary overseas migration.[11] It is striking that Sir Richard Hawkins, who was acting vice-admiral for Devon and was eventually himself to be removed from office for colluding with the pirates operating there, should comment in 1608 that, in attempting to remove the pirates from the coast of England, the king's actions had forced them to relocate instead to Ireland.[12] Many, as accomplished mariners, were familiar with the Munster coastline. Indeed the seas off the south coast of England and along the southern coast of Ireland witnessed their own phase of piracy during the previous century under Elizabeth I (reigned 1558–1603).

Contact between the ports in southern England and those in Ireland continued throughout the period, and while intermittent,[13] a certain continuity existed in the practice of piracy along the Irish coast, where, as we shall see, some members of the pirate alliance commenced and pursued their careers. A large number of pirates had been legitimate sailors, seamen or commanders, and many in government from 1603 under the new king may therefore have considered the migration of these mariners to the southern coast of Ireland as the continuation of the civilising efforts in the new phase of the Munster Plantation. This Atlantic Alliance of Pirates, however, was much

FACING PAGE, FIGURE 1: Portrait dating to 1625 by John de Critz of King James VI of Scotland after he had acceded to the throne of England as James I. The jewel on his hat, known as the 'Mirror of Great Britain', was commissioned to commemorate the union of the crowns in 1603. © PG 561; NATIONAL GALLERIES OF SCOTLAND

more than that: the relocation of the locus of piratical operations formed part of a maritime framework for commercial expansion that was to have international colonial and trading dimensions across the Atlantic world.[14] As trade routes opened up, ships grew in size and capacity and, in turn, the pirates were able to enhance their capabilities through the acquisition of larger and faster vessels of their own and through increased access to ordnance, supplies and of course goods to plunder.

Many of these English mariners previously served aboard the ships of those 'glorified state pirates' Sir Francis Drake and Sir Walter Raleigh, Elizabeth's celebrated 'privateers'.[15] Those who became pirates during this period therefore can best be regarded as active agents within the wider milieu of an emerging modern British state, with the actions of many frequently perceived as beneficial to the greater cause, particularly when they attacked the ships of the traditional enemies of England, namely those of the Iberian powers. Undertaking a form of 'piratical imperialism' within the context of the Munster Plantation itself and the wider Atlantic world in general, they served the purpose of expanding English trade and settlement while at the same time broadening their own social and economic situations. When at sea, of course, reality was much different and plunder often occurred for nothing more than plunder's sake, with no sense of patriotism towards crown or country, though it was offered as a defence by many of those who were eventually captured for their piracy (see Chapter 3).

The men who came together as a cohesive band of marauders from 1608, and who were individually active as pirates from at least 1604, were more than acquainted with the ports and harbours of Munster. They would have called to its shores and sailed its waters over several decades, finding ready markets, a cooperative populace and safe havens. The changes that occurred under the new king, as well as changes in the men's own circumstances, led them to utilise the coast of Munster and establish their North Atlantic pirate headquarters there. The pirates became amphibious in nature, with some settling, albeit outside the formal plantation areas, in the remoter regions of the Munster littoral.

Piracy tended to flourish during times of weak rule and in isolated places. These conditions favoured proscribed operations that facilitated legitimate businessmen tapping into less legitimate trade in goods and services. New opportunities in tandem with traditional patterns of predation, where piracy and smuggling became part of the life of coastal communities over time, saw episodic periods of piratical activity on a scale that influenced socio-political,

FIGURE 2: Map of Ireland showing key locations around the coast frequented by the pirates of the alliance. COURTESY OF NICK HOGAN, UNIVERSITY COLLEGE CORK

commercial and, at times, global affairs. In 1521 Henry VIII's lieutenant in Dublin documented the importance of Ireland to the piracy then prevalent in the Irish Sea region, requesting a commission to 'put to death all rovers of the sea taken in this land', and warned that Ireland was 'the very land of refuge that English pirates most resort to'.[16] The problem of piracy within the group of islands making up the Atlantic archipelago of England, Scotland, Wales, the Isle of Man and Ireland and their adjacent isles during the sixteenth century stemmed from a period of disorder in the preceding century, primarily during the 1480s and 1490s, which led to an increase in piracy and general maritime lawlessness.[17]

Predation on the water was a feature of Gaelic-Irish rule throughout the millennia, whether in the coastal territorial waters or the inland waterways of Ireland.[18] The ruling Gaelic lords either commanded their own ships, primarily galleys and pinnaces, or had access to other shipowners; when not protecting their lands and waterways from foreign attacks, they frequently waged a floating war as a means of patrolling shipping within their own waters, controlling trade or protecting their coastal domains. Along the southwest coast of Ireland the two leading maritime lordships were those of the O'Sullivan Beara and the O'Driscolls, who owned their own fleets of ships and were engaged actively in maritime activities both regional and transatlantic. Others – such as the O'Mahony lords, who had little or no formal shipping capacity – seem to have had a symbiotic relationship with their Gaelic-Irish neighbours and therefore were still in a position to regulate those who used their waters, by controlling anchorages, landing places, harbour usage and other maritime facilities.

The later piratical activity is best understood when considered within the context of former ruling Gaelic-Irish lordships, taking into account maritime trade, communication, territorial expansion, internecine warfare and fickle loyalties. The history and archaeology of the O'Sullivan Beara lordship and its territories to the west has been covered extensively in the work of Colin Breen and it is not the intention to repeat it here.[19] The pirates of the alliance primarily utilised as their headquarters the coastal lands and waters of the O'Driscoll and O'Mahony lordships, an area of the County Cork coast known as West Carbery, essentially extending from Castlehaven in the east to Crookhaven in the west. As early as the 1380s, admirals had been appointed in the various ports around Cork to deal with this 'menace to merchant shipping' and were commissioned 'to fight with God's assistance the nation of the O'Driscolls, who constantly remain upon the westerly ocean preying on passing ships'.[20] The plundering of other ships formed part of the tradition of seafaring by these maritime lords, with the exploits of the O'Malleys in Connacht well documented.[21] Lords such as the O'Driscolls may well have served as maritime mercenaries, possibly under 'hire' by those rulers with little or no maritime capacity. Their piratical activities were perhaps interchangeable, with a fiscal as well as a personally acquisitive basis to such transactions. Indeed, the maritime lords may have exercised a more formal maritime function, with their fleet of ships available to others, and the lords ruling equally as both waterlords and landlords.[22]

The allegiances of the Gaelic-Irish lords could be unpredictable, as is apparent towards the end of the sixteenth century when the Munster Plantation began to take hold following the downfall of many of the leading Gaelic-Irish rulers in the province during the Desmond Rebellions of the 1580s. These wars either forced or encouraged residual lords such as the O'Driscolls in west Cork to submit and accept their lands through the surrender and regrant system.[23] From the time of Elizabeth I, ruling lords had handed over their lands to the crown, to be returned to them under this policy. The O'Driscolls of West Carbery are documented as having done so, some at a very early stage of the Desmond Rebellions. Sir Peter Carew's letter of 1568 stated that 'Fynnye O'Driscol [Fineen O'Driscoll, chief of the clan] and others, whose ancestors never came to any Deputy, are come in, of their own accord'. A letter sent from Lord Deputy Fitzwilliam to Lord Burghley in March 1573 noted that Fineen O'Driscoll sought to retain control of his territory by complying with the new dispensation. In September of that year, Fineen petitioned the queen to accept the surrender of his lands and to return them to him. Consequently, Fineen agreed to take his lands by letters patent and swear fealty to the crown of England, and he accepted a knighthood.[24]

By 1582 the O'Driscolls were, on the face of it anyway, co-operating with the crown, with a letter from Sir Warham St Leger to Lord Burghley relaying that Conor O'Driscoll has supplied information about a Spanish vessel that had surveyed the coast near Castlehaven. The information included details of the Spaniards having landed on the island at the mouth of Castlehaven (Horse Island), their intention to erect a fortification there. Similarly, a letter of 1583 from St Leger to Walsingham recounted that Fineen O'Driscoll 'has loyally behaved in this dangerous time and [has] animated the Chieftains of Carbery to the finding of 100 soldiers. His good actions against pirates is noted.'[25] By contrast, a deposition from the High Court of Admiralty Examinations dated March 1582 shows that Fineen recovered and retained

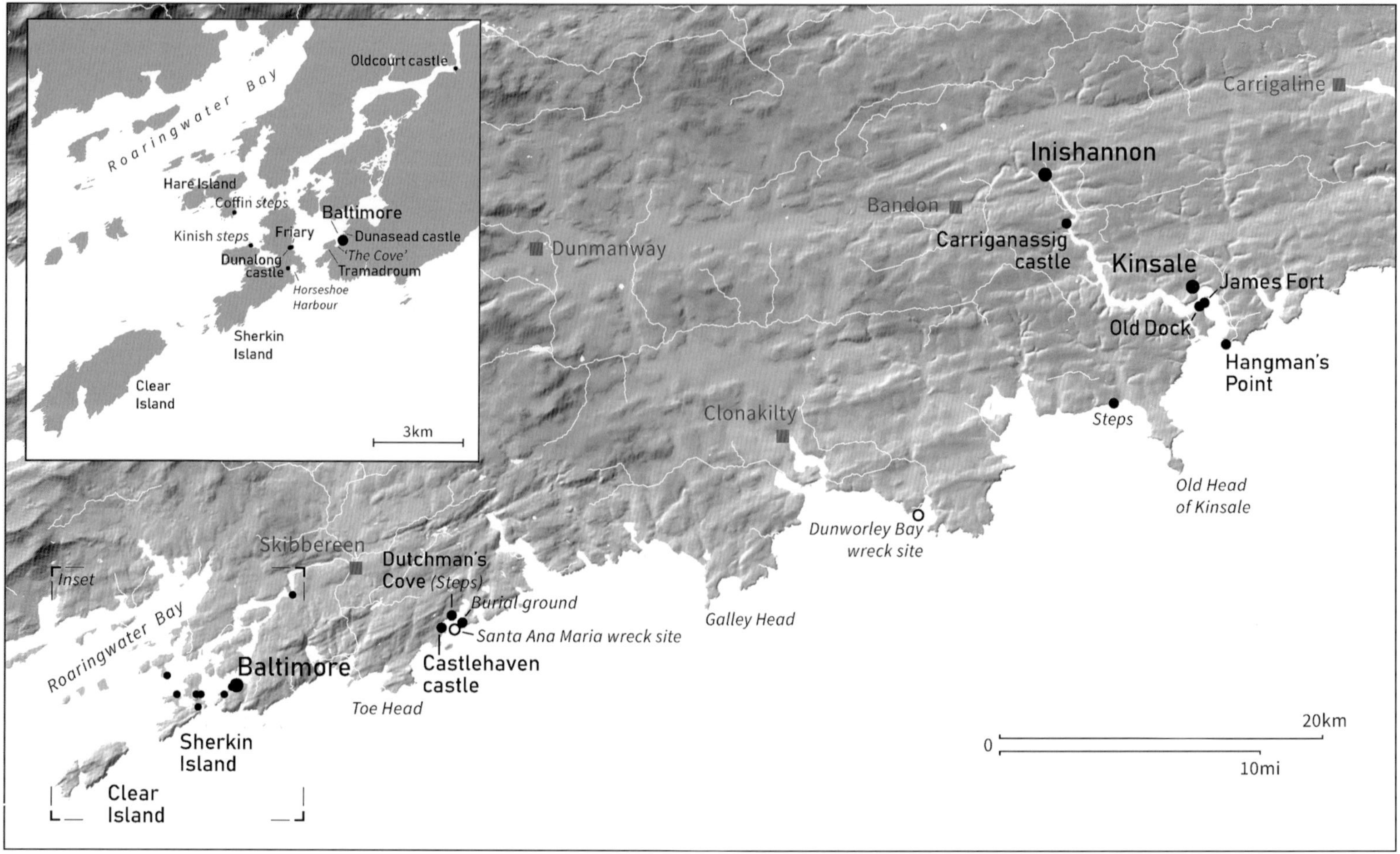

FIGURE 3: Map, with inset, showing harbours in southwest Munster from Kinsale to Baltimore; indicated are the main bases and places utilised by the pirates along this particular stretch of coastline. COURTESY OF NICK HOGAN, UNIVERSITY COLLEGE CORK

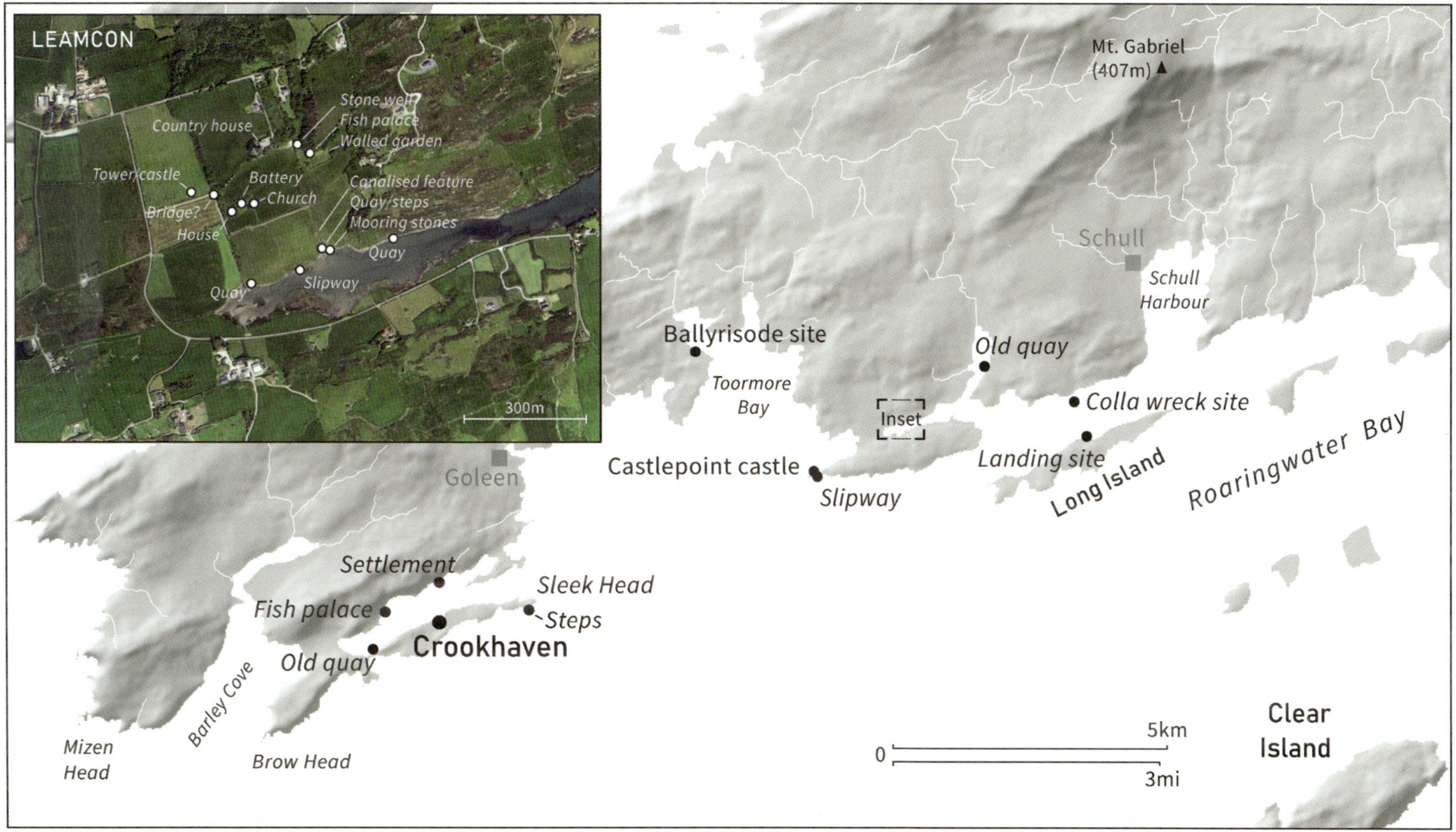

FIGURE 4: Map, with inset, showing harbours in southwest Munster from Schull to Crookhaven, with specific archaeological sites highlighted; inset shows main sites in Leamcon where William Hull had his estate. COURTESY OF NICK HOGAN, UNIVERSITY COLLEGE CORK

goods from a 'bark' operated by English pirates that had been wrecked on Sherkin Island off Baltimore, and that he had previously bought a small bark of 150 tons then trading in the harbour and sold it to the English pirates there.[26] Old habits die hard, as they continued to support piracy and the trade in illegal goods, though they may have adapted to and, indeed, adopted new ways and new affiliations; relationships, of necessity, were fluid.

Strategic areas began to attract more attention, and coastal locations such as 'Carberie' in west Cork, given the importance of its havens, became the focus for speculation as confiscated territories were allocated to new settlers. It was notable too that the remaining native Irish were in such a weakened state that the king could successfully lay claim to such territories by persuading them to lease their lands to prospective undertakers and settlers along the 'Sea Coasts'.[27] However, as Marc Caball has commented in his studies of the province for that time, there was relative cultural and social continuity across substantial areas of post-plantation Munster. Though allocations of land opened the way for an influx into Munster of newcomers, including individuals who were to become synonymous with men of the alliance, the pirates also arrived into a land where Gaelic-Irish traditions persevered.[28] New settlements developed under government-sanctioned schemes, including Baltimore under Thomas Crooke, Crookhaven under Thomas Roper and the Leamcon demesne of William Hull in Schull, who became the kingpin in the operation of the alliance. Natives adapted to the new arrivals, but, in turn, these newcomers adopted prevailing patterns in social and economic norms when it suited their wider agendas. The pirates who arrived did not look to introduce new ways to plunder; they needed only to adopt existing practices and to build on them.

PIRACY AND PRIVATEERING

To understand maritime operations fully – and by extension, piracy – and the function of ships at that time, the nature of warfare at sea requires more detailed consideration. From the late-medieval period to the early-modern era in Europe, ships operated in various ways when under sail on the high seas. They functioned as public (that is, state-owned) vessels, as military ships (engaged to transport troops and supplies as part of amphibious warfare), and as privately owned or as merchant vessels. The latter could be commissioned (or indeed requisitioned) by a state or ruling order to supplement public ships in times of war or as reprisal vessels to target enemy shipping (and seize them as prizes) in times of peace. All ocean-going ships of that time had to be individually prepared for warfare at sea, and were therefore armed.[29] Heavily armed merchant ships could be owned by merchants who held a commission, while others operated as 'interlopers' – that is, without a commission – or were owned by unlicensed traders who focused their trade on areas or locations allocated to monopolies or chartered companies, such as the English East India Company (also known as the Honourable East India Company or, less formally, John Company) or the Dutch East or West India Companies (respectively abbreviated as VOC and WIC).[30]

By definition, piracy is any act of robbery at sea, with a pirate thus defined as anyone who commits piracy. In reality, however, there have been grey areas that over time have served to blur these definitions, and piracy therefore needs to be defined within the context of what is taking place economically, politically and socially at any given time. Privateering has become synonymous with Elizabeth I's private sea captains, but it should be noted, as emphasised by maritime historian N.A.M. Rodger, that the term itself was coined only in the mid to late seventeenth century as a legal expression for privately owned ships that held a state's commission to attack an adversary. In sixteenth-century Europe there were a number of mechanisms in place to permit a privately owned ship to capture another vessel: either by the issuance of a 'proclamation' that referred strictly to ships of a named enemy, by the issuance of 'letters of marque', or 'letters of reprisals'.

Letters of marque, technically, permitted a commissioned ship to enter foreign waters to capture ships belonging to other nations. Letters of reprisal, on the other hand, authorised the taking of captured vessels back to the home port of the merchant who commissioned the ship, the captain who recaptured the vessel, the state that issued the reprisal commission, or other vested interests who had been economically disenfranchised when the ship was captured in the first place. Reprisal commissions permitted those who had been robbed at sea the opportunity to commission ships to seek out those who had targeted them, and to seek the return of their property or to be recompensed to the value of that property when other legal solutions were either unavailable or unavailing. Letters of reprisal tended to be issued only after a failure to obtain justice through the courts.[31] Privateering, therefore, was considered a legitimate basis for predation – the taking of a 'prize', as it were – as opposed to open piracy, which operated where there was no state-sanctioned commission in place and was thus, by its very nature, opportunistic.

Those who committed piracy in all its manifestations – whether referred to as pirates, bandits at sea, sea robbers, swashbucklers, sea rovers or, in the Dutch, *zeerovers* or *watergeuzen* (sea beggars), were far from clearly defined, and legitimate commissioning was often unforthcoming from a convoluted and corrupt admiralty.[32] Essentially, a government might choose to ignore outright piracy, so that acts of plunder went unpunished because it suited the political and economic purposes of that particular state at that moment in time.[33] Examples include the frequent attacks – by nations such as England, Holland and France – on Spanish treasure fleets coming from the New World. 'Commercial piracy' is that invested in or facilitated by legitimate merchants, traders or government officials, or, indeed, by communities who existed beyond direct government control and who traded with pirates 'as a major economic exercise'. Emerging states such as 'Great Britain' – a term coined by King James in 1604 when the crowns of Scotland, England, Wales and Ireland had been joined – were unable to control or police the old trade routes and merchants, as emerging economic powers, could not afford to be alienated from developing mercantile empires. They were thus forced to ally themselves by whatever means they could to ensure they remained integral to, and formed a part of, these commercial westward networks. Government officials, many of them involved in merchant ventures, ignored the law, and the merchant class followed suit, resulting in piracy becoming a commercial venture tapped into by all concerned, it being sustained as a highly lucrative amphibious enterprise.[34]

A third type of piracy was defined as 'deep-sea marauding' or 'high seas plundering' that equated with either organised piracy on the high seas or anarchistic marauding. Some pirates were involved in both, but organised piracy tended to involve individuals attaching themselves to a specific port or base, while anarchistic pirates tended to sail without a base as a focal point, sometimes spending years at a time at sea. The Atlantic alliance incorporated most elements of the types of piracy defined above, bar perhaps anarchistic marauding.[35]

A fourth element linked directly to piracy and which must be examined here, particularly when considering the semi-aquatic nature of the Atlantic pirates' operations and the landscape within which they operated, is smuggling. The thin line between pirates at sea and smugglers on land was frequently crossed and criss-crossed. Smuggling – the import or export of goods without paying lawful customs or excise duties – goes hand in hand with piracy. If pirates could not land their goods to trade, victual their ships or avail of ready markets, they would very quickly cease to be active pirates able to make a profit from the goods they plundered. The use of specific bases enabled individual pirates to live locally, whether transitorily or permanently, with a reliance on local accomplices to enable the landing or lading of goods or men. The landscape, too, just as it facilitated piracy, facilitated the success of smuggling.[36] Like piracy, smuggling was an issue not just around Britain and Ireland, but also throughout the oceans wherever piracy took hold.[37] The reverse is also true: smuggling symbiotically interrelates with piracy.

As elsewhere, smuggling in Munster evolved as a thriving commercial enterprise akin to piracy itself. Evidence from ports such as Bristol supports this, where well-established smuggling activity became an important business for local merchants, with the incentive to engage in smuggling dependent on the level of demand for a product and the relative cost of legal, as opposed to illegal, commerce.[38] The practice therefore became more economically viable in remote places and where liminal existence facilitated engagement in the business of smuggling and piracy. Though the pirates of the alliance would frequently use their ships as ready markets when either at anchor or on the high seas, thus avoiding the need to land goods, smuggling remained integral to their operations and the local populace depended on it; ex-pirate Sir Henry Mainwaring, for instance, informed King James that the native populace in Munster received exaggerated rates for goods supplied to the pirates to victual their ships.[39] With new and exotic goods arriving via the pirate ships, smuggling flourished; those on land crossed boundaries with those at sea, each functioning as supplier and consumer in the business of predation, distribution and economic advancement.

CONSIDERING THE TERM 'ALLIANCE'

The term 'alliance' can be used interchangeably with nouns such as 'coalition', 'confederacy', 'association' and 'union'. An alliance generally refers to the grouping, banding or coming together of like-minded individuals with a common, mutually beneficial goal. The term is used here in relation to the pirates operating out of Munster, in the early seventeenth century, because it serves to define their operation. Contemporary writers referred to individual bands of pirates as 'confederates', and certainly the pirates functioned as a 'unified' force, in that they could operate as a single unit when required, when plying the waters of the North Atlantic and when conducting their business along the southern coast of Ireland.[40] This ability to come together as one demonstrated an allegiance to leadership, an appreciation of, and agreement regarding, objectives, and a willingness to work as a group towards a common goal – ultimately an economic one. This banding together also ensured safety in numbers, protection for their power base, and supported success in the task at hand.

Clive Senior, in his seminal work on English piracy in its heyday, referred to those operating in the North Atlantic as 'the Confederation of Deep-Sea Pirates' and noted that the coming together of so many men was the first time in North Atlantic pirate history that 'pirates enjoyed such strength, independence and unity of action'. Senior credits Captain Richard Bishop with bringing the men together into a 'loose confederation' and with organising the pirates' operations.[41] Though this would appear to be the case, it was more complex than that, as will be seen in the following chapters. Before returning to northern European waters from about 1607, Bishop was lieutenant for arch-pirate John Ward, who was primarily active in the Mediterranean.[42] Bishop's election as admiral of the pirate alliance was strategic and timely, and indicative of forward-thinking with regard to crimes, punishment, negotiations and pardons. Although the independent exploits of the pirates continued unchanged, where each pirate could plunder when opportunity presented itself, under Bishop, for a period of some three to four years, they also came together to fight as a single force when needed, under an agreed hierarchy of command.[43]

For this period the names of particular captains are regularly recorded, including those of Admiral Richard Bishop, Peter Easton – who became vice-admiral under Bishop and later took over as admiral when Bishop was pardoned – and Thomas Francke who was elected rear-admiral. Other leading English captains included John Jennings, James Harris, William Harvey, Gilbert Roope, Tibalt Suxbridge, William Baugh, Robert Stephenson and Robert Walsingham. Irishman Captain Patrick Myagh was based in Crookhaven, and Captain John Fleming may also have been Irish. All commanded fully crewed ships.[44] Collectively, they formed a formidable force that stirred Sir Ferdinando Gorges, keeper of Plymouth Fort, to declared in 1611:

> These men thus furnished threaten the world and gives yt out they expect to be called in verie shortlie by his Majestie's pardon for 40,000 pownds, of whome not whitstanding, they speake verie aprobriouslie, but withal they say yf they bee not, they will take and spoyle all they meete with.[45]

The 'alliance' went beyond the coming together of men engaged in piracy to include collusion with natives and newcomers alike. The forging of such relationships was inherent in piracy during all eras, particularly as pirates grew in power and strength. Part of the 'pirate cycle', as identified by Philip Gosse in his *The History of Piracy*, was the building of alliances with other powerful individuals, groups, states or governments to the mutual benefit (usually economic), of all concerned, and this in turn allowed enlargement and growth.[46] Thus, the North African corsairs, generally referred to in historical texts as 'Barbary corsairs', allied themselves with the Ottoman Turks when menacing trade in the Mediterranean, and the Chinese pirates of the China Seas worked with their maritime state officials to overturn the Dutch East India Company's control of Taiwan.[47] The North Atlantic pirates adhered to this pattern of piracy, allying themselves with resident government officials, landed gentry, businessmen and locals as a mechanism for strengthening their hold on their base of operations and extending their network of vested interests. Petty officials in ports and harbours were more than willing to be bribed to ignore the committing of offences, and, as Gosse states, 'they began to think of it as a principal perquisite of their office'.[48] The pirates of the previous century operating out of Cornwall and Devon, as noted earlier, were no different, and allied themselves closely with the landed gentry and local officials there; thus connections and networks between Ireland and England continued into the period of the alliance.[49]

The men of the pirate alliance in Munster seem, for the most part, to have upheld a principle when at sea in that they targeted ships sailing under the flags of their common enemies, primarily Spain and Portugal, though ships of other trading rivals were also attacked, including those of the Dutch and French. In the case of the latter two nations – who themselves would have attacked Iberian shipping – the pirates of the alliance were also targeting already plundered goods.[50] No written evidence of a 'code' that governed their actions exists, or whether members of the alliance drew up 'articles', as was the case in later times by such notable pirates as Alexandre Exquemelin and Samuel Bellamy.[51] The success of their operation, however, suggests that an agreement of some sort governed the actions of the men in the alliance, both when targeting ships and in organising their business, including the sharing out of booty (see Chapter 5 for further discussion on this). Contemporary sources provide information about the operational approach of the alliance, including papers relating to High Court of Admiralty (HCA) examinations of pirate leaders, among them Admiral Richard Bishop and Captain Henry

Mainwaring. These valuable sources refer to the leading pirate captains being bound by this maritime arrangement, whereby a certain honour code guided their piracy.

The operation of the alliance was complex, and it was not merely for the plundering of ships at sea. Many of the pirates, with family and kin, had settled in the coastal areas of Munster, and led an amphibious lifestyle. This lent a familial permanence to their operation, with pirates having developed a social set-up onshore. Inadvertently, this supported the plantation efforts of the crown and, in turn, semi-legitimised the activities of the pirates. It also assisted with the commodification of goods and services within local communities, albeit using piracy and smuggling as the means by which this exchange took place. Though they were pirates under the strict letter of the law, it could be argued that they were perhaps regarded as private operators, acting without formal commissions but with the tacit permission of the local admiralty officials.[52] Adopting an allied approach that was underscored by a code of operation enhanced the standing of pirates in the community and affected how officials dealt with them. They successfully evolved from independent predators or small marauding groups to an aligned, coherent band of organised and adaptable amphibious sea robbers. In working as an alliance, with close economic and familial ties to their shore bases, their strength increased to the point where they became intrinsic to the coastal settlements in southwest Munster. This, in turn, ensured their safety, not just because of their numbers but also because tackling this budding piratical empire would have meant impinging on legitimate local revenues, customs and territory.[53]

CHARTING A 'PIRATE' LANDSCAPE

Though the pirates used specific ports and harbours around the Irish coastline when required, the expanse along the southwest coast of Cork formed the hub of their operations. Stretching from the small harbour of Castlehaven westward to include Baltimore Harbour, Schull (Skull) and Leamcon harbours, and as far west as the small harbour of Crookhaven, it covered a distance of approximately thirty nautical miles. Within this section of Roaringwater Bay are located a multitude of islands, collectively known as 'Carbery of the Hundred Isles', and which include Sherkin, Cape Clear and Long Island. This is an ancient maritime landscape with the ruins of many of the O'Driscoll and O'Mahony castles dotting the littoral fringe. These sentinels once stood guard over the seas and controlled their respective territorial waters, but fell into disuse or were garrisoned by English soldiers following the fall of the Gaelic Order after the Battle of Kinsale, 1601–2. Thereafter, this remoter part of the southwest coast, outside the official area of plantation, witnessed an influx of new settlers and traders who exploited the maritime resources and forged mercantile links across the Atlantic. The pirates, too, made this their landscape, where secrecy, seclusion and seasonal operations were assured. The pirates' theatres of operations extended across the seas to include other bases, among them Harbour Grace in Newfoundland and Mamora in northwest Africa (previously called al-Ma'mura, now known as Mehdia), both of which became valuable strategic pirate nests. The Atlantic pirates also developed a network of ports and harbours beyond the straits within the Mediterranean, including, when required, Tunis and Algiers in 'Barbary' (modern-day Morocco, Algeria, Tunisia and Libya). Smaller harbours in southern Spain and islands off the Atlantic coasts of Spain, Portugal and Africa also formed part of this commercial chain, as did the multitude of islands within the Mediterranean, including the Balearic and Greek islands. Each harbour and each location offered a variety of operational benefits, such as careening places, fresh water sources and, more strategically, ready seasonal markets for pirate plunder.[54]

Mamora served as an entrepôt in which the pirates could trade openly with the sanction of the ruling Sultan Mulay Zidan, beyond the control of the Ottoman Turks, who ruled the area traditionally referred to as the Barbary Coast, and thereby limiting the ability of pirates to trade freely in ports such as Tunis and Algiers.[55] The three key bases of Munster, Newfoundland and Mamora ensured a triangular trading and raiding route within the North Atlantic, where ships of all nations could be intercepted, plundered or captured. In a sense the Atlantic was the pirates' playground. They could base themselves, as the seasons dictated, in any of the three harbours, where men and supplies were readily available. The Atlantic trading world had bigger and faster ships plying routeways to newly discovered lands. Dominated by the maritime fleets of Europe, including England, the Netherlands (Holland), France and Spain, these armed merchantmen returned with their holds full of exotic goods, precious metals and rich cargoes of bullion from the mines of Mexico and South America. Resident merchants on the north and northwestern coastal regions of Africa – among them displaced Moriscos from southern Spain – engaged with the pirates in processing booty

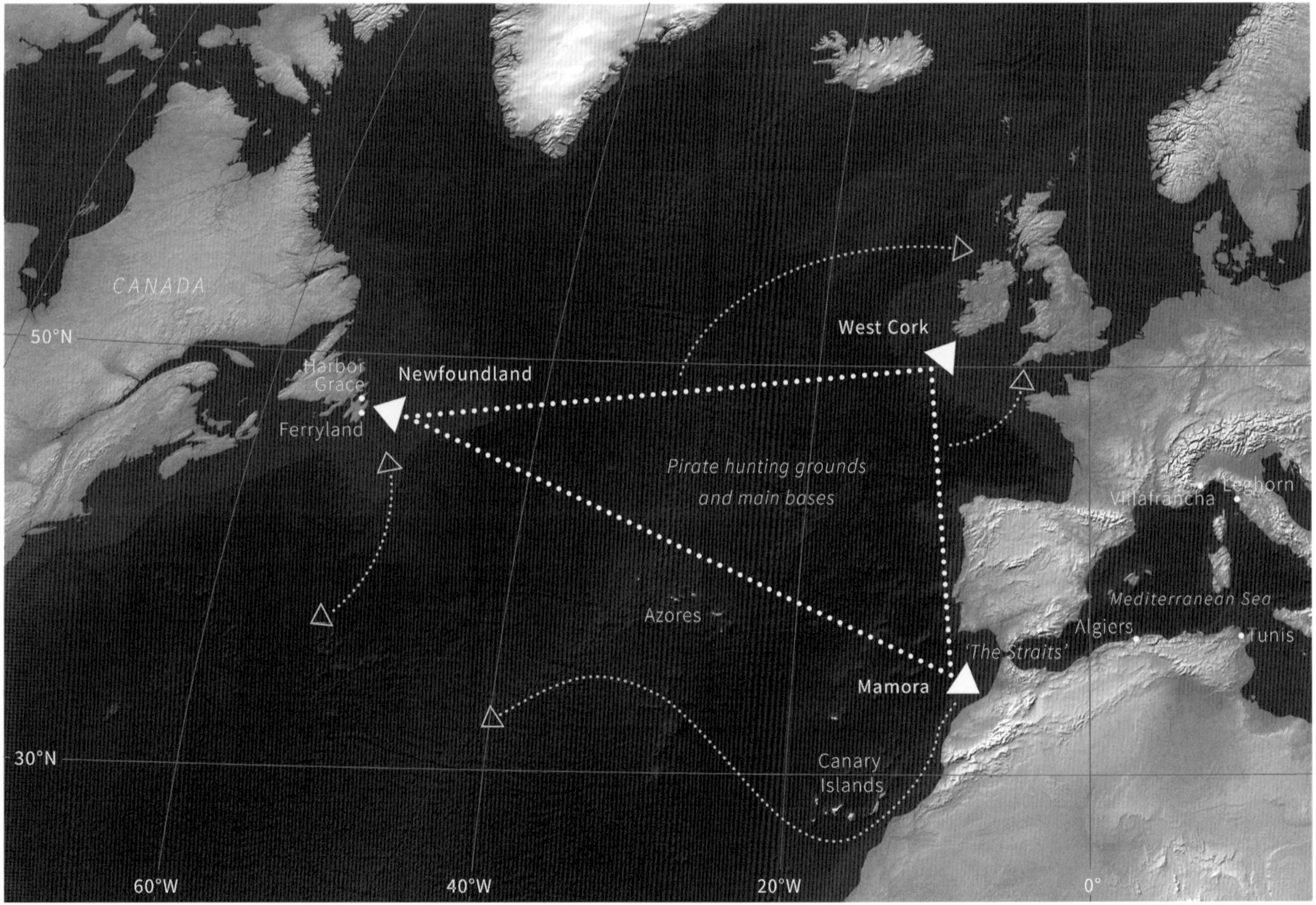

FIGURE 5: The Alliance of Pirates' hunting ground within the North Atlantic. The area stretched from bases in southwest Munster to northwest Africa to Newfoundland, and formed a triangular theatre of operations that devastated trade and shipping. COURTESY OF NICK HOGAN, UNIVERSITY COLLEGE CORK

from plundered ships belonging to the Christian states. Backed by the ruling Muslim leaders, the pirates were guaranteed ready markets in the harbours of the Mediterranean and Africa, where they could also carry out necessary repairs to their ships and re-victual them.

No pirate story is complete without an associated map or chart. These nautical items generally form part of the fictional or embellished tale of a given pirate, but in the case of the Alliance of Pirates, an actual map is linked directly to it. The 1612 Dutch chart of the Munster littoral is contained within a document printed in Old Dutch and titled *Beschrijvinghe van de Zeecusten ende Haenen van Yerlandt*, which translates as 'Description of the Seacoasts and Ports of Ireland'. Rediscovered in 1924 in the Library of Georg-August University of Göttingen in Germany, the chart forms part of a 'rutter' or *leeskaart* (sailing directions) published by the Dutch East India Company's hydrographer Hessel Gerritszoon, with the charts drawn by English cartographer John Hunt, assisted by Dutch mapmaker Dirck Gerritsz.

The chart of the southwest coast was commissioned by the Dutch States General to inform their men-of-war patrolling the waters around England, Scotland and Ireland at that time in an effort to purge the area of pirates.[56] The chart should, perhaps more appropriately, be called an anti-pirate chart because, within the document, it is stated that it is John Hunt's chart of the 'roof-havenen', or pirate havens near Cape Clear, and was thus clearly generated to target those harbours. A view of the contemporary landscape is provided, albeit obliquely drawn, with various elements depicted in colour, including the harbours, islands and prominent features along the coast, such as fortifications.

The chart provides a lens into the cultural landscape of the time, with invaluable details about the types of buildings and other features that were there then. Indicated are the main O'Driscoll and O'Mahony castles and tower houses, and also churches, industrial buildings, houses, cabins, anchorages and even ships.[57] Many of the depicted structures remain traceable archaeologically, while others – such as the chapel on the headland at the entrance to Castlehaven Harbour – have left no above-ground trace.

Cartographic sources are central when considering the cultural mentalities of pirates and those chasing them. These 'pictures' into past landscapes and seascapes provide invaluable insight into the harbours and havens used by the men of the alliance, as well as the locations where they anchored their pirate ships and landed their plundered goods. In particular the 1612 Dutch *leeskaart* of the southwest radiates a combined sense of purpose and mystery.

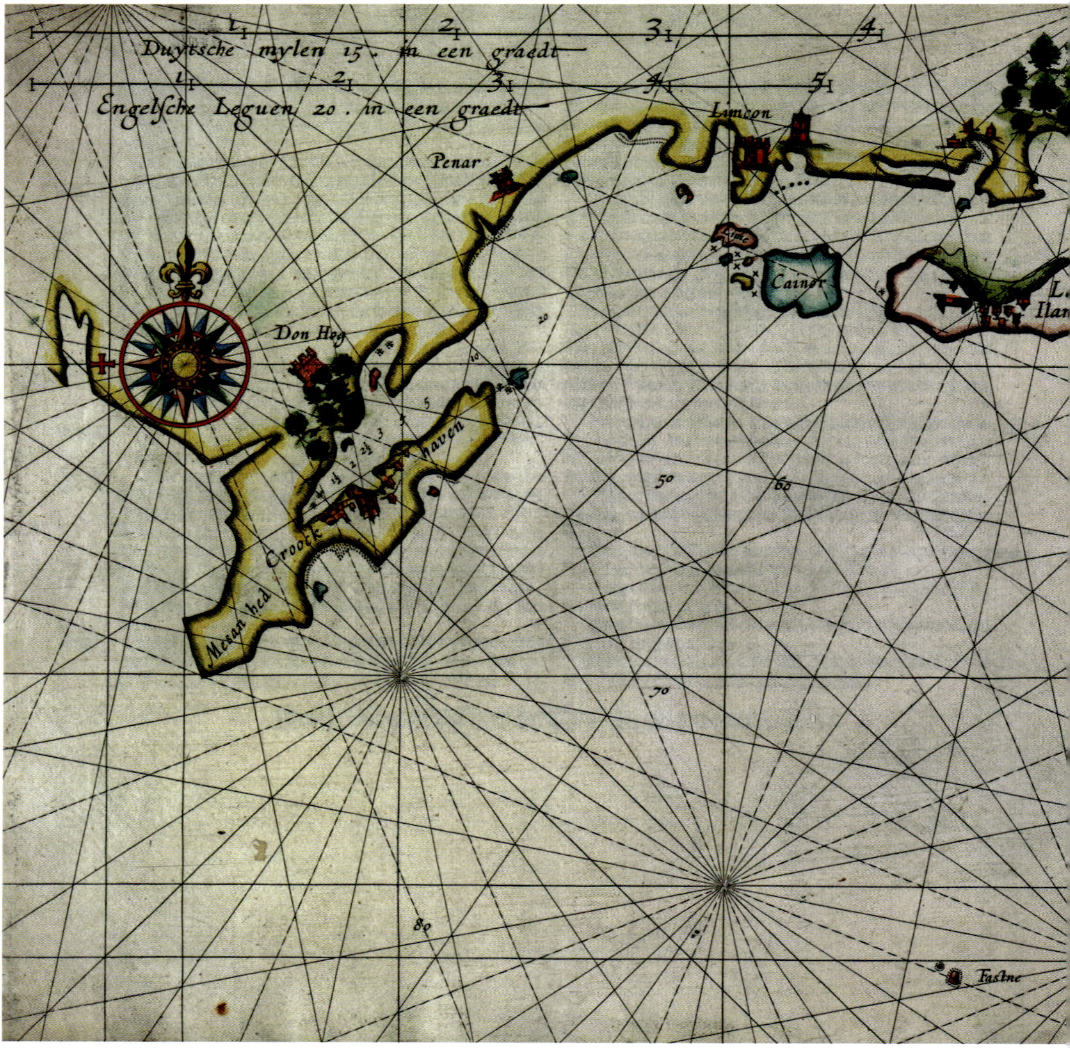

FIGURE 6: The 1612 chart of southwest Munster and the area of Roaringwater Bay drafted by English cartographer John Hunt. Commissioned by Dutch hydrographer Hessel Gerritszoon on behalf of the States-General, the chart is one of four found within a *leeskaart* written to inform on the harbours of Ireland in an effort to rid them of pirates.
SUB GÖTTINGEN, 4 H BRIT P III, 6 RARA, UNIVERSITÄTSBIBLIOTHEK, GÖTTINGEN, GERMANY

The chart's real value lies in providing evidence of the many structures within the landscape, particularly those that have since disappeared, which, in turn, aids our understanding of the historic landscape of the time. It shows a land in transition, with residual Gaelic-Irish sites interspersed with sites

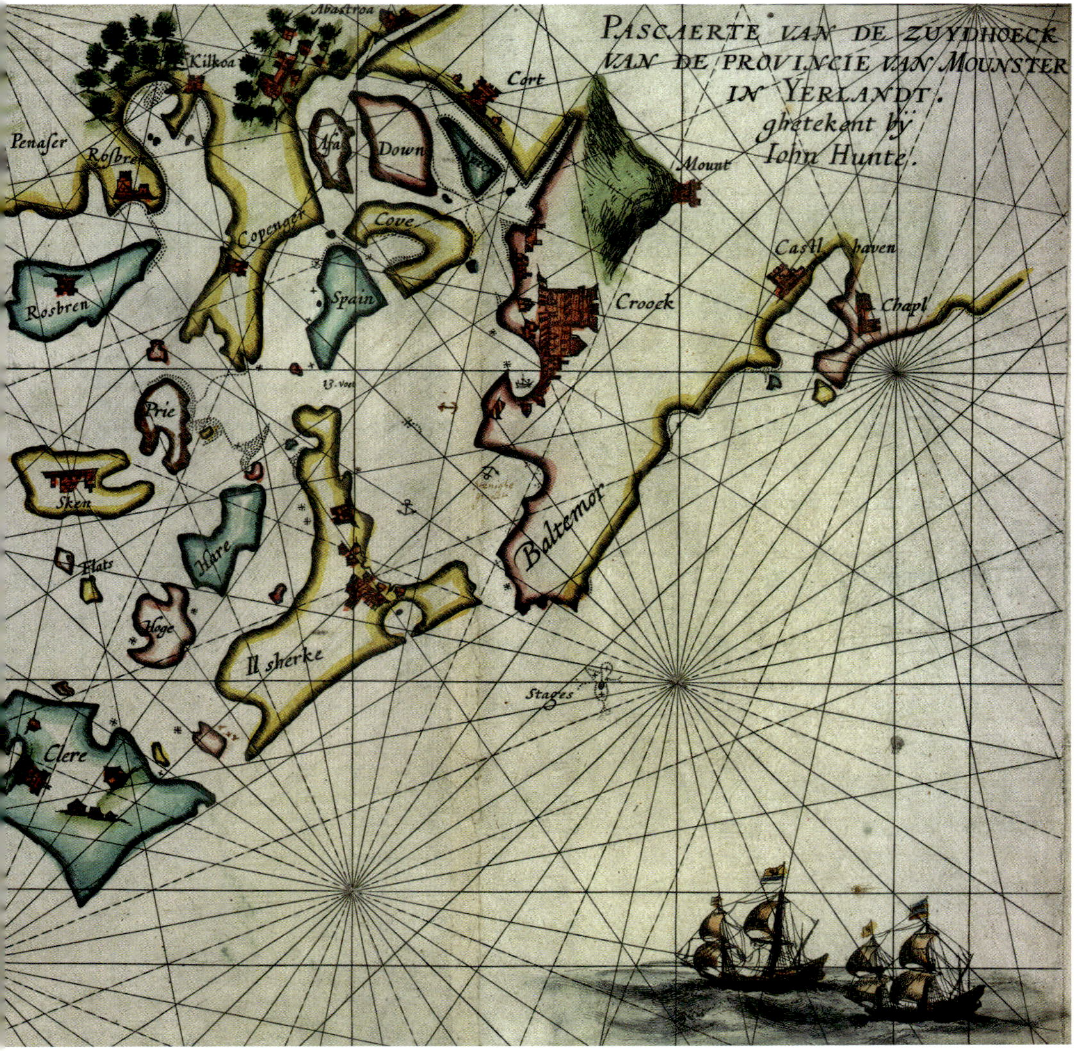

associated with new arrivals under a colonial policy of plantation, investment and improvement.

Integrated within this changing setting were the pirates who made it their own. The chart brings alive the time and the place in which the alliance was at its strongest, and its colourful simplicity and attention to detail achieves its objective – to inform on the coastal areas of Munster within which the pirates operated – but in so doing, it also succeeds in displaying the cultural coastal landscape of the alliance of Atlantic pirates.

THE VALUE OF PIRACY AS A BUSINESS AND WAY OF LIFE

When considered in modern terms, the considerable wealth that could be accrued from the business of piracy (discussed in Chapter 5) was astounding. In addition to financial contentment and the accumulation of material goods, wealth brings power, and the incentives for remaining active as pirates were clear to the men directly involved, and also for conspiring partners. Above all else, piracy was a business, and for any business rooted in trade there was a need to establish networks of communication and knowledge that would ensure that ready markets were in place to handle goods. Throughout this book, the values attributed to goods plundered are those recorded in contemporary sources. However, in order to gain an economic understanding of the value of piracy as a business during the time of the alliance, it is worth considering what these values would equate to in modern terms.

The National Archives (TNA) Currency Converter was used to convert values from the given period to current pound sterling equivalents,[58] while the XE Currency Converter was used to obtain average euro equivalents.[59] Caution must be applied, however, when considering contemporary values given in depositions or as transcribed by court clerks as they could contain inaccuracies or may have been deliberately inflated, depending on the agendas at play at the time. The following examples are therefore indicative, but also striking.

In 1607 arch-pirate Captain John Ward and his fellow captain Anthony Johnson sent £200 in Barbary gold to England in the safe-keeping of the master of the ship *Husband* for their respective families.[60] The modern equivalent of this amount is £26,819 sterling or €30,680, an indication of just how much money was being sent ashore for the support of families and why wives and mothers sought recompense from officials if they did not receive it. In 1610 pirate Edward Higgins deposed that when he was serving as ship's surgeon on board pirate Captain Richard Robinson's vessel *Bull, Bear and Horse*, he was entitled to three shares worth '4li–11s' (four pounds and eleven shillings) per share.[61] From one plundering venture his payment amounted to the equivalent of about £610 sterling or €700 in modern values. This is quite a return for one crew member, and from just one voyage.

When in Dublin at Mistress Suxbridge's residence, her brother, pirate Henry Orenge, had on his person a large 'carbuncle' (most probably a garnet) that was stated to have been worth between £20,000 to £30,000. Orenge was on his way to London to sell the jewel, along with many others he had stolen from pirate Captain William Baugh when in Kinsale in County Cork (the story of Orenge is discussed in detail in Chapter 5). If the amount is to be taken at face value, and depending on the price per carat for precious jewels on the current market, for the carbuncle alone the modern value could be in the region of £3.4 million sterling or €3.9 million. It is easy to see why there were ready markets for goods, including fencing houses in London and other places, when such wealth could be earned from just one haul of precious jewels.[62]

The motivation to remain a pirate even when offered a pardon by the English king can also be understood by taking into account monetary recompense and, indeed, security of income for services rendered. In 1613 Captain Thomas Tucker, who had been one of Vice-Admiral Peter Easton's captains in the alliance, chose to serve as a soldier in the service of the Duke of Savoy in Villafranca in Italy (now called Villefranche-sur-Mer and in France, on the French–Italian border, it was then in Italy as part of the Duchy of Savoy, ruled over by the duke, Charles Emmanuel I).[63] During his time there Tucker earned a wage of twenty-five crowns a month, equivalent to about £825 sterling or €924.[64] No details on payments are provided for Peter Easton, but no doubt he earned a much more substantial 'wage' reflective of his success as a mariner and a pirate, and he too refused a pardon; rather, he settled in Villafranca, and acquired the title of 'marquis'.[65] The opportunity for a steady, substantial and legitimate income, the potential to acquire a title, and the security of operating under a foreign flag would certainly have been attractive to men who stood to gain not much else other than the paper on which the pardon was written should they have chosen to remain in the Atlantic.

SOURCES FOR SECRET LIVES

Extensive use of historical documentation, both published and unpublished, has provided contemporary insights into the world of the men of the alliance, and also their movements. Among them are the invaluable High Court of Admiralty papers (HCA) containing examinations and depositions taken from the pirates and their cohorts, as well as letters and correspondences held in the relevant state papers. Commander-turned-pirate Captain Henry Mainwaring's *Discourse* (the fragmentary remains of which are housed in the Cottonian Collection in the British Library) lays out the operational details of these men and provide a first-hand recounting by one of their fellow pirates of the places they used and the tactics they employed. These contemporary accounts immediately connect the reader with the men of the alliance, and their wider retinue.

Cultural evidence found in the landscape, as discussed above – including newly discovered sites – provides a tangible link to the time of the alliance. Physical assessment of these sites and features depicted on the available contemporary maps and charts, together with an appraisal of the hidden insights held within the key historical sources for the period, has underpinned the cultural history approach when researching and writing this book, and has provided a multi-layered understanding of the pirates and the world in which they operated.

Chapter 1 provides a description of the nature and extent of the English-dominated Alliance of Pirates in Munster during its heyday. It places the alliance within the setting of transplantation of men and operations from the English West Country to a still-demonstrable Gaelic-Irish landscape in the remote regions of the southwest of Ireland. Its situation within the wider Atlantic world and beyond is discussed, including continued links with the Islamic world that were a strategic part of Elizabethan policy. Chapter 2 traces the genesis of piracy, from the explorations and merchant ventures of Elizabeth I's 'seadogs' to outright piracy under King James, when from 1604 all privately commissioned war at sea was regarded as piracy. The emergence of piracy during the process of plantation is integral to understanding the men and their motivations, and flesh is put on the bones of many of those who formed the alliance, with leading captains and their operations considered. This coalition of men stretched beyond the pirates themselves, and the officials and associates who provided tacit approval and overt assistance are also considered in Chapter 3, with certain key individuals standing out as intrinsic to the story of the alliance.

Without a secure place to establish pirate nests, a crucial element of the pirates' operation would have been missing. A cultural approach is employed in Chapter 4 when considering the landscape within which the pirates lived and functioned. Physical evidence for places that hold traces of these men or their associates is presented, including potential associated shipwreck remains on the seabed (this is further developed in Chapter 8). As discussed above, Chapter 5 looks specifically at piracy as a commercial venture involving the pirates, their cohorts and their families, and provides a more familial perspective on the lives of these men when onshore. This social world is further expounded on in Chapter 6. Consideration of the amphibious nature of their lives, and of their kinfolk who joined them and settled in Munster – some of whom became integral to the business of piracy – indicates a more cohesive operation. The women are also discussed, lending a voice to individuals who have for so long remained invisible in the sources, and with reflection given to the strategic place held by them as wives, daughters, mothers, prostitutes or pirates themselves. The strength of the pirate alliance was such that the English crown had to devise innovative methods to tackle it.

Chapter 7 delves into the mechanisms put in place by the English king and his officials for dealing with the pirates. These included amending the legislation on piracy in Ireland, an extensive issuance of pardons to pirate leaders, the granting of commissions to the Dutch to attack pirate ships within the harbours of Ireland, and the execution of less senior captains and ordinary crew members in the pirate fleets as a disincentive to others who may have considered piracy as a way of life. Although the alliance went into decline from 1614, piracy did not end. Certain individuals continued their pirate ways in distant waters, and piracy itself was transformed. The final chapter considers how piracy changed, taking on a much more frightening aspect with the advent of Turkish-dominated piratical attacks in North Atlantic waters, where human cargo then formed part of the 'goods' plundered. The Algerine raid on Baltimore in 1631 is reconsidered and reinterpreted from a cultural perspective, and we discover how, in an ironic twist of fate, former pardoned pirates or their families who then lived as legitimate settlers in Baltimore may themselves have been taken captive by the North African corsairs.

The Alliance of Pirates was instrumental in shaping a unique period in the cultural history of Ireland and in North Atlantic piracy. Though a singular phenomenon in its own right that developed due to a multitude of circumstances, its wider geopolitical and economic influences and repercussions cannot be ignored. The heyday of the alliance coincided with a cosmopolitan period in Munster's history, when extant Gaelic-Irish traditions were mixed with newly arrived philosophies under a plantation agenda. The alliance comprised formidable individuals who set their own agendas and who, upon suppression and demise, stepped into legitimate roles or continued as pirates under foreign flags. While the alliance was unique, the piracy it encompassed was not. Akin to other eras of piracy, the pirates of the alliance served, ultimately, but one master: themselves. At a time when markets could dictate the lives of men, the sea was the only constant in an often-merciless maritime world.

CHAPTER 1

Deeds and Misdeeds: The beginnings

Unto must also be added the convenience of the place [Ireland], being that the South, the West, and the North Coasts, are so full of places and Harbours without command, that a Pirate being of any reasonable force, may do what he listeth.[1]

Piracy in Munster was at its peak during the period 1605–1614, during the reign of the Stuart King James VI of Scotland when he ascended to the throne of England as James I. As well as intensive pirate activity, there were widespread pirate executions, petitions considered and pardons granted. The change in attitude towards the naval fleet and Britain's seafaring capability under James' rule was marked, with an immediate decline in funding and support. It was a situation that allowed for an increase in clandestine activity within the waters of the North Atlantic, though the expansion of English-dominated piracy on the high seas and the use of remote places 'on the edge of empire' had their roots in the second half of the sixteenth century.[2] Events took place that opened up new opportunities for trade and profit. English maritime incursions into Iberian-held territories in the New World (Americas) from the 1580s, and later to the East and West Indies from 1600, led to significant expansion in private-investor ventures and privately operated ships at sea. England's early explorations coincided with the excommunication, by Pope Pius V in 1570, of Elizabeth I, forcing the crown to forge new trade agreements with Persia and the Ottoman Turks.[3] The concerted plantation policy in Munster at the close of the sixteenth century created new prospects for settlement within which extensive wealth could be made from maritime trade but also predation nearer home. These colonial considerations from the late sixteenth century onwards were paralleled by piratical activity rooted in the English-dominated piracy of the southwest coast of England – in Elizabeth's West Country.[4]

WEST COUNTRY ORIGINS

During the queen's reign, financing of the navy (state-owned vessels) was prioritised, with her ministers, from the outset, engaged in forward planning. The steady investment in shipbuilding infrastructure, cartographic and navigational expertise, supported by sufficiently trained crews (made up of both sailors and soldiers), led to the formation of a formidable fleet. The strategic outlay ensured maritime success, not alone in naval power but also through encouragement of merchant shipping, and the success of the navy was assured through its augmentation by a requisitioned merchant fleet when the need arose.[5] This of course was true both in times of war and in times of peace, with Elizabeth's armada further improved by commissioned privately owned vessels, the accomplishment of which was demonstrated in the many exploratory voyages to the continent and the New World. These 'sea dogs', as they came to be known, persistently transgressed the divide between commissioned 'privateering' and acts of outright piracy, not surprising considering their central motivation was profit through plunder.[6]

The Catholic Iberian empires of Spain and Portugal shared the world. Under a papal bull of 1493 and the Treaty of Tordesillas a year later, they had devised a trade line that stretched from the Cape Verde Islands and the Islands of Cuba and Hispaniola (Haiti and the Dominican Republic). In 1529 they completed the full encirclement of the globe under the Treaty of Saragossa, with the Portuguese dominating trade in Asia, India, the East Indies, and West and Sub-Saharan Africa. Spain established colonies and exploited the local resources that the New World and West Indies (Caribbean Basin) had to offer, particularly the extensive silver mines in Mexico and Peru. The richest silver mine in the world at the time was to be found high in the Andes at Potosí, in Peru (now part of Bolivia). Sixty per cent of all the silver mined in the world during the second half of the sixteenth century was produced at Potosí, and Spain wisely engaged private-venture capitalists to operate their mining industry. The Spanish crown, in turn, took a substantial percentage of the profits through taxes. Whether it was the immense profits that the Portuguese could accrue from the exotic spice trade with the East Indies or ivory and slaves from Africa, or the bullion mined by the Spanish from the mines in the New World, over the course of half a century both empires amassed immense wealth, which they doggedly guarded. It ensured that Spain, in particular, remained the most powerful maritime empire of the time.[7] As Spanish ships returned with their treasure, in the latter half of the sixteenth century, 'sharp-eyed adventurers and pirates' operating out of the ports of North Africa were waiting to seize their cargoes. These included 'Muslim raiders', while attacks by European marauders also began to proliferate. As argued by Peter Frankopan in his formative reassessment of world history, 'A New World had been discovered overseas, but a new world was also being created at home, one where vibrant new ideas were encouraged, where new tastes were indulged, where intellectuals and scientists jostled and competed for patrons and funding.'[8]

Private speculators from other nations, who identified opportunities, not only for significant commercial advancement, but also for political elevation if established trade routes could be interrupted and undermined, began to intrude into these Iberian-dominated territories. The Hawkins family of Plymouth and the Killigrews of Falmouth, for example, operating out of the strategic harbours in the southwest of England, made their livelihoods from maritime trade and plunder. For decades members of both families had been regularly accused of acts of piracy, but they now recognised the chance to capitalise both individually and collectively on global mercantile ventures that could be allied with colonial strategies at home.[9]

West Country residents included Walter Raleigh and Francis Drake, both of whom had been commissioned by Elizabeth to operate privately owned ships on her behalf. Both also had hereditary ties with the Hawkins family, while Raleigh and his half-brothers Humphrey and John Gilbert became leading investors in merchant venture companies, and established fledgling settlements in Newfoundland and North America. The term 'pirate', however, in this context needs consideration. Mark Hanna's study of colonial piracy notes that referring to anyone in the 1590s West Country as a 'pirate oversimplifies the complexities of Elizabethan maritime careers'. Men could be suspected or found guilty of 'piracy' but were rarely accused of being 'pirates', and this, Hanna points out, is indicative of the difference between their deeds and their character.[10] Piracy, and what would come to be called privateering, went hand in hand, and at any given time an act of piracy on the high seas could be considered legitimate privateering when a rich prize was brought back to eager merchants and local accomplices in a West Country port. The remoteness of these harbours, along with the network of knowledge-based collaborators, facilitated economic success, with central government, and particularly the admiralty, being unable to police or control maritime affairs in geographically distant locations. The targeting of the overseas economic and colonial interests of Portugal and Spain by ships from the West Country was to threaten Iberia's imperial hold on global trade and settlement while opening up enormous opportunities for private investors to advance geopolitical and economic agendas. This growth in English piratical activity from the latter part of the sixteenth century, as discussed by Hanna, formed part of the global expansion of trade and empire but importantly set the scene for the explosion of piracy that was to become a fixture of maritime operations for the following half century in the North Atlantic region.[11]

ISLAMIC LINKS AND STRATEGIC ENTREPÔTS

Jerry Brotton's study of England's links with the Islamic world provides valuable context for the use of ports and harbours by the emerging pirate alliance. The forging of commercial agreements and the opening up of trade routes between Elizabethan England and the Muslim world provided those involved in piracy with opportunities for exchange of plundered goods, trade in exotic commodities and strategically located entrepôts to use as piratical bases when required. Such trade links had begun from the time of Henry VIII, and as noted by Brotton, 'by the end of Elizabeth's reign (in 1603), thousands of her subjects were to be found in the Islamic world, some working in trade and diplomacy, others as pirates'.[12] English pursuits of wider trade agreements with both the Ottoman Turks and Moroccan Sultanate allowed access into the Mediterranean, as well as overland into Asia and India.

Morocco in particular was attractive due to its political independence from the Ottomans but also from Spain and Portugal; this facilitated free trade, and the country had autonomy to negotiate trade agreements, particularly in English cloth in exchange for Moroccan sugar (a reported favourite of the queen). By 1571, when Elizabeth had been excommunicated, trade with Morocco was returning such profits that it involved over thirty of London's most powerful merchants. In the same year the decisive Battle of Lepanto took place, when the Christian League of Europe defeated a 300-strong fleet of the Ottoman Turks. The celebration by the Christian states of the 'marvellous and glorious Christian victory against the infidels' was short-lived, however, with the realisation that Protestant interests within this Muslim world continued to grow both economically and politically.[13] These links were to be key in enabling the later pirate alliance of the early seventeenth century to freely use the ports of northwest Africa for legitimate trade and the exchange of purloined goods, and to establish certain of those ports as seasonal bases of operations. Mainwaring, in 1616, advised the king that it would be prudent to maintain good relations with both the Moroccan Sultanate and Ottoman Turks. He pointed out that the Ottomans would attack English ships, primarily for the goods carried rather than as a source for slaves or to capture vessels, preferring to release the ships once the cargo was removed, but he counselled:

FIGURE 7: *Abd al-Wahid bin Muhammad al-Annuri (Abd el-Quahed ben Messaoud ben Mohammed Anoun), Moroccan ambassador to Queen Elizabeth I*, 1600. Al-Annuri was in London at that time as secretary and ambassador to Muley Hamet (Ahmad Al-Mansur) to negotiate a trade and military alliance with the queen. BIRRC-AD427; BRIDGEMAN PFH1166942; RESEARCH AND CULTURAL COLLECTIONS, UNIVERSITY OF BIRMINGHAM

> Though this be a great injustice, yet I think it is necessary to hold quarter with them, for if we should have Wars with Spain, there is no place for our Merchants that trade that way to relieve themselves in any distress betwixt Sicily and Gibraltar so convenient as those places.[14]

Intricately interwoven into the late sixteenth-century maritime events were privately owned ships operated by both Barbary-based merchants and English-based ship owners or operators, who availed of the open roadsteads that were now accessible around the north and northwestern coast of Africa. With crown support, predatory activity burgeoned throughout the two decades following the 1570s. A predacious programme by English ships, predominantly privately owned or operated, and targeting Iberian shipping in particular, provided employment for thousands of mariners from all strata of society; it enabled the engagement of legitimate men of the sea with piratically inclined seafarers, all with a common goal of profit by means of aggressive marauding and plunder. This in effect was a mechanism by England to wage unofficial maritime war on its traditional enemies while availing of the increasingly expanding diversity of cargoes crossing the Atlantic each year. This private war at sea was effectively backed by the powerful merchants of London and the West Country, with the tacit approval of the crown, under the guise of legitimate trade within the commissions of their business interests, including the Levant and Barbary Companies.

In 1577 Sir Humphrey Gilbert submitted two proposals to Elizabeth to target Spanish shipping, and in 1579 and again in 1584 John Hawkins designed a plan that would see crown and privately operated ships attack the Spanish treasure fleet and increase maritime assaults on Spanish global trade.[15] It was in this period too that Elizabeth's counsellor with responsibility for advising on voyages of discovery and trading ventures, John Dee, devised the term 'Brytanici Imperii' for the first time, and the concept of a 'British Empire', first within the Atlantic but then expanding into the New World, was conceived.[16] As the final decade of the sixteenth century drew to a close, men-of-war continued to engage in aggressive maritime behaviour. Pirates and privately owned vessels scoured the seas of the North Atlantic and continued to make excursions into the Mediterranean in collusion with the Ottoman Turks – at the same time expanding trade agreements with the Moroccan Sultanates – but they now also began to turn their attention to places like the Caribbean. Thus began the transformation from persistent prize-taking nearer home into transatlantic piracy, which set the stage for what was to become the golden age of pirates in the eighteenth century.[17]

EVOLVING NATIVE LANDSCAPES AND SEASCAPES

During the same period, the political and economic landscape of Ireland had also changed. With the fall of the Gaelic Order following the crushing of the Desmond Rebellion in the 1580s and the subsequent defeat of the Spanish at the Battle of Kinsale in 1601–2, remote areas such as the southwest of Ireland were now open to targeted settlement and exploitation of resources. The Gaelic-Irish lords had hitherto held these areas as peripheries of native control, located outside the 'official' colonial remit.[18] The plantation of Munster, which began in the 1580s, was focused on forfeited lands. Though the actual movement of people into Ireland was slow during Elizabeth's reign, much of the mapping of confiscated territory took place during this time, with a variety of inquisitions carried out. One example, dating to 1586, was *The Plot from England for the Planting and Peopling of Munster*.[19] It was during James' administration, however, that the plantation of Munster gained momentum, and though not to the same degree or intent as that undertaken in Ulster, it progressed steadily, with the 1611 commission survey indicating its extent at that time.[20]

Prior to their demise, the ruling Gaelic-Irish lords rigorously commanded their territories, and the fortunes that were to be made from the sea in particular was well documented. The strategic nature of the harbours along the southern coast of Munster was specifically identified. Maritime Gaelic-Irish lords, including (though not limited to) the O'Donnells of Donegal, O'Malleys of Mayo, and in the southwest of Munster the O'Sullivan Beare and O'Driscoll lordships, retained the capacity to hold sway over their waters, with their attendant fleet of ships. They exerted extensive control over all activity within the jurisdiction of their coastal and maritime territories, and appear from contemporary accounts to have had a localised and semi-formal administrative approach in place, with some lords acting as admirals of their own or neighbouring harbours.[21] The larger and more urban harbours and ports still retained their charters through the English chancery, but the Gaelic-Irish lords controlled the more rural and peripheral harbours.[22] The remote nature of these harbours was a mitigating factor for these ancient lordships in their efforts to retain control for much longer than those that had fully succumbed to the Anglo-Norman feudal system during the medieval period; from the sixteenth century, submission of their lands under surrender and regrant would have given an extended lease of life to rulers who would have lost everything had they refused.[23] The terms of regrant for these lords, following the surrendering of their lands to the crown, as part of the plantation policy, would no doubt have included co-operating with local government officials then in place, including paying dues to the crown annually.

Other Gaelic-Irish clans, though not having an obvious maritime capability, still amassed substantial wealth and maintained extensive landholdings, including men and horses. Integral to the story of the pirate operations in the southwest were the O'Mahony lords, whose main territory was located in Kinelmeaky and Ivagha, areas that included Schull, Leamcon and Crookhaven. The O'Mahonys, ruling from their strongholds in the far southwest, including the castles of Rossbrin, Ardintennant and Leamcon (Black Castle), were of such strength that they could muster a larger contingent of horsemen than the combined efforts of their neighbouring lordships of the O'Driscolls, O'Donovans and O'Sullivan Beara.[24] Whether this was borne out in practice or not, records indicate that lords such as the O'Mahonys, who had no maritime capabilities in the way of a fleet of ships, maintained a strong force on the ground. A record from the 1540s, listing the armed forces of the Irish rulers at that time, refers to 'O'Maghond' having 16 horse and 120 'kearn', while the O'Driscolls retained 6 horse, 200 kern, 'who useth long galeys'.[25] Curiously, an inquisition taken in Cork in 1576 refers to the execution some fourteen years earlier of 'Donal MacConogher O'Mahonye, of Rossbryn, gentleman', who was apprehended in Cork for an act of piracy relating to his chasing of a ship of the crown into Cork Harbour.[26] Whether this was a ship belonging to the O'Mahonys of Rossbrin Castle in west Cork, and thus inferring some sort of maritime capacity, or else a vessel on which Donal O'Mahony was serving, remains unknown. What is clear is that these coastal lords, like their maritime counterparts, sustained their wealth and strength in land, men and links with the sea. The tower houses of the Gaelic-Irish lordships, including those of the O'Mahony lords, were positioned to monitor not alone coastal activity but also the associated hinterlands. So whether a coastal lordship had the capacity through dedicated ships or not, collectively they had the ability to control anchorages and landing places, monitor maritime movements, and police the provisioning of fleets within their territorial waters.[27]

A major transformation in the socio-economic and political landscape from the 1590s was marked by resource availability, the industrialisation of the landscape – particularly in the southwest – and land exploitation by arriving English settlers. The ability of the local populace living around the coast of

PARTE OF THE PROVINCE OF CONNOGH
AND IS PARTE OF TOMMOND
THE PROVINce OF MOVNSTER
Skennan
Enish Skoth
O KONNER
GANCORBERRY
CLANMORRISH
Kerry head
The Bayes of Trelee
The 3 Systers
CORKEAMENE
The Sound of Blasket
The Bay of the Dyngel
COVNTY OF DESMOND
MVSKERE
KARBERE
DOWALLE
COVRTNE
St. WILLIAM
CHARLES HARBERT
SLEVELOGHAR
BAWTERE
The Hand Valench
The Skellites
Commabee
Corweand Calfe
The great Ilande
Beare Hauen
Island Fyde
Kymeslande
Croke Hauen
Cape Clere
Dorsey

FIGURE 8: The province of Munster, Ireland, dated c. 1595, artist unknown. The chart shows Munster with lands targeted for resettlement under the plantation following the failed Irish rebellion and fall of the Gaelic order. Also shown are ships of various types and sizes, as well as a sea monster looking towards Waterford harbour.

E9078 P/49(27); NATIONAL MARITIME MUSEUM, GREENWICH, LONDON

the province, and in particular the ruling native lords, to adapt and conform to these changing times facilitated the continuation of their native rule for longer than in many other parts of the country.[28] These lords sustained their income and power by extracting payment from those who were exploiting the marine resources within their respective territorial waters, and they were not going to let changing times prevent them from continuing with their accustomed way of life.[29] A relationship evolved between the native rulers and those administrating admiralty jurisdictions locally, to control and manage the ports and harbours in their respective peripheral places.

The inquisitions carried out under King James, particularly that of 1609, provide first-hand evidence of the wealth of some of these lords, and give valuable insight into the means by which they prospered. The O'Driscoll lords of West Carbery, from early in the fourteenth century, retained control of their harbours and the territorial waters along the coastline through the use of their own fleet of ships, including galleys. In what capacity the maritime lords were allowed to retain the fleets following submission of their lands has yet to be fully assessed, but certainly the O'Malleys retained the use of galleys, albeit on a fluctuating basis, during the late sixteenth and early seventeenth centuries, though the true nature and extent of their maritime activities remains obscure. Grace O'Malley (anglicised as Granuaile from the Irish Gráinne Mhaol), characterised in more recent times as 'the Pirate Queen' and who is perhaps the most renowned of all recorded Irish pirates, continued to use her fleet of ships as a means to exert local power, though such usage was increasingly affected by the shifting political situation in the west at that time.[30] Piracy, as noted, was one of the ways in which Gaelic-Irish leaders like O'Malley could exercise influence through disruption of trade and control of shipping, used in effect as one of the 'arts of survival'.[31] Grace O'Malley was distinctive in her capacity as a woman leading a Gaelic lordship and as the 'most famous femynyne sea captain' commanding her own fleet of ships in a traditional patriarchal world. A female's direct involvement in piracy was even more unusual.[32] In general conformity with most of the other coastal lordships around Ireland at that time, Grace chose to acquiesce to the crown in 1576 under surrender and regrant in respect of her own territory, including the seas. Like the other maritime lords, she retained the use of her fleet, and continued local raiding and control of fishing, smaller shipping and users of immediate coastal waters.[33] In such ways these resident Gaelic lords maintained certain autonomy while paying the requisite dues and revenues to the local government agents or admiralty officers, to enrich

FIGURE 9: View of the O'Driscoll castle of Dún na Séad, Baltimore; from 1607 it was the administrative residence of Thomas Crooke. IMAGE: CONNIE KELLEHER

the central exchequer in London. The returns could be considerable, and the appeal of these earnings and the opportunity they afforded for substantial profits did not go unnoticed by either the pirates or the governing officials.

The 1609 inquisition details the O'Driscoll's income from management of their territorial waters.[34] These waters traditionally extended from the Fastnet Rock off Cape Clear to the rocks known as the Staggs, some 3.2 nautical miles east of the harbour of Baltimore, with dues exacted from local, regional and foreign ships. The O'Driscolls were entitled to:

> … every ship and bark that comes to anchor in any part of the said harbour of Baltimore, to pay the chief Lord of the time four-pence sterling. The lord hath been wont to be Admiral of the Harbour and to have all wrecks within the harbour and country time out of mind … to include a royalty out of a butt of wine landed in any part and that no man may draw a seine [i.e. fish] in the harbour without a licence first obtained from the lord.
>
> Every ship or boat that fishes there is to pay the lord in money sixteen shillings and two-pence, a barrel of flour, a barrel of salt, a hogshead of beer, a dish of fish three times a week from every boat and if they dry their fish in any part of the said country to pay thirteen shillings for the rocks. For every beef they [those using the harbour] kill they are to pay eight pence, and for every sheep and pig that is killed likewise one penny to the lord.

> That every boat that is let in to the harbour to fishermen, that the lord is to have of the latter six shillings and eight pence for every hundredth white fish and every barrel of herrings or pilchards.[35]

The O'Driscolls sought to retain control of their lands, and the later inquisition illustrates why they were eager to do so: in order to retain their income stream. Following the crown's return of their lands to them, including rights of the sea, the relationship between Gaelic-Irish lords like the O'Driscolls and the local admiralty officials is informed by considering how admiralty matters were organised in the local towns, such as Kinsale:

> … the town of Kinsale was wont to appoint an admiral for the fishing season and that he and the lord [O'Driscoll] would join in settling orders for the fishing, and keep Admiral's Court every Monday, and all pecuniary punishments for breaking the orders agreed upon were to be equally divided between the Lord and the Admiral, but if Kyngsale did not send one Admiral then, the Lord might appoint one, and take the same course alone.[36]

As underlords to the MacCarthy Reagh in Munster, the O'Driscolls would traditionally have paid dues to them, while maintaining their own wealth and power through territorial self-rule. These dues were still in place, even following the surrender and regrant of their lands, and the Lord O'Driscoll provided annually to the earl of Desmond 'eight beeves or eight nobles sterling, at the ellecction of the said O'Driscolls, to be paid at the feastes of All Saints'. To the MacCarthy Reagh 'duties … of fower poundes, thirteen shillings and fower-pence sterling, Irishe. Also a rente, called in Irishe by the name of Dubh Chios or black rent, three poundes, two shillings and two-pence halfe penny sterling … and certain tribute at Samhain and Bealtaine.'[37] The ruling Gaelic-Irish overlords thus retained ultimate control through tribute, while the lesser lords presiding within their own territories could extract huge profits either directly from fees or fines from users of the sea and its resources or through positions within a local admiralty set-up. These positions, like that of acting admiral in Kinsale, allowed them to issue orders and extract monies that were distributed through a clearly agreed and traditional administrative construct, albeit one that was evolving to adhere to changing times within wider colonial movements.

NEW ENGLISH ARRIVALS AND NATIVE ADAPTATIONS

The English population grew steadily in Munster from the 1580s, though not to the degree hoped for by Elizabeth's government and its plantation strategies; this saw further increase from the late 1590s. It was estimated that 5,000 settlers were in the province in 1610 and by the 1630s this had risen to nearly 22,000.[38] This influx of English venture capitalists and settlers would change the landscape of the southwest not just economically and politically (particularly from an administrative perspective), but socially too. With any enforced plantation, loss of land and loss of freedom is inherent, and displacement of local populations, formed part of the process. With the growth of towns and trading centres related to entrepreneurialism and investment by new arrivals, native populations migrated to these new market places, and peripheral settlements of native dwellers became features outside, but immediate to, the main trading centres.[39] The native Irish who remained in their remote areas, particularly those living along the coast, quickly recognised new opportunities and the need to adapt to new social norms introduced by

FIGURE 10: Illustrative painting showing a fully-rigged pinnace of the period under sail leaving Baltimore Harbour, with stylised beacon on the headland. © DR PETER MURRAY

the new arrivals. Equally, however, they continued with what would have been traditional coastal living where engagement with ships and their cargoes allowed for exchange, improvement and profit.

The closing years of the sixteenth century and emerging years of the seventeenth marks the transition from Gaelic-Irish-dominated Munster into the modern historic period, with diversification and advancement in trade and shipping, expansion of markets and towns, and changes in domestic architecture and lifestyles becoming evident within the landscape. In the early part of the seventeenth century new settlers began to inhabit certain ports along the southwest coast of Munster, stretching from Courtmacsherry to Bantry. New markets sprang up, with 107 grants issued by 1610 to hold markets throughout the province, the majority of these in the county of Cork. Though certain markets were held outside newly expanded towns, some went hand in hand with mercantile centres that became crucial to commerce and trade during this period. One of these was Bandon in west Cork. Referred to at the time as Bandonbridge (in Irish: *Droichead na Bandan*) or 'The Bridge', prior to its expansion into an urban centre it was a small village with a bridge located at a strategic fording point in the River Bandon. The region was ruled over by the Gaelic-Irish O'Mahony lords and McCarthy overlords. The lands around Bandon were granted, by Elizabeth I, to the English prospector Phane Beecher in 1588 but it was not until the opening years of the 1600s that the development of Bandon as an urban centre began in earnest. The walled plantation town was designed and built by Richard Boyle, perhaps one of the leading speculator and venture capitalist of them all in an Irish context. Bandon was to become the hub in west Cork through which all forms of merchandise could be traded, siphoned and exchanged.[40]

It was into the remote areas southwest of Bandon from 1603 onwards that officials such as William Hull and Thomas Roper came to acquire lands and develop the fishing industry, to advance their own commercial interests.[41] The locating of their respective industries in isolated areas was deliberate, and served the purpose of those who wished to reside outside the watchful eye of central government. Others, who similarly identified the opportunity to turn a profit from coastal commerce – whether legally or otherwise – quickly joined them. They included mariners whose private careers on the seas were extinguished by King James' administrative policies, and they arrived into Munster as piratical outcasts, though some also chose to become settlers.[42]

ROYAL ACTIONS AND CONSEQUENTIAL REACTIONS

The growth in organised piracy took place within a 'colonial context' intermingled with both official and unofficial expansionary efforts into distant regions of Munster where local conditions dictated the law. While certainly the extension of English piracy into Ireland may be considered a formative stage in the development of transatlantic piracy and plunder thereafter,[43] such piracy – and many of those involved in it – was a feature of life throughout that period around coastal 'Great Britain'. Those same pirates frequently made landfall in Ireland prior to James taking the throne in England, and were thus familiar with the place.[44] Piracy was accordingly an integral part of maritime life within the northern Atlantic fringe for millennia, despite various attempts by the crown and the admiralty to suppress it.[45]

James' neglect of the navy, stemming from a lack of financial input and indeed interest, was influenced by his brokerage of peace with Spain shortly upon his assuming the throne of England.[46] This coincided with his outlawing of privately commissioned ships – regarding private commissions and piracy as one and the same – though complaints by the Spanish crown about the impact that private war at sea was having on its shipping also influenced the king's actions. Cumulatively, these actions (or inactions) undermined England's seafaring capabilities at the very time when maritime trade routes were opening up and the commodities markets throughout the continent, Greater Europe and the wider world were expanding. James' vision of himself as a king of peace, underscored by his vacillating nature, was to depress the very legacy bequeathed to him by Elizabeth – that of the English naval fleet.[47] His indecisiveness and weak actions impacted specific business interests elsewhere. Charles Howard of Effingham had been made lord high admiral in 1585 and, following his command of the fleet during the expedition to Cadiz in 1596 and as a particular favourite of Queen Elizabeth, was given the title earl of Nottingham in 1597.[48] Nottingham was one of the longest-serving lord high admirals, holding the office from 1585 to 1619. He continued in this capacity under James and in 1609 he also assumed the role of vice-admiral for Munster. While he was instrumental in building the navy into a maritime force during Elizabeth's tenure, he was equally guilty of accelerating its demise under James. The reasons for Nottingham's actions are best explained by considering his personal involvement in all matters maritime, particularly the wealth he had accrued through inducements from the commissioning of private vessels in Elizabeth's time, as well as outright

piracy. As private commissions were no longer lawful under James' rule, the depletion of the navy suited Nottingham's purposes, in that it allowed him to continue to reap rewards from the business of piracy.[49]

The new king, prior to the 1613 Piracy Act, issued a number of proclamations in tandem with commissions in his initial attempts to curb pirate activities.[50] These efforts at prohibiting not only piracy but also those aiding and abetting it, including government and admiralty officials, sought to tackle the problem at home and abroad and to indicate to foreign governments that the issue was being addressed.[51] Indeed, it appears that under James, two main areas were dealt with by the court of admiralty – cases following the war with Spain and Holland, which raised important questions of international law, and cases dealing directly with piracy. The latter were the most notable feature of the court records for this period, with many cases highlighting James' 'feeble attempts to suppress them'.[52] The king revoked all letters of marque and made it illegal to serve on commissioned vessels, declaring such practice to be an act of piracy.[53] The effect was immediate; in 1603, just three days after the official cessation of commissioning privately operated vessels, the mayor of Plymouth wrote to the English Privy Council describing the situation there:

> … there do daily resort heither such a great number of sailors, mariners and other masterless men, that heretofore have been at sea in men of war, and being now restrained from that course do still remain here and pester our town which is already overcharged with many poor people. And some of them do daily commit such intolerable outrages as they steal and take away boats in the night out of the harbour and rob both English and French.[54]

Government action went a step further in 1605, when a proclamation outlawed any English citizen found in the employ of foreign shipping and who was acting under a letter of marque from a foreign ruler.[55] This in effect meant that, where previously English sailors and seamen had the option to serve aboard privately owned foreign vessels, this too was now banned. Whereas a

FACING PAGE, FIGURE 11: Charles Howard of Effingham, 1st earl of Nottingham and lord high admiral, 1536–1624, studio of Daniel Mytens the Elder, *c.* 1620. Nottingham is shown in garter robes and a gold-embroidered skull-cap with the English fleet in action against the Spanish Armada depicted behind him. BHC2786; GREENWICH HOSPITAL COLLECTION, NATIONAL MARITIME MUSEUM, GREENWICH, LONDON certain number of sailors and men of the sea were always attracted to unlawful activity, it is open to debate as to whether such high volumes would have turned to piracy if the king's obdurate approach had not been so immediate.[56] Indeed the king's intolerance for any such activity appeared determined and became more targeted as time passed, with proclamations being issued that increased penalties against piracy and those in collusion with it. James' dislike of piracy seems to have been both personally and politically motivated. While this tough approach was designed as a mechanism for addressing the pirate problem, in practice it had little if any effect, and in fact led to increasing numbers becoming involved in piracy in the North Atlantic.

Nottingham was also in a dilemma and had no option, if his supplementary income was to be maintained, but to engage more actively in black marketeering. Thus the king's actions directly contributed to the increase in, and encouragement of, corruption and complicity by his officials. Nottingham's collusion with pirates and smugglers operating out of the many harbours along the southwest coast of England prior to James assuming the throne assured a steady and lucrative income through his network of agents and vice-admirals on the ground.[57] This was highlighted in 1603 when James, not long after he assumed the crown of England, came under international pressure. Foreign ambassadorial complaints of predations at sea by marauding English ships intensified, and they became increasingly irritated over collusion of admiralty officers at the highest level of government. The Venetian ambassador, Giovanni Scaramelli, for example, complained in that year to James that Lord High Admiral Nottingham was in cahoots with the English pirates who were preying on his merchant ships, proclaiming that 'it was the Admiral himself who had a part of the plunder in his hands, and what is more, he admitted it'.[58]

The king's outlawing of commissioned ships and his targeting of admiralty and revenue officials in charge of ports and harbours in southwest England had two immediate impacts. Firstly, as highlighted above, it seriously undermined the entrepreneurial earnings of powerful bureaucrats like Nottingham. Secondly, it led to large numbers of seafarers – commanders, captains, commissioned sailors, ordinary seamen, legitimate mariners and general crew – finding themselves out of work, the majority of whom knew only life at sea. This sudden socio-economic change forced thousands to look to less legitimate means to ensure survival.[59] The huge numbers involved can be gleaned from the recorded figures for 1582, which show that 16,306 men were engaged in maritime activity in England that year.[60] Many were willing to go to sea at any cost once they were provided with some hope of a living, and it is estimated that as many as 50,000 men, numbers having substantially increased due to two decades of war, were by 1603 'treading the boards' in ports and harbours looking for any work that might come their way.[61] The king's 1609 enquiry into the actions of officials, which led to a clampdown on activities in the West Country harbours, resulted in the pirates relocating their base of operations from the southern coast of England to the distant ports and harbours of the southwest coast of Munster.

The escalation and organisation of piracy in the waters of the North Atlantic highlighted the inadequacies of admiralty jurisdiction to deal fully with such activity but also reflected a successful sub-culture that extended from England to Ireland, and that involved admiralty officials, English settlers, merchant venturers, landed gentry, willing locals and the pirates themselves.[62] The inability of the admiralty to fully address the pirate problem, together with James' attempts to curb piracy, certainly encouraged the transplantation of pirate operations to southwest Ireland. This is understood best when considered in light of the innate nature of maritime fraud, economic incentives – particularly with regard to colonial speculations in Munster ongoing at that time – and blatant business dealings between government officials and the pirates. While the king may have strongly disapproved of piracy, he certainly could not prevent it.[63]

THE LEGALITY OF ILLEGALITY

An ambiguity in Irish law meant pirates or those aiding and abetting them could not be tried in Ireland but instead were transported to England to stand trial.[64] Though individuals were pursued, captured and examined during the period, this legal loophole facilitated pirates in operating freely along the southwest coast of Munster.[65] The king uncompromisingly regarded piracy as any act of robbery or violence undertaken by anyone at sea, around the coast, along creeks or in rivers that fell under admiralty jurisdiction. This applied equally to the waters around Ireland when, following the establishment of a separate admiralty court for Ireland in the 1570s, the principal interest of the court was in dealing with pirates and their captured prizes. Things became more intense after 1603 with the establishment of the provincial court of admiralty of Munster, attesting to the heightened activity there.[66] The problem caused by the ambiguity in the primary legislation was aired in the 1606 correspondence between the lord deputy, Sir Arthur Chichester and the earl of Devonshire; Chichester pointed out that the pirates in Munster, who apparently well understood the law, were of the opinion that the law could not hurt them and so flagrantly pirated merchants and their ships in the area. This was reiterated by Chichester in 1610 when he again requested that the law be extended to Ireland to allow for 'the adjudging and execution of pirates'.[67] The legislation was finally changed in 1613 with the enactment of the Piracy Act, which brought admiralty legislation in Ireland into line with that in England, though it still allowed for dual jurisdiction where pirates could be either tried and executed in Ireland or transported to England and prosecuted there.[68]

Prior to this, commissions could be issued to the lord deputy in Ireland to deal directly with piracy, but individuals would still need to be sent to England for trial. This ensured that the lord high admiral retained control of events, including the disposal of plundered goods and ships.[69] In the early sixteenth century in England a specific statute prohibiting piracy was enacted with the passage in 1536 of the Offences at Sea Act (also known as the Act of Henry VIII, 28 Hen. VIII, c. 15) that made all 'treasons, felonies, robberies, murders and confederacies' committed within admiralty jurisdiction subject to trial by commission according to the course of the common law.[70] The act, however, did not extend to Ireland, though there appears to have been an unsuccessful attempt to draft a commission under the Henrician act to allow for execution in Ireland.[71] In the latter part of the sixteenth century, attempts were made by the queen and her council to suppress piracy, with the establishment of commissioners and the issuing of commissions that primarily targeted the coast and waters around England, Scotland and Wales. Though this move initially had some effect in reducing the occurrence of piracy in those waters, it had little or none on piracy in Irish waters. Over time it proved to be ineffectual overall due to a combination of convoluted bureaucracy, rivalries of jurisdiction and the continued problem of corrupt officials.[72] While the scale of piracy in Irish waters during the sixteenth century may not have been on a par with the opening decades of the following century, or indeed as organised as the North Atlantic pirate alliance subsequently became, officials were highlighting the problem from an early period. Henry VIII's lieutenant in Dublin in 1521 commented that Ireland was 'the very land of refuge that English pirates most resort unto'.[73]

DEVELOPMENT OF THE IRISH ADMIRALTY AND ISSUES OF JURISDICTION

The origins of the Irish admiralty and its attendant legislation lay within the jurisdictional powers conferred on the lord high admiral in London, with, in practice, these powers exercised by a deputy acting as judge. Until the enactment of the Piracy Act of 1613, all administration of admiralty business in England and Ireland, including court proceedings, was carried out centrally from London, with pirates and other felons extradited to England to stand trial. The need for legislative provision to govern those using the seas and tidal waters of Great Britain and Ireland in the late sixteenth and early seventeenth centuries was twofold. Firstly, to control the Atlantic waters around Britain and Ireland and defend them from enemy ships. This was primarily administered by the central admiralty in London and included overseeing the provisioning of ships to patrol these waters. Secondly, the whole issue of maritime legislation in Ireland – the 'law maritime' – which governed all acts of pillage or seizure on the sea or coast by pirates, as well as death at sea, wages of crews, orders to ships' masters and captains, salvage, wreck, collision at sea and other disagreements that may have arisen while on the water.[74] The issue of jurisdiction at sea, however, was a longstanding debate between the common law courts and the admiralty. This intensified under James with an escalation in complaints by foreign courts. The necessity to have authority on the high seas, including over ships that were plundered and taken as prizes became all the more urgent as international markets opened up and cargoes increased in value.[75]

Sources suggest that there was a High Court of Admiralty in England since the 1340s, primarily established to deal with increasing problems of piracy at that time.[76] Many seaport towns, on the other hand, had their own local administrative 'marine' or 'port' courts and the common law courts similarly dealt with cases relating to maritime issues, which served ultimately to complicate matters.[77] In the 1530s the powers of the High Court of Admiralty were strengthened and appear to have been more formally established, with the office of lord high admiral coming into existence at that time.[78] This coincided with the enactment of the Offences at Sea Act, after which all maritime matters were dealt with more directly, though not necessarily any more efficiently.[79]

In Ireland a separate admiralty court was not established for a further four decades, but when it was set up in the 1570s it was strictly under the direct supervision of, and as a subordinate court to, the High Court of Admiralty in England.[80] This need to control maritime affairs in Ireland by central government was evident in 1573 in the case concerning Sir John Perrot, then lord president of Munster, who was accused of seizing a French ship in Youghal Harbour and distributing the rich cargo on board, including keeping some of it for himself. Called before the High Court of Admiralty in London, he was able to show that he held a commission from the Dublin government to impound the ship and dispense with its cargo as instructed. Though he was acquitted, the government in Dublin was severely reprimanded for making independent decisions and issuing commissions beyond its authority, and by so doing, overriding the authority of the London court.[81] This authority was regularly challenged with respect to the jurisdiction of the London admiralty court and that of the common law courts.[82] Sir Edward Coke, as chief justice from 1606, seems to have been particularly averse to allowing the court of admiralty any leeway in matters of jurisdiction. Coke argued that admiralty authority was on the high seas only and any issue relating to other areas, whether coastal, estuarine or on the inland waterways, fell under the auspices of the king's court of common law:

> Be it enacted, that all Contracts, Pleas and Complaints, and all other things … arising within the bodies of the Counties as well by Land as by Water, as also of Wreck of the Sea, the Admiral Court shall not have any conusance, power, or jurisdiction, nevertheless of death of a man, and of Mayheme done in great Ships, being in the main stream of great Rivers, onely below the Bridges nigh to the Sea, and not in other places of the same Rivers.[83]

In Ireland, however, the issue of jurisdiction and its attendant powers was problematic from the beginning. Officials in Ireland seem to have perceived it as being more substantial than just a vice-admiralty court, though not of the same standing as the High Court of Admiralty, while the lord high admiral and his officials in London categorically regarded the Dublin court as subordinate to central government. The vice-admiral in Ireland could appoint his own officials, but these engagements were by direct sanction of central government in England.[84] As the earl of Nottingham held both positions, he was best placed to attempt to control and, more importantly, influence admiralty business on both sides of the Irish and Celtic Sea. By the time the three crowns were joined under James in March 1603, the lord high admiral himself had long ceased to hear cases; instead, appointed deputies or judges heard and administered cases for and on behalf of the high admiral, including sanctioning those in Ireland. The desire to maintain central control over appointments and commissions had its basis in the profit to be made from a wide range of payments and charges that could be exacted and imposed, as well as shares from cases relating to 'sea casualties' such as flotsam, jetsam and wreck. These were collected on behalf of the lord high admiral by his deputies. Additionally, he received a tenth of all prize monies taken by privately owned English vessels; the amounts were substantial, with the value of prizes seized during Elizabeth's war with Spain estimated at over £100,000. Control in matters of the admiralty prize courts was thus in the interest of individuals like Nottingham.[85]

BLURRED BOUNDARIES AND LOCAL LAWS

With the expansion of English piracy along the southwest coast of Munster from 1603 and the opportunities for increased profits from pirated goods and ships, the need to maintain rigid control of the appointment of admiralty officials in Ireland was all the more urgent. Persistence for central London control frustrated Irish-based officials, who also recognised the opportunity (and indeed it became the norm to avail of such opportunities) to make profit from the pirate community. The link between law and profit led to a blurring of the boundary between public and private interests.[86] Comprehensive evidentiary material for cases undertaken by the admiralty court in Ireland is rare, particularly during its early period of existence, due primarily to the fact that the court records for that period do not survive as complete papers. Indeed, it is only on rare occasions that a case brought before the admiralty court can be followed through from beginning to end, from the first issuing of a warrant to sentences handed down.[87] This was a direct result of the ineptitude and corruption of admiralty officials on the ground, their failure to hold regular courts and – often a deliberate act – failure to keep annual accounts. The reluctance of local admiralty officials to take direct action against the pirates in Ireland also influenced the number of examinations that were taken or extent of records made.[88]

Ambrose Forth was the first judge of the admiralty court in Ireland, appointed in 1575, and he served for nearly thirty years. From the beginning of his appointment he had to contend with challenges from the chancery court and common law courts in respect of jurisdictional matters, while at the same time contending with pervading issues of piracy.[89] As a lawyer himself and master of the chancery in Dublin, he was perfectly positioned to ensure that procedures would be followed as judiciously as possible in an effort to curb piracy, albeit in the absence of direct legislation to tackle it in Ireland.[90] Such measures would, in theory anyway, be compliant with the High Court of Admiralty in London.[91] Little is known of Forth during his tenure, though he did report to London on the state of affairs in Ireland and seems to have held court on a number of occasions.[92] He is accredited with establishing the Munster court of admiralty, and it was he who appointed Henry Gosnold as his resident deputy judge in 1608. Gosnold was judge of the presidential court of Munster and was MP for Clonakilty at that time. It is not clear though whether he was judge for the separate (provincial) court of the admiralty of Munster as commissioned by the lord admiral, or a deputy of the national court of admiralty and acting as Forth's deputy in Munster.[93]

The operation of the court was sporadic, due in no small way to the absence of an established court structure in rural areas. The lack of specific law also inhibited the hearing of cases as they arose, though Forth tried to argue that the Offences at Sea Act of 1536 also extended to cover Ireland and thus allowed him to hear cases and try pirates in Ireland. Following the successful apprehension in 1587 of a Captain Cawfeld (Caufield?) and his pirate crew in Drogheda and their incarceration in the jail there, Forth stated that:

> The pirates are all committed there to the number of one and fifty. We have no commission in Ireland for their trial according the course of Her Majesty's laws; neither are the statutes made anno H. VIII 27 and anno H. VIII 28 for trial of pirates of force in Ireland, according the common opinion of our Justices. Howbeit I construe (consterr) them to extend to all Her Majesty's dominions, for offences committed upon the main seas.[94]

The Dublin government did not agree, and Forth's pleas to the lord high admiral fell on deaf ears. Nottingham's need to control the transfer of merchandise and money continued to inform his decisions to have pirates and their goods brought to England for trial. Should power be ceded to Dublin, there was a risk that maintaining control of pirate trials and, more importantly, pirated goods would have been virtually impossible due to the remoteness of the bays and harbours in Ireland.[95]

The transplantation of many of the English-based pirates to Ireland can therefore be regarded as reciprocally beneficial, but this shared relationship was not limited to admiralty officials alone. It was embedded within a wider social landscape that permeated undertakers, settlers and government officials who looked to Munster as a means to obtain land and wealth, and – in many instances – to escape the authority of central government.[96] London continued to issue commissions for the apprehension of pirates in Irish waters without consulting with Forth. One such letter was issued to the lord justice of Ireland, Sir William Pelham, to ensure he was prepared in advance when instructions were given to Sir William Winter to send ships to patrol the coastal waters of Ireland, and in particular the Shannon region, to apprehend pirates if they were encountered.[97] Forth wrote to Sir Julius Caesar in 1586, who was then general commissioner on piracy, detailing his concern with regard to pirates infesting several towns and pleading for a commission to be sent to try the pirates in Ireland. This again seems to have been ignored.[98]

Another issue thwarting Forth's progress was the claim by some incorporated towns and cities to their right to admiralty administration. It is interesting to note that some town and city officials were clever enough to have the right to carry out their own admiralty business written into their charter of incorporation. In 1578 for instance, Galway officials ensured that:

> ... mayors of the said town, so long as they shall be mayors of the same, shall be admirals of us, our heirs and successors, and every of them, for the time he shall be mayor of the said town, as long as he shall be mayor of the same, shall be admiral of us, our heirs and successors within the port, bay, town, liberties, franchises and suburbs of Galway.[99]

Similarly in 1582, when Dublin's charter was being confirmed, granted to its mayor, sheriffs, commonalty and citizens was 'the office of Admiralty, and all matters pertaining to it'. Stipulated was that 'the jurisdiction and authority of Admiralty [was] to be exercised by the Mayor for the time being'.[100] This insistence by cities and towns to claim admiralty jurisdiction seems to have remained a persistent and unresolved issue, as evidenced by the inclusion in Youghal's charter that the mayor was 'to have a further grant of office of admiralty from Ardmore and Caple Island to the Island at Toorene with Jetsam and Flotsam, to the use of the Town ...'.[101] The control of admiralty matters was thus retained at a local level, which further exacerbated governmental handling of pirate matters. Harbours like Youghal would have been among the most important in the southwest throughout the medieval and post-medieval periods, along with Cork and Kinsale. The smaller towns and harbours equally appear to have had an administrative set-up throughout this period, albeit on a more localised level, that governed maritime affairs, including admiralty jurisdiction.[102] Many of these retained legislative controls similar to those of the seaport towns in England. In place since medieval times, they operated in the same way as the systems of revenue governance for the main coastal towns and harbours, which included dealing with ongoing problems of piracy. This system had its origin in the feudal administration under the Anglo-Normans and continued under later English control, covering the area on the eastern seaboard of Ireland known as the Pale.[103] With the demise of the Gaelic Order at the turn of the seventeenth century, further laws were enacted to control trade and shipping in Irish ports and harbours in general. These tended to concentrate on revenue and exchequer returns on goods imported and exported, not just relating to the merchant community and their ships but also to those settlers and natives who supplied much of the goods to the port towns and harbours.[104]

Youghal, as well as other Munster ports at the time, was regarded as an ideal location from which to develop a vibrant export trade, in livestock and other agricultural produce, with tobacco planters and other plantation owners in the colonial New World settlements like Virginia. In turn it was hoped that such a development in trade would entice settlers to the province. Ships on their way to the developing settlements in the New World frequently stopped off at Munster ports, and some merchants, such as Symon Gibbons who had settled in Youghal, traded tobacco from the West Indies to that port.[105] Revenue streams on both exported and imported goods therefore began to grow exponentially as international markets expanded, and the opportunity for greater profits grew accordingly, as did the prospect for plunder.

THE PROVINCIAL COURT OF ADMIRALTY IN MUNSTER AND FURTHER MATTERS OF JURISDICTION

In 1613 the English legislature sought to address the legal hiatus in Ireland, and on 20 October a bill came before the Irish parliament in Dublin, gaining passage into law in 1614 as the 'Act for the Punishing of Pirates and Robbers at Sea'.[106] From that time in Ireland both the High Court of Admiralty and Irish parliament could then deal directly with piracy and, more importantly, the pirates themselves, on home ground. Following the establishment of the Irish admiralty in Dublin, local vice-admiralty courts were set up in the four provinces. The Munster vice-admiralty court was the earliest established in Ireland, with Sir John Norris (Norreys), lord president of Munster, acting as vice-admiral from 1586 to 1598, with the provincial courts established in the seventeenth century. The Munster Provincial Admiralty Court was the first established, in 1608, and the remaining three provinces had vice-admirals appointed from 1635 onwards. Though the Irish courts of admiralty remained subordinate to the High Court of Admiralty in London, and if the need arose cases could be appealed to England, attempts were made by the Irish government to exercise sole jurisdiction without due regard to central government.[107]

The constitutional status of the Munster admiralty court was clearly that of a satellite administration of the national court in Dublin, which was in turn meant to be a regional or vice-admiralty court of the High Court of Admiralty in London. Essentially it was to be an extension of central admiralty governance in Ireland, or at least this seems to have been the viewpoint from London.[108] But issues pertaining to jurisdiction prevailed. Vice-admirals held their positions more or less on an honorary basis, and many were absent and held other high-office roles (the earl of Nottingham, for example), with deputies appointed to carry out the work in the regions; deputy vice-admirals therefore effectively acted on behalf of the absent vice-admirals in the provinces.[109] Sir Arthur Chichester, for example, was vice-admiral of Ulster from 1607 to 1628 while he also held the office of lord deputy of Ireland (1605–16), succeeding Charles Blount, 1st earl of Devonshire. In Munster, Sir John Norris was succeeded by several individuals who resided in England, the most relevant to the pirate operations being Nottingham himself.

Between the ending of Norris' tenure in 1598 and Nottingham's appointment in 1609, a number of others held the post. Henry Cowper is cited as acting vice-admiral in 1598 and the following year George Wadham was in office. In 1606 Humphrey Jobson is referred to as servant of the lord admiral, but he and others also acted as deputies for the London court at the time, rather than being officially appointed as vice-admirals in Munster.[110] In 1627, Jobson is also referred to by Viscount Falkland (Lord Deputy Henry Cary) as 'Deputy Vice-Admiral in Munster and Secretary for Admiralty Causes to the Earl of Nottingham', to which is added that he was expelled for bad behaviour.[111] Jobson and many others remained in place over extensive periods, which afforded them the time and opportunity to become deeply rooted in pirate affairs. Viscount Falkland himself was acting vice-admiral in 1619 and was replaced in 1634 by Thomas Wentworth, later earl of Strafford.

The Munster court of vice-admiralty was organised in a more structured way than the other provincial courts, due to the intensity of pirate activity around the coastline there. The geographical location too, within the direct line of the transatlantic trading routes, was another mitigating factor in the complexity of organisation, as the Munster court proved to be the most profitable of the four provincial admiralty courts.[112]

CULTURAL EVIDENCE FOR ADMIRALTY AFFAIRS

When considering where such administrative centres were located, and to provide a physical link to those events, it is to be presumed that the location for the 'Admiral's Court every Monday' in Kinsale was either Desmond Castle, located in Kinsale town or Castlepark, on the southern side of Kinsale Harbour. Now named James Fort, Castlepark was originally known as Castle Ny Parke and also called Old Fort, when construction began in 1603. Its name changed following the visit to the area of James II in 1689 during his Irish campaign.[113] The fortified tower of Desmond Castle, built in the late fifteenth or early sixteenth century, was used as an official town residence and functioned as the custom house during the sixteenth and into the seventeenth centuries. It operated as a powder magazine for the commander of the Spanish fleet, Don Juan del Aquila, during the Battle of Kinsale in 1601 and thereafter was used as a prison, since known as the French Prison, Kinsale. The castle commands an excellent view of the harbour from its battlements and would have been the centre of activity for wine, wool and tobacco imports during the latter part of the sixteenth century.[114]

Though at a distance now from the harbour front, in the early seventeenth century the shoreline would have been closer to Desmond Castle. In the intervening centuries the town of Kinsale has expanded seaward, with quay extensions and reclamation of foreshore pushing the land outward, leaving sites like Desmond Castle more remote from their original setting and functional maritime context. It now houses the International Museum of Wine, providing historical information on Ireland's wine trade with Europe and the wider Atlantic.[115] The castle comprises a three-storey keep and storehouses to the rear, with domestic offices on the first and second floors, where the business of customs and excise and admiralty duties would have been carried out. Castlepark (James Fort), discussed in more detail below, probably marks

FIGURE 12: Desmond Castle, Kinsale. The tower house was built by the earl of Desmond in the sixteenth century as a custom house and was used as an ordnance store during the Battle of Kinsale in 1601. It may have functioned as an administrative fort or custom house at the time of the pirates; it is now a national monument in state care.

the site of an earlier fortification and hence its earlier name of 'Old Fort'.[116] It was here that Sir Henry Skipwith was stationed as admiralty officer during the first decade of the seventeenth century and from where he had direct dealings with the pirates in west Cork, maintaining a close working relationship with many of them. He became one of the leading admiralty officials linked with the pirate alliance.[117] By 1607 Skipwith was the commissioned constable in Kinsale and had a lieutenant reporting to him, along with a gunner and twenty soldiers. While the complement of men stationed at Castlepark was relatively small, it did ensure Skipwith could control movements very easily, both of persons and goods inward and outward.[118]

Castlepark and Desmond castles, both national monuments in state care, provide important upstanding archaeological evidence for the probable location of admiralty operations when piracy was in its heyday in Munster. It was from sites like these that official business was administered, but also where more furtive deals took place, which allowed the pirates' operation to sustain through the legitimate cloak of admiralty jurisdiction and admiralty affairs.[119]

AN END ... AND A BEGINNING

The genesis of the piracy that was to become so endemic in Ireland can be traced to late sixteenth-century Tudor explorations dominated by privately operated ships – Elizabeth's 'sea dogs' – who successfully waged an aggressive maritime war on traditional enemies. At the same time, England's forging of trading links with the Ottoman and Moroccan empires would open up ports in northwest Africa for English pirates to use as seasonal headquarters. King James' outlawing of privately commissioned ships from 1603 meant there was no legitimate work for thousands of mariners, most of whom turned to piracy. His targeting of the ports and harbours of the southwest of England in an effort to curb piracy there forced those involved to transfer from the West Country to Munster. The coastal landscape of the southwest of Ireland was more than conducive to the piratical flow of monies and goods, as the ruling Gaelic-Irish lords had previously controlled their harbours and territorial waters in a similar fashion to safeguard revenue streams; arriving speculators and settlers within a colonial context tapped into these local processes. The extension of the English pirate base of operations to the southwest coast of Ireland in the early seventeenth century was facilitated by legal loopholes that permitted this activity to flourish, and encouraged men of the sea to come together and form an alliance.

CHAPTER 2

A Piratical Alliance

Ní neart go cur le chéile.[1]

The mariners who were active in the North Atlantic in the early seventeenth century, to enable them to operate productively as a marauding group, required organisation and a dedicated command system. Such a system needed to allow for individual autonomy, equality and manoeuvrability, but, importantly, it also needed to be sufficiently structured and ordered to merit loyalty and the coming together of all ships to operate as one when the need arose. The English-dominated piracy in the southwest of Ireland at that time had just that – a hierarchy of command and leadership that was formal yet fair, officious yet democratic, structured and cohesive. The chain of command within the ranks of the pirate crews, coupled with the eagerness of those on land to accommodate them, was vital to their operations. When all these variables came together within a coastal landscape that was conducive, agreed relationships were established and accords made – and hence an alliance was formed. This union of mutually aligned individuals became, for a specific period of time, a unique, powerful and extremely successful body. Together they dominated and dictated maritime events within their main sphere of operations in the North Atlantic, but this activity also had more far-reaching global economic and political impacts.

In the previous chapter the mechanisms that led to the formation of the Alliance of Pirates were discussed, with broader geopolitical and maritime events providing the backdrop. It is necessary to delve deeper into the sources to gain a better understanding of how the alliance operated, the individuals involved, and what their motivations were. Though accounts of the numbers of pirates operating around the coast of Ireland at the time vary, most if not all indicate that such numbers were high. Realistically, though, it is only possible through historical research to arrive at an estimate.[2] In 1609, for example, admiral of the Atlantic Alliance of Pirates, Richard Bishop, reportedly commanded eleven ships and over one thousand men, while his vice-admiral, Peter Easton, entered Villafranca with a fleet comprising nine hundred men.[3] In the same year, Lord Deputy Sir Arthur Chichester, writing to the earl of Salisbury, Sir Robert Cecil, solemnised that 'they are grown to a height of strength and pride that he doubts his endeavours will hardly prevail without the assistance of some of His Majesty's good ships'.[4]

What can be said with some certainty, and as identified by Richard Moryson, then acting lord president in Munster,[5] is that the pirates were of such numbers that they operated openly, without fear of prosecution and in such a way that they were facilitated by natives, settlers and local government officials alike, whether readily or through compulsion.[6]

It is possible to identify approximately seventy individuals active in piracy in Ireland during the early seventeenth century. These were either directly involved and with a firm focus on using Ireland as a base, or indirectly by calling into bases and places in Ireland during the course of their operations but with their main pirating activity focused elsewhere, in places like the Mediterranean, Newfoundland and North Africa.[7] This number reflects only those individuals who can be discerned in the records as being in Ireland for the period 1603–31, and includes captains and senior crew members (such as ship masters or lieutenants), along with some individual men. The numbers are thus not exhaustive. Similarly, numbers of ships associated with captains are traceable, but again, a complete record is not possible as ships frequently changed hands or their names changed, went unrecorded or were mistranscribed at the time. Neither can it take into account those who spent part of the year working legitimately as fishermen, labourers, carpenters, shoemakers or other now 'invisible' professions in the local areas and who dipped into piracy when opportunity presented itself, essentially leading a deliberate amphibious lifestyle.

One can, therefore, only guess at the overall actual number of pirates operating in southwest Ireland in the early part of the seventeenth century. Indications of actual numbers as well as organisational details can be obtained from contemporary and often first-hand sources, particularly the HCA examinations and indictments, the state papers, and of course Henry Mainwaring's *Discourse on Piracy*.[8] Mainwaring outlined the situation clearly for the king when he wrote:

> ... although these things happen more often in England than Ireland, by reason there is plenty of Ports and Shipping, as also more abundance of Seamen, yet in proportion Ireland doth much exceed it, for it may be well called the Nursery and Storehouse of Pirates.[9]

Care needs to be taken when considering such accounts, however, and the numbers represented. Between the years 1603 and 1640, for example, there were 1,031 men indicted on charges of piracy in the High Court of

A note of the Pirates,

Captaine Richard Bushope his mr name is Richard Thornton his mate George [illegible] of Ratclif. Capt Lewis Plumley, Henry Pope, Ellis Beast, George Willington, Pemberton [illegible] a youth [illegible], Lodwick Barry [illegible]

[illegible]

Captaine Peter Easton his mr name is Martin Williams his Liefetenant one fford, Edward Jhnes, walter Frayes,

Capt ffrancke his mr name Gabriell his mates Capt Ellsetone of [illegible], on Jhn Ellis

Captaine Woolmert

Capt Stephenson his mr name is George his mates [illegible] Jhn Bryan one Thomas Hussy, Arthur Capp

Captaine Parker his mr name Jhn Hill, wth him Captaine Martin & one Goddard of St Katherines & Kinge his Liefetenant one Moone of Plimouth and one Adams

Peter a Dutchman, wth him many Dutchmen, his Liefetenant Jhn Perkinges,

Captaine ffinge, most of his Company out landishe men, Severs one Skerry of Plimouth [illegible]
of good meanes buyer of such commodities & seller [illegible]

Captaine Halsey his mr name Edward

Capt Halsell of Plymouth

Rich Kerry

(105)

FACING PAGE, FIGURE 13: 'A Note of the Pirates', *c.* 1610 by Richard Kerry, agent to the vice-admiral of Munster, the earl of Nottingham, listing the primary pirate captains of the alliance, and their leading crew members then active in Roaringwater Bay. TNA, HCA EXAMINATIONS 1/47, F. 105

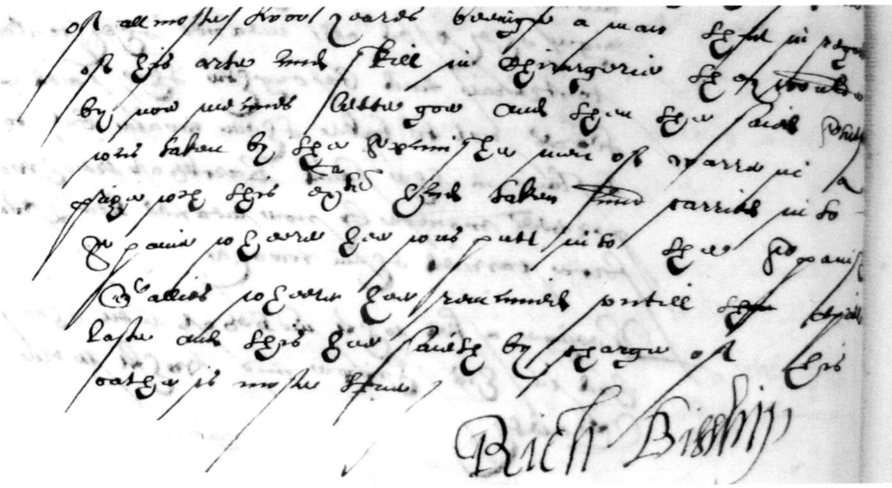

FIGURE 14: Detail showing signature of pirate Admiral Richard Bishop taken from High Court of Admiralty Criminal examination opening: 'Rich Bushopps of Skull in Ireland, aged about 52 years, 17 August, 1614'. TNA HCA EXAMINATIONS 13/98, F. 213

Admiralty, but of these, some had been indicted more than once. The true figure, therefore, was only 728 men. This averages out at less than twenty men a year and as Clive Senior in his study points out, this would not have amounted to one third of the compliment of a well-armed pirate ship.[10] The Venetian ambassadors to England, Marc' Antonio Correr and Zorzi Giustinian, reporting in 1608, again provide some insight when they wrote that the English king had stated that there could be up to 500 pirate vessels active in the Atlantic.[11] James may have included all pirate vessels here – Dunkirkers, Spanish, Dutch, Ottoman Turks, as well as English – and therefore, again, the numbers given may be misleading.

For the year 1610, Richard Kerry, agent to the vice-admiral of Munster, the earl of Nottingham, travelled to Leamcon in west Cork. There, in the company of Deputy Vice-Admiral Humphrey Jobson and his brother Richard Jobson, Kerry recorded details of the men active in piracy. His account suggests that three main leaders had been elected at that stage, who held titles of command to reflect their roles. A second contemporary list, again by Kerry, though Captain Edmund Flint had been replaced by pirate Captain Sammes, confirms this. The lists are striking, giving details of the pirates and their ships.[12]

Richard Bishop is referred to as 'Admiral', commanding a ship of 240 tons with 35 guns and 120 crew; Peter Easton is titled 'Vice-Admiral', with a French ship of 140 tons, 35 guns and 50 crew; 'Rear-Admiral' Thomas Francke commands a Dutch flyboat of 200 tons, 16 guns and 90 men; Captain Robert Stephenson a French vessel (no tonnage given), 7 guns and 27 men; Harvy (Harvey) captains a Dutch ship of 100 tons, 9 to 10 guns and 30 crew; Sammes is in charge of a Biscayner of 80 tons and 35 crew (ordnance not listed); Parker (Richard) is in command of a Dutch ship (size not listed), 3 guns and 35 crew; Pieter, a Dutchman, captains a French 'bark' of 30 tons, no guns but 27 crew; and another Harvey has a Dutch ship of 100 tons, 16 guns and between 30 and 40 crew. There were two pirates named Captain Harvey at the time: Philip Harvey from Plymouth and William Harvey, who settled in Schull.[13] Taking the numbers listed at face value, and bearing in mind that not all the subordinate pirate captains and their crews are listed by Kerry, the number recorded as active pirates for a given period in one year amounts to 454 men serving on nine ships that collectively carried up to 114 guns or more. A formidable force of men indeed.

PIRACY BEFORE THE ALLIANCE WAS FORMED

The change in the political and social landscape of Ireland in the latter part of the sixteenth century created opportunities for the exchange of legitimate and illicit goods. Not all changed completely, however, as has been discussed in the introductory chapter, particularly in remote areas where native Irish continued to live within a dispersed landscape familiar to them. Newcomers were arriving but social norms, and in many cases lifestyles, remained unchanged.[14] Certainly the native Irish still living in the distant coastal areas of southwest Munster were more than accustomed to, and indeed continued to be intricately involved in, maritime activities. Many were engaged in the fishing industry, originally as tenants of Gaelic-Irish lords and then of newly planted landlords, and essentially made their living from the sea, so although remote, this was not an 'uncivilised' landscape.[15] This distinction separates the settlement of areas of Munster from other examples of colonial expansion elsewhere in the New World. The pirates who came to do business along the Munster coastline in the early part of the seventeenth century did not enter an unknown, uninhabited land but essentially extended their base and system of operations, were received by those native Irish living there, and connected with new settlers and entrepreneurs within a plantation process.[16]

Many of the men who agreed to come together and serve under the combined leadership of Bishop, Easton and Francke had forged a name for themselves as pirates before that. They operated primarily on an individual basis but co-operated when the need arose, in what appears to have been very much autonomous ventures within a small but loosely associated assembly. The High Court of Admiralty indictments provide details on the early activities of some of the pirates who a few years later became synonymous within the more structured alliance, but who were known to the authorities well before that.[17] Names for the years 1603–7, some of whom are discussed later, include William Pierce, Thomas Tompkins, Thomas Tucker, John Ward, Thomas Salkeld and Richard Robinson. It is from 1608 that more familiar names are recorded, including Tibault Suxbridge (at times spelled 'Saxbridge'), John Jennings, James Harris, Thomas Coward, William Baugh, as well as Peter Easton and Richard Bishop. Of these, Jennings, Coward, Harris, Tucker, Easton and Bishop appear most regularly during the years 1609–12, and thereafter new names enter the record. Other pirates disappear from the records early on but who were active before Bishop began to lead them as an organised group.

In 1606 Chichester noted that a pirate named Captain Connello (possibly Connolly) had arrived into Wexford in a 'barque' with seven or eight others, whereupon they were duly captured.[18] Chichester was concerned that the pirates would receive benefit of clergy and escape conviction by this means, declaring that 'they will be admitted their "cleargie" by the laws of this realm [Ireland], and then he is sure the chiefest of them will escape with life, for they can read well'.[19] The reference here to their ability to read reflected the requirement that when using benefit of clergy, they had to be able to read, with the first verse of Psalm 51 generally read aloud to fulfil the process:

> Have mercy on me, O God, according to your steadfast love;
> According to your abundant mercy, blot out my transgressions;
> Wash me thoroughly from my iniquity and cleanse me from my sin![20]

Chichester recorded that Connello, his master and one other are 'notable offenders of that kind', and he provided a list of some of their plundering. This included robbing ships in and around the harbour of Barnstable in Devon, and taking oils and wools. Connello, a mariner of Devon, had previously used his influence with Lord High Admiral Nottingham and was acquitted, and Chichester was again worried that the pirate captain would, once more, try to do the same. The lord deputy wrote that the pirates 'conclude that the law [in Ireland] can do them no hurt', and he looked to the earl of Devonshire, lord lieutenant of Ireland, to intervene. Chichester, in his correspondence, suggested that change was needed in the law in Ireland in order to prevent pirates from exerting their influence on officials, as they had previously done in England.[21] The hiatus in the legislation in Ireland allowed the pirates more freedom to operate and encouraged officials to turn a blind eye when it suited them. Where trade in contraband was concerned, therefore, and as noted in the previous chapter, this legal loophole facilitated the growth in the underground black market in illegal goods and supported ongoing commerce with the pirates.

Captain Thomas Coward was also active in the area from about 1604 onwards and his influence with admiralty officials in both England and Ireland emphasised the difficulty in dealing with the pirate problem under the English monarch during the early part of his reign as James I. Coward was imprisoned in 1604 in Bristol, charged with piracy against French and Bristol merchants, but no charges were subsequently brought and he was released. In 1606 he was acting under letters of marque from the Dutch and it is only in 1607 that he is first mentioned as a captain of his own ship.[22] Recorded as a Bristol mariner, Coward had a long and successful pirate career that straddled the time just prior to and during the main period of piracy in southwest Ireland.[23] In 1607 he was operating off the Munster coast and was captured in Youghal through the efforts of the deputy vice-admiral Humphrey Jobson and Sir Richard Boyle, who, at that time, was serving on the regional Council of Munster. A Bristol man named Hampton, who manned a small vessel in the harbour, was engaged by them and hidden below deck were eighty men. They surprised Coward, overpowered him and his crew (of which his lieutenant and three of his men were killed), and captured his ship, a Flemish vessel of 60 tons and well equipped with ordnance and supplies. Coward's ship was handed over to the vice-admiral, the earl of Nottingham, for use as a naval ship and the ordnance was sent to Sir Oliver St John, master of the ordnance for the admiralty. Coward and his men were sent to prison to await trial.[24]

During his stay in prison in Ireland, he garnered support from the lord president of Munster, Donogh O'Brien, 4th earl of Thomond, who made representations to the Privy Council on Coward's behalf saying that his experience as an able seaman and an excellent pilot should instead be utilised.[25] The lords of the Privy Council in London, when enquiring in March 1608 as to the whereabouts of Coward and his fellow crew, learned that not only had he been released but that Thomond had engaged his services as a mariner. Replying at the end of the month, Chichester explained that the Chief Baron of the Exchequer, Humphrey Winch, when he arrived at the court in Cork, could not find a good reason to hold Coward and his crew.[26] Shortly thereafter, however, Chichester received directions from the Privy Council in England to have Coward transported there. Coward was sent to London in the *Lion's Whelp*, under Sir William St John, but was, once again, acquitted and released.[27]

A prominent pirate captain, who seems to have had the wherewithal to dodge execution, Coward operated extensively in the Atlantic. In 1609 he served under the command of Captain William Harvey in a 140-ton captured Dutch ship. Not long after and acting as a free agent, he joined Peter Easton's crew for nine months and was given command of the ship *John*. Coward, at this point, seems to have been part of the emerging alliance, with a letter from the mayor and aldermen of Bristol referring to the 'piracies committed by him and his confederates'.[28] Such was his success and integration thereafter into the pirate alliance and local society, that it is documented that he built a house on William Hull's estate in Leamcon near Schull, though unfortunately few details of his arrangement with Hull are recorded.[29] William Hull, deputy vice-admiral in the Schull area, had business and familial connections with strategic players within the context of the Munster plantation at that time and became a central figure in the alliance. He is discussed in detail in the next chapter.

The inter-dependence of those within the emerging alliance is clear when we consider the ship *Grace Bonaventure* of Bristol, which was the focus of Easton's and Coward's attention in early 1610. Easton brought the ship from Bristol into Berehaven in west Cork, where he plundered its cargo of packets of wool and linen, damask to make sails, the cable for the bower anchor and other cordage. He held captive the master, the boatswain, the carpenter and two boys to serve as crew on board his own ship and left on board the *Grace Bonaventure* just two mariners and the purser. Easton then released the ship but Coward intercepted it rounding Mizen Head, and helped himself to the 'shipp's boate, two musketts and six pikes, one buckett and a canne (cane)'.[30] Both pirates were thus operating within the same area and within the same confraternity, but they also functioned independently of each other, with Coward taking the pickings left over from Easton's work. It was this juxtaposition between independence and inter-dependence that was the cornerstone of the alliance's success.

Men like Thomas Coward were active from an early period, progressing through times of war and legitimate maritime activity at the turn of the seventeenth century and, while successfully continuing to operate as individuals, also made the transition to being part of an alliance that acted in unison as a powerful pirate force. This was perhaps best illustrated in 1608 when Captain Williamson in the king's ship *Tramontane* was attempting to open fire on pirate Captain Tibault Suxbridge in Baltimore Harbour. Within moments:

> Captaine Jennings and Captaine Bishoppe with theire shippes came downe to the saied Williamson, and anchored the one of his bowe and the other to his quarter within pistol shott, And the said Williamson beeinge then as it seemed not fitt to fighte with them putt for a flagg of Truce ....[31]

INDIVIDUALS COME TO LIGHT

Little is known of the lives or background of most of the pirates who formed the alliance, and indeed it is only for a select few that there is any information that allows an informed overview of who they were and what possibly motivated them. Clive Senior has compiled a comprehensive list of the primary English pirates active around the coasts of England and Ireland for the early part of the seventeenth century. Of these, approximately seventy-four are known to have frequented the southern coast of Munster, either as a stopover point or as their permanent summer base.[32] Captain Richard Bishop from Yarmouth (though other indictments refer to him as of London or Dartmouth) seems to have been a learned man, judging from his prowess as a sailor and commander, and his ability to broker deals with the establishment, while at the same time having a successful career as a pirate. His joint petition with his pirate colleague Captain William Wollmer, which has suffered from fire damage, is undated but was clearly signed by him. His value as a seaman, and the contribution he could make to the crown as a legitimate commander, ultimately led to a king's pardon, though no actual details of the issuing of the pardon are known.[33]

Bishop is described as 'a man of such parts, and experience in that profession [mariner] that, if his courses of life were any way suitable to them, good use might be made of him in His Majesty's service'.[34] In a deposition taken in 1614, Bishop is described as a 'gentleman of Skull [Schull], aged about 52 years'.[35] Lord Deputy Chichester referred to Bishop as 'by farr the most sufficient man amongest them all [the pirates], both for Cowncell and Commaund'.[36] As a pirate leader and as a man whose services could be utilised thereafter, Richard Bishop seems to have been respected by all sides. Formerly a naval officer who served under Sir John Norris (Norreys) in the latter part of the sixteenth century, Bishop would have been familiar with the coastline of Ireland as part of his duties on board Norris' coast fleet, tasked with patrolling the seas around Ireland, ironically in search of pirates and privately commissioned ships from other nations. If Bishop were of that age in 1614, he would have been born sometime around 1562 and he could conceivably have been involved in several of the key naval and maritime events during the intervening period before he became admiral of the Alliance of Pirates. These could have included serving under Sir William Winter at Dún an Óir in Smerwick, County Kerry, in 1580, or being on board one of the English ships in the Channel engaged against the ill-fated 1588 Spanish Armada campaign. Or, indeed, he could have been part of the Counter-Armada of 1589, while the attack on Cadiz in 1597 would have involved mariners like Bishop in lesser command positions. He might also have played a part in the English engagement with the Spanish at the Battle of Kinsale in 1601, in Castlehaven Harbour. Bishop would thus have risen up the ranks of command, acquiring his expert knowledge of seamanship along the way; this could explain why he was treated with such favour once he sought a pardon from the king, but also why he was elected pirate admiral of the alliance by his peers.

It is conceivable that Bishop found he was conflicted from 1603 onwards following James' prohibition of the licensing of privately owned ships and as a consequence allied himself with his former naval colleague John Ward, one of the most successful pirates of that era. Ward, who had deserted from the English Navy, had by then turned to outright piracy, with the Mediterranean as his primary theatre of operations. During his heyday Ward assumed celebrity status, the 'classic' archpirate, and indeed this has sustained in literature, art and movies ever since.[37] Ward is variously referred to by several names, including John Ward, Jack Ward and Yusuf Reïs, the last of these denoting his conversion to Islam in 1608. In that year he 'turned Turk', an action regarded as the ultimate insult to the Christian world. By so doing, he was viewed as turning his back on all things civilised, but in reality his conversion was an expression of full allegiance to the Ottoman rulers and secured his position as a commander within their fleets. It was about 1608 that Bishop was selected to lead the alliance, with Captain John Ward handing over power in the

North Atlantic to Bishop, perhaps coinciding with Ward's conversion to Islam and decision to focus his operations in the Mediterranean. Little is known of Ward before 1603 apart from him serving successfully as a sailor in the navy out of Plymouth; possibly a native of Kent, he too rose up through the ranks and then operated as a successful captain of his own ship under letters of reprisal issued by the queen against Spanish shipping. By 1603 Ward was back in Plymouth, down on his luck and with no money. He re-enlisted on the King's ship the *Lion's Whelp* based in Portsmouth but this did not last long, and as the drudgery and harsh conditions of naval life became a reality once more, he persuaded the crew to mutiny. Taking the *Lion's Whelp*, they sailed to Tunis, where Ward began life as a pirate.[38]

It is reasonable to consider that both Ward and Bishop knew each other when serving in the navy or under letters of marque/reprisal, and indeed they may have served and sailed together at some point. It would explain why Bishop joined Ward in piratical pursuits. However, accounts put him as Ward's right-hand man from about 1607 onwards, leaving a hiatus of some four years from the time of James' outlawing of commissioned ships. There are hints that Bishop was part of Ward's crew earlier than this, when Ward was active as a North African pirate. Ward accepted an offer from the ruling Pasha in Algiers to command an Ottoman ship, in concert with janissaries, the élite infantry who served the Ottoman sultan's personal household, and among the most feared soldiers in Europe. Members of the crew too were North African corsairs, whose fleets were called upon by the Ottoman Turks to augment their own, to the mutual benefit of both. While Ward's venture should more correctly be regarded as an Ottoman-commissioned one, his organisational skills and ability to unify diverse but aligned sailing interests led to one of the earliest accounts of janissaries and North African corsairs sailing under a former Christian and indeed non-Ottoman captain. Ward's expertise as a mariner and his ability to unite and lead ingratiated him with the Ottomans and corsairs alike.[39]

At this time, too, Dutch pirate Seimen Dansiger, anglicised more frequently as Simon de Danser, was based in Algiers.[40] Later known as Simon Reïs following his conversion to Islam, Danser, like Ward, also commanded ships of the North African corsairs. Such was the Ottoman and 'Barbary' world of pirates into which European sailors entered; these men came to play key roles in the history of maritime predation, forming part of a network of multi-cultural mariners that, in turn, influenced piratical activities in North Atlantic waters and life along the southwest coast of Munster. Many of these

FIGURE 15: *An Algerine Ship off a Barbary Port*, by Flemish artist Andries van Eertvelt, seventeenth century. The scene shows a typical ship of the time, moored in an unidentified harbour, and smaller tender vessels being used at the quayside. BHC0751; PALMER COLLECTION, NATIONAL MARITIME MUSEUM, GREENWICH, LONDON

seafarers were colleagues with shared motivations who formed a confluence of operations that connected the North Atlantic with the continent, North Africa and, in turn, the Americas. The knowledge base informing the operations of the pirate alliance was cosmopolitan and global.

THE ALLIANCE EXPANDS

Bishop served as lieutenant on board Ward's ship, with one commentator in 1609 noting that '[Ward's] chief of trust in [all] his practices' was Bishop, 'whom [Ward] employed to go forth and bring in prizes at his pleasure'.[41] Ward's sphere of operation remained along the coastline of north and northwestern Africa and among the Mediterranean seaways, with his base in Tunis under the protection of the ruler Cara Osman, who was also head of the janissaries. Osman was assassinated in 1610, and thereafter Ward operated under Youssef Dey.[42] Ward's acumen as a commander of men and his success in piratical expeditions may have influenced Bishop in his organisation of individual pirates and their ships into a cohesive coalition in the North Atlantic. Accounts record that in the waters along the Munster coast in 1609, Ward accompanied Bishop, along with other principal pirate captains. These included John Jennings and Thomas Salkeld (also spelled Sockwell), the latter becoming famous when he proclaimed himself king of Lundy Island off Bristol in 1610, where he set up his base.[43] In their own right, captains such as Jennings and Salkeld were noted for individual acts of piracy along the southern coast of England and Munster and were to join with Bishop and Ward at Tunis in 1609, before sailing back to Munster.[44]

A number of entries in the contemporary Venetian state papers provide detail on the working relationship between Bishop and Ward before Bishop and the others left Tunis for bases in the North Atlantic. One recounts that at El Arisch (Larache):

> … he [Ward] fell in with two English captains, one called Bishop, the other Michael. Michael went home to England, and left his crew with Ward, including his lieutenant, Anthony Johnson. Bishop abandoned his own ship, which was rotten, and joined Ward, and these two, Bishop and Johnson, have been his constant companions in drinking and plundering.[45]

The account, given by the English ambassador to Venice, Sir Henry Wotton, reveals further insights into the English pirates operating in Tunis. Wotton's report, informed by one of the sailors there, continued by outlining that 'the Turks had recently separated them [Bishop and Johnson] from him [Ward] and they carry on their trade on their own account, the one going out to plunder and the other staying behind in Tunis as a hostage'. The other pirate upon his return to port, it seems, ransomed the pirate on shore. This was not something new to Bishop, as he had redeemed several of his fellow crew over the years, including his associated adventurer Captain James Harris in the closing years of Elizabeth's reign when Harris found himself in the bagnios as a galley slave of the North African corsairs.[46] It was no doubt also a way by which the Ottoman Turks maintained control of their own fleets, ensuring at any given time that only a select number of Englishmen or non-Turks sailed, and therefore would not be in a position to assume unofficial command or influence a mutiny on board an Ottoman ship.

Several of the pirate captains who sailed with Ward and Bishop became leading captains in the North Atlantic alliance. Contact was maintained between Ward and those in Munster, under the leadership of Bishop, thus retaining the network across the Atlantic and into the Mediterranean. In 1609, the Venetian ambassador in England, Marc' Antonio Correr, wrote: 'Ward has fourteen ships, and is on the point of going to Ireland where he will find both friends and shelter.'[47]

A HIERARCHY OF COMMAND AND AN UNWRITTEN CODE?

Later sources on pirates provide an understanding of the operational setup and the status of the men engaged in the activity, the type of ships used, and the social makeup beyond the confines of their wooden world when not on board their vessels on the high seas. Importantly, these sources reveal the codes of practice, or 'articles', that were in place that governed the operations of the pirates at the time. Certainly Alexander O. Exquemelin's history of *The Buccaneers of America* is one such source, providing a first-hand account from the latter part of the seventeenth century of the pirates active around the Caribbean islands.[48] No such written evidence has come to light for any formal written code or 'article' governing the operations of the pirates in the alliance, though their tactics and their business dealings among crew certainly suggests a system was in place, albeit perhaps a verbal agreement. Henry Mainwaring's *Discourse* contains details of individuals, their theatre of operations, their sailing tactics and their social perspectives, all of which helps to flesh out those men who by design remained deliberately hidden within a world masked by secrecy and silence. The *Discourse* does not contain any mention of a written code of practice, but it certainly shines a light on how they operated their ships, including having agreed signs that governed when to give chase, where to meet, and how to know one another at a distance when at sea. The flag they used was not a black flag or what would later be referred to as the 'Jolly Roger'; instead, Mainwaring wrote, 'they commonly show such colours as are most proper to their Ships, which are for the most part Flemish bottoms ...'.[49] It seems therefore that the tactics of the alliance were pragmatic, with the focus on successful plunder. The flags used and signals agreed all formed part of their operational strategy.

The men in the alliance accepted certain characters to lead them, such as Richard Bishop, but how he, or his vice-admiral Peter Easton, for example, were elected to their command also remains a mystery. It can be presumed that it was undertaken in an open way, as democratic election of individuals to lead them was common among pirate groups, and was a means to retain order and ensure fairness and control. Life on board a pirate-operated ship needed to be representative as it was essentially a business setting – their place of work, as it were. The greater the return on the business, the better for all crew involved. The crew on any pirate ship would have needed to have confidence in their captain. They would have had to trust his ability to command, and also his knowledge of navigation and seamanship. It is to be presumed therefore that it was in everyone's interest to ensure a system was in place to regulate and democratically elect leaders, to distribute the agreed allocation of goods plundered so that each man and their families received their fair share, and to ensure each man had a voice. From sources that do exist, it is obvious that there was a mechanism in place for each crew member to receive their share in goods according to their position on board, as is discussed in more detail in Chapter 5. How this arrangement was agreed, however, can only be hypothesised. It may be that there was an oral agreement in place, an 'oral code of practice' as it were, that included selecting or electing certain seasoned men of the sea to lead them, as well as governing tactics and share amounts. Each ship or fleet of ships within the alliance seems to have had its own system, as suggested by the records relating to Captain William Baugh, discussed below. Each member of crew would have agreed the structure, or put in place an understanding, that regulated their respective roles, ensured a return on their actions, and with new crew abiding by the agreed 'code'.

This approach may have become more formalised over time, as was the case with pirates in the Caribbean and North America, where 'articles' were written and signed, and from which the archetypal 'pirate code' has become synonymous with the pirates of the Caribbean in particular. Such agreements, whether oral or written, would have been detailed enough to ensure not only order but also encouragement to perform. They would have sought to inspire men to act as a coalition with the singular aim of successful plunder. The incentive was in the agreed shares per man, meaning that each could begin to gauge, on a personal level, the potential return on pirated goods or ships. That an understanding was in place is suggested in the 1612 account of pirate Captain William Baugh, one of the pirates of the alliance. Baugh's vice-admiral Richard Millington, along with other members of the crew, argued that they did not receive their rightful shares from goods plundered and sought redress from Captain Baugh.[50] The captain was answerable to his men, though as was seen in Baugh's case, such understandings did not always work out.

This wider social aspect to the rules of engagement governing a pirate ship and its crew has tended to focus on the later piracy of the Caribbean and North America, and has only recently been properly explored. It is indicative of a much more complex and organised system, however, rather than the traditional view of outcasts functioning within an 'uncivilised' and unruly society.[51] The command system that governed the pirates operating out of Munster is more difficult to determine in the absence of written evidence, but from sources that do exist it can be said with a degree of confidence that it was consistent with and no doubt informed by the calibre of men active within it and their experience as seasoned mariners.

MEN OF THE ALLIANCE

Twenty-one pirates are identifiable as settled in the area, most in Leamcon on Deputy Vice-Admiral William Hull's lands near Schull, as well as in Crookhaven and the Baltimore area (including on the islands of Sherkin and Ringaroige).[52] Many others who remain undocumented would have lived along that general stretch of coastline, including on the other islands scattered across Roaringwater Bay, but outside of the main villages. This dispersed settlement is inferred by a proposal to depopulate areas, including the islands, in an effort to rid them of the pirates, their families and fellow conspirators. The proposal was rejected, deemed potentially too disruptive locally to the plantation efforts.[53] In 1609, Sir Richard Moryson was forced to suspend any attempt at suppression, being concerned that it may have provoked 'this unruly multitude into [carrying out] any act either of spoiling or burning the country'.[54] This was further borne out by naval commander Sir William Monson, in charge of the Irish coast fleet tasked with the eradication of piracy, who perhaps best reflected the situation when he noted that Moryson was in fact too powerless to take steps against the pirates.[55]

Richard Bishop left Ward's main fleet in Tunis in late 1608 or early 1609 to lead the alliance in the North Atlantic. His title, that of admiral, denotes the highest rank of a naval commander and perhaps was an attempt to attribute a more legitimate or respectable status to the leader of the pirates, which, in

FIGURE 16: View from the Cove across to Baltimore village, with Dún na Séad Castle elevated in centre of image. Thomas Crooke's main settlement was at a distance from the smaller settlement in the Cove, which was the focus of attack by the Algerine pirates in 1631. IMAGE: CONNIE KELLEHER

turn, may have assisted in negotiations on pardons and subsequent lawful settlement ashore. In his capacity, Bishop did have the power to assign men to particular ships, if captains were in need of men or if ships were in need of repair, for example. These could include carpenters, surgeons and gunners. This movement of men within the pirate fleet would still have required majority agreement whenever any given moment dictated.[56] The adoption, in principle at least, of a certain code of practice, including not attacking their fellow English mariners and agreeing instead to target the traditional enemies of the crown – predominantly Spanish, Portuguese and Dutch shipping – may have served in the long term to work in their favour, for example in the subsequent issuing of pardons to so many of the pirate leaders.

Peter Easton went on to forge an illustrious career as a pirate, and, after Captain John Ward, became the most famous pirate of his day. Easton emerged as one of the most powerful – and the richest – of the Atlantic pirates. It may be the case that he took over from Bishop in 1610–11, though Bishop may have retained a seat of power at the pirate table, as he is not recorded as taking his pardon until after 1611. Records from 1610 show Easton as leader, heading a fleet moored in Leamcon Harbour; the flotilla was described as formidable, comprising thirteen ships, with a complement of 400 men and 250 guns, with Easton's own ship being the captured English prize the *Concord* of London.[57] His piracies ranged from Ireland across the Atlantic to North Africa, the Mediterranean, south to Guinea in western Africa and west to the shores of Newfoundland. It was in Newfoundland's waters, off Harbour [Harbor] Grace, that Easton wrought havoc on the French migratory fisheries, but where he also established a base of operations.[58] His election to the 'office' of vice-admiral suggests he commanded a level of respect within the pirate coalition during its heyday, no doubt based on his success in predatory ventures. He adopted a liberal attitude, however, and his command role was not without its issues. Easton was less concerned about who he attacked, choosing to ignore any agreement to not attack English shipping. He considered most ships as fair game – the 1611 capture and subsequent command of the *Concord* of London as his own – being an example. On several occasions he fell out with his fellow crew members. In 1612 when in west Cork, he quarrelled with Captain Richard Robinson, another of the leading Atlantic pirate captains, and made off with one of his ships. Again, in 1612, a large number of his men deserted him in Newfoundland, and on another occasion two of Easton's men clashed on board his ship and had to be placed on separate vessels.

Easton's successes as a pirate, however, surpassed his flaws as a commander, and he became a menace to all shipping along the Atlantic trade routes from Africa and the continent to the southern coast of England. Easton's first command when he took over from Bishop in the alliance was the 160-ton, 22-gun flyboat *Fortune* and he lead a fleet of pirate ships in the company of his fellow captains Gilbert Roope from Devon and William Harvey (who by then had been made vice-admiral of the pirate fleet by Easton, replacing Thomas Francke, who served under Bishop, and is discussed below). Within just one year, the pirates took successive ships as prizes, including the *Greyhound* of London, bound for the Canaries, taking its victuals, tackle and cargo of wine; the *St Nicholas* of London bound for Zante in the Greek islands, plundering the cargo of salmon; they also captured the *William and John* of Weymouth-Malcombe Regis that was on its way to Galway in Ireland from Spain.[59] Easton held the latter for seven weeks and the pirates consumed its cargo of wine. Following that, he captured a Biscayner ship, which he converted to a man-of-war in Mamora, and placed Captain Gilbert Roope in command. In the closing days of 1610 the pirates pillaged the *Gift of God* and mistreated the English sailors on board; Easton reputedly declared that he was going to be 'a scourge to Englishmen, as he had no Englishe blood in his belly and therefore esteemed Englishe men no other than as Turckes and Jewes'. He continued his prowling of Atlantic waters, sailing to the Azores, the Canaries and the Cape Verde Islands.[60] Easton and his pirate fleet captured ships of several nations, including English, Dutch and French.

In 1611 he seized the *White Swan* of Rotterdam returning from Tenerife with a cargo of Canary wine, sugar, syrup, preserves and Spanish wool. He brought the ship to Leamcon in Ireland where it became his man-of-war, giving the *Fortune* to Roope.[61]

Thus did the business of piracy continue under the leadership of Easton but with a more expansive and aggressive targeting of potential victims than hitherto under the command of Bishop. The threat from the pirate alliance and the impact of their activities in Atlantic waters thus continued, and complaints from foreign ambassadors to the court of James increased accordingly. Easton and his men, including those who continued to serve under him following Bishop's 'retirement' in and about 1611, were to prove cunning adversaries. Bishop was actively seeking a pardon by that year, or at least had begun negotiating for pardons generally, including his own.[62] Easton's taking command of the alliance could have been a tactical move, allowing Bishop to adopt a more 'legitimate' role to enable negotiations to progress, while also ensuring the continuation of the successful business of piracy in the Atlantic. Central to this was consistency in the type of pirate serving in the alliance, men who were experienced in doing business with foreign ports and ruling officials. Thus, while Easton appears to have assumed the role of admiral, seasoned captains who served under Bishop remained to lead and maintain the alliance as a marauding force.

Little is known of Thomas Francke, including his background or what supported his election as rear-admiral of the alliance. He is first mentioned in 1606 as a 'bosun' on Dutch pirate Arthur Adyn's ship the *Golden Phoenix*, but then no record until his election as rear-admiral about 1609.[63] Richard Kerry's account indicates that Francke captained a significant ship – a Dutch flyboat of 200 tons – and had some 90 men under his command, a forbidding force in itself.[64] In January 1611, Anthony Bull testified that following his capture by Peter Easton and serving two months aboard his ship, he managed to leave when in Baltimore. He was attempting to get back home to England aboard a ship from Minehead when the vessel was captured by Captain Francke and Bull was again taken captive to serve aboard Francke's ship for a further six months.[65] In July 1611 Francke was in the company of fellow captains Richard Stephenson and Arthur Gay off Ushant in the English Channel, when he was joined by Peter Easton and his ships. Easton had captured the 240-ton *Concord* of London, and he had also taken the *Philip Bonaventure* of Dover. The full fleet, numbering seventeen ships or more, returned to Ireland in August.[66]

By this time, the combined pirate fleet of the alliance was formidable and was inflicting serious damage to shipping in the Atlantic. The capture of the *Concord* triggered uproar within the mercantile community in England, particularly from those who had vested interests in the safe passage of ships across the Atlantic. Sir Ferdinando Gorges, English naval commander and governor of Plymouth, sent the examinations of five Englishmen to Robert Cecil, the earl of Salisbury, in 1611 and they provided specific details on the capture of the two ships by Easton and his fellow pirates. The examinants warned that, with the strength of the alliance, 'These men thus furnished threaten the world' and 'they will take and spoyle all they meet with'. Gorges' correspondence continued by saying 'there is in all [the pirate force] to the number of 40 sayle, and 2000 men, all English'.[67] The Privy Council and admiralty were forced to consider pardoning the pirates, particularly the leading captains: Bishop, Easton, Francke and others, as Gorges pointed out that: '… the daily outrages and enormities committed upon the coast [are] by pirates of our own nation …'.[68] As a main stakeholder and key financial backer of the Plymouth Company, a merchant venture enterprise engaged in colonial expeditions to the New World, Gorges had a personal motive in seeking to solve the problem of the pirate alliance.

PIRATE HUNTER TURNED PIRATE

Henry Mainwaring was one of the leading pirates of the time, holding key positions in northwest Africa and Newfoundland. Mainwaring could be described as a reluctant pirate and one who, while directly linked with the piracy of the first quarter of the seventeenth century, was not central to the activity along the Munster coastline. His career as a pirate dates to the second decade of the seventeenth century and towards the end of the main active period of the pirates in southwest Ireland. Born in 1587 in Ightfield in Shropshire, England, he attended Brasenose College in Oxford and in 1602 received his bachelor of arts degree there, at fifteen years of age. He was the second son of Sir George Mainwaring, an MP in Shropshire, and Anne, daughter of Sir William More, also an MP and vice-admiral of Sussex. Mainwaring thus came from a well-established and politically connected family, which no doubt influenced his actions during his career as a captain and commander, and possibly during his time as a pirate as well. In 1604 Henry Mainwaring was admitted as a law student at the Inner Temple, Four Inns Courts of Law in London and went on to serve in the Low Countries as a soldier.[69]

In 1610 he took up the post of captain of St Andrew's Castle near Southampton, though he did not accede to it and was given a commission by Lord High Admiral Nottingham to proceed against pirates, targeting ships in the Bristol Channel and, ironically, the predations carried out by pirate Peter Easton.[70] Mainwaring fitted out a number of ships for the task, including his own, the well-armed, medium-sized *Resistance*. At this time too Sir Robert Shirley, adventurer, had returned to England after spending time in court in Persia and he recounted tales of commercial riches and political power potential there. Mainwaring's interest in the expedition grew, and he may have volunteered or been commissioned to accompany Shirley on his return to the Persian court in 1613. Intervention by the Spanish ambassador, however, fearing that the ships fitted out for the voyage would be used to attack Spanish shipping, led to James prohibiting Mainwaring's involvement in the voyage. Such was his annoyance at this Spanish interference, that Mainwaring began targeting Iberian shipping, and it is from this year that his career as a pirate can be traced.[71] Though his piratical career came at the very end of the main period of activity of the alliance, Mainwaring's involvement with many of the leaders of the alliance places him as a strategic player within the world of pirates at that time, and integral to the story of the alliance itself.

The concern of the Spanish ambassador may have had some basis, as such expeditions, particularly under the guise of pirate hunting, often masked more commercially orientated ventures on the high seas; consequently, the Spanish suspected that such voyages would in fact target the lucrative trade to the Indies and the Americas.[72] So successful was Mainwaring in his taking of Spanish ships and as a commander in his own right, he eventually led a substantial flotilla; he was noted as a gentleman when handling captured crews and not targeting his fellow Englishmen. Accounts vary as to his exploits and fleet numbers, one recording his arrival in 1613 in Newfoundland, where he fitted out three ships.[73] Another dates his arrival to 4 June 1614, with eight ships.[74] The latter date would seem to be the correct one, as from 1613 Mainwaring had made Mamora his primary base of operations, where no doubt his success at plundering Spanish and Portuguese ships would have ingratiated him with the merchants of the port there. It was during his absence in Newfoundland that the Spanish took the opportunity to attack and capture Mamora in 1614, thus taking control of one of the three main bases used by the pirates. Mainwaring, however, in turn attacked the cod-fishing settlement in Newfoundland and used it as a recruiting ground for crew, as

FIGURE 17: The east coast of Newfoundland, off the Avalon Peninsula; this stretch of water was a favoured hunting ground for pirate captains Peter Easton and Henry Mainwaring – for men, supplies and as a location where they established their Newfoundland base.

well as for provisioning his ships. Some willing settlers joined his crew while others did so under duress, and Mainwaring, along with his then colleague Captain Peter Easton, regarded Newfoundland as the perfect recruiting ground for such men.[75]

With no entrepôt in northwest Africa, as all other ports were either under Ottoman Turk or Iberian control, Mainwaring took refuge in Villafranca. Mainwaring was probably sailing in consort with Easton at that point, with both captains selecting to use Villafranca, as it had replaced Mamora as a free port for the pirates in the Mediterranean.[76] From Villafranca, Mainwaring sailed to Newfoundland with five vessels, and continued his targeting of Iberian shipping. Such was his impact on trade that James feared Mainwaring's actions would lead to a breakdown in the peace with Spain and Portugal. Given his connected background and his acumen as a fleet commander, the king issued a royal pardon to Mainwaring in 1616 and a knighthood followed in 1618.[77] He went on to be a leading vice-admiral in the English Navy from 1621 and was elected to parliament that year representing Dover. He served until the end of 1622.[78]

Wider familial connections may have served Henry Mainwaring well throughout his career, with potential links to speculative interest and grants of land in Ireland deserving far greater scrutiny. Examples include that of Leixlip in County Kildare in 1579 granted to a Roger Mainwaring and Fedamore (Fanningstown) in County Limerick in 1588 to Edmund Mainwaring. The latter sold the whole of the seignory of Fedamore to the 4th earl of Thomond, Donogh O'Brien, in 1620, who is discussed in more detail in the next chapter, including his links with the pirates. Edmund Mainwaring, from Peover in Cheshire, came from the same branch of the clan as Henry, the latter's family moving to neighbouring Shropshire in the fifteenth century.[79] Whether connections existed and the individuals were acquainted, or indeed related, or the grants of land were a mere coincidence, remains to be ascertained.

A somewhat swashbuckling account of Mainwaring is given in Jean Chevalier's mid-seventeenth-century sketch. Chevalier, it seems, visited the former pirate at his residence in Jersey when Mainwaring was in his mid-seventies. Retold as the 'heroic feats of Sir Henry', the narrative recounts how the emperor of Morocco gave Mainwaring a castle in order to protect his fleet of ships; it projects an image of the emperor and the pirate as close cohorts, to the point that they called each other 'brother'. It praises his success as a captain when, on one occasion, Mainwaring's fleet is attacked, but finding he is out of ordnance, he defeats the attackers by loading his guns with pieces of eight.[80] It is Mainwaring's own *Discourse* that provides the most vivid insight into the organised squadrons of pirates operating in the Atlantic at the time; each of the five chapters relays specifics about those involved, where they operated and how they functioned.[81] Of course, acting as he did as pirate hunter turned pirate, Mainwaring had first-hand knowledge of the pirates and their operations at that time. Perhaps more than anyone else, he has provided historical evidence of the thin line that existed between legitimate lives, political collusion, commercial ventures and proscribed routines of everyday coastal life.

FIGURE 18: The seagate at the Kasbah Mahdiyya (Mehdia). Located near the Moroccan city of Kenitra at the lower reaches of the River Sebou, it commanded the outer harbour. Dating from the tenth century, it became a vibrant entrepôt and was the primary northwest African base for the Alliance of Pirates in the early seventeenth century when it was then known as Mamora. © PROF. RICHARD PENNELL

CONNECTIONS EXPAND AND EVOLVE

Those central to the pirate alliance were well placed to influence official mindsets when the need arose, and to cobble favour for themselves when absolutions were sought. Mainwaring's familial connections certainly placed him in good standing with the crown, while Richard Bishop had the maritime expertise and necessary connections to ensure that he could operate without fear of capture by governing officials and could also negotiate pardons when the time was right. Bishop, as leader, could perhaps correctly be called the pirates' broker as he successfully bridged the gap between legitimate and criminal, middleman to the middlemen. His close ties with admiralty officials, strategically William Hull of Leamcon, who is discussed in the following chapter, confirms this, and indeed if it were not for Hull, the pirate alliance would not have developed into the threat that it became. Hull therefore is key to understanding the pirates in the North Atlantic, a central figure in this organised coalition. But he was not alone in official complicity, and the success of the Alliance of Pirates depended on a network of land-based agents and conspirators. Hull epitomised well-connected individuals who strategically established themselves in the remote regions of the southwest, providing safe havens and safe houses where the pirates could trade, socialise and settle. The alliance was a force to be reckoned with, but it was the 'land pirates' who ensured that all involved reaped rich rewards.[82]

CHAPTER 3

Honourable Crimes and Corrupt Times

I pray your Lord to signifie what shall be don with these [pirates] in Prison, for we have no Law to hang them here, & it will require charge to send them into England.[1]

A significant number of governing officials involved in maritime business in Munster were also involved in fraudulent affairs. This was a matter of course, and if an individual were not willing to 'avail' of opportunities and facilitate black market commerce, there were plenty who were ready to step in and do so. The roots of clandestine industry ran deep in such areas, the level of such furtive business was significant, and corruption was on a grand scale, though within a functional arrangement. While some officers and agents had only a peripheral input, others were key figures in the very operation surrounding the trade in contraband goods. Regarded by their contemporaries as land-based pirates, albeit hiding beneath the canopy of government and admiralty jurisdiction, these men successfully muddied the waters between legitimate affairs and shady contacts. Local participation in piracy in remote areas permitted access to markets and goods that were out of economic reach through legitimate trade for most emerging communities. While this was nothing new, as demonstrated by England's West Country piracy, Mark Hanna has correctly identified that acceptance of and involvement in pirate business also underscored far deeper issues 'regarding political power, the rule of law and oppressive market regulations'. While men in high office worked from the centre to expand empires through global maritime enlargement, pirates and their cohorts operated from the periphery to impact and influence those same expanding empires.[2] Piracy and corruption were essential bedfellows, particularly within an international colonial context.

SEA SHARKERS: PIRATES BY DEFAULT AND BY DESIGN

As discussed in the previous chapter, agreement on operational tactics – whether as a definitive adoption of a code or as guidelines that governed their actions – whereby English ships were generally not targeted, meant that many of the leading pirate captains of that time, when seeking a pardon for themselves or their men, hoped that their acts of piracy would be considered as a lesser offence than the 'ordinary' crimes that came before the civil or common courts of law. Captain Henry Mainwaring adopted the term *pulchrum scelus* or 'honourable crimes' when describing their deeds in his *Discourse* of 1616. He suggested that they should not be dealt with as pirates fighting the crown but instead should be treated more leniently.[3] Several of the resident government officials, while not outwardly supporting the concept of 'honourable crimes', made representations that argued the pirates' value to settlement and that their service instead could serve to solidify the crown's plantation efforts in Munster. In addition, it meant that knowledgeable mariners were in place in these isolated harbours to encourage trade and to partake in economic advancement, and were, in theory at least, acting on behalf of the official governing regime. Such symbiotic arguments sought to justify the intensifying collusion that was taking place between officials resident in Munster and the pirates using it as their base. As records below show, several officials, both native and newcomer, chose to deliberately ignore orders from central government in favour of the pirates themselves.

In a dispatch from Cork in 1608 to the earl of Salisbury, Lord Danvers wrote that he had to agree terms with the pirates, such was their numbers:

> Now turning from land pirates, he [Danvers] must trouble his Lordship with 'sea sharkers'. Upon the departure of the King's ship, commanded by the deputy for the northern service, one Robinson arrived here [in Baltimore] with 40 men, poor, as they pretended, through the falsehood of their own companions, Eston and others. [The pirates are] daily reinforcing themselves … [that] he was forced to confirm a treaty.[4]

The common link between those on land and those at sea is clearly apparent in contemporary letters sent to central government from resident governing officials. There is an almost resigned tone common throughout these dispatches, with the scale of collusion dictating the degree to which effective action could be taken, either by deputies for the admiralty or captains of the king's ships then stationed around the coast. Certainly, Baltimore was considered one of the main hubs of piracy at that stage, with 'weak inhabitants' providing relief to the pirates and their ships. It is equally interesting to note the interchange of terminology by Danvers between 'land pirates', referring not only to natives but also to colluding officials, and 'sea sharkers' – the pirates themselves.

LAND PIRATES: OFFICIAL COLLUSION AND COMPLICITY

Issues of jurisdiction dominated the workings of the Irish admiralty, not just between the High Court of Admiralty in London and those officials in Dublin tasked with the administration of Admiralty affairs in Ireland, but between Dublin and provincial agents. Several deputy vice-admirals, who were based in the southwest, operated for the most part within a framework of semi-autonomy and inherent self-interest. Such relationships appear to have filtered down to the very heart of these peripheral locations, and is recognised in a proclamation issued by James in 1608, where the potential for collusion between those outside the law and official personnel is plainly stated:

> … having lately found by many pregnant circumstances, that most of the great faults [piracies] are continued by the connivence, or corruption in many [of] the subordinate Officers, especially such as are resident in and neere the Ports and Maritime Counties.[5]

A specific example from the same year relates to Sir Richard Hawkins, acting vice-admiral for Devon, who was removed from office for conspiring with pirates.[6] There was growing pressure from central government on key officials in the West Country to comply or be removed from office, a situation that encouraged the transfer of pirate operations to Munster, and with it, continued collusion. Lord Deputy Chichester notes this clearly in 1612:

> It is not only the Irish Inhabitants upon the Seacoasts here that do cherish them [the pirates] when they arrive, either in consideration of the benefits they receive by Exchange of Vituells for commodities or ready money … but Men of our own Nation under colour of Treaty do usually and familiarly converse and commerce with them, and have therefore taken convenient places for the purpose upon the Western Coasts of this Realm, either in the Ilands or upon the Maine, in which they are well provided for.[7]

It was a point made by several individuals over time, including in 1616 by then ex-pirate Henry Mainwaring in his *Discourse*.[8] The profits to be made from admiralty matters were potentially enormous, and officers were sent to Ireland, and in particular Munster, to oversee the acquisition of goods and cargo from ships, and in many instances the controlling of individual ships using the harbours along the southwest coast.[9] Clive Senior notes that Humphrey Jobson, who was appointed vice-admiral of Munster early in 1607, was as corrupt as Hawkins had been in Devon. Secretary to Lord High Admiral Nottingham, he had been tasked with investigating reports of corruption in the vice-admiralty in Devon in 1606. He would thus have been well informed of the workings of rural politics and familiar with most of the leading pirates there at the time, the majority of whom shifted their attention and activities to Ireland from 1607 onwards.[10]

Jobson was used as a proxy by Nottingham in England to take in pirate goods and make a profitable return on them, with the lord high admiral no doubt reaping a comparable reward.[11] Nottingham fulfilled a similar role in Ireland, where he administered his office through vice-admirals and deputy vice-admirals. Jobson, as vice-admiral, engaged his deputies to assist him, primarily his brother Richard, though both acted more on behalf of the pirates than in their official capacity.[12] Of course the vested interests of those involved influenced decisions, and had its beginnings in the 'commercialising of colonisation' in the time of Elizabeth I. It became particularly focused during James' tenure as king, and continued on into the reign of Charles I (from 1625). Integral to this was plunder, either through piracy, privately operated ships, or 'semi-official expeditions' overseas. Certainly, it seems, high-ranking admiralty officials were more concerned with making a profit than with keeping law and order at sea.[13]

Jobson was a cog in the wheel of admiralty business, but he also had links elsewhere. He was connected to William Hull, one of his deputy vice-admirals in Munster from 1607, through the marriage of his daughter Hester to Hull's brother Henry, who at that point was resident in Clonakilty in west Cork and was actively engaged in developing the settlement there. In June 1608, Humphrey's brother Richard was also in Munster in the capacity of deputy-vice admiral, a post he held until February 1610. Richard was tasked with undertaking the same inquiry in Ireland as his brother in England – to examine officers who 'favoured, relieved, consorted, ayded and abetted' with pirates. Little came of either investigation, as both brothers were overtly predisposed to gain from pirate booty.[14] The extent to which they colluded during that time was staggering, with Richard issuing 'passports' to the pirates to enable them to travel unimpeded.[15] William Thompson, possibly a Yorkshire man and active as a pirate in Munster in 1607, was so involved in local business that Humphrey Jobson engaged him to serve on jury duty during a session of an admiralty court hearing on Sherkin Island.

Indeed, this is probably the same Thompson referred to by Richard Jobson when suggesting that he be pardoned:

> ... that it is well knoween hee is the onely pirate this daie in the Sea, for his true understandeinge of all remote harbors bothe in Engelande, Irelande and all other Countries where men of therie wicked condition resorte or are fitt to be resorted unto ....[16]

Such accounts again highlight the weakness (whether deliberate or otherwise) of the English state in dealing with piracy, and the ambivalent attitude of the admiralty and, by default, the crown. Not to mention the manipulative, mutually driven measures that could be used by locally based officers when required.[17] Humphrey Jobson was examined in London in 1609 for his handling of events relating to the taking of goods from the ship *Pearl*.[18] The vessel, carrying a cargo of hides, cochineal, indigo, ginger, leather, pearls and Spanish coin, was captured on its way to Calais in 1607 by two pirate ships under the captaincy of Alexander Vaughan and William Blanch. The High Court of Admiralty in London commissioned Paul de Cuper, a German merchant resident in London, to recover the goods and arrest the pirates. De Cuper travelled to Ireland when he learnt that the pirates were stationed there, but rather than arresting them, he seems to have spent time in their company without, as can be inferred from Jobson's deposition, keeping the resident deputy vice-admiral informed. De Cuper recovered the goods, which was the primary aim of the admiralty, but Jobson's deposition provides evidence for continuing complaints surrounding commissions made by central admiralty officials without the knowledge of local admiralty officers. It is more probable, however, that Jobson was relinquishing responsibility for the activity and hiding behind proclaimed ignorance in an effort to absolve himself of complicity.[19] In any case, Humphrey Jobson was imprisoned, and his brother Richard dismissed in 1610, both on the same charge – their ineffectual handling of, and collusion with, pirates in Ireland – though those who succeeded them did not stray too much from the same course.[20] Humphrey retained his interests in southwest Munster, however, and research by Dr David Heffernan of Queen's University Belfast has shown that he leased a house and one ploughland called East Tawnagh in West Carbery from Sir Richard Boyle on 17 November 1620 for a period of twenty-one years. In 1628 the lease was assigned from Jobson to three of Deputy Vice-Admiral Sir William Hull's sons, Boyle, Henry and John Hull.[21]

FIGURE 19: Portrait by artist William Holl of Sir Richard Boyle, 1st earl of Cork, 1566–1643, date unknown. © EP II 280.2; PRINT ROOM, PORTRAIT GALLERY, NATIONAL GALLERIES OF SCOTLAND

Of all the admiralty officers stationed in Munster, one stands out: the above-mentioned William Hull, a Devon mariner who held the post of deputy vice-admiral in Munster from 1607 until his death in 1643. Hull arrived in west Cork in the early part of the seventeenth century. As with Henry Mainwaring, Hull's family connections most likely worked in his favour, particularly when he was accused of corruption or suspected of collusion with pirates. His father Henry was a prominent merchant and shipowner, with commercial links to France and Spain; indeed William may have served aboard some of his father's ships when trading with the continent. Henry also served as mayor of Exeter in 1605.[22] William Hull may have been involved in acts of piracy in his early days, or, more appropriately, engaged in commercial maritime trade as a private operator, as is suggested by an earlier proclamation issued by the king:

> Whereas it hath appeared vnto vs by the Records of our high Court of the Admiraltie, That William Hull Captaine of a Ship called the Talbot of Topisham in our Countie of Deuon, … with diuers others … respectiuely stand indicted, for that they in Nouember 1602, … did rob and spoile a Ship called la Serene of Olona in France, and the goods therein laden.[23]

Though it may be the case that the William Hull mentioned was a different person to the gentleman who became deputy vice-admiral in Munster, the possibility that Hull may have had prior experience as a pirate would certainly lend itself to understand better his ability to 'seize' opportunities, including liaising so easily with the main pirates in his area.[24] It is highly probable that the individual in question is the same person, who was absolved of any misdeeds in the Mediterranean through his familial connections and the deathbed confession of Captain Philip Ward, a fellow captain sailing in consort, who absolved Hull of any wrong-doing. The case against Hull was dismissed in 1607. This opened the way for him to pursue his commercial and personal agenda, and he came to settle in Leamcon, to the west of Schull in County Cork, leasing the lands from the Gaelic-Irish O'Mahony lords. He may have previously identified the potential of the area when he visited Leamcon as early as 1601, when in receipt of a grant of money from the crown, possibly for naval services. In Leamcon he acquired the lands of Crookhaven from the church and rented out the O'Mahony castle there for £100 per annum.[25] A detailed list of lands either claimed or leased by Hull, taken from the information recorded by Bishop Dive Downes during his visitation to Cork in 1699, shows that the lands of Crookhaven were part of the bishopric of Cork when leased. Hull was serving as deputy vice-admiral to Nottingham very shortly after his arrival in west Cork, and from this time until the outbreak of the 1641 Rebellion he became one of the most influential and wealthy settlers in the area. He acquired large tracts of land, was directly involved in several business ventures, including trade and fishing, and his liaisons with the pirates supplemented his escalating prosperity throughout his tenure as deputy vice-admiral, and in fact may have been the fiscal basis for his wealth as indicated in his 1641 deposition.[26]

Hull's entrepreneurial spirit brought him into direct contact with Sir Richard Boyle, with whom he went into business in 1616, primarily in the fishing industry, with Hull maintaining his commercial interests in Bandon, the town developed by Boyle.[27] Richard Boyle pulled out of the fishing venture at an early stage, but probably acted as a silent partner or provided financial backing when required. Hull operated alongside Thomas Roper, who between 1610 and 1620 had established fisheries in Schull, Crookhaven and Bantry, and the 1622 commission reports that he had planted several hundred families at Crookhaven. Roper, who was ennobled as Viscount Baltinglass in 1627, shifted his focus to the plantation efforts in Ulster from 1610 onwards and thereafter Hull acquired his commercial interests and eventually more or less monopolised the resources in west Cork.[28] Roper was to influence much of the industry in the southwest during his time there, including cloth production and the fisheries, while his authorising of specific establishments as a mechanism to control profits is clearly demonstrated in his licensing of alehouses in Ulster.[29] Roper was not averse to receiving goods out of pirated vessels. In 1625 he obtained 700 pounds of sugar from the ship *Hope* of Rotterdam, and in the same year goods that included fifty tons of salt out of a Dutch ship brought into Kenmare that was taken off Portland.[30] As an absentee, Roper acted through agents, and a Mr Crosse is mentioned as his servant. He thus ensured control of the acquisitions of pirated goods in his own interest.[31]

Hull's deposition, which covers his losses by 'rebels' during the general unrest of the Irish Rebellion period in 1641, and though no doubt exaggerated, provides detailed evidence for his proclaimed wealth, with the majority of his stated losses to do with the fishing interests he took over from Roper: '… he Loste, was robbed and forcibly dispoyled of his goods and Chattells to the severall values following … 7679 besides the proffitts of his lands & leases worth 1148 li. Per annum'. It is also noted that he was receiving £250 per annum rent from the fishing enterprises in Crookhaven.[32]

FAMILIAL AND COMMERCIAL LINKS

Hull's rise through the ranks of the landed élite was rapid, due primarily to familial and economic connections, but his dealings with the pirates in Munster were just as extensive and rewarding. In 1621 he had been appointed to the Council of Munster, and was also awarded his knighthood in that year, while during his long tenure as deputy vice-admiral his role was extended to include a customs post in Kinsale in 1622. By the early 1620s, Hull seems to have been functioning as rent collector in the southwest for Sir Richard Boyle, with whom he had strong family and commercial ties; Boyle had by that time been created the first earl of Cork.[33] Other family connections (to the daughter of Humphrey Jobson, through his brother Henry), and his business links with both Lawrence Parsons (Boyle's cousin) and Thomas Roper, no doubt also contributed to Hull's success.

He married Boyle's sister-in-law Elizabeth in 1622; she was the widow of Boyle's brother, the deceased Bishop of Cork. Boyle himself chronicled the event: 'January 1622. My brother the late Bishop of Cork's widow was by me given in marriage to Sir William Hull, and married together in the study at Youghal by Mr. Goodwin.'[34] Boyle's matchmaking, indicative of course of his ability to increase his own business interests and expand his sphere of influence, is also indicative of how well connected Hull was locally. He was deemed acceptable to marry into the Boyle dynasty, no doubt influenced by his success as a planter and business entrepreneur. Perhaps his ability to successfully make a profit from his trade with the pirates was another persuading factor for a businessman like Boyle, seeing the merits of bringing individuals like Hull into the commercial fold. This would also of course have enabled Richard Boyle to profit from the business of piracy while ensuring he remained at sufficient remove to avert implication. In a peculiar act of loyalty, Hull named his only son by his second marriage Boyle, in respect of the family connection, and another son, by his first marriage, also named William, went on to marry into the Boyle family.[35] Hull's older daughter Mary, by his first marriage, married Edward Boyle, son of the deceased bishop of Cork and Hull's second wife. This occasioned the somewhat intriguing family arrangement whereby Hull's daughter married her stepbrother and her stepmother was also her mother-in-law. As affirmed in John Appleby's study of Hull, his bond with Boyle afforded security through the patronage of the earl, while, 'for Boyle the relationship contributed towards the creation of an extensive rural power bloc …' and 'provided Boyle with a dependable agent on the western margins of his extensive estates who could look after his commercial and other landed interests …'.[36] It also ensured a safe buffer between Boyle and any involvement in pirate affairs, with Hull serving as broker to both sides.

The High Court of Admiralty papers contain abundant accounts of Hull's encounters with – as well as his victualling of and benefitting from – the pirates that utilised his shores; one denounces Hull as 'a notorious harboror of piratts and receavor of theire goodes'.[37] He came under direct scrutiny in 1610 when an arrest order was issued and carried out by Sir Richard Moryson, who reported that he had 'apprehended the deputy vice-admiral of the province, Captain Hull'.[38] Rather than being tried for collusion, the value of Hull's intelligence was recognised in terms of the pirate activity, as was the strategic nature of his lands in the midst of such activity, and he was instead given authority to 'parley and go aboard any pirates [ship], the better to enable him to give accounts of their proceedings'. In fact while in England at that time, Hull received a commission to entreat with the pirates in an effort to encourage them to accept pardons, whereupon he assumed a more conciliatory role in this respect. This was, of course, much to the annoyance of Moryson, who cautioned that 'it cannot be but hurtful to the service [admiralty], for they will never be able to constrain this misunderstanding people to think commerce a fault with them, when they shall see any by authority converse with them'.[39] In September 1611 the Council of Munster sent a garrison of crown forces to Hull's castle at Leamcon in an attempt to control activities there. This was presumably the O'Mahony tower house on Castle Point rather than Hull's own fortified house, but in a very short time garrison soldiers were engaging in deals with pirate Captain William Baugh, his men and their booty.[40]

FIGURE 20: Detail from the 1612 Dutch chart showing two castellated structures at Leamcon; the one on the lower headland is the O'Mahony tower house, known today as Leamcon Castle, and the other, to the right, is the fortified house of William Hull, the upstanding remains of which are now gone.
SUB GÖTTINGEN, 4 H BRIT P III, 6 RARA, UNIVERSITÄTSBIBLIOTHEK, GÖTTINGEN, GERMANY

Hull's own deposition of 1613 reveals the extent to which he was involved in negotiating with pirates for pardons. For example, he stated that he boarded the ship of Captain Robert Stephenson when the pirate and his crew arrived at Leamcon seeking his majesty's pardon, and confirmed

FIGURE 21: Gold Spanish colonial two-escudo coin discovered during archaeological excavation at St James' Church and graveyard, Dublin, and dated to the seventeenth century. Minted in the Bogota mint in the Andes mountains of Colombia, the coin was associated perhaps with a wealthy pilgrim or patron travelling between Ireland and Spain or may represent wider trading connections, in legal or perhaps even illicit trade. PERS. COMM. AISLING COLLINS; IMAGE © AISLING COLLINS ARCHAEOLOGICAL SERVICES LTD (ACAS), DUBLIN

that Stephenson paid Captain Middleton in Mamora £200 to secure the pardon from the king, a fact that Middleton denied.[41] Roger Middleton was a naval captain tasked by the admiralty to act as official negotiator on pardons in the period 1611–14. His main focus was in west Cork, and Mamora in northwest Africa. He was suspected on several occasions of extracting payments from pirates in return for pardons, actions that resulted in many who distrusted his motivations refusing to accept the pardons offered.

The London government was cautious in its dealings with individuals like Hull and was circumspect about his liaisons with pirates. Its determination not to undermine his success in settling large tracts of land, or his business ventures, which were a consistent and increasing source of revenue to the crown, was tempered with ensuring individuals were not compromised by his 'double-dealing' when it came to trading in pirated goods. Hull's interaction with the pirates provides key insights into the everyday activity of those involved. As Appleby has termed it, several were 'pirates-cum-settlers' with Richard Bishop's settling at Leamcon, and Captain William Baugh at Innishannon near Bandon, just two examples.[42] Many others are similarly recorded as settling and working legitimately in the southwest following the issuing of pardons, though Hull's primary tenants may have been the pirates and their families throughout the period when the alliance was most active. Certainly, the available sources reveal that many of the pirates availed of the opportunity to partake in 'legitimate' work, particularly those who had families in the area. Similarly, local fishermen, seeing opportunities for profit through piratical ventures, joined as pirate crew. These amphibious lifestyles are well accounted for, not alone in Munster but also, for example, among fishermen in Newfoundland at that time.[43]

Though abusing their official positions for their own interest, men like Hull were useful to the crown in that they were in a perfect position to exert local pressure and influence on the pirates. It served to diminish piracy to a certain degree by slowly encouraging the pirates themselves to settle and live locally, the prevailing opinion being that even though these were brigands, they were also English, so better an English settler to support the crown's plantation endeavours in Munster than the prevention of such settlement when it was needed. Exasperation in England continued, however, and indeed heightened as time passed, as the pirate problem became directly linked to escalating corruption among officials. The Privy Council, writing from Whitehall in November 1612, stated:

> As to the general subject of the pirates, it has hitherto been supposed that their means of support and countenance come from two quarters only, the coast of Barbary and the west coast of Ireland [Munster]; the former of which is beyond all rule and justice, being wholly given up to barbarism, while the latter is inhabited either by natives, who, from motives of interest or of fear, are ready to supply their necessities, or by persons of our own nation who have taken places there with the express purpose of commercing with the pirates with more convenience and security.[44]

Hull was strategic in his dealings with individuals on every side of the 'civilised' divide. Throughout his time in west Cork he encouraged settlement in places like Crookhaven to the west and Clonakilty to the east, where Hull's brother Henry oversaw the expansion of the towns of Bandon and Clonakilty throughout that time. Hull never sought to establish a formal settlement on his own estate or its wider environs, and this in itself is informative. To do so would have brought official attention to the area, with obligations governing revenue, taxes, and administration relating to a plantation scheme.[45] He did, however, follow English standards in building, as supported by contemporary accounts, and built houses in the required styles and thus brought colonial influence to the wilds of west Cork.[46] That being said, to have established his residence in a discreet demesne, situated in the centre of a complex coastline, guaranteed that Hull could conduct his business in relative isolation away from official scrutiny and with whom he so pleased – residual Gaelic-Irish, Old English or New English settlers, merchants and investors and, of course, the pirates who considered Leamcon not alone vital to their own operations, but many who began to think of it as home.

THE SETTLEMENT IN BALTIMORE

While Hull was establishing his foothold in the wilds of Roaringwater Bay, Thomas Crooke had identified the opportunity to acquire land in Ireland and establish a formal settlement at Baltimore, to generate legitimate profits through plantation. He would no doubt also have recognised the prospect of enjoying economic benefits on a more unofficial level. Crooke arrived and settled in Baltimore in 1605–6 supported by an existing agreement with Sir Fineen O'Driscoll of a twenty-one-year lease of his lands, totalling some thirty-four and a half ploughlands.[47] Crooke paid an entry fee of £2,000 and rent of £56 per annum.[48] Fineen O'Driscoll was impoverished at that point, with his petition of October 1606, taken by the lord deputy, stating, 'Owing to the poverty of himself [Fineen O'Driscoll], and of his wasted country, he is scarse able to pay His Majesty's composition.'[49] Crooke had the backing of Sir James Lancaster, interestingly the commander of the East India Company fleet of ships who was commercially linked to the development of the settlement in Dundaniel, one of Richard Boyle's primary industrial investments near Bandon in west Cork.[50] Lancaster's, and indeed Crooke's, connections with Baltimore would appear to go back farther than this, however, with both having a stake in lands in the area from O'Driscoll as early as 1600, and with further letters of 'feoffement' issued in 1605 and 1606 to both parties.[51]

Crooke was linked both professionally and personally to the Winthrop family, with a John Winthrop settling in Munster in the late 1590s. He had lived in Aghadown to the north of Baltimore, where he died in 1613, and would have been perfectly placed to identify the opportunity for undertakers and speculators, following the fall of the Gaelic Order, and it may have been this connection that brought Crooke to the area at the turn of the century. Winthrop's son, also John, formed what MacCarthy-Morrogh refers to as the 'Baltimore syndicate' comprising John Winthrop, James Salmon and Thomas Crooke. Salmon had familial ties with Crooke and possibly also with the Winthrops. The motive for the three of these New English settlers to move to the south coast, apart from the resource potential of the area, seems to have been freedom of religion, with all three looked upon in England as non-conformists. Relocation and settlement in remote places such as the west Cork coast could afford religious freedom without fear of political or ecclesiastical recriminations.[52] The opportunity to express and practise their beliefs more freely was raised as an issue, with Richard Moryson, in 1611, writing on matters relating to conformity of religion and the penalties that should be enforced on those not complying.[53]

Within a very short time of settling in Baltimore, Crooke had been granted a lease to hold a weekly market and two annual fairs. By 1609 he had established a vibrant settler community there with two towns, the main one centred round the castle of Dún na Séad, which Crooke now used as

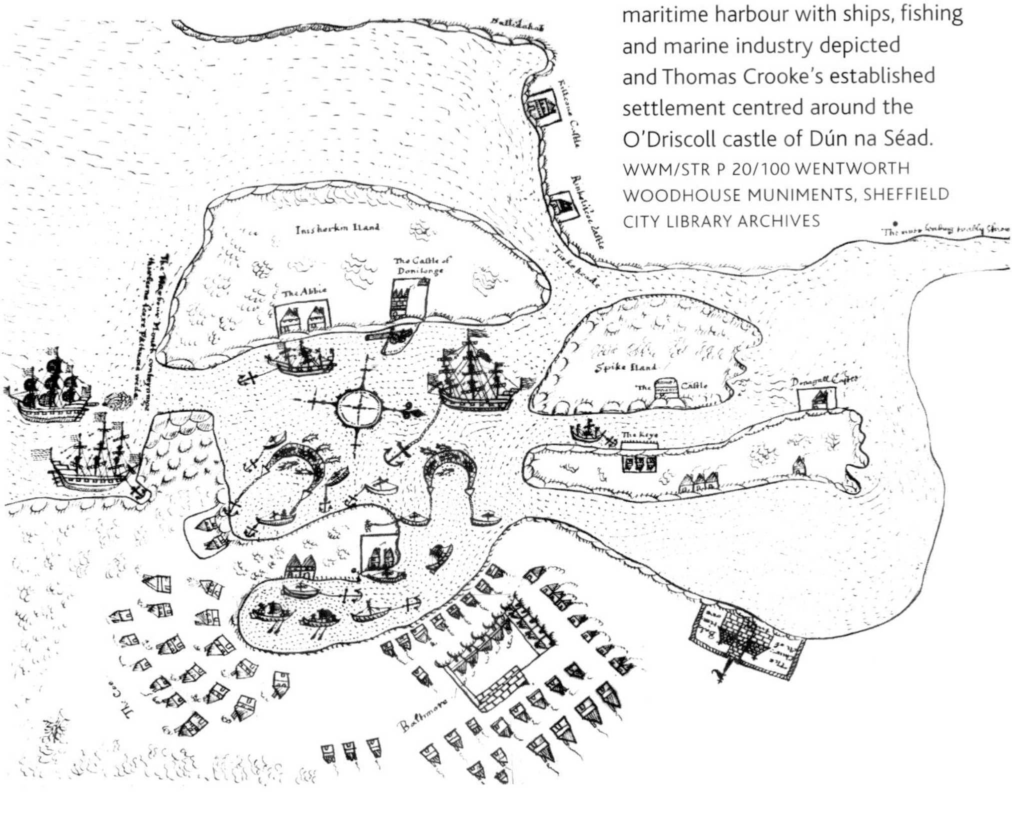

FIGURE 22: Strafford Folio 'Mapp of Baltimore' reflecting a vibrant maritime harbour with ships, fishing and marine industry depicted and Thomas Crooke's established settlement centred around the O'Driscoll castle of Dún na Séad. WWM/STR P 20/100 WENTWORTH WOODHOUSE MUNIMENTS, SHEFFIELD CITY LIBRARY ARCHIVES

his administrative centre. The second community was a smaller, less defined town in the area known as the Cove, to the southeast of the main town and which would have been the location of the original medieval settlement of Baltimore. The contemporary Dutch chart of 1612 and map from the Strafford collection show Baltimore's settlements at that time (Figures 6 and 22).[54] The 1612 chart provides more detail on the main settlement, including the possible earlier O'Driscoll tower house, with attached rectangular structure, most probably the hall or administrative building used by Crooke and built by him when he established the settlement there shortly after arriving. The map of Baltimore in the Strafford Collection/William Woodhouse Muniments (Figure 22) depicts a large rectangular building only, with the earlier tower house gone by then.[55] To the east of the main fortification, within an enclosing wall, various attached buildings are illustrated with what appear to be two flanking towers indicated on the 1612 chart (Figure 41).

Both sources have depictions of buildings in the second settlement area by the Cove. Two buildings, leading down to another structure beside the water's edge, can be seen on the Dutch chart, while the Strafford map records nearly twenty houses alongside possible industrial buildings.[56] One of the two structures illustrated on the water's edge, adjacent to where the vessel is anchored on the chart, may represent industrial sites associated with Crooke's fishing interests, which he developed and expanded.[57] This large rectangular building depicted to the bottom of the image is substantial, with a possible spire, turret or gable on one end. On the Strafford map, a site is indicated within an enclosing wall. While these representations may be of structures now long gone, in this general area the archaeological remains of a fish palace, developed by Crooke under the auspices of Richard Boyle, are recorded. A series of beam-hole niches cut into the rock face, with twenty-nine holes in a line, *c.* 1.2 metres above the present ground level, are now all that remain of this industrial site. These would have housed the beams used to press and extract the train oil from the pilchard into barrels, which was then traded as a commodity in its own right.[58] Further cultural evidence has revealed itself in the immediate area in recent times, with the basal remains of a quay, slipway and cobbled trackway emerging from the gravels on the shoreline of the small stony inlet called Tramadroum, which can be found due south of the fish palace, leading from the Cove.[59] Whether these new archaeological sites are contemporary with Crooke's industrial works await confirmation through archaeological investigation, but what they do indicate is that boats and ships could access Tramadroum in times past, providing a

FIGURE 23: View across the small inlet of Tramadroum, Baltimore, where the basal remains of a slipway and old quay can be seen along the water's edge. They provide cultural evidence for maritime infrastructure, suggesting that Tramadroum was a working cove at some point in the past. IMAGE: CONNIE KELLEHER

direct route to the Cove, the settlements and industrial sites there.

The issue of ownership of the lands around Baltimore was confusing and contested. In 1607 Fineen O'Driscoll had made a lease of sixteen ploughlands to Walter Coppinger, the Catholic entrepreneur who had arrived in Ireland looking to build an empire for himself and had seen such opportunities in the lands around Baltimore, Bandon and Clonakilty. Coppinger paid £1,700 for his lease but problems arose when it became clear that those lands leased by Crooke and Coppinger overlapped, with each prospector claiming the rights. Protracted arguments ensued, with Coppinger resorting to bullying tactics and, at times, illegal methods in an attempt to undo Crooke's settlement and hold on the land. By 1610, though petitions had been sent to the lord deputy from various persons, including Fineen O'Driscoll, in relation to dues and commissions owing on their lands, Coppinger was accepted as the representative to collect the said dues for the crown.[60] Coppinger may have taken undue advantage of his position, however, with complaints about his methods and actions later made by settlers in Baltimore: '... his malicious and covetous desire to supplant the said plantationers and get their possessions has, by very many forgeries, champerties, maintainers and other like corrupt and unlawful courses ... gotten several pretended titles to all their lands'.

Crooke and Coppinger sparred over the following three years, but by 1616 Coppinger had been jailed and fined for his transgressions.[61] Such tactics seem to have been the norm for Coppinger as he had also been in trouble in 1613 for sabotaging the works at Dundaniel in an attempt to force the English East India Company's scheme to fail and to undermine Richard Boyle's commercial ventures there.[62]

By 1612 the Baltimore plantation under Thomas Crooke had government approval, receiving a royal charter the following year; Crooke was appointed sovereign and was supported by a council of twelve burgesses, among them James Salmon. As sovereign, Crooke held court for minor offences and civil actions and with his council could enact byelaws; he was invested with the duty to send two officers to the king's parliament held in Dublin that year and, essentially, was empowered locally, which he exploited to the full.[63] At this point and following some form of tentative agreement between O'Driscoll, Crooke and Coppinger, the lands around Baltimore were rented to Thomas Bennett of Bandon, who it seems had functioned as executor for Crooke in 1610 during inevitable ongoing issues of land ownership.[64] As early as 1608, not surprisingly, Crooke was under suspicion of colluding with the pirates, and letters of complaint about his extra-curricular commercial activities with individuals in the harbour ensued. In a postscript to a letter sent by the lords of the Council of Munster, writing to Chichester in 1608, we read:

> They understand that one Thomas Crooke, of Downshead, Esq., dwelling not far from Baltimore, has been a chief maintainer and abettor of Coward [pirate Captain Thomas Coward] and other notorious pirates, and that having been often sent for by process out of the Court of Admiralty, he could not hitherto be brought to his answer for it; wherefore they pray his Lordship to take notice, and to give order that he [Crooke] may likewise be apprehended and sent over hither, for he little knows how much they have to do for the satisfying the ambassadors of foreign princes in their complaints against pirates harboured in Ireland.[65]

Some months later the lord president of Munster also took issue with Crooke:

> … fforasmuch as Thomas Crooke of Baltimore in the Countie of Corck Esquier beinge accused before his Maiestes most honorable privy Councell in England for Divers matters. Wherevppom yt hath pleased their Lordships to send for him for annsweringe thereof before them, and by the

> Dirrection of the Lord Deputie of this kindgome, I am to send him ouer accordingly....[66]

In the same month, however, Chichester supported Crooke in his dealings with the pirates, suggesting, in a letter, that he was falsely accused and his actions misconstrued. During an onshore excursion by the pirates to obtain supplies, they had burned a house and Crooke had boarded one of their ships to seek restitution for the damage; for this, he was accused of liaising with the pirates.[67] The bishop of Cork also wrote to exonerate Crooke of any wrongdoing: '... he is bold to recommend him as more serviceable to His Majesty, in respect of his ability and sufficiency in many ways, than any man in those parts ... and has been, for the service in that behalf, commended by their Lordships and hated by pirates'.[68] This letter was quickly followed by a report of the return of Crooke to Baltimore, 'declared free of all imputations'.[69]

The suspicions were, nonetheless, well founded. The High Court of Admiralty papers contain several entries showing Crooke openly trading with the pirates. In partnership with James Salmon he was provisioning the pirates in Baltimore Harbour, reportedly supplied them with over 200 beef, slaughtered by a local butcher in Crooke's yard, as well as mutton and beer, in return for sugar and other booty. He was also closely tied in with Sir Ralph Bingley, a soldier and undertaker who acquired lands in Donegal and who was tasked with planting settlers there. He was also brother of Sir Richard Bingley, chief surveyor of the king's ships and commander of the Irish Coast Fleet. Bingley was involved with the Virginia Company and overseas colonial speculations, but was also suspected of acts of piracy.[70] In 1607 Crooke willingly received goods off the ship *Triall*, which, scheduled for a voyage to Virginia from London, was boarded by Bingley in Dublin and diverted by him into Kinsale.[71] In what is described by Kenneth Andrews as one of the most notorious cases of a captain turning pirate, and seemingly with the full knowledge of the lord president of Munster, Sir Henry Brouncker, Bingley proceeded to trade the goods on board with the pirates in the port.[72] Indeed, Ralph Bingley did not content himself with taking the goods from the *Triall*; while in Kinsale with some of his crew, using the longboat from the *Triall* he entered Cork Harbour and captured another ship that was moored in the River Lee.[73]

In that same year Crooke refused to hand over goods to Humphrey Jobson that Bingley had plundered from a French vessel.[74] Bingley, surprisingly, was never tried for piracy and continued in his ventures unimpeded by either the pirates or indeed the establishment in London. In 1611, the States-Generals of the United Provinces in Holland had received sanction by King James to pursue the pirates, being issued with a commission to do so. Orders were sent to all vice-admirals and their deputies around the coast to assist the Dutch fleet but the Dutch complained that Crooke had 'uncourteously refused' to furnish them with pilots to guide them into the harbours around Munster.[75] Though it seems that Crooke was still serving two masters, his petition to the lord high treasurer in 1612 pleading his case against his accusers appears to have found sympathetic ears because by 1613 he had been acquitted and awarded a knighthood.[76] He was created a baronet in 1624.[77]

Connected to Crooke, both personally through family ties and officially as a prospective undertaker in Baltimore, James Salmon arrived into Munster at the same time as Crooke. Though there is less information available about him, he is recorded as being from Suffolk and was married to one of Crooke's daughters.[78] He worked closely with Crooke, and from letters that passed between both gentlemen it is clear that Salmon kept Crooke appraised of shipping activity; for example, Salmon thought it right to inform Crooke that he was suspicious of a ship in Baltimore. He confirmed that the crew comprised 'Irishmen, who could speak but little English'. The letter is signed from 'Ould Court', with an additional note, 'To my loving father, Mr. Thomas Crooke, Esq'.[79]

FIGURE 24: Detail from the 1612 Dutch chart of Oldcourt tower house in Baltimore, marked as 'Cort' and with two smaller buildings also depicted. An O'Driscoll fortification, it may have been from here that James Salmon carried out his deputy vice-admiral duties in Baltimore. SUB GÖTTINGEN, 4 H BRIT P III, 6 RARA, UNIVERSITÄTSBIBLIOTHEK, GÖTTINGEN, GERMANY

There are two Oldcourts in Baltimore: the O'Driscoll tower house of Oldcourt, which is located along the lower reaches of the Ilen River, about one kilometre north of Baltimore village; and the nearby Oldcourt House, a predominantly later Georgian house that was built on the site of an earlier tower or possibly a tower house the very lower courses of which remain subsumed within the family residence that is extant there now. The top two storeys were taken down when the Jennings family took over the house in the mid-eighteenth century, acquired from Henry Becher who was landlord in the area at that time. The larger Georgian house was then built onto the earlier, much-altered structure.[80] Little if anything is known about this earlier tower, so it cannot be stated with certainty if this is the site depicted on the 1612 Dutch chart or if it is a later fortified structure not directly linked to the O'Driscolls or indeed Salmon. What is certain is that the structure depicted on the Dutch chart is crenelated, and if assessed alongside other known fortification sites on the chart, such as Leamcon or Castlehaven, then it suggests that it is the O'Driscoll tower house that is illustrated. Further supporting this argument, the structure indicated on the chart is placed at the confluence of the Ilen River and estuarine limits of Baltimore Harbour, exactly where Oldcourt Castle is located. Its depiction suggests importance, named as the 'Cort' or courthouse.

Not all Salmon's dealings with the pirates were self-serving, however, and in 1608, in his legitimate role as deputy vice-admiral, he sent goods that pirates Bishop and Jennings had plundered from the ship *Almanac* back to Bristol to their rightful merchant owners.[81] Such 'official' actions were carried out concurrent with liaisons with pirates, and as late as 1624 in papers dealing with interrogatories recorded on behalf of the lord high admiral, several responses refer to goods taken from pirates in Castlehaven by 'Mr. Salmon, an Englishman'. One, an interrogation of a suspected pirate, queried a ship called the *Neptune* that was captured and brought into Castlehaven, where its goods, including salt, were sold to James Salmon for money and other victuals to the value of £250.[82] By 1627, Salmon was resident in Castlehaven, though he seems to have had direct connections with the place prior to this. In that year his name is logged in the patrol journal of the naval ship the *St James*, when the vessel and its crew took shelter in Castlehaven from bad weather.[83] Salmon was a man of wealth at that point, if a letter from Sir Richard Aldworth describing the misery and poverty of the soldiers stationed in County Cork at the time is considered. It suggests that the 'rich Englishmen of the province should be written to and asked for a loan'. One of the gentlemen he lists is Mr James Salmon.[84]

Salmon's later involvement in a number of legal cases relating to ships either plundered or wrecked off the coast of Cork confirms that he was still employed by the admiralty at that stage. One concerns the loss, in 1628, of the Spanish galleon *Santa Ana Maria* in Castlehaven Harbour and perhaps provides one of the most informative accounts of not alone Salmon's official duties locally, but the workings of the admiralty courts in general. While not specifically a case of piracy, it concerns the capture of the 1627 Spanish treasure fleet by Dutch West India Company Captain Piet Hein; while en route to Holland, the *Santa Ana Maria* was separated from Hein's fleet by a storm and was captured by an English privateer, the *Dragon*. When on its way to Bristol, it was lost, due to more bad weather, in the outer harbour of Castlehaven. The convoluted legal wranglings that ensued on rights of prize, ownership of goods and salvage operations makes for interesting reading and confirms that, irrespective of the questionable trading affairs of individuals like Salmon, they still managed to remained in their official position.[85]

ASSOCIATED OFFICIALS

Several other characters working in an official capacity in Munster during the early part of the seventeenth century were also involved in illegal activity. Captain Henry Skipwith was one of them. Listed in 1610 as one of the crown's undertakers in Ireland, he succeeded Humphrey Jobson as vice-admiral, but no sooner had he assumed the post in Munster than he too was suspected of receiving pirate goods and selling them to his deputies, one of whom was William Hull.[86] Skipwith had arrived earlier, however, and from Fineen O'Driscoll's petition of 1606 we learn that he acted as a commissioner to enquire into O'Driscoll's lands. The petition is counter-signed by Chichester and seven other individuals, including Captain Henry Skipwith.[87] By 1610 Skipwith was stationed at Castlepark in Kinsale though he is also associated with Carriganassig Castle in Inishannon which he seems to have used as a familial residence.[88] In 1613 Skipwith received wheat and rye out of a ship named the *St Saviour* of Lübeck. The vessel had been seized by pirate captains William Baugh and William Wollmer and brought to Leamcon, no doubt with William Hull as broker to the deal. Skipwith distributed the goods to his tenants on the understanding that they pay 'two for one at the nexte harveste followinge'.[89] Skipwith, like many of his contemporaries in west Cork, was duplicitous. While no doubt accommodating piratical activity, in several of his official communications he is also frustrated at his inability to prevent local engagement with pirates. In one, for example, he makes reference to the smaller fishing boats of Crookhaven and the fishing community there claiming they are 'forced' to victual the pirates, though he suspects that this is more a ruse to cover what they would have intentionally done in any case.[90]

Skipwith is mentioned throughout the main period of activity of the pirate alliance, and he had a particular link to pirate Captain William Baugh. On one occasion he advised Baugh to sail to Kinsale where he could anchor

FIGURE 25: Aerial view of Castlepark or James Fort, Kinsale, showing the star-shaped bastioned fortification where Vice-Admiral Captain Henry Skipwith held many meetings with pirate Captain William Baugh.

safely and stay in the fort at Castlepark, under the protection of the lord deputy, Chichester, while negotiations took place on Baugh's pardon. It was on the understanding, however, that Baugh leave '900 pieces of eight at Captain Bishop's house', in Leamcon, for Skipwith. The examination of two of Baugh's crew, pirates John Huskins and Richard Millington, state that 'the Boatswaine told this examinant that [the money] was to be delivered to Captaine Skipwith to procure the lo deputy's protection'.[91] While the exchange of monies suggests that an agreed mechanism was in place for the pirates to 'buy' their pardons, and thus inadvertently contribute to crown revenues, if such monies were instead bribery, it points to corruption that led all the way to the lord deputy himself. It also informs on how central a figure Richard Bishop was within the Alliance of Pirates, not alone acting as their admiral when on the high seas or their broker when negotiating pardons, but also the agent who administered monies between individual pirates and admiralty officials, albeit on the understanding that it was part of the negotiation process. The fact that Bishop was living on William Hull's estate in Leamcon ensured that all deals were carried out under his watchful control and where his demesne was the filtering place for bribes, goods and knowledge.

Lawrence Parsons, very much a background but nevertheless constant figure from the first decade of the century, took on a formal position when he assumed the role of judge of the Irish Admiralty Court in Munster in 1619, taking over from Henry Gosnold. Prior to that he was legal clerk of the crown, peace and assizes for Munster, 1604–16, attorney general for Munster, 1612–24 and then judge of the admiralty and deputy vice-admiral for Munster, 1619–28. He was an absentee adjudicator, however, who relied fully on others to function on his behalf.[92] He acted as inspector for the 1622 commission that sought to examine all aspects of the plantation, including land acquisition and undertakers' activities. It is ironic that one of the main findings of the commission was criticism in regard to absentee undertakers, a fault for which Parsons himself was found guilty. In 1620 Henry Cary was named Viscount Falkland and shortly afterwards was appointed lord chief deputy of Ireland. In 1618 he had been appointed vice-admiral of Munster, taking over from Nottingham, and he complained that Parsons was essentially doing little or nothing in his post as judge. This complaint also had a fiscal basis, with Adam Loftus later also using Parsons' ineptitude to support his own cause, estimating that no more than £10 sterling profit had been made during Parsons' tenure in office. In 1612 Loftus succeeded Ambrose Forth, who died in 1610, as judge of the admiralty in Ireland. The admiralty court in Ireland, in the two years between the death of Forth and the appointment of Loftus, remained out of commission, a hiatus no doubt that was exploited to its fullest by both the pirates in the southwest and the complicit officials in residence there.[93] It is telling that it was during that period when most of the pardons were negotiated and issued. Within just a few years of being in office, however, Loftus benefited from the passing of the act for punishing pirates 1613–14. He was thus able to take a hands-on approach to the piracy problem in Munster, which he appears to have done more or less straight away.

Parsons, a cousin of Richard Boyle, had bought Walter Raleigh's estates in Youghal and subsequently sold them on to Boyle and Parsons may have initiated introductions between Hull and Boyle, as suggested by John Appleby.[94] Throughout his career Parsons was suspected on a regular basis of corruption.[95] In 1621 the High Court of Admiralty papers lists his receipt of goods, including 'barrels of suckets' from the ship *Exchange*, and again in 1623 he gave permission for Dutch privateer-cum-pirate Captain Yope to land goods in Leamcon, to revictual his ship and take on board thirty men to augment his crew.[96]

Not all government officials were English; as noted above. In June 1607 Donogh O'Brien, 4th earl of Thomond, an Irish nobleman and high-ranking soldier, was provisionally appointed joint lord president of Munster, with Sir Richard Moryson, following the death of Sir Henry Brouncker. Sir Richard Boyle, in his position as privy councillor for Munster, proposed Thomond as a candidate.[97] As evident from his dealings with the pirate Captain Thomas Coward, the earl of Thomond played at being both poacher and gamekeeper, though it could be argued that he was in fact just following instructions during the course of his office. The sources suggest his interactions with members of the alliance were on a peripheral basis, stepping in and out of events without being directly complicit. These encounters may have had a wider context, however, if considered in terms of Thomond's efforts to expand his economic holdings and rental income from developing settlements along the course of the River Shannon. Similarly, his attempts to have the county of Clare included as part of Munster rather than Connacht, which it was at that time, fitted with his desire, as lord president of Munster, to control his possessions in that county.[98] Boyle and Thomond maintained mutual interests, particularly in land speculation, and indeed so much land was changing hands in 1610, the earl of Salisbury received complaints that 'the Earl of Thomond and Sir Richard Boyle are at this present passing so many parcels of land as the particulars contained in a roll of parchment reach 16 yards in length'.[99]

In late June 1607, in correspondence with the earl of Salisbury, Thomond apologised for not writing sooner and promised to continue the good works of Brouncker, principally with respect to purging seminarians and Jesuits in Munster; interestingly, he remarked on the need to fortify areas to ensure control, and blamed the undertakers for not carrying out their settlement requirements as commissioned.[100] It is from March 1608 onwards, in letters that issued back and forth between the English Privy Council and Lord Deputy Chichester, that we get some inkling into his engagement with the pirates. One suggested Thomond was too lenient towards pirates who were cruising the reaches of the River Shannon right up to Limerick City. As a postscript to one letter, the lords of the council accused Thomas Crooke of maintaining links with the pirates, and specifically naming Captain Coward in that dispatch. The pirates were able to sail between Limerick and Baltimore, while openly dealing with resident officials, in this case one in west Cork and the other in Limerick, the latter the lord president of Munster himself.[101]

Thomond's leniency towards the English pirates may have been influenced by his desire to promote all things English, including customs, law and settlement, something he was frequently commended for by senior government officials during his tenure in office.[102] As a result, he may have been less rigorous in his dealings with the pirates, once again, like others had, recognising the potential for advancement of the plantation policy through encouraging them to settle. Chichester was careful to point out that Thomond only kept Coward engaged for a short time until he was able to deliver the pirate to the lord deputy himself.[103] This explanation seems to have worked, as subsequent letters from the king to Chichester praised Thomond highly and suggested that the lord deputy give the earl 'special consideration'.[104]

In February 1609, Chichester instructed Thomond to apprehend the pirate John Jennings who was anchored at the mouth of the River Shannon. If interception were not possible, the lord deputy suggested that some alternative means to hold Jennings in the area should be used, until such time as Jennings and his crew's intent to submit to a pardon could be legitimised – a period of some twenty days was expected before such corroboration would be forthcoming.[105] This is curiously similar to Thomond's handling of Coward, and suggests that an 'unofficial' policy of negotiating with the pirates was already in place in early 1609. By the end of February, Thomond had taken Jennings prisoner, but the earl was injured during his storming of the pirate's vessel, losing the use of his right arm during the encounter.[106] The pirates were targeting merchant ships travelling along the course of the River Shannon up as far as Limerick City, ships that were trading with the satellite towns established by Thomond within the estuary, including Kilrush and Ennis. These coastal towns and their marine facilities allowed foreign traders to avail of the rich supply of timber in the hinterland and exploit the abundant fishing resources to be found within the waters of Ireland's largest river.[107]

When Captain Jennings entered 'the river of Limerick' (the Shannon), he did so with a rich cargo plundered from a Dutch ship. He proceeded to harass the local towns along its course and 'impeached even their ordinary trade'.[108] The value of the goods on board Jennings' ship and the potential value of selling off confiscated cargo would not have gone unnoticed by Thomond, and the necessity for the admiralty to make a decision on its fate was emphasised when he wrote that 'the charge of the ship, her keepers, and others will eat up all, or the greatest part, of the goods in short time'.[109] Indeed, in a deposition a few days later, Deputy Vice-Admiral Richard Jobson was to go to Limerick to meet Thomond and take delivery of forty-nine chests of sugar left by Jennings.[110] Thomond was thus receiving pirated goods officially, but the question remains, was he also doing so personally?

Ultimately, Thomond emerges as a loyal subject of the crown, confirmed when he was made lord deputy of the Council of Munster in 1615.[111] His associations with Boyle, his speculations in developing maritime trading towns within his jurisdiction, and his involvement, albeit indirectly, with admiralty business through his interception of pirates could suggest a more calculated participation, and possible wider associations that cannot be readily traced within the existing sources.[112] It is interesting to note that Dr Thomas Singleton, principal of Brasenose College, Oxford, wrote to Thomond in August 1607 recommending that Thomond's sons should return to Ireland, as they were intent on doing so and thus there was no point in keeping them at the college any longer.[113] This was the same college attended by Henry Mainwaring, who graduated from it with a bachelor of arts degree in 1602.[114]

Such coincidences, with close associations and wider professional and personal links, whether familial or otherwise, were widespread. These were times when knowledge and networks were critical to success in political as well as personal life, and the intermingling of relationships across the official and unofficial spectrum of players is telling. This was a landscape where who you knew and who you could influence was the key to advancement, power and wealth. When considering this interplay between the official and illicit worlds of politics and business, the pirate alliance, rather than being outside the system, was in fact best placed to benefit from within it, and those officials who colluded with them facilitated access to the heart of administrative affairs. It is within the context of colonial worlds, in particular the need to generate venture capital or profit from goods plundered, that the relationships between government officials and the Atlantic pirates is best placed. Knowledge of those who were involved, on all sides, provides background to the men and their motivations, but understanding the landscape within which they operated is crucial. It is to the wilds of west Cork, therefore, that we need to look to identify how the suitability of landscape was a key to their success.

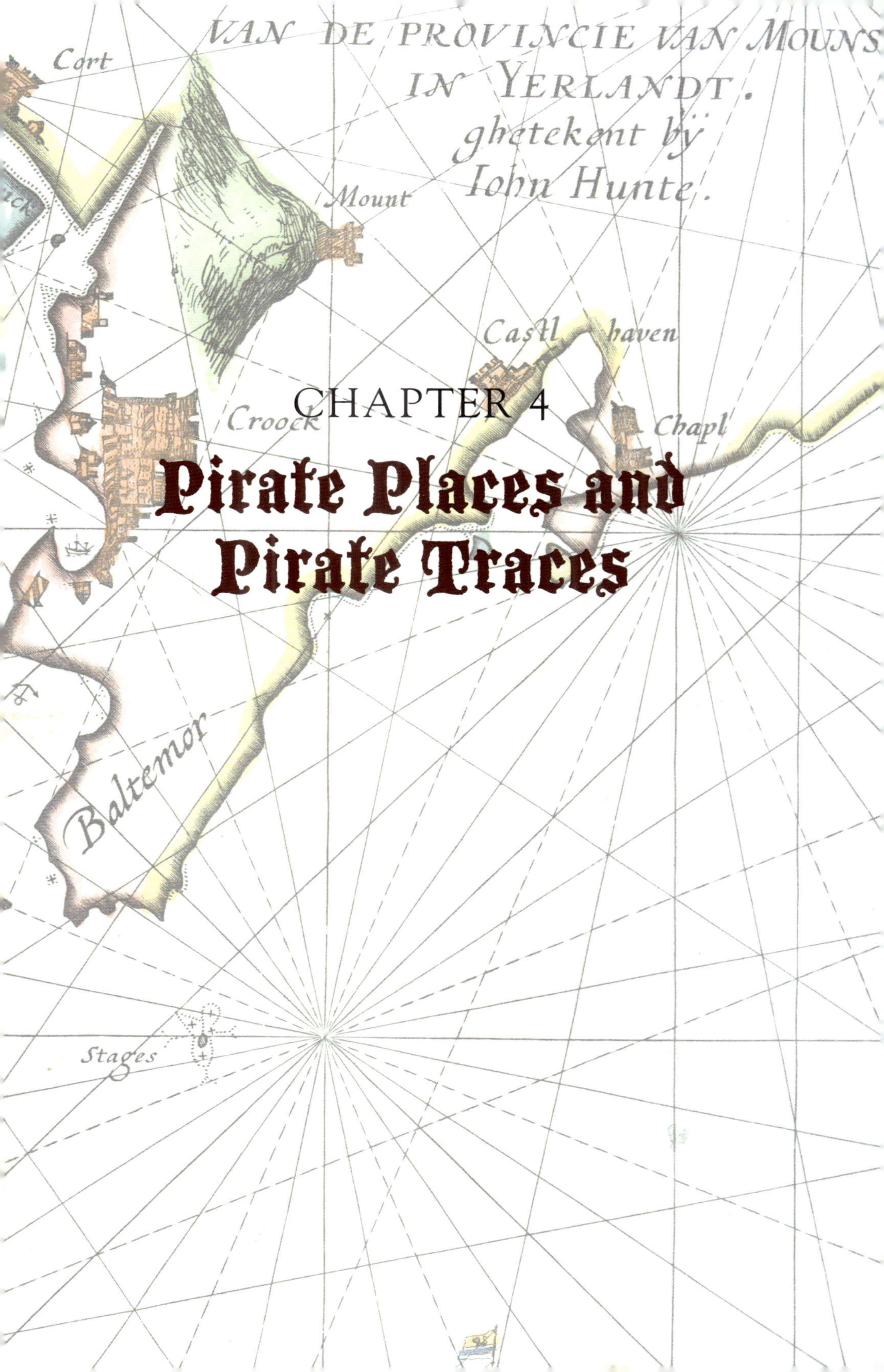

CHAPTER 4

Pirate Places and Pirate Traces

Volcht de Caerte van de Roof-havenenaen C. Cler .[1]

The coastal regions within which pirates operated comprised both landscape and seascape. Some locations bear striking names that immediately suggest this activity, though such names should not always be taken at face value. One of the many islands that make up the British Virgin Islands, for example, is Dead Man's Chest. Although a location for much pirate activity over the centuries, it is the island's coffin shape that gives it its unusual toponym. Ireland too has a multitude of provocatively named bays and beaches, including Grab-All Bay near Crosshaven in County Cork, Wine Strand in Dingle, County Kerry, and Murder Hole beach near Downings in County Donegal. These names evoke images of illegal acts in remote places beyond the reach of the law. Whether this was true or not, the names of places around the coast can point directly to maritime activity in the past and inform on wider connections: Newfoundland Bay located between Cork Harbour and the Old Head of Kinsale comes to mind. Indeed the name in the Irish language for Newfoundland is equally informative: 'Talamh an Éisc' or 'The Land of the Fish'. Names can vibrate with past associations and are thus important markers when considering what events actually took place, what connections are relevant and how the coastline was utilised through time.

What made a landscape suitable for piratic activity, and what within that landscape contains evidence for this activity, are questions that have only recently been considered fully from a cultural perspective, though historians have dealt with elements of them in earlier writings.[2] Cultural signals within any given landscape can be ephemeral, even more so with covert activities such as piracy, and its partner, smuggling. The example above illustrates that place-name evidence alone cannot be trusted, and that, instead, the physical world within which the pirates lived and worked must be included in any considered examination of 'pirate places' and 'pirate bases'.

Members of the alliance skirted most of the coastline of Ireland at one time or another, using a variety of harbours, havens and river courses right along the west and northwest coast, including the Shannon Estuary, but also Clew Bay and Broadhaven Bay in Mayo and Lough Foyle and Lough Swilly on the northern coastline. Certainly, Clew Bay would have been known to the pirates, with piracy under the O'Malley clan still ongoing there, though not to the same extent as that prior to Grace O'Malley's death in 1603.

Broadhaven too was a favoured haunt. It was there that several pirates awaited their pardons, including Henry Mainwaring. In a curious act, and indicative of how familiar Broadhaven must have been, William Monson, admiral of the Narrow Seas fleet and tasked primarily to eradicate pirates, impersonated Mainwaring in Broadhaven in 1614, in a successful effort to gain access to the local Gaelic-Irish family of Michael Cormack and his castle, most probably located at Inver. This he did with ease as the lord, his family and the locals openly welcomed him and his crew thinking it Henry Mainwaring and his ships full of booty. Prior to that, in 1613, pirate Mathew Gunter was also in Broadhaven seeking a pardon, and as late as 1626 Dutch pirate Claes Compaen (Anglicised in the sources as Claus Campane) was recorded there with two other ships to trim and victual.[3] This certainly points to a location that pirates – some of whom were also active in Munster – visited over a number of years, with perhaps similar infrastructure and trading networks in place as in west Cork. Critically, it provides evidence for the scope of operations of the English-dominated pirate alliance and their engagement with resident Gaelic-Irish beyond the boundaries of transplantation and plantation, on an equal footing and to the mutual advantage, no doubt, of both.

It was the southwest that was their preferred haunt, an area stretching from the small harbour of Castlehaven westward to include Baltimore Harbour, Roaringwater Bay, Schull (Skull) and Leamcon harbours and as far west as Crookhaven. Covering a distance of approximately thirty nautical miles, the area includes the islands of Sherkin, Cape Clear and Long Island. It represents an ancient maritime landscape ruled over for centuries by the Gaelic-Irish lordships of the O'Driscolls and O'Mahonys, discussed earlier. Dotted along the coastline are the ruins of many of their castles, sentinels that in the past stood guard over the Atlantic, controlled their territorial waters and commanded the harbours and approaches. These too fell into disuse or were used as garrisons by English soldiers following the fall of the Gaelic Order after the Battle of Kinsale in 1601–2. Thereafter, the southwest coastline witnessed an influx of new settlers and traders who availed of the rich maritime resources and forged mercantile links across the Atlantic. This was a landscape favourable to maritime activity and operations, and was readily identified as such by the pirate alliance. It was distant enough to ensure security, traditionally vibrant enough as a focus of maritime trade to warrant expansion or establishment of settlements, and as a base for industry was seasonally sustainable and, most importantly, commercially viable.

THE SEASONALITY OF PIRACY

The southern coast of Ireland was an ideal location for a pirate headquarters, on a number of levels. Its position within the temperate Atlantic waters on the periphery of northern Europe, combined with its strategic placement along the emerging Atlantic trading routes, permitted the interception of ships outward from Britain and Northern Europe to the continent and Americas and then likewise on their homeward journeys. Its multitude of harbours, ports and bays ensured an ideal northern headquarters for the members of the alliance (see Figures 2 and 5). Writing from Youghal in 1609 to Sir Robert Cecil, the lord lieutenant of Ireland, Richard Moryson, vice-president of Munster, despondingly noted:

> … [the] continual repair of the pirates to the western coast of the province [of Munster], in consequence of the remoteness of the place, the wildness of the people and their own strength and wealth both to command and entice relief, is very difficult for them to prevent or remedy.[4]

Familiar with the rugged nature of the landscape, the Irish climate afforded the pirates a strategic summer base.[5] Sailing to Ireland from early May, they based themselves primarily along the south and southwest coast until the weather began to change in August. At times during this period, if the weather proved too inclement they would stop instead for a time in Newfoundland. Here was a favoured recruiting ground for pirate captains Peter Easton and Henry Mainwaring.[6] Easton was a former private operator under Elizabeth I who held a commission to provide protection for the migratory fishing industry in Newfoundland. Familiar with the area, when he eventually turned to outright piracy after 1604 he based his operations there. He used it as a 'springboard' from which to operate and as a location that he could fall back on when needed.[7]

In August the pirates would move south again, and until February would spend their time in a number of key locations in North Africa, including their main base of Mamora. From here they could venture as far afield as the Caribbean waters of Barbados and the West Indies via the Azores. Contact continued too with bases within the Mediterranean, among the most visited being Leghorn (Livorno in Italy), then under the rule of the grand duke of Tuscany, Ferdinando de Medici; it served as a free port to encourage trade, freedom of religion and settlement. Algiers and Tunis were sometimes used as revictualling ports, though not as free ports, and strictly under the imprimatur of the Ottoman Turks.[8] Mainwaring explained that 'Within the Straits of Gibraltar, there is not any place for Pirates to resort to, but only Algiers and Tunis, where they may be fitted with all manner of provisions and to ride safely from the Christian forces'. From February to May the pirates focused their activity primarily among the warmer waters north of Africa, skirting the coasts of Spain and Portugal.[9]

This tradition of seasonal travel had a number of advantages. It availed of the most suitable sea and weather conditions; it avoided spending long periods in one place, thus impeding capture by the English navy; and as far as possible it coincided with Iberian treasure fleets and other European merchant shipping that followed the trade winds homeward in the autumn with their rich cargoes. This is borne out by Chichester when, writing in August 1613 in response to notification of the planned embarkation of the king's ships to Ireland to clear the coasts of pirates, he informed Lord High Admiral Nottingham that due to the time of year, pirates would no longer be found to populate the area. He went on to specified where the pirates went from spring onwards:

> ... [the] most opportune time of the season is allredy spent, and that Pirates here do take new Enterprizes in hand very Early about the end of Spring, if not before as divers have done this yeare and so enabled themselves against the Winter to Adventure Southwards towards Spain and Barbary, where they become Expert and hard to be dealt with all afterwards, and from whence again when the heat of the Sun and the Gallyes there do threaten to prosecute them, they return hither (to refresh themselves for the time) or towards the Newfound Land, which seems to be a safe retraict [retreat].[10]

As with all weather-dependent activities, operations could change as the need arose; at times some of the pirates could find themselves revictualling and repairing their ships in Ireland in January or February if the weather allowed them to travel that far north from their winter base in Mamora. The North Atlantic pirate alliance was therefore organised to maximise opportunities for capturing vessels, over-wintering in sunnier climes and avoiding engagement with the king's ships.

THE RECEIVING LANDSCAPE

Of all the harbours along the southwest coast, during the latter part of the sixteenth and first two decades of the seventeenth centuries, Baltimore appears from the documentary accounts to have been among the most favoured by pirates. Indeed in 1608 this was noted by Chichester when he wrote to the lords of the English Privy Council: '… though all of them [the harbours in Munster] be very commodious and safe for pirates to come unto, yet Baltimore is most frequented by them'.[11] No doubt it was the willingness of the local populace that encouraged the use of Baltimore, including acquiescence by remaining members of the Gaelic-Irish O'Driscoll lords, though by then they held little sway. More importantly from a knowledge point of view, it is suggested that it was the maritime capability of lords such as the O'Driscolls that enticed pirates to frequent Baltimore rather than, for example, Kinsale or Cork, the main ports used by the king's ships in the south. The fact that there had been an O'Driscoll fleet and other local boats using Baltimore Harbour meant that some form of infrastructure was probably in place to accommodate such vessels. This would have included slipways, landing places, careening and repair facilities, and men who had the knowledge and ability to carry out such work. This would, no doubt, have been well known throughout the maritime community at the time. In 1602 it was noted that in front of Dunalong Castle on Sherkin Island, there was '… a deep pool about half a league over, where infinite numbers of ships may ride … and a good place to careen ships'.[12] The use of harbours like Baltimore therefore has to be regarded in terms of the geopolitical landscape, where environment, topography and local ruling polity inevitably allowed illicit activity to continue as it always had, as part of the everyday life of the area, from the earliest of times. Piratical pursuits were thus, it seems, consistent; it was only the pirates themselves who changed over time.

The importance of Baltimore for the provisioning of ships was identified from a much earlier period. In 1550, an instruction was given by the crown to Sir Anthony St Leger to seek out the best harbours for gathering customs returns, with particular attention to be paid to 'Valentimore, Knockfargus, and Strangforde' (Baltimore, Carrickfergus and Strangford).[13] In 1582 an entry from the High Court of Admiralty lists a Spanish vessel coming into Baltimore in need of new masts and general repair,[14] while in 1585 the great woodland in Munster is mentioned with a good store of timber available in Youghal for shipbuilding, where local shipwrights and mariners were also available and two ruined abbeys were to be used as storehouses for the timber.[15] Harbours like Baltimore may therefore have had requisite localised or indeed improvised vessel repair and maintenance facilities with larger ports like Kinsale and Youghal maintaining more commercially organised infrastructure for the building and refurbishment of ships. This is confirmed by the examination of suspected pirate John Lee, taken in May 1610, where he mentions a ship then being built in Kinsale, on which he hoped to gain passage to Fowey.[16] Contemporary seventeenth-century cartographic sources also support this, by depicting such facilities, including a graving dock and quays in Kinsale located below the fortified site of Castlepark (James Fort), which would have controlled and protected them and those using them.[17]

The identification of a careening site in the Cove area of Baltimore substantiates the historical evidence for more localised services that were available to mariners. Significantly, though, it provides the archaeological evidence for these site types that generally leave very little or no physical remains in the landscape. The site is on the southwest side of the Cove, on the foreshore, and is accessible at low water. A natural sloping rock outcrop was used, with four well-carved rock-cut rope holes and associated putlog holes visible. The mechanism to careen (or clean) a vessel was to run a vessel ashore at high tide and when the tide receded, the vessel was pulled onto its side by tying ropes to the upper part of the masts, once the rigging and sails had been secured. It was supported from tipping too far over by means of timber planks placed between the hull and foreshore or nearby rock. The site in the Cove was perfectly located for the task, with the rock-cut holes accommodating the ropes that pulled the vessel onto its side; the putlog recesses held the supporting timbers between the ship's hull and rock. Careening involved the removal, from the outside of the hull, of marine crustacea such as barnacles, or repair of ship timbers that had been damaged through impact, rot or marine borers, the ubiquitous 'shipworm'. Re-caulking and re-tarring could also then be carried out if needed. When work on one side of the vessel had been completed, it was refloated on the next available tide, turned around, and the opposite side similarly attended to. Careening was a necessary evil for all mariners if their ships were to sustain, but it left the vessel vulnerable and its crew literally stranded until the job was completed. For pirates, who needed to ensure their ships were exposed for the least amount of time, a careening place ideally had to be secluded yet accessible, familiar but not well known. These sites also had to have protection from the prevailing winds, and were usually located in areas of calm water, to allow for

FIGURE 26: Evocative watercolour depicting a three-masted ship in the Cove, Baltimore, awaiting low water so that it can be careened (cleaned); archaeological evidence for a careening site has been identified in the Cove. © DR PETER MURRAY

proper operation of the wooden platforms that were hauled close alongside the vessels for crew to clean the lower hull.[18] Certainly the site at the Cove in Baltimore had all these requirements, and documentary sources point to other locations used by the pirates having similar facilities, including across the harbour at Dunalong and in Croagh (pronounced 'Crewe') Harbour, which lies to the west between the harbours of Schull and Leamcon.[19]

Contemporary accounts refer to the natural attributes of the bays and harbours along the southwest coast, with Gerard Boate, writing in his *Ireland's Naturall History* in 1657, reflecting that Bantry, in west Cork had 'severall good Harbours and Roads', Berehaven in County Cork being 'a very good and safe port' and that the 'rest of the Harbour and Sound, is everywhere very clean and clear, and very good anchor-ground, ten, twelve and thirteen fathoms deep'. He describes Dunmanus, in west Cork, as being great and wide and, though not comparable to Bantry, has a 'very commodious Road to save ships in and good anchor ground everywhere'. Though not named, Boate refers to Roaringwater Bay as one 'far greater than those three forenamed' (Kenmare, Bantry and Dunmanus) within which are located Crookhaven and Schull, with Baltimore the most easterly. These are described as 'great havens'. He singled out Baltimore as 'surpassing all the others in bigness'.[20] His detailed description of Baltimore Harbour referred to its narrow entrance, with a rock to the east that endangers shipping. This is now known as the Looe Rock, at the eastern side of the main entrance to Baltimore, so named following the wrecking of the English man-of-war HMS *Looe* there in April 1697.[21]

Boate's account of the harbour is interesting, as his description suggests that he may have been observing Baltimore and the landscape in the region from the sea rather than from the land. He refers to 'Baltimore-Haven' and 'the Iland' (probably Sherkin Island) as within Roaringwater Bay; there is no mention of a town or village that would indicate settlement of any consequence visible at that time. The town of Baltimore went into decline following the raid by Algerine pirates in 1631 when they captured over 100 of its inhabitants, an event discussed in Chapter 8. Boate also drew attention to Baltimore's two access points. The fact that Baltimore has two entrances, its main one to the south and a second that lies between Sherkin Island and Spanish Island, was a strategic factor in its use over the years, as it provided an escape route from the harbour, if required, and also an alternative exit or entry point should weather conditions prevent the use of its main southern entrance. Natural navigational hazards were well known, such as the previously mentioned Looe Rock or the aptly named Lousy Rock in the middle of the harbour, and these were noted on cartographic sources, in sailing directions or pilot guides, called 'rutters', and commented upon in documents. Carew described the harbour in 1602 when he was surveying the coastline there after the Battle of Kinsale:

> ... the haven's mouth of Baltimore is caused by the island of Inisherkin, two leagues to the east of Cape Clear and the harbour is ten fathoms at low water but exceedingly narrow, by reason of a great rock lying in the same (always above the water) which, being within half a caliver's shot of the better shore, gives good opportunity to secure a port. At the other end of the island, with good pilotage a ship of two hundred tons may safely come in by day but not by night by reason of sunken rocks that lie in the entrance.[22]

Such detail was again worthy of mention from a strategic perspective when Chichester reflected that in Baltimore:

FIGURE 27: Sketch by John Windele of Dún na Séad Castle in 1835 with ruin of the O'Driscoll castle and later Thomas Crooke's house elevated, and also showing the lower battery tower. The tower was located where the fisheries pier in Baltimore is now built.
RIA MS 12M 15(169), ROYAL IRISH ACADEMY, DUBLIN

> … [the pirates] might be easily kept out thence, by the advantage of the narrow entrance in at the mouth thereof, where there is a rock naturally made to contain ordnance that would be able to sink any ship coming within reach of their shot as of necessity it must, if it will come in. A small charge, with three or four pieces of ordnance and a few warders, will make it inaccessible to any.[23]

Chichester is probably referring to either the high cliff at the northeast of the entrance where the beacon is now located, or Sherkin Island, at the southwestern approach to the entrance, where there is the remains of a lighthouse, but where a battery formerly stood. A second battery was extant below Dún na Séad Castle, on a rocky outcrop, commanding the inner harbour that is still known as Battery Point today, though it has been built upon over the last three decades or so for the extension of the main pier. It stood directly across the harbour from Dunalong Castle on Sherkin Island, where yet another battery was located.

The Spanish emplaced these inner harbour batteries in 1601 when they garrisoned the castles there during the lead-up to the Battle of Kinsale, but Chichester's comments suggest that there was no actual battery at the outer entrance to the harbour itself. Their strategic nature, maritime facilities, allied with the abundance of resources available within harbours like Baltimore, both from the sea and from the land, was such that Vice-Admiral Skipwith reported to Chichester that the pirates in Munster could be facilitated there free of charge for at least three months.[24] He added that men brought provisions to the pirates from other parts of Ireland under the guise of supplies for the fishermen of Crookhaven. One, Henry Cook of Cork, brought twenty-two barrels of beer to the pirates at Leamcon.[25] It was not supplies in the form of food, drink or timber for the repair of their ships that drew the pirates to Munster, but the availability of ready recruits; local men who were unemployed sailors were willing to become part of a pirate crew in the hope of rich rewards, and the pirate captains welcomed them into their company. Resources in coastal Munster thus spanned the natural, physical, cultural and social spectrum to sustain an industry fast expanding by stealth.

THE NORTH AFRICAN BASES

When not in Ireland, the pirates turned their attention to the warmer waters off the Iberian coast and along the Atlantic coastline of northwest Africa. They would only remain along the coasts of Spain and Portugal while onboard supplies lasted and ships were in good repair, presumably so that if given chase, they could make it to a suitably friendly port on the Atlantic coast of Morocco. Several of the smaller ports along the Moroccan coastline provided open markets for the pirates' goods as well as provisioning and stopover points when needed. Mamora served as an entrepôt and winter base for the Atlantic pirate alliance. In 1611, Ferdinand Gorges' correspondence to the Privy Council mentions that the Atlantic pirates' 'comon harbour is at Mamora in Barbarie where they have merchants of all sorts that trade with them for all kind of comodities'.[26]

Havens north of Mamora included Cape Spartel, Asilah and Larache, all located south of the larger port of Tangiers.[27] Those south of Mamora were Salé and Rabat, Fidallah, Safi, Mogador (now Essaouira), Santa Cruz (now Agadir) and Massa. The ports along this Atlantic coastline were under the governance of the Moroccan Sultanate, and were open to trade following the crushing defeat of the Iberian forces in 1578 and the ending of the Hundred Years War for Morocco. Mainwaring explained that:

> At Missa [Massa], 5 leagues to the Southward of St Cruce [Cruz] they sell goods very well, and have fresh victuall & water, but they ride far off, and the Road dangerous, so that they must be beholding to the Moores [Moors] for their nosaveries [necessaries]; else they can doe nothinge, and this is the farthest Southward that they use upon the Barbarie coast, unless very rarely some goe to Rio-dore [de Oro], where they can have nothinge but water.[28]

Portugal abandoned most of its coastal fortresses along the Atlantic coast of Morocco thereafter.[29] The Portuguese held on to the areas below Massa, from Rio de Oro southwards, with the coastal regions there remaining under the Iberian Protectorate, rendering it unsafe for English mariners, including pirates. The men of the alliance rarely sailed south beyond the Canary Islands, primarily because it meant that their ships would have to be fully provisioned for such a long journey and would thus be heavier, slower and more vulnerable to attack in open water.[30]

While the pirates were free to trade in most of the above-listed ports, in some, like Massa, for example, they could sell their booty only with the agreement of the local tribal leaders who in turn were trading with the permission of the ruling sultan. This ensured control on goods and activity throughout the ports, as well as over individuals and commodities connected to the trans-Saharan trade, and critically, it safeguarded a valuable source of revenue.[31] Mainwaring provides specific details in Chapter 4 of his *Discourse* on the routes taken by the pirates around the coast of Africa and into the Mediterranean Sea, including the need to obtain sanction from the Ottoman Turks: 'At Bona and Bougie which are under the command of those of Algiers, Pirates may be very well refreshed with victual, water, and bread, and also sell goods well, … but they dare not trade with any unless they bring with them the Letters of Algiers'. Other ports were also used when needed, such as Tripoli 'in Barbary they shall be entertained and refreshed, and ride in command; but these are dangerous people, and the entrance bad for ships'.[32] Mamora remained one of the primary northwestern African bases for the pirates until it fell to the Spanish in 1614, after which Mainwaring, Bishop and their cohorts moved focus south to Salé and Rabat.[33]

There were certain pirates who adopted Muslim ways, including learning the Arabic language, clipping their beards as the Muslims did, or dressing in traditional North African clothes. As discussed above, pirates like John Ward and Sir Francis Verney decided to adopt the culture fully and converted to the Muslim faith.[34] Conversions were viewed with fear and horror by particular Christian power houses in Europe, both Catholic and Protestant. On a religious level it was considered blasphemy, idolatry and damnation of the soul, while politically the fear was that it could lead to the Islamisation of Europe. It was such an emotive issue that contemporary religious and literary writers expressed their views in sermons, plays and prose, often with underlying geopolitical motivations. Shakespeare's *Othello* of 1604 or Daborne's *A Christian Turn'd Turk*, written in 1609 and relating specifically to the conversions the previous year of pirates John Ward and Simon Danseker, are among the most obvious.

The expanding cross-cultural interaction between Christians and Muslims, whether through legitimate trade or piratical trade, was a growing worry for those in power in Europe, particularly the Catholic rulers of Iberia.[35] The Atlantic pirates forged ever-stronger links with the Moroccan and Ottoman rulers, merchants and corsairs of North Africa, through commercial dealings and shared knowledge of maritime resources, merchant fleet movements and shipbuilding technology. With the expulsion of the Moriscos – former Muslims who had been coerced into converting to Christianity – from southern Spain to North Africa in 1609, many Spanish Muslims (commonly referred to as the 'Moors' at that time) willingly engaged with the English pirates against their common enemy, Spain. At least two communities of Moriscos established themselves in port areas on the Atlantic coast of Morocco.[36] This may have facilitated the Atlantic pirates in accessing the ports and harbours of North Africa, but to suggest that this communal bond was based primarily on an anti-Christian, anti-Catholic ethos alone would be overly simplistic. Individual agendas, the prevailing political circumstances, and economic factors would have been the real dictators of events. Longstanding suspicions and mistrust prevailed too and were ever ready to seep into relationships to undermine agreements.[37] The fluctuating geopolitical environment within which the pirates functioned underlined their motivations and dictated successes or failures, as did their amphibious lifestyles within coastal landscapes of change, whether in the North Atlantic, in the warmer climes of northwest Africa or in the Mediterranean.

A 'PIRATE' LANDSCAPE?

Contemporary and modern writers alike have identified the strategic nature of particular places and the suitability of the topography of these landscapes to piracy. The physical characteristics of a particular coast presented opportunities for pirates to operate, but there was also a corresponding need to have social and economic components present within that landscape. Places of piracy may have had geographical, social and spatial similarities: remoteness of coastlines; the presence of offshore islands; wind and current correlations; local resource parallels; willing local populations; and political and social transformations. Peter Galvin certainly identified patterns with respect to the geography of landscape in his study of Caribbean piracy. He appropriately identified 'labyrinthine' characteristics of coasts whereby pirates 'traded and smuggled as often as they robbed' and were thus dependent on local factors to achieve their goals, and this was critical to understanding how they operated.[38]

The southwest coastline of Ireland, though unique in its own right, had close parallels to other pirate haunts, with Tortuga among the most infamous. Ellen Semple, in her study of pirate coasts of the Mediterranean, succinctly noted that, with Mediterranean piracy, 'the sea hunter … knew various points where he was sure to bag his game'.[39] Pirates knew a good coastline when they saw one. Contemporary writers noted the geographical importance of prominent 'pirate' harbours, including Baltimore's dual entry and exit points, Leamcon, Croagh, Long Island Sound, and Crookhaven Harbour to the western extremity of the pirates' hunting ground.[40]

Mainwaring similarly reported on these qualities as piratical requirements, inferring that, as with the other principal bases used by the pirate alliance (Harbour Grace in Newfoundland and Mamora in Atlantic Africa), the harbours of Ireland successfully met such needs, 'in regard of the general good entertainment they received there [and] supply of victuals and men which continually repair thither out of England to meet with Pirates'. It was thus well known that the southern coast of Munster was an open receptacle for the pirates and their goods, and it seems the locals ensured that this remained the case. Mainwaring continued: 'they [the local populace] have as good or rather better intelligence where your Majesty's Ships are, than contrariwise they shall have of the Pirates'.[41] Some contemporary commentators referred to these harbours as primary bases, 'their headquarters at Baltimore', where negotiations could take place for pardons.[42] Leamcon played a central role also in the daily activities of the pirates, referred to as the northern equivalent of Mamora and likened to 'a wild place, more like a frontier town than an Irish village'.[43]

Local knowledge was as valuable a commodity to the pirates as any other service, and a benefit to be used by the locals when negotiating with the pirates on goods and services. Familiarity with the coastline gave an immediate advantage to those navigating its waters, as the many islands and sunken rocks, particularly within Roaringwater Bay, were hazardous for all but the most experienced mariners. Many havens required pilotage for safe access, a service that locals were only too pleased to provide for a cost or that the pirates provided for themselves by either pressing pilots to join their crews or welcoming willing pilots as fellow crew members. Mainwaring refers to 'perforstmen', those forced to join crews, such as carpenters, surgeons and pilots, but also noted that, while many claimed they were pressed into service, they were in fact there by choice.[44]

HARBOURS, ANCHORAGES AND MARITIME FACILITIES

In order to utilise any bay or harbour, knowledge of access was necessary to ensure safe passage. Local information, as discussed above, was sought, bought or forced, with accessing complex places like Roaringwater Bay dependent on navigational know-how. Sailing directions, if available, were closely guarded as they provided specific information that could steer a vessel around natural hazards and furnish essential guidance on anchorages, foul ground and other important geographical and topographical features.[45] The description of Baltimore in the 1612 Dutch leeskaart provided essential directions for a captain of a ship, if he were to navigate its waters safely:

> The haven of Baltimore, one can run in and anchor well sheltered on both sides: sailing along the westlands one may lie sheltered in the bay before Castle Croock [Dún na Séad Castle]: in the middle of the waterway, to sail the backway around the island Ils-hercke [Sherkin Island], lies a cliff, that is dry at low tide.
>
> The narrows between the islands Spain and Ils-hercke is very shallow and at half tide only 13 feet of water; [a floaty ship[46]] no more than 10 or 11 feet, in addition it is somewhat foul, but one can go through it with small ships with a spring tide.

> The gap that lies on the west-side of the Island Clere [Cape Clear] is so foul, that one may not go through, so the fishermen say.[47]

Charts too could accompany the sailing directions, providing information on geographical features and other necessary details, including hazards and depths, location of islands, anchorages and access to 'watering places' (such as streams, rivers, springs or wells). Baltimore and Crookhaven were known to have primary anchorages. Baltimore is shown with four on the available early charts and maps: the deepest lay just off Dunalong Castle on Sherkin Island, another at the Cove area, a third at Tramadroum and another within the inner harbour immediate to the castle of Dún na Séad.[48] A ship is shown within the inner harbour at the Cove near where the careening site is located, and two possible house sites are depicted there also, overlooking the sea. These are similar to two other buildings that are indicated below the main tower, and may represent settler houses, as they look to have one and a half to two storeys with hipped roofs. They were thus possibly built in the 'English style' – timber-framed, of stone or brick infill, with slate or tile roofs and brick chimneys – and adhering to plantation standards. Leamcon Harbour, unlike Baltimore, is very much enclosed, apart from its one entrance to the east. Curiously, the 1612 Dutch leeskaart provides little if any mention of Leamcon, apart from detailing: 'There is a haven called Skolhaven which lies from Fastne[t] N by W 5 leagues.' Hunt's accompanying chart shows 'Skolhaven' [Schull] to the east of 'Limcon'. No details of anchorages or other topographical features are shown (see Figure 6).[49]

The nearest deep water anchorage was located at the north side of Long Island, and indeed Captain Martin White's sailing directions of the early nineteenth century indicate two main anchorages adjacent to the northern shore of Long Island.[50] Archaeological fieldwork undertaken by the author at Leamcon has identified a number of previously unrecorded features and structures that provide evidence for maritime infrastructure: the basal remains of an old quay, known locally as 'the long dock'; an associated eroded slipway; steps attached to a second stone pier, with the local name of 'the boathouse field'; three stone mooring posts which show distinct wear patterns from ropes, suggesting a long use period. The harbour is narrow and shallow, but records from Hull's time, as discussed below, of vessels docking and discharging goods, either for his legitimate fishing business or for pirate business, suggest that it was deeper, and the archaeological and placename evidence may support this, with maritime infrastructure in place to service

FIGURE 28: The archaeological remains of Leamcon long dock or quay, below Leamcon House; the quay was substantial and indicates the presence of harbour facilities that would have accommodated the loading and unloading of goods and people. IMAGE: CONNIE KELLEHER

vessels using its quays and slipways. It is in the intervening period, therefore, that the harbour has been subject to inundation and today, only small vessels are able to navigate its course at high water, with the main anchorage for larger boats still located on the northern side of Long Island.

The historical sources are replete with references to trade and shipping taking place at Leamcon, but it is quite possible that Leamcon encompassed the area comprising Long Island Sound, the entrance to Leamcon Harbour, and Leamcon itself. This is suggested in 1627 when Dutch pirate Captain Yeape [Yope] came to 'Long Island near Limcon', where he revictualled and offloaded cargo for William Hull.[51] Smaller craft may have ferried goods and individuals between Long Island and Leamcon, with the larger ships mooring in deeper water within Long Island Sound. At the time, therefore, the name Leamcon probably referred to the entire waterway between Schull Harbour and where William Hull had his demesne (Figures 4 and 6). On the eastern side of that demesne, and directly associated with the quay and mooring stones, is a canalised feature with dry-stone walling that leads from the foreshore northward, for a distance of over 100 metres. It would have originally provided access to a spring well, but the latter was destroyed by farming activity in the 1980s. The discreet but dedicated canal would

FIGURE 29: Stone steps of a second quay that lead down to a canalised channel, with associated mooring stones, again point to extensive maritime activity taking place at Leamcon. IMAGE: CATHAL TWOMEY

have allowed small vessels to ferry cargo from the shore to facilities within Leamcon demesne, as well as providing access to fresh water. It could also have allowed shallow rafts to transport goods to or from vessels at the quays, perhaps towed by a draught animal. On the western perimeter, a second man-made watercourse tracts inland for over 500 metres and connects with Leamcon Lake to the north. Perhaps constructed to channel fresh water from the lake to the foreshore, the linear feature, while not large enough to accommodate boats, intersects a stone-built bridge that incorporates an ancillary stone structure with three channels that allow the water to flow through it.

The function of this feature is open to interpretation but it may have served as a holding pond for fish and may therefore have been associated with William Hull's legitimate fishing operations. Directly linked to this industry, at Leamcon, is the recorded remains of one of his fish palaces.[52] Hull's 1641 deposition refers to the many 'fishhouses' and 'fishing sellars' [cellars] that were on his land at 'Lymcon' and also mentions 'the fishing on the land' there.[53] It is possible that fish were kept in Leamcon Lake, to the north of his fortified house, or stored in ponds on his demesne but it could also refer in general to his industrial fishing operations there or within the context of the wider harbour area, including at Long Island and in Schull. In the absence of archaeological excavation, it is not possible to attribute a specific date to these newly identified sites, and they could well be from a later period when William Hull's sons and successive family members continued to operate from Leamcon. It is reasonable to deduce, however, that formal quayside infrastructure was in place to service Hull's own fishing industry, but whether the newly discovered sites are contemporary with this is the question that remains to be answered.

Artefactual evidence has provided dating to at least the same century. Numerous pottery sherds recovered from the foreshore during wading surveys by the author contain both utilitarian and more exotic wares, including a sherd from a seventeenth-century Tuscan oil jar recovered adjacent to the man-made watercourse on the western side of the harbour. The pottery wares were found dispersed over a wide area and could have been washed in or brought in during later periods. One can speculate at connections to settlement and trade and certainly the Tuscan ware suggests connections with the continent. Whether this was during the period of the pirate alliance or from a later period remains unknown.[54]

The solitary battery tower that now stands sentinel overlooking the harbour at Leamcon, which would have formed part of Hull's fortified demesne, controlled activities taking place along the foreshore and its watercourse below.[55] The harbour, now deeply silted, retains the potential for further remains to be found, both artefactual and structural, perhaps even the remains of a vessel that once plied the waters beside the quays. In 1612 pirate Captain William Baugh was in Leamcon seeking his pardon, before proceeding to Kinsale.[56] In the same year, the lords of the English Privy Council wrote in reference to a letter from the French ambassador, who was looking for restitution on behalf of the French owners of certain goods brought into 'Limecon' by Baugh and his pirate colleague Miller. Baugh and Miller are referred to as 'the late pirates', suggesting they had received their pardons at that stage.[57] In 1613, when Robert Stephenson was offered a pardon, he brought his ship into Leamcon Harbour, where Captain Middleton boarded it during the course of his negotiations with the pirate captain. In the same deposition William Hull mentions that Stephenson arrived at Leamcon about 2 March 1613 and anchored in the harbour, and that they met at the 'Battering place' in Leamcon, when the pardon for Stephenson arrived.[58] What is meant by the 'Battering place' – whether it refers to the Battery, the only extant remains of Hull's fortified house and ancillary defensive towers, or to another location, perhaps off Gun Point on the headland to the south-east of the entrance to Leamcon Harbour – is open to discussion. The place-name is certainly suggestive of a gun emplacement there at some period, and such an installation would have secured the entrance between Long Island and the mainland at Gun Point.

Croagh Harbour is similar to Leamcon in that it too dries out considerably at low tide and is only fully accessible at high water. Here too are the remains of two large quays and stone moorings similar to those at Leamcon. The sites are located below the early eighteenth-century country house of Seafort and its complex of farm buildings.[59] The current house dates to around 1740 and is thought to have been owned by a William Hull in 1814, a relative of Sir William of Leamcon.[60] It is quite possible therefore that an earlier house stood at Seafort that was directly associated with Sir William Hull, his familial and commercial interests. As has been discussed above, Croagh was a harbour known for its careening places and thus strategic to Hull's and the pirates' operations.

ISLANDS AND RIVERS

Derwent Whittlesey in his work on political geography *The Earth and the State* was one of the first to identify the importance of islands and river courses to pirates. Whittlesey suggested that islands were 'springboards' with political significance as they had the qualities to ensure unity of settlement, isolation to guarantee non-government interference, and were tactical locations for control of waterways and for advancing political or piratical power.[61] Many of the islands in Roaringwater Bay were utilised by the pirates at one time or another. Their strategic importance is indicated by their mention in the 1612 Dutch document and inclusion on the 1612 chart. They also provided choke points within the chosen landscape – narrow areas between individual islands or between headlands and islands that could be used as strategic ambush points.[62] Baltimore's two entrances, the entrance to Crookhaven, and many key locations between the islands in Roaringwater Bay would have made excellent choices as choke points from which to await unsuspecting ships.

Of the many islands within Roaringwater Bay, the three largest are Long Island, Sherkin Island and Cape Clear. The most southerly is Cape Clear, though the Fastnet Rock lies beyond Clear, and is marked on the Dutch chart as 'Fastne'. Cape Clear is specifically referred to in the 1612 Dutch document as the 'pirate havens on Cabo Cler', but its designation reflects the general Roaringwater Bay area. Cape Clear island receives relatively little mention in other contemporary sources in relation to its use by the pirates. When it is mentioned it is often as a visual marker, for example when a French ship was captured by pirate John Ellis in 1618 'off Cape Clear'. Again, it is mentioned as an outpost from which to spot returning merchantmen but it is afforded little else in descriptive detail compared to other islands within the Roaringwater Bay area, such as Long Island and Sherkin Island.[63]

Long Island, on the other hand, was used as an island base by the pirates. It provided sheltered anchorage in the sound from the prevailing southwesterly winds, and would have also protected the entrance to Leamcon and Croagh Harbours, both visible from the southwest end of the island. Long Island would have been the focus of legitimate settlement when members of the pirate alliance were eventually pardoned. In 1615 Richard Boyle engaged Denis O'Driscoll to set up the pilchard fishery on Long Island and perhaps it was in such industries, and on such islands, that the pirates found gainful employment, overseen perhaps by a resident native O'Driscoll.[64] Certainly from the representation of Long Island, written as 'Long Iland', on the 1612 Dutch chart, there was a vibrant community there, with substantial structures as well as settlement shown, primarily focused around its north harbour and adjacent to the safe anchorage in the sound. Sherkin Island, like Long Island, provided protection to shipping in Baltimore Harbour from the prevailing southwesterly winds and attendant sea conditions. Sherkin's strategic importance to the pirates and those using the harbour is obvious. As with Long Island, the main settlement on Sherkin was on its northern extent, around the O'Driscoll castle of Dunalong and the Franciscan friary to the south, at what had been the traditional landing place on the island (see Figure 42).

Rivers functioned as avenues of penetration, allowing settlement from the coastal regions into the interior and accommodating a network of trade, transport and communications inland, encouraging settlement and expansion.[65] The Ilen River, which winds its way through the town of Skibbereen and enters Baltimore Harbour from the north of Church Strand Bay, has been used over the centuries by smaller vessels and lighters to ferry people and goods, including a vibrant industry in the transportation of sand in the early part of the twentieth century. No doubt illegal merchandise also formed part of these cargoes at times. Its representation on the early charts and maps of Baltimore denotes its importance as a conduit inland and indicates that mariners were aware of it and its usage potential.[66] Knowledge of fresh water, marine features and resource availability was essential if ships were not to be lost when in the process of doing business.

TO LAND OR NOT TO LAND: REMOTE COASTAL ACCESS POINTS

Accessing the coast in remote areas, whether on the mainland or on islands, required planning, innovation and competence in seamanship. The smaller coves and inlets afforded shelter and seclusion but also the risk of stranding or wrecking; other areas, particularly on islands, could be open to the sea and elements and required more precise knowledge if safety were to be assured. Best described as coastal access points, specific sites were needed to function as nexus sites within a littoral hinterland between land and sea. Excluding landing places with formal slips and quays, these access points include sites carved out of bare rock. Many have been identified along the southern coast of Ireland, though examples are to be found all around the coastline. They present with a variety of forms and features: most are cut out of the natural rock and include rock-carved steps, slipways and ledges where goods could be landed; and rock-carved niches for lanterns or candles and recesses akin to putlog holes to house timbers for possible wooden platforms. Several such sites also have associated sea caves. While sites are found individually, for example an isolated set of rock-cut steps, other sites can retain a number of the identifying features, with rock-cut steps, platforms and slipway all occurring together.[67] Some rock-cut sites are associated with known monuments, particularly castle sites, and therefore their function is observable by association. The steps leading up to Dún na Séad Castle in

Baltimore, for example, would have been the main access point into the castle when occupied by Thomas Crooke and his Gaelic-Irish predecessors.

Other coastal access points are located in remote places, away from any established settlement or formal residence, and constructed in isolated, almost inaccessible areas that, while not perhaps being the only function of the sites, would certainly have accommodated covert activity. The reality is that these sites could facilitate a multitude of uses, including access to fresh water from a well, spring, river or stream outlet, and were thus availed of by all manners of mariner, including pirates, and for manifold reasons. When sailing in warmer climes during the summer, in the Mediterranean, for instance, Mainwaring described some of the places accessed by the men in the pirate alliance and hinted at the function of some of those sites. One such place was 'Lampedusa', an uninhabited island midway between Malta and the coast of Tunis, where the pirates could 'safely water there'. 'Porto Farina' (Porto Feryn) in the Gulf of Tunis also had 'very good watering, and [was] a good place to careen in, being land-locked'.[68] The pirates would have had the same needs and therefore similarly identified places and sites when in Ireland. The importance of such resources is obvious from Captain Martin White's 1817 chart of Crookhaven Harbour, where he depicts 'watering places', where rivers or streams emerge onto the foreshore.[69]

These coastal access sites would therefore have been the focus of repeated usage over time, which could have ranged from the collection or offloading of goods and people in remote parts of the coastal mainland and islands, to piratical and smuggling activity. One small cove that is specifically linked to a pirate is Canty's Cove. Strategically located on the northern side of the Mizen Peninsula, in the townland of Dunkelly West, it faces directly out at Dunmanus Bay. With high rock ledges enclosing the cove on all sides, excluding the northwest where the entrance is located, rock-carved steps, ledges and a slipway can be seen, alongside several related caves. Within the cove, golden sands, tinged aquamarine from copper prevalent within the geology in the wider bay area, give Canty's Cove an almost Mediterranean hue.

Little is known of this haven from a historical perspective, but during the first quarter of the seventeenth century tradition recounts that an individual named Canty, a 'known pirate', whose first name is not recorded, operated from his castle which stood there. Two sets of rock-cut steps were originally located within the harbour. One led to a spring well and was accessible from the slipway; known as the 'Buan Well', the steps were unfortunately destroyed in the 1950s, though the well is still extant. The other set are precipitous,

FIGURE 30: Caves at Canty's Cove, in Dunmanus Bay. The aquamarine waters were the focus of pirate activity in 1629 when Captain Canty had his castle on the headland, where he would lure unsuspecting captains before capturing their ships. IMAGE: CONNIE KELLEHER

leading down to a tiny inlet beside the main harbour, and has the Gaelic name *Cuasanstaighre* or 'Cove of the Stairs', though also referred to locally as 'the pirate steps'.[70] The cove is just over eight miles northwest of Leamcon overland, which would have enabled local residents in the general area of Canty's Cove, including Canty, to have knowledge of or indeed be directly involved with the pirate activity in Leamcon. On what basis this interaction would have been remains unknown. It is interesting to note that in his 1641 deposition, a 'Daniell Canty Landlord of Donkelly gentleman, Owyn Canty of the same, *gentleman*' are mentioned as attacking Hull's demesne.[71] In 1629 Canty, a Gaelic-Irish sub-lord to the O'Mahony lords, was recorded as resident at the cove, where he had his 'house' and 'garden' and exerted dues from those using the sea within his territorial area.[72] His 'house' and 'garden' were located on the promontory overlooking the cove and Dunmanus Bay. These high points in the landscape were ideal as lookouts for coastal defence and exploitation.[73] This information on Canty, like that on his counterpart Michael Cormack in Broadhaven Bay, provides the opportunity to consider the interaction between the resident natives and newcomers, whether the latter were settlers or visitors, looking to trade or plunder. Unlike Cormack in Mayo, however, there is no information on any direct contact between Canty and the pirates of the alliance.

Local lore recounts that Canty was a rather disingenuous individual, and it could be said that he was not really a 'pirate' in the true sense of the word. His reputed tactic was to encourage captains to anchor in his cove, at which point he invited them to his house for food and wine. When sufficiently intoxicated, and on the pretence that he was escorting them back to their ship, he led them out through the back door of his house, which overlooked the cove, and pushed them over the cliff. He then proceeded to plunder their ships moored in his harbour. The story is steeped in myth and no doubt has been embellished over the centuries, but the basal remains of a structure in the place where his house is thought to have stood is compelling, though most of the stone from the building was used to construct the pier at the cove in the 1920s.[74] On the pre-Famine 1840s Ordnance Survey map for the area there is also a building indicated, referred to as 'Canty's House, in ruins'. The cove area itself is, if one were a pirate, ideal for that activity as it is sheltered, secluded, provides depth of water for small boats and has several key vantage points, but it does not in any way lend itself to more extensive operations, as a nest for more than one pirate. The rock-cut steps with associated platforms and sea caves could have been utilised for all manner of activity, not just potential smuggling, and in the early part of the twentieth century, for example, the 'pirate steps' were used to access the little inlet where sand was extracted; a derrick set up overhead assisted with pulling up containers full of sand. Canty's Cove was also a vibrant fishing place, with fish landed and mackerel catches cured on the quay there in the 1920s.[75] Specific dating of these sites remains an issue, as they are known from all periods of antiquity and within a global context, with pirates' dependent on the landing of goods to ensure success. They would therefore have used existing access points within any given landscape; indeed the use of such common sites could have provided the pretence necessary to allow surreptitious activity take place under the guise of legitimate business.[76]

Though Canty's Cove fits well into the geographical and archaeological template, in that it contains several 'markers' that could point to it being a 'pirate place', the presence of these elements at sites does not in itself equate to clandestine operations. Examples exist that show different associations. For example, a set of beautifully carved rock-cut steps and platforms are visible on the western side of Boat Cove in Saint Finian's Bay, in

County Kerry. Traditionally, this site is linked to the monks that lived on the offshore island of Skellig Michael. The World Heritage Site lies some 8.6 nautical miles off the coast and the early medieval monks are said to have used the bay when travelling to and from the island. The coastal routeway led to Ballinskelligs Abbey to the southeast, the site directly associated with the monks on Skellig. Indeed, a whole series of precariously cut steps are to be seen on the island of Skellig Michael, carved and used by the monks to access their monastic site, the sea and other areas that they used as part of their penitential repose and life on the island.[77] It is clear therefore that rock-cut steps could have an everyday, practical use and could be utilised throughout the centuries that followed.

While one cannot be too prescribed when considering their many uses, in relation to the geographic location of some sites one can ponder whether they were deliberately carved to facilitate piracy and smuggling. Mainwaring noted that the local populace in Munster, no doubt both native and settler, assisted the pirates in landing and storing goods in secluded bays. This involved coming to an agreement with the pirate captains as to where goods could be dropped off or collected by the pirates under cover of darkness: that they 'privately with the Captain will appoint where he shall in the night find so many Beeves [beef] or other refreshments that he shall need'.[78] Secluded sites were therefore a necessity for the exchange of goods and were, it would appear, well communicated. Similar tales are told of the Saltee Islands off Wexford, a noted pirate sea base, where they would store their goods while awaiting collection or redistribution.[79]

Certainly the location of some of the sites identified seem to have been chosen to deliberately conceal their use. Dutchman's Cove in Castletownshend is one example (Figures 3 and 31).[80] It is a small inlet located some 7.5 nautical miles east of Baltimore on the western side of Castlehaven Harbour. The name itself is provocative, conjuring up thoughts of the Flying Dutchman and his mysterious pirate ship. Local tradition, however, links it with a Dutch ship lost in the outer harbour in the mid-seventeenth century.[81] What actually exists is a series of rock-cut steps running up the side of the cliff from the water's edge. Fourteen steps run parallel with the shore and ascend north, where they meet a carved flat surface in the rock; a second set of five steps then turn northwest and ascend to another carved flat surface. Here they connect to a defined path leading inshore along the coast. To the west-southwest of the upper flat rock are three steps that allow access to two light niches carved into the sheer rock face overhead. Their purpose

FIGURE 31: Rock-cut steps and platforms and two light niches cut into the rock face at Dutchman's Cove, Castlehaven. The niches accommodated candles or lanterns that were used to guide a ship's boat safely into the little cove, where goods could be landed by night. IMAGE: CONNIE KELLEHER

was most likely to direct light southward across open water, to signal smugglers and pirates and guide ships' boats safely to shore. The site at Dutchman's Cove with its light niches is, to date, unique in Ireland, as no parallels have so far been identified. It seems clear that the location of the site was chosen and its rock-carved features fashioned to ensure anonymity and to fulfil its purpose – to allow the movement of goods and individuals within a remote part of the landscape without being seen or captured.

A more discernible site is located at the very tip of Gokane or Alderman Point on Streek Headland, to the southeast of the small village of Crookhaven (Figures 4 and 32). The site comprises eleven rock-cut steps, though there may have been more in the past that have since eroded or collapsed. Carved precariously out of the sloping rock that adjoins the sheer rock face, the angle of the steps is so acute as to be almost vertical. They overhang a drop to the sea below and are carved just wide enough to allow one person at a time to use them. They do not appear to have descended all the way to water level

FIGURE 32:
The precipitous steps on Streek Head at the eastern edge of Crookhaven village were hewn out of the sheer rock. They lead down to a cavern that runs through the headland and out to the open sea.
IMAGE: CONNIE KELLEHER

but are carved to allow access to a cavern that runs beneath and through the full length of the headland and which is open on both sides to the sea. Local kayakers on calm days travel through the cavern, and this allows a view of the steps overhead. The Streek Head steps are amazing and terrifying at the same time, and prompt a number of questions: Who cut them? Who would have taken on such a dangerous task? How exactly did they function? It is to be supposed that they were used in conjunction with ropes to move goods up and down and no doubt to secure the individual using them. A winch or derrick may have been in place to assist with the lifting of goods, suggesting a collaborative effort, as is traditionally noted at Canty's Cove for the steps there, as discussed above.

The nature, extent and location of the steps gives a sense of purpose to the site, with planning, expedience and co-operation required to ensure maximum and safest utilisation. Prearrangement, communication and knowledge of movement would have been critical to guarantee that individuals, boats and goods were in place at the designated time. The site is located within an archaeological monument, a coastal promontory fort, and therefore could be associated with it, perhaps suggesting a prehistoric or early medieval date for its construction.[82]

Without doubt, however, this site would have been used in later periods for illicit activities. The motivations of those who physically cut these sites out of the natural landscape are impossible to determine. It is likely that they were designed for use by a diversity of stakeholders, not just mariners seeking fresh water or the resident locals to gain access to the sea, but also the pirates and smugglers frequenting the coastal waters in their ships, seeking to land or seeking to raid.

SHIPS FOR PLUNDER

Perhaps the most obvious requirement, and indeed a primary need of a pirate to fulfil their role successfully, was ships and boats: ships to carry out their function as predators on the high seas, and boats to land their goods and ensure an economic return on their pirated 'booty'. With the neglect of the navy by James, compounded by his ineptitude in dealing with corruption among his leading officials, including the lord high admiral, the earl of Nottingham, the pirates in Munster were more than capable of out-manoeuvring the two or three naval vessels sent to patrol the Irish coastline each year.[83] In 1608 such was the depleted state of the king's ships that they were described as 'for the greatest part manned with aged, impotent, vagrant, lewd, and disorderly companions; it is become a ragged regiment … of common rogues'.[84] The deteriorated state of the English fleet was clearly illustrated when captured pirate vessels were utilised to augment the king's squadron. When Vice-Admiral Humphrey Jobson took possession of pirate Captain Richard Robinson's ship in Baltimore in 1608, Lord President Danvers commented that the 120-ton ship, armed with twenty cast guns, would make a fine vessel for service in the navy, to remain upon the coast, to support the king's ship *Tramontane*, which 'is outsailed by every pirate'.[85]

Of the naval vessels sent to patrol the coast of Ireland at that time, the *Lion's Whelp* and the *Tramontane* were the principal ships, under the general command of Sir William St John. Generally only two or three were sent to an area, for example the southwest coast, which was the key reason why the king's ships had no impact on the pirate activity there. Others included the *Moon*, the *Antelope*, the *Rainbow* and the *Phoenix*, the latter two under the command of Sir Thomas Button.[86] Both the *Lion's Whelp* and the *Tramontane* saw long service; *Tramontane* was built in 1586 under the auspices of Elizabeth and the *Lion's Whelp*, of 90 tons burthen, was built in 1590, but was 'rebuilt' in 1608 under orders from the king.[87] This Irish coast fleet comprised several pinnaces, a vessel that could be either small or medium in build, ranging from 100 to 500 tons. The smaller vessels could also have oar power; they were generally single-masted and were often used as tender vessels. The larger pinnaces were mostly fully rigged, akin to a medium-sized man-of-war. These tended to be fast, seaworthy and could carry heavy ordnance.[88] They were thus readily suitable as naval coastal patrol vessels, but also ideal for pirates. Indeed, pinnaces were popular from the earliest times, though their design altered somewhat, with the main body of the O'Driscoll fleet made up of such vessels; fifty-three were recorded as wrecked in Baltimore Harbour in 1538 following an attack by feuding mariners from Waterford, though the number lost is likely inflated.[89]

Logistically, the pirates required vessels that were fast, seaworthy, generously armed and efficiently crewed. While many pirates began their days with small, ill-equipped vessels, they enhanced their power, as reported by Mainwaring, by judiciously targeting slightly bigger ships and thus they slowly 'reinforce[d] themselves' and built up their strength until they had command of their chosen vessel.[90] The ship types favoured by pirates were those around 80–300 tons burthen, though some captains did command larger men-of-war, for their prestige value. Details given on the ships listed as part of Mainwaring's flotilla include general size ratio for the vessels, led by his own 160-ton *Resistance*, and with a mixture of French, Flemish and English-built ships making up his fleet. The preference by the pirates for certain vessel types was stressed by Mainwaring, saying that the pirate ships often consisted of 'Flemish bottoms, if they can get them' and '…in regard that generally they go well, are roomy Ships, floaty [draws little water] and of small charge'.[91]

Pirate captains would have had more than one ship, with subordinate captains commanding additional vessels and their crews. They were thus capable of sailing in packs, with safety in numbers. A second ship type that seems to have been well favoured was the Dutch flyboat or *vlieboot*.[92]

FIGURE 33: Dutch 'Yachts' illustrated on the 1612 Dutch chart; they represent the types of ships used by Dutch Captain Moy Lambert and his crews when they carried out their decimating attack on the pirates in Crookhaven in 1614. SUB GÖTTINGEN, 4 H BRIT P III, 6 RARA, UNIVERSITÄTSBIBLIOTHEK, GÖTTINGEN, GERMANY

The flyboat was originally developed as a cargo carrier, primarily operating over short distances as a North Atlantic trader. It had good depth of hold and was sturdy in the water, and was modified to a more speedy design towards the end of the sixteenth century. It traded across the Atlantic to Newfoundland, Africa and the New World. Around 1595 the Dutch 'fluyt' was designed, which was more roomy and cheaper to build. This ship type grew in popularity, and was favoured by the later Ottoman pirates of North Africa.[93] The Dutch ships depicted on the 1612 chart by John Hunt provide visual evidence for the types of vessels used by them at the time, not just during the attack on Crookhaven two years later, but as ships favoured by them generally. Illustrated are two typical late sixteenth-century or early seventeenth-century Dutch 'yachts' that are essentially smaller and fleeter versions of the larger, ocean-going vessels used by the Dutch East India Company or other joint-stock venture companies in those early years of exploration. The illustrator, possibly John Hunt, has applied details, showing the Dutch ships flying both provincial and local flags.[94] Barques or 'barks' were also favoured, both by the navy and by pirates as they too were speedy and agile crafts and could easily sail into small bays and harbours. Of a barque provided by Ralph Bingley to Sir William St John in Baltimore to assist the *Lion's Whelp* there, Chichester notes that it was 'as fitter to go in and out among those islands than His Majesty's ship'.[95]

Sources provide evidence of the advancement of pirates within the alliance, with Rear-Admiral Thomas Francke given his first command by fellow pirate Captain Robert Stephenson, and taking over the vessel *Fortune* as commander.[96] Others, such as pirates William Hughs and Thomas Hussy, took part shares in an individual ship, in this case the *Black Raven*, a Flemish vessel of 160–200 tons and carrying twenty-eight guns. The pirate Gilbert Roope, during the course of his piratical career, commanded several ships including the *St John Evangelist*, the *Bishop* and the *Katherine*.[97] When Easton and his crew captured the London ship *Concord* in 1611, he made the ship his main vessel: 'being a tall shippe and verie well fitted with ordinaunce and municion'; during the encounter he lost his own ship (the *White Swann*) of 200 tons and twenty-four guns but very quickly replaced it with the *Concord*. Skipwith wrote that Easton, whom he referred to as the general of the fleet, refitted the *Concord* for his own use including altering it 'for better fight and mounted much ordnance more into her'. Easton's captains included William Hughs, William Baugh and William Wollmer, each captaining a vessel of 160 tons and carrying eighteen guns; William Harvey was in a 60-ton vessel with eight guns; Gilbert Roope was also present but the type and size of his ship is not recorded, though it was probably Easton's former command, the *Fortune*, 160 tons and twenty-two guns.[98] It is obvious from the contemporary accounts that Easton's subordinate captains favoured smaller vessels, of 160-ton size or less, each of which carried similar amounts of ordnance. This allowed for the inclusion of small, swift and well-armed vessels within the combined pirate fleets, adding critical support to the primary ships commanded by the leading pirate captains, such as Easton's larger vessel; this strategy enabled the pirates to venture safely into areas like Roaringwater Bay and its multitude of islands and inlets, while the larger ships of those in command could anchor in the bigger bays like Baltimore.

The pirates targeted ships as replacements, as supplementary vessels to add to fleet numbers, or for the guns that were carried on board. Easton, in the same year, attacked the *Hercules* of London in the *Concord*, whereupon he stripped the ship of its guns and ammunition. At this point Easton was in command of seventeen ships in Ireland and noted as 'grown very strong'. Pirate captains were open to changing their vessels frequently and upgrading to larger ones when the opportunity arose or having the use of several sizes of ships when required. Pirate captain William Hughs is again recorded as manning a 250-ton flyboat in 1611, which carried twenty-eight guns comprising demi-culverins, sakers, minions and six fowling pieces.[99] Mainwaring, in discussing the Turkish corsairs of Algiers, wrote that they went about in fleets of some eight or nine ships, with between twenty and thirty pieces of ordnance on each vessel.[100] The large number of pirate-operated vessels plying the waters of the North Atlantic during this period inevitably led to ship losses. Whether through weather events, engagements with other ships, prizes plundered and deliberately sunk or abandoned, vessels became victims of circumstance. Identifying where these losses took place and establishing if newly discovered wrecks are connected to pirate activity is where the real challenge lies.[101]

SHIPS WRECKED AND WRECK SITES

When using the historical sources to enlighten on the types and sizes of ships used, accuracy is obviously a consideration. Mainwaring's *Discourse*, written by a man who was not only a master mariner himself but uniquely placed to know the details of the vessels used by his fellow pirates, being an ex-pirate at that stage, can be trusted in terms of accuracy of information. The details he provided on the construction of the ships, such as where masts were located to allow greater speed and manoeuvrability, is important to any nautical study and could assist with comparative analysis should archaeological evidence be discovered for a potential pirate-associated wreck from this period.[102] Certainly contemporary sources can provide details on size of ships, cargoes carried, crew numbers and encounters at sea; further, they can inform on ship losses, and potential locations for those wrecks.[103] Nine ships with connections to pirates or acts of piracy are recorded as wrecked between 1582 and 1631, with a spatial distribution eastwards along the west Cork coastline from the harbours of Berehaven, Crookhaven and Schull and on to Baltimore, Castlehaven and finally Dunworley Bay.[104]

In 1609 Captain Sammes was part of Richard Bishop's crew when they came into Leamcon. Little information exists on Sammes the individual, and he seems to have had a short piratical career, killed in 1610 during the capture of another flyboat off the Munster coast. His ship is described as 'bulged' at the entrance to 'Berehaven' in 1609, but whether this is the Biscayan ship of 80 tons and twenty men that accompanied Bishop into Leamcon in that year is unclear.[105] The exact location for the wrecking of Samme's ship is also unknown, and the reference to 'Berehaven' unfortunately is too general to pin down exactly where the ship may have been lost within the confines of Castletownbere. More specific locations for other ships lost during alliance-related activity is known. When the Dutch, under Captain Moy Lambert, attacked the pirate base of Crookhaven in 1614 some thirty individuals were killed, both on land and in the harbour. A number of the pirate vessels were destroyed, including Captain Patrick Myagh's 180-ton ship.[106] The admiralty records do not detail if there were any Dutch casualties that would add to the potential archaeological record for other vessels. The ships represented on the cover of the 1612 Gerritszoon leeskaart and on the accompanying chart for the southwest provide a visual representation of what these vessels may have looked like (see Figure 33).[107]

Captain Myagh's ship exploded and was on fire after the Dutch attack, burning to the waterline. Lambert was then able to remove the sails, and all the goods and coin on board; it was only what was on the lower deck or within the hold that was inaccessible. What the Dutch captain did manage to take included: three whole pieces of satin, three whole pieces of silk grosgrain, about one whole piece of velvet, 120 whole pieces of Holland cloth, twenty-four whole pieces of canvas, one chest containing about 300 turbans, two great chests of sugar, one chest of sweetmeats, silver and gold, coined and uncoined, to the value of £3,000. The goods taken were given an overall value of some £5,000.[108]

The diversity of goods that were carried on board the pirate ship is illustrated in the High Court of Admiralty document, but it also gives an indication of what may yet remain on the seabed. This could include the guns, the anchors and their cables, residual material remains of the cargo or what belonged to the pirate crew, along with evidence for the ship itself. Salvage of the wrecked vessels would inevitably have taken place immediately, and over the following years, but cultural material in the form of the actual ship structure or artefactual material may still remain buried beneath the seabed in Crookhaven Harbour. Recent wreck discoveries that may be associated with pirate activity include two from the west Cork area. First, the Dunworley Bay wreck, dating to the first half of the seventeenth century, was discovered in 2004 as a consequence of illegal treasure-hunting activity at the site. The wreck has the potential to link directly to one of possibly two pirate-related events. One connects to pirate Captain John Nutt, who with his brother Robert was active around the southern coast in the 1620s. He reportedly lost his ship, the *Black Mary*, in Dunworley Bay (Nutt and the wreck site are discussed in Chapter 8). The second and more infamous event is that of the 1631 Algerine raid on Baltimore. Prior to the attack, the Turkish fleet was sailing from Kinsale to Baltimore when one of its ships is reported to have been lost in or near Dunworley Bay. Dating evidence from the guns recovered from the site places it within the correct time period. The site may therefore provide the archaeological link through time to one of these pirate events.[109]

FIGURE 34: Painting by artist Johannes (Jan) Abrahamsz Beerstraten (1622–66) showing a Dutch flagship, in broadside, and a fluyt running into a Mediterranean harbour, *c.* 1660. Also depicted is a Mediterranean galley leaving the harbour between the two Dutch ships. BHC0811; CAIRD COLLECTION, NATIONAL MARITIME MUSEUM, GREENWICH, LONDON

The second wreck discovered in Cork is that generically referred to as the Coconut wreck, named after the archaeological evidence from the site. Discovered in 2012 during the archaeological monitoring of dredging works for an outfall pipeline, the site is located across the sound from Long Island, west of Schull Harbour and east of Leamcon. The remains are in a very good state of preservation; lying in about 10 metres of water at high tide, most of the hull, from the lower deck down, is intact. From the underwater archaeological investigations so far undertaken by the director of the project, Julianna O'Donoghue of Mizen Archaeology, the hull timbers appear to be exotic wood, possibly suggesting the ship was built in one of the New World colonies; artefactual material recovered includes barrel remains, quern stones, Iberian pottery (Majolica ware, Merida ware and Seville olive jars) and seven coconuts. Collectively, the finds, once again, point to either transatlantic trade or goods plundered from a merchant ship that traded to those places. Several wooden crates are visible stored together within the hold of the wreck, and this cargo awaits further detailed investigation in due course.[110]

An early seventeenth-century date has been indicated based on the artefactual assemblage – a Type B olive jar, for example, similar to one found in Fermeuse Harbour in Newfoundland or indeed from the wreck of the *Santa Ana Maria* lost in 1628 in Castlehaven Harbour, and discussed above.[111] The dating period corresponds to just one recorded wreck for the Leamcon/Schull area.[112] In 1615 Claes Compaen lost one of his pirated ships after he offloaded its goods at Leamcon, including providing booty to William Hull. The contemporary report records that 'Campane's prize had sunk in the harbour of Lymecon in three or four fathoms'.[113] The depth would certainly correspond with that of the Coconut wreck, as would the date for the remains as currently known. The Coconut wreck may, however, be the remains of another ship from that period, lost without record, and demonstrates how caution must be applied when analysing wrecks like this, to avoid falling prey to wishful thinking.

How sites like wrecks or rock-cut steps came to be located where they are, who manned or built them, and what their primary use was, are all questions that need to be considered when looking for patterns in the archaeological remains and evidence for pirates within a given landscape. It is clear that the geography and topography of a certain environment was important to pirates, and they certainly identified particular types of landscape that suited their purpose. Rugged remote coastlines; secluded harbours and bays; islands that served as staging posts and provided choke points, close to a trading route; and willing coastal populations to facilitate their operations were all key attributes that drew pirates to a particular place. These coastal characteristics were critical for the pirates of the alliance, and the study of certain identified sites may provide traces of the places where they operated.

A landscape that was favourable provided viable commercial opportunities, and the pirates recognised the Munster coastline as encompassing the necessary attributes. Opportunistic plundering by individual pirates was to change into a tactical predatory business, the impact of which could be significant and rewards from which could be substantial.

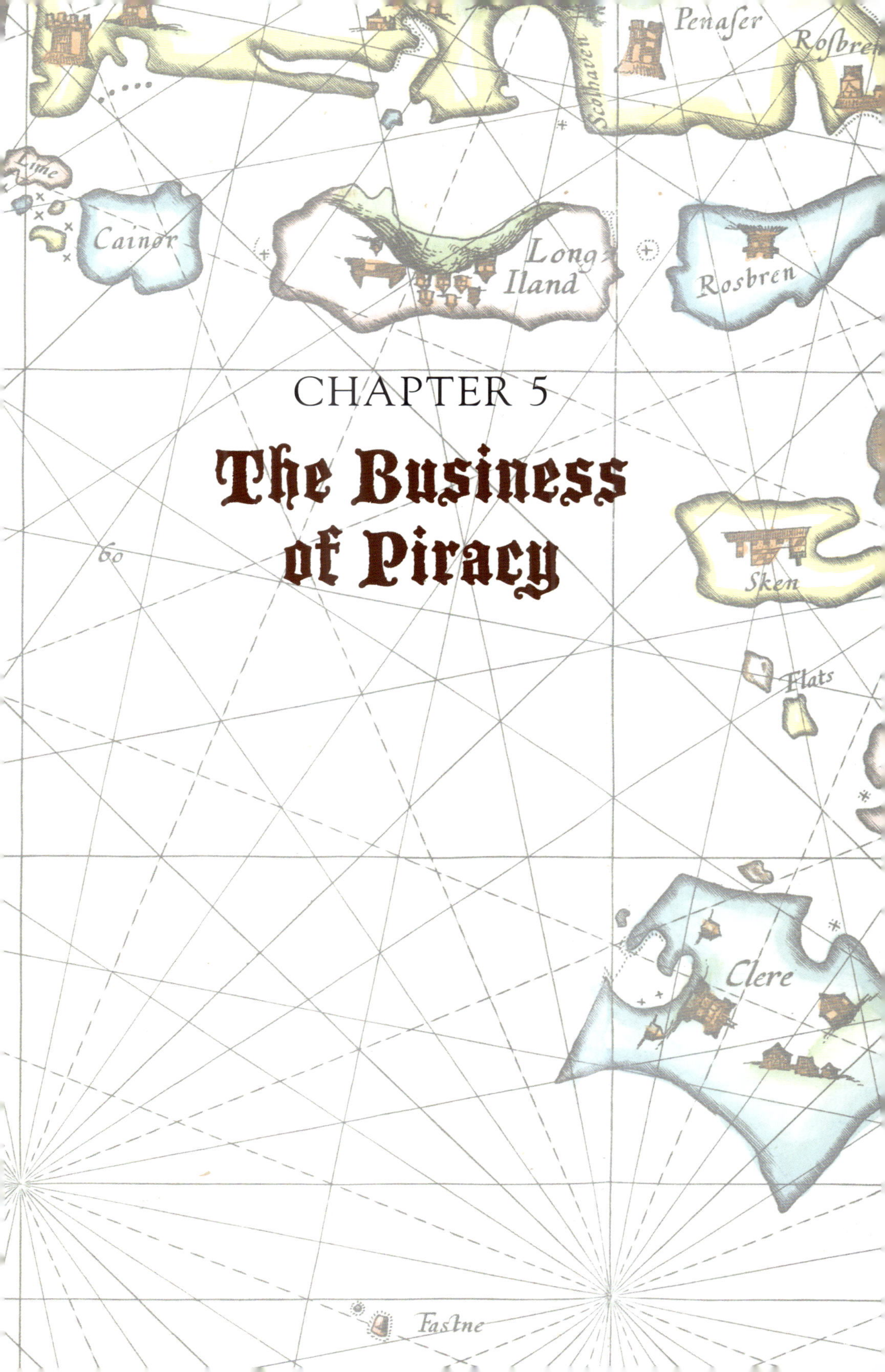

CHAPTER 5

The Business of Piracy

... that which altogether passeth here [in Munster] – is rialls of 8, Barbary ducketts & dollars, and yt is thought som treasure [be] here buried on land by some of the Pirates.[1]

The level of wealth that can be attributed to any given member of the pirate alliance is difficult to assess. Little is known of the actuality of personal ill-gotten gain, for obvious reasons. Instead, contemporary sources can contain details of the value of cargoes or individual items of specie, including at times the calculated worth of ships used or taken as prizes by the pirates. The indictments of the High Court of Admiralty are among the most valuable sources for the potential worth of both individual and collective predation across the broad spectrum of piracies carried out in the first half of the seventeenth century. Listed are the names of pirates, locations of action, and details of ships targeted, goods taken and purported value placed on plunder. As Clive Senior points out, however, the value figures provided are frequently conservative because the indictment might only mention goods relating to one merchant and ignore those of another taken out of the same ship. Adding to the information supplied in the indictments, Senior's study of them lists which of the plundered ships were retained by the pirates and which were left behind, either for recovery by the merchants/owners or to the fate of the elements.[2] By perusing the indictments one can, by degree, begin to gauge the nature, extent and cost of piracy and, by extension, the wealth that was accrued from the activity for that period.

The impact of the pirates' actions on trade similarly informs on economic disruption in terms of value, and in turn, reward to the pirates. Of the many piracies carried out between 1603 and 1640 as indicated in the indictments, the most valuable and thus most impacting have been attributed to pirate captains John Ward, Richard Robinson, John Muckill, Thomas Tomkins and William Baugh. John Ward was among the most prolific in his predations, and in one of the most lucrative prizes recorded at the time, in 1607 he took the Venetian *Reniera de Soderina* to the value of £100,000. This would be equivalent to about £13.4 million sterling or nearly €15 million in modern value. Ward kept the *Soderina*, as it is frequently referred to in the sources, as his own flagship. Thomas Tomkins plundered the *Black Balbiana* off Cyprus in 1603 to the stated value of £30,000. John Muckill in 1605 in his ship

Catherine took the *Jonas* of Emden near the seaport town of Cowes on the Isle of Wight, worth £10,000. Richard Robinson, one of the leading alliance captains, in the same year, and indeed at the same time, took two ships, the *St Anne* and the *Janet* of Roscoff, off the Isles of Bayonne. Both ships carried cargoes of wine, raisins and Spanish coin and were given an estimated collective value of £10,510. Captain William Baugh, who is discussed in detail below, in 1612 took the *Bull* of Dieppe off Cape Clear with a proclaimed value of some £20,000. Other pirate captains, by their actions collectively over time, were to have an equal if not more devastating impact on trade and political relations overall, but singular events, like the capture of the 600-ton argosy *Soderina* by Ward, could strike to the core of merchant shipping. With its valuable cargo of cotton, indigo, silks and cinnamon, the incident caused turmoil across the Mediterranean. The Venetians valued their loss as high as 500,000 crowns, while other contemporary accounts estimated the cargo was '... worth two millions at least'.[3]

The recorded wealth of some officials, including the nobility then resident in Ireland, can assist in understanding the 'actual worth' of what was accumulated through commercial ventures, albeit with returns on ownership of lands often included in wealth accrued by the nobility. Nevertheless, the yields on legitimate business can comparatively inform on the potential worth of the leading pirates. William Hull's deposition of 1641 totals his losses, following the attack on his demesne and wider estate, as £8,927. Of that, £7,679 covered loss of goods and 'chattel', with £1,248 from rent of his land and rent of his leases and mortgages.[4] The majority of his claims are related to his legitimate business dealings and are no doubt inflated in places, but the value given nevertheless is substantial for that time. Other estate records and depositions can be likewise considered. Richard Boyle's annual wealth by 1641 was calculated to be between £18,000 and £20,000 from business interests and rental income, with his overall wealth, to include personal and commercial income, from all his estates, estimated at £300,000. The earl of Thomond's annual income before the Irish Rebellion period was £7,000, while the average income for most of the lesser noble families at the time was between £2,000 and £3,000.[5] What is unclear in these figures is the level of income generated from trade in commodities, and particularly clandestine goods, that would have supplemented legitimate wealth.

There are only a handful of pirates from the time whose income is suggested or stated. The Venetian state papers contain numerous entries on Captain Peter Easton, particularly after his move to Villafranca, then in Italy.

Along with acquiring the title of marquis in return for his expertise as a master gunner and service as a commander, in March 1613 the Venetian ambassador, Vincenzo Gussoni, reported that 'The English Corsair' (Easton) had bought a palace there and was living in it. Easton had secured warehouses for his goods, and so full of jewels and coin were they that Gussoni believed they had a value upward of £2 million in gold. The report concluded that Easton, having amassed such riches, may have wished to give up his pirating ways and settle in Villafranca.[6] At this point, Easton certainly was the leading pirate of his time and his success is reflected in his amassed fortune. As discussed further below, other leading pirate captains such as William Baugh, for example, could have had significant means at times, only to lose them just as quickly when corruption from within his own ranks and between rival officials entered the ring. For some of the leading nobles, such as Sir Richard Boyle, the figures given were most probably conservative. The fact that pirates like Easton, Baugh and others could be on an equal financial footing with, or indeed surpass in prosperity, many of the ruling élite or nobility of the time would have bestowed a certain degree of power, standing and autonomy. The impact on Atlantic trade was more palpable, however, and the increasing cost of this over time was where the real issues lay. It is easy to see why the business of piracy was so critical to the success of those in the alliance and their accomplices, and why it was of such concern to officials and merchants in London.

PIRATE TREASURE: COMMODITIES AND COMPLEXITIES

It can be gauged from the cargo brought back to Ireland in 1612 by pirate Captain William Baugh, then rear-admiral to Peter Easton, just how diverse and valuable plundered booty could be. The case highlights perfectly the potential riches that could be made through piracy and smuggling, but also the inherent issue of corrupt officials, along with corrupt colleagues. John Appleby has published the account in detail, reflecting that 'the Baugh case ... illustrates in dramatic form just how complex this problem [with corrupt officials] could be, involving the often rival interests of the administrations in London and Dublin, as well as those of local officials in Kinsale'.[7] The degree to which the affair was documented at the time indicates how significant it was and how seriously it was regarded by central government in London.

Over the course of several months, from April 1612, when on his way back to Ireland from Mamora, Baugh and his fleet of three ships carried

FIGURE 35: James Fort, formerly Castlepark, in Kinsale, and the covered way that leads down to the blockhouse and water's edge. Vice-Admiral Henry Skipwith was stationed here in the early seventeenth century and was notorious in his dealings with the pirates.
© CON BROGAN, NATIONAL MONUMENTS SERVICE

out one of the most successful marauding operations of the North Atlantic Alliance of Pirates. A number of ships were plundered of their goods and others captured as prizes; these were first brought into Leamcon and then onto Kinsale, where remaining goods were to be placed in Castlepark under the orders of Vice-Admiral Henry Skipwith. Baugh was seeking a pardon at this stage and was looking to agree terms. Skipwith was acting as negotiator on the matter with the lord deputy, Chichester, who had agreed protection for Baugh in Kinsale, if he were to accede to a pardon. As a part of the terms, Baugh wished to retain some or all of the booty he had captured, on agreement that he and his crew would give up their pirating ways.

The ships plundered included two Dutch vessels, taken off the coast of Spain, one that carried five bags of pepper, forty-eight bags of silver and gold coin, a hogshead of purston ware (stored for transport) and other goods. Out of the other Dutch ship, also taken by Baugh off Spain, were plundered '41 plates of copper, 3 or 4 packs of bedtikes, a pack or two of diapers and various other goods'. These too were placed in Castlepark.[8] A third Dutch ship from Amsterdam, returning from the West Indies, was taken off Ireland in May and Baugh took out of it a 'chest of branched damask [branched design], two pieces of redd velvette, a piece of sattin, seven paire of silke stockings, and some other goods'. These too were placed in Kinsale. Baugh had also, within the previous twelve months, removed from a Flemish ship plundered off the coast of Spain '21lb of gold and silver twiste', and had brought the ship into Kinsale.[9]

The '*Grayhounde*' [*Greyhound*] returning from La Rochelle was also captured in May off Ireland carrying linen, silks, canvas and other goods. Out of Baugh's own ship the *Archangel*, and scheduled to be placed in Castlepark, were the following listed goods:

> 28 bolts of Holland [cloth]
> vi pieces of Stayes
> certain silver & gold wire
> certain satin
> velvette & damaske in bolts
> 170 bolts of silk garters[10]

Other goods recorded as plundered during Baugh's pirating spree included sugar, Brazil wood, cotton wool and precious stones out of the *Bull* of Dieppe. Another French ship laden with 'forty nine chests of sugars, some wood and other goods' was also relieved of its merchandise. Baugh had also placed on board his own ship and that of his rear-admiral, the *Lion*, some thirty or more pieces of ordnance, taken out of one of the Dutch ships, the *Nightingale*, and out of the Flemish ship. Some of the goods were initially landed at Leamcon, including coin to the amount of £3,361 that Baugh shared out among his crew. As vice-admiral under Easton and captain of his own fleet, Baugh received a third, plus fifty pounds to cover his agreed shares. From previous monies shared out from the plundering expedition, the examination of John Huskins, one of the pirate crew, reports that the captain had the following:

> … between three and four thousand pounds ready money as well as [silver] plate, broken silver, ringes, jewels, two chains of golde, a peacock made of pearls pinning the wings and the legge wire was of gold.

Huskins concluded that where Baugh 'conveyed his said wealth he knoweth not'. The pirate captain was eager to share gifts with locals and others too. In a boat at night, he sent ashore two chests of sugar and a bag of pepper; another boat with one or two chests and canvas followed, also under the cover of darkness. Baugh seems to have instructed his crew to bring members of the local community onboard the *Lion*, where they were given gifts, including Holland cloth, taffeta, garters and ribbons. The boatswain, again on the instruction of Baugh, brought goods ashore, similarly comprising ribbons and garters, and gave them as gifts to the garrison there: 'horsmen, footmen, trumpetors, mustians [musicians] & many others of his knowledge'. In an attempt to curb the activity of pirates in Leamcon in 1611, the Council of Munster had placed a garrison of soldiers in the castle [Leamcon/Black Castle on Castle Point], under Captain Povey, accompanied by the royal ship the *Lion's Whelp*, at anchor in Leamcon Harbour. Baugh, however, sent a chest of sugar to the ship, where, by all accounts, it was not rejected.[11] The pirate captain seems to have agreed, rather quickly, trading terms with Povey and his men, and later again, when in Kinsale, Baugh provided similar merchandise to the king's men stationed in the fort there, including ribbons as a wedding gift for one of the trumpeters.[12] Baugh clearly stated that the gifts sent ashore 'should all come out of his own shares'.[13] Certainly, issues arose with shares among the crews of Baugh's ships, as Richard Millington, who was Baugh's vice-admiral and served with him for over four years, had recently sought recompense from Baugh as part of his pardon negotiations. Several of Baugh's crew members subsequently sought legal redress for loss of what they argued was their rightful shares, accusing Baugh's trusted shipmate John Horse of taking goods to Captain Skipwith's house on behalf of Baugh.[14]

Baugh, as we have seen above, received advise from Skipwith to sail to Castlepark in Kinsale, where he would receive protection, though it was with the proviso that he deposit money and goods with Richard Bishop in Leamcon, to serve as retainers for the lord deputy's protection and to guarantee his pardon. Apart from the '900 pieces of eight' to be left there, other booty included a chest of sugar and a bag of pepper also taken to 'Richard Busshopp's house', and William Hull received two chests of sugar. While official protection was being offered, it appears that a vibrant protection racket was part and parcel of the negotiations for pardons between pirates and government agents. When in Kinsale, Baugh delivered goods to Skipwith's 'house' including 'two pieces of red velvett, one piece of tufted satin, six boults of branched damask, four barrels of powder, a French bedstead, about 60 bundles of silver and gold twist, some plate, and a great kettle or two'.

There were suggestions at the time that Baugh wished to marry Skipwith's daughter and he plied Mrs Skipwith with gifts to win her blessing. This included 'a silver basin and ewer of silver, a piece of branched damask to make her son Edward a coat, a piece of holland [cloth] and a pack of lynen [linen]'. During the course of events, one of the barrels of powder that had been deposited with Skipwith 'was put on fire' and exploded, causing severe damage to Skipwith's house, but whether this was deliberate or not is unclear.[15] This may refer to where Skipwith was stationed in Castlepark fort but may also be his other residence at Carriganassig Castle, in Innishannon, as one deposition mentions goods 'taken up river to captain Skipwith's house'.[16]

Baugh, at that point, had negotiated the terms of his pardon with Roger Middleton in Mamora but, when he surrendered himself in Leamcon, Skipwith informed him that the terms of the pardon had actually expired and that he needed to remain under his [Skipwith's] protection pending the negotiation of a new pardon.[17] Though William Baugh was eventually granted his pardon, he did not receive a share of his goods, a key element of the negotiations which had been agreed with Chichester.[18] Sir William St John in the king's pinnace the *Speedwell* arrived into Kinsale, and though he was meant to wait there on the instructions of the lord deputy, he had been given a counter order by the English Privy Council to arrest Baugh and take command of his ship and goods. This he did but proceeded to help himself to the pirate's plunder. The lord president of Munster, Sir Henry Danvers, and his vice-president, Sir Richard Millington (distinct from Baugh's cohort of the same name), are said to have similarly sequestered goods out of the fort in Kinsale.[19] To add further confusion, instead of arresting the pirates as instructed, Sir William St John, accompanied by Baugh, went to see Lord Deputy Chichester. This act set in train a series of disputes between Baugh and his men, who viewed with suspicion the captain's actions. Chichester too was concerned about perceptions and attempted to distance himself from dealing directly with the pirate. The crew's understanding was that, once their pardons came through, they would be allowed to retrieve their goods and monies, which had been placed in the fort in Kinsale.

The whole affair escalated into a confused conflict between the pirates, local admiralty officers and governing officials, with Baugh subjected to blackmail by William St John and most of the pirates' goods dispersed in the meantime. The lord deputy was incensed by the whole affair.[20] It was agreed at the meeting with Chichester that Baugh's crew would receive the agreed share of their booty on the understanding that they first return home to England. Most of the men refused and waited in Kinsale for the arrival of their pardons. Frustrations mounted as the pardons were delayed, as did suspicions that their goods were being continually pilfered by not alone St John and his men but by Baugh himself. This had some substance. On one occasion, the pirate captain went on board the *Lion*, which was under arrest in Kinsale, with one of Skipwith's sons, and they proceeded to fill their 'breeches with pieces of silks, garters and ribbons & carried them ashore'.[21] Baugh later argued that he did it to incriminate William St John, but fears and doubts among his crew at that stage continued to alienate him from his men. Baugh blamed the lord deputy for the debacle. Chichester sought permission from the Privy Council to determine the affair and return the pirates their goods as per the terms of their pardons, which had yet to arrive. He feared that more would return to piracy if he did not uphold the agreement or honour the protection that he had provided for the pirates. When the pardons arrived, they were devoid of the promise to return the goods, a critical change by which Chichester was completely compromised.

By mid-1613 most of the remaining goods in Castlepark had been returned to their original owners, with little or no recompense for the pirates. Those who remained in Kinsale, including Baugh, were by then in dire straits and several of his men returned to piracy. Baugh may have eventually received some cursory payments as suggested in an order of 4 November 1613 referring to a sum of £2,310 16s. 8d. paid to him. It is not, however, entered as a payment out of revenue until 1 July 1615.[22] Baugh settled in Innishannon, up-river from Kinsale, following acceptance of his pardon in 1613, referring to himself as a 'gentleman of Inishoon' (Inishannon) in his examination of that year.[23] Whether Baugh built a house, and thus became owner of a property, albeit perhaps as a tenant, or if he were 'accommodated' by Skipwith in Carriganassig Castle on the banks of the Bandon river, is not stated in the sources. In 1619 he is recorded as destitute and 'discontent' in a debtors' jail, possibly in the marshalsea in Bandon, where he eventually died.[24] The Baugh affair certainly offers a frame of reference for the amount of goods and their value that could be found on the pirate ships or on those ships taken as prizes. It also provides first-hand information on the types of goods available for plunder on the richly laden merchant ships crossing the Atlantic and why the illicit trade in these commodities was so important to local communities. What is certain is the impact of the affair, with its complexities, level of corruption and resultant fallout among the pirates themselves, it understandably deterred others from taking their pardons, particularly Vice-Admiral Peter Easton and his men, preferring instead to make their own decisions on how they were to determine their lives.[25]

GOODS AS PLUNDER

By 1609 Captain John Jennings was seeking a pardon. It seemed he had tired of pirating and looked to the earls of Clanricard or Thomond to act as intermediaries on his behalf. The previous year he had voiced his distrust of the government's pardon initiative, stating that he and his fellow pirates 'might be hanged with their pardons about their necks'. He obviously had a change of heart and subsequently submitted his ship and its booty to Thomond.[26] Offloaded at Limerick from Jennings' 300-ton vessel were 150 chests of sugar, thirty-six cases of cinnamon ('some double, some single') and twelve packs of pepper. In his own keeping (personal goods) were small diamonds and pearls, and in his chest was 140 pounds worth of Spanish silver (presumably referring to 'reales' or pieces of eight), while other packs full of pearls and money, but not diamonds, were also noted. His clothing, part embroidered with Barbary gold, was valued between £400 and £500, and 'he had on him' £40 worth of doubloons and 'dymondes and a number of rubyes'. The examination recounts other, miscellaneous booty taken by Thomond as amounting to some £2,000.[27] When they surrendered with Jennings, goods belonging to Captain Gilbert Roope and his lieutenant, Arthur Drake – 'his lieutenant being a blacke man dwelling in Plimouth' – were also found to contain precious jewels and coin.[28] Some of Jennings' goods had been taken to Thomond's house while more had been sent to Leamcon in the custody of brothers Humphrey and Richard Jobson.[29]

The precious jewels and coin may appear to be the most valuable commodities on board, in today's terms, but at the time, of equal if not of more value would have been the spices – in particular, pepper. It became one of the oriental condiments, along with cinnamon, cloves, nutmeg and ginger, which were central to the international race for mercantile domination from the close of the sixteenth century onwards.[30] The establishment of the Honourable East India Company by the English in 1600 and the Dutch East India Company or VOC in 1602 began a rivalry between the two nations for supremacy of these emerging global markets that was to have a profound commercial and colonial impact at home and abroad.[31] Sugar too was highly prized. Carried within the holds of the pirate vessels, it may well have been the product of plunder, but equally may have been 'legitimately' traded by the pirates when in North Africa in exchange for European goods. As defined by Kenneth Andrews, the trade in such exotic goods fuelled 'the growth in luxury consumption. The luxury trade boomed, feeding the appetites of the rich with silks, satins, linens and other fine cloths, wines, sugars and spices, gold and silver ware, jewellery, perfumes and medicament.'[32]

A slightly later but nevertheless relevant example that illustrates the diversity of goods brought into Leamcon in 1625, including the subsequent dispersal of cargo, is that of Dutch pirate Captain Claes Compaen, mentioned briefly in the previous chapter.[33] Not unlike the events that overtook Baugh, Compaen's dealings at Leamcon similarly involved claims of theft and embezzlement. The list of goods on board his ship and offloaded at Leamcon was substantial in size and diversity. It included: '864 hydes, 5,820 weight of iron, 30 dozen earthen dishes, 30 dozen hangers and girdles, 2 pieces of golden [gilted] leather, 3 pieces of Holland [cloth], 16 pieces of cloth for sails, 14 pieces of silk, including 12 pairs of silk stockings, 300 weight of tobacco, 1 barrel of tobacco, 2 kettles, 11 hats, 8 pistols, 7 pieces of ordnance, 6 pieces of murderers [cannon], 10 barrels of powder'. During the course of discharging the goods, Compaen claimed that some had been embezzled, and he sought restitution from William Hull. Of the items 'stolen' were fifty pairs of hangers, three pieces of 'silk stuff' and two pairs of silk stockings, one barrel of tobacco, six barrels of iron and six dozen earthenware dishes.[34]

An accompanying document containing the names and details of individuals who 'legitimately' bought goods from Compaen on the quayside is even more informative. Titled 'The Names of those who Bought Goods of the Pirate Campane at Lymecon, in the West of Ireland',[35] it provides firsthand evidence for the intricate network of individuals involved in acquiring, transporting and moving goods, including 'carriers' who trafficked their own and others' merchandise. William Palmer of 'Clanghannakelty' (Clonakilty), for instance, is named as a carrier, who bought 'many things of the Campane, and carried many men's goods'. A James Stanley is listed as a 'searcher' whose job it may have been to identify the locations where pirated goods were landed, either to assist those looking to trade or in an official capacity to gain intelligence on this underground operation and those involved. From the list and locations given, the distribution network stretched from Kenmare in County Kerry, to Cork, Waterford, Plymouth and London.

The document also states that 'men of power thereof made admissions', and refers to men like Lieutenant Jacques of Cork, who acknowledged that he had pilfered goods from the pirate, including 16 pounds of 'massy' gold.[36] 'A 'Mr Gregory Symson, at Snail in the Cheapside' is included as a witness to the signing of a partnership deal between a Mr Harman and Justice Brady of Cork, where Harman bought €200 of goods from Compaen, including pepper and wax.[37] The identification of these individuals perhaps provides the clearest indication of how the trade in pirate goods had infiltrated all echelons of commercial, administrative, military and naval offices and how the concept of 'crime' was distorted when in the business of purloined goods. Among the usual suspects named are William Hull (who had been knighted at that point), his brother Henry in Clonakilty, along with a Joshua Boyle of Waterford, and Sir Lawrence Parsons. Joshua Boyle was, quite probably, a relation of Richard Boyle and may have been the same individual who was elected Member of Parliament for Mallow, in County Cork, in 1641 and later became MP for Ardee in County Louth. He bought 'one chest of camphor, 500 weight at least, 14 rolls of tobacco, 1,000 weight of pepper, 212 lbs. of cloves, 3 elephant's teeth [tusks], 5 doz. Red Muscovy hides'.[38] These were all men of established or official positions but who were directly involved in a grey market fuelled by pirated luxury goods. Another gentleman named Henry Turner of Bandon is traceable within contemporary sources; on 16 July 1625 he was under suspicion of trading in pirated goods and admitted to buying sugar from Joseph Carter, a merchant in Baltimore, but clarified that he did not know where Carter got the goods.[39] Lawrence Parsons and William Hull were subsequently called to explain what had become of the cargo from Compaen's ship: 'to enquire what became of all the great quantity of goods pepper cloves sugar & c that was landed … out of Campane's shipp? What quantity was sent to France, … what was sent to the L. Deputy, what to Lawrence P's men and what was with Captain Hull … ?'[40]

The link with Snail in Cheapside is revealing as it was the main street for goldsmiths and jewellers at the time, near Fleet Street and the financial quarter of modern day London; a list of jewellers for the period working in Cheapside includes several Symsons, Simons and Simmons.[41] It is worth considering that there may well have been a system in place for moving bullion and precious jewels, with a 'fence' or middleman collecting the 'product' at an agreed time and place. This would certainly help in understanding how goods seemed to disappear when landed, and would also clarify why it was so critical to have a trusted intelligence network that informed on when the

FIGURE 36: The Cheapside Hoard discovered in 1912 in London is the greatest single collection of Elizabethan and Stuart jewellery in the world. Comprising over 500 gemstones and jewels from across the globe, it is theorised that some or all of it could be part of pirate booty. © IMAGE ID: 379194, THE MUSEUM OF LONDON COLLECTION

goods were arriving, where they were to be landed, what the cargo comprised and who should be in place when the ships docked.

The range and scope of actions surrounding the arrival of just one cargo that came into Long Island near Leamcon in 1625, its subsequent dispersal and the information on those involved with wider commercial links, is striking. It is interesting to note that Compaen had been given protection by

Parsons, on the understanding that the pirate agree to submit. Vested interests also influenced such protection, and the security levied on the pirate was confirmed in a letter from the lord deputy, Henry Cary, Viscount Falkland, to Sir William Hull, in February 1625. Discussing the submission of Claes Compaen, Falkland suggests that Compaen make a petition for a pardon but to include details of his wealth: 'where his wealth lies, and [if not in Ireland] that he will make a voyage to sea to fetch it'.[42] The pirates by all accounts had safe harbours and safe places where they kept their personal wealth. Peter Easton was provided with warehouses for the storage of his goods in Villafranca, and, no doubt, William Hull in Leamcon and Henry Skipwith in Kinsale did the same.[43] The individual pirate captains would have had their own 'secret places', however, where they would store their goods and sources suggest, reinforcing the stereotypical view of pirates, that booty could be simply buried. Writing to the earl of Salisbury in August 1611, 'In the harbor at Longe Ilande nere Limcolme', Roger Middleton wrote:

> … that which altogether passeth here – is rialls of 8, Barbary ducketts & dollars, and yt is thought som treasure [be] here buried on land by some of the Pirates.[44]

Middleton's report also states that many of the pirates 'have wives and children in this place about Limcolme'. It immediately conjures up images of chests full of gold, silver and precious jewels, though the use of the term 'treasure' at the time could refer to all moneys, both legitimate and otherwise.[45] What is remarkable about it is the picture it paints of what appears to have been more or less a cosmopolitan existence at Leamcon, where international currencies were in circulation, passed around by multinational crews on board the pirate ships, but at the same time within a familial landscape in a remote region of Munster.

THE ADMINISTRATION OF PIRATE BOOTY

While the pirates had their own administrative system for the distribution of booty among themselves, an arrangement of compensation and compositions was attempted between the admiralty and the leading captains of the alliance, by which they could keep all or a portion of their plundered cargo if they agreed to submit to a pardon.[46] It was alluded to in the list of names discussed above, when such an agreement was reached with Claes Compaen, and where Mr Symson from Cheapside 'was at the composition making'.[47] It was meant as an enticement to pirates to submit but, as with Baugh and Easton, was not always successful. At times too local officials could be at variance with their responsibilities relating to compositions. Humphrey Jobson was in disagreement with Thomas Crooke as to who was entitled to take into care pirate booty. Crooke, who liaised with fellow speculator Ralph Bingley in the distribution of plundered goods, was determined to prevent others, including Jobson, from trading with the pirates.[48] It therefore seems that local officials could be in competition with each other when vying for control of this lucrative black market trade. The ease by which pirates like Richard Bishop or John Jennings could land their goods, and the acquisition of such commodities by the local Irish and settlers alike, goods to which they would normally have no ready access, symbiotically supported this thriving market. Government agents 'officially' intercepted such goods for the crown, but equally dispersed select, but yet substantial, amounts for themselves.

The transporting of some of Jennings' goods, by Humphrey Jobson, to Leamcon from Limerick, where Jobson was stationed, speaks volumes about the overt nature by which such booty was distributed among those involved. It is equally obvious from examinations that payment in kind using products such as pepper was as acceptable as using coin of silver or gold – if not more so. It was noted by Chichester that the local populace benefited from the 'exchange of victuals for commodities, or ready money'.[49] Mainwaring also described how members of local coastal communities in Munster arranged privately with the pirate captains suitable locations for the exchange of goods. This was done at night and such victuals often included beef, hides, butter and 'other refreshments'. In turn, the pirates dropped off money and goods worth, as was expected, two or three times the value of what was being supplied to them.[50] Willing locals, as remarked by Chichester, 'receive payment to the double valewe, and by that meanes thinke to be freed from the penalty of divers proclamacions forbidding commerce with them …'.[51]

Knowledge of places ancillary to the main harbours where goods could be easily handled and exchanged was vital to the pirates' operation, and it is in this context that sites such as Canty's Cove, Sleek Head steps or Dutchman's Cove, discussed in the previous chapter, are best understood – purposefully located and familiar to locals and pirates, allowing business to continue as usual.

FIGURE 37: View of Calicut on the coast of Malabar, southwest India, in 1572 taken from Georg Braun and Franz Hogenberg's atlas *Civitates orbis terrarium*. The scene shows several types of craft in the bay along with fishing activity, and expanding colonial settlement in background. Places like Calicut became major centres in the spice trade from the sixteenth century onwards. WIKICOMMONS

THE 'HOLY TRINITY', OTHER CONDIMENTS AND COMMODITIES

Of the commodities traded at the time, spices were among the most highly prized. Through the ages, spices have always held a value, with the Chinese, Arabs and Indian Sultan rulers closely guarding the locations of where they were grown. They shrouded them in mystery, and tales of deified dangers for anyone intent on seeking them out, to ensure their own trade, sustained.[52] Certainly, bullion formed part of any specie, but condiments, as the lists of goods carried in the holds of plundered ships show, were among the most

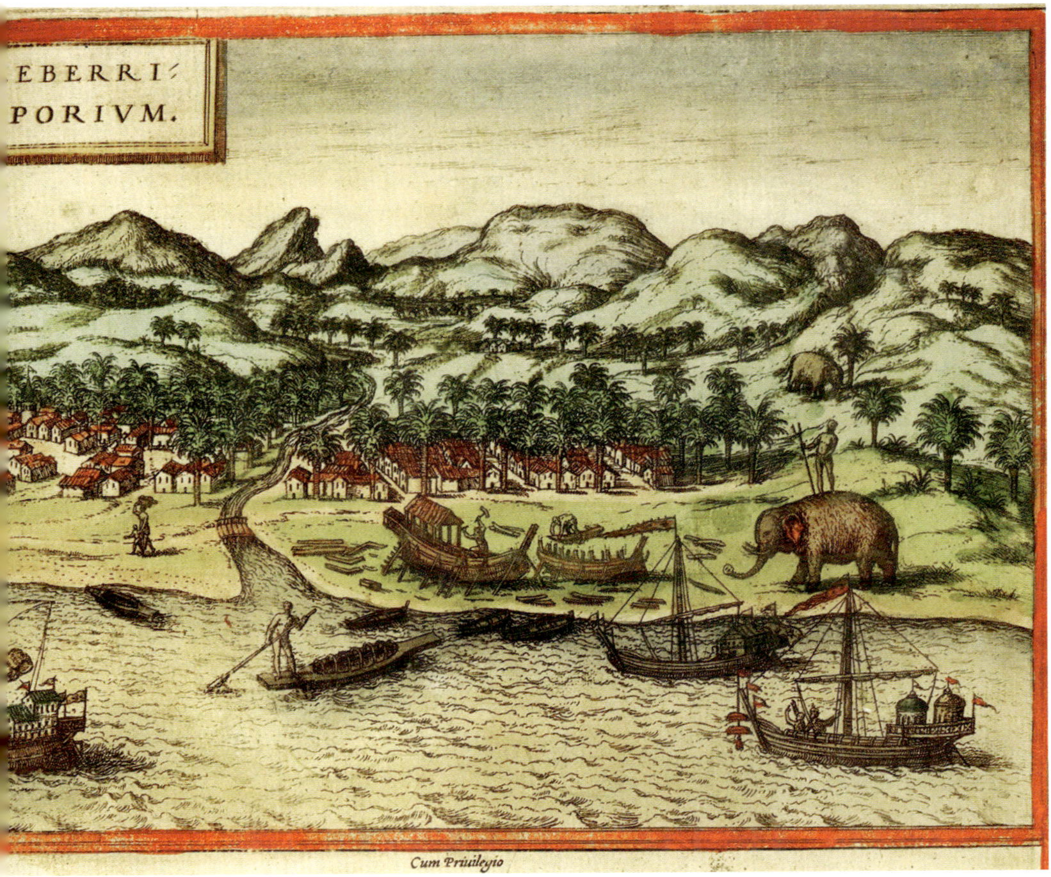

common items, and the most sought after. Those regularly listed are cloves, nutmeg and mace – known as 'the holy trinity' as they alone grew in the Spice Islands – along with cinnamon, pepper and sugar. Dyestuffs too such as cochineal beetle, saffron (now one of the most expensive spices) and indigo were favoured, but it was the pungent spices that were traded most.

The Spice Islands, comprising the Moluccas group of islands in northeast Indonesia within the Indian Ocean, were famed for their nutmeg, cloves and mace. The 'holy trinity' were desired for differing reasons in Europe, not alone for gastronomical use, but also for their medicinal and aphrodisiac qualities. Nutmeg, for example, was thought to fight off disease, including the plague, which explains why consumers were prepared to pay such enormous prices.[53] Cinnamon was indigenous to Ceylon and China. With ginger, which also originated in southern China, these spices were transplanted to

Southeast Asia and the Malay Archipelago and from there to east Africa and the Mediterranean, between the first and seventh centuries BC.[54]

Pepper is probably one of the earliest-known spices and was by far the most traded. Worth its weight in gold, and referred to in trading terms as 'black gold', such was pepper's worth that it was used as a currency when specie was scarce or unavailable. It was used for gifts, bribes and dowries, to pay bills, tributes and taxes, to purchase land and to indicate wealth – large quantities of pepper in a household denoted prosperity, with lack of pepper representing poverty. Originally from the forests of Malabar and Travancore in India, it was eventually propagated in Southeast Asia, from Sumatra to the Philippines.[55] While cinnamon, nutmeg and cloves were by far the most expensive and most sought-after of the spices in the early part of the seventeenth century, with annual demand in Europe approximating one million pounds, pepper was handled in greater quantity. From the sixteenth century into the early seventeenth, for example, Portugal imported from Malabar some two million kilograms of pepper annually, while European usage increased to around three million kilograms.[56] Such was the demand in the late sixteenth century, however, that the Portuguese could not maintain supply, and prices rose accordingly. This motivated other maritime empires, not unexpectedly the Dutch, to look to the trade in spices to secure their own supply, in order to meet demand and control their own prices. The age of joint-venture merchant trading companies to the Spice Islands thus began, and with it changes in ship design that accommodated greater volumes of merchandise carried in the holds of armed merchantmen.

Pepper remained the most traded spice throughout the sixteenth and seventeenth centuries, and only declined in the eighteenth century when other commodities entered the marketplace.[57] Silver was used to buy pepper, and was thus usually part of a cargo on any trade ship dealing in spice as commodities. Price varied according to season, wars, and so on, but in the early sixteenth century 1g of pepper was bought for the equivalent of 1–2g of silver in Malabar; in Alexandria it was 10–14g of silver; in Venice 14–18g of silver; in Lisbon traders would have to pay 16–20g; and the final European consumer would have to pay 20–30g of silver for 1g of pepper.[58] It too was traded for its culinary, medicinal and aphrodisiac properties. Specific storage space was allotted for spices in the holds of Portuguese ships; contained in sealed crates, pepper was carefully marked and packed.[59] Such was the tight storage provision for some spices that when trade ships were captured, pirates often by necessity had to retain the ship as a prize to transfer the goods on

FIGURE 38: Collection of coconuts recovered during archaeological excavation on the Coconut shipwreck, Schull, County Cork; each one is stamped with a plantation or merchant's mark which may assist in identifying where they originated. © MIZEN ARCHAEOLOGY LTD, CORK

shore as doing so at sea could prove too time-consuming or too difficult if the weather was inclement.

From the list of goods bought from the pirate Captain Claes Compaen, as discussed above, it is clear that pepper was the most highly prized commodity. Pepper is variously described, with Thomas Neale of Bandonbridge buying two bales containing 700 [lbs] weight, at 8d per pound; Martin Harman, in partnership with Justice Brady of Cork, bought pepper at a cost of 6½ pence per pound; Nicholas Atwood bought 6,000 [lbs] weight, Mr Newcomen of 'the Bridge' (Bandon) bought 800 [lbs] weight and Sir William Hull sent '40 horse loads of pepper to Kinsale'.[60]

Contemporary archaeological evidence for pepper as cargo has been recorded at several wreck sites, including the Portuguese *nau* generically named Pepper wreck lost at the mouth of the River Tagus, in Lisbon Harbour, in 1606 and a second, recently discovered wreck found near Cascais, close to Lisbon, that dates between 1575 and 1625. Among other artefacts, pepper was scattered over a wide area at the Pepper wreck site and in such quantities that it formed a blanket of peppercorns. Valuable evidence is provided by the Pepper wreck for the Portuguese trade to the East Indies, when they still retained a monopoly on the spice trade there, while the shipwreck near

FIGURE 39: One of two Iberian olive jars from the Coconut shipwreck, Schull, County Cork, recovered by local fishermen in the 1980s when scallop dredging and recorded during the archaeological work on the wreck site. © MIZEN ARCHAEOLOGY LTD, CORK

Cascais is believed to have been on its way home from India. Both wrecks afford important insights into the types of ships used at that time.[61] Cultural evidence in Ireland may be found in the remains of the Coconut wreck, discussed in the previous chapter, whose crates in the lower hold could potentially have contained pepper. The exotic timber used in its construction could point to an East Indies or at least New World origin for the ship, and the fact that both the Pepper wreck and Coconut wreck were also carrying coconuts may indicate corresponding trading activities.[62]

Trade by its very nature needed to be reciprocal, and goods like wine, wheat, beer, beef and wax were primarily European in origin, though hides, which are frequently listed, could have had a wider derivation. These products were also needed to feed the colonial markets of the New World: exotic spices could be used to satisfy the tastes of a growing élite, while the common settler needed leather for shoes, wax for candles or beef for sustenance. Sugar too was highly prized and was imported into England from the sixteenth century (250 tons of Moroccan sugar imported each year, for example), and such was its market price that it became a target for plunder.[63] Sugar was also brought from Jamaica from that early period, while it only began to be traded from places like Barbados from the first half of the seventeenth century, where it formed part of the triangular commercial trade in human cargo from Africa – the slave trade. Venture capitalists sought access to these exotic goods to advance their own investments, through legal routes or otherwise. As will be outlined below, many officials tasked with combatting piracy, and in particular tackling the pirates of the alliance, were themselves compromised by their own commercial interests.

PIRATE BUSINESS OVERSEAS

With the fall of Mamora in 1614 to the Spanish, the pirate alliance was forced to move its bases of operations, not only to ports like Villafranca in the Mediterranean or Harbour Grace in Newfoundland, but also to Algiers and Tunis. There they came under the control of the Ottoman Turks, as described by Henry Mainwaring, and could no longer behave with such freedom within these port cities. This proved little deterrent, however, and they essentially sailed in partnership with their fellow North African corsairs on board the same ships, albeit with many of the European (primarily English) pirates now outnumbered by their North African counterparts.[64] Mainwaring confirmed that 'Ships are ... manned out by the Turks, after the proportion of 150 Turks to 20 English, yet the English in their persons are well used and duly paid their shares.' Some, like Mainwaring, had built up such a relationship with the Turkish pirates in Algiers and Tunis at that stage that he was readily accepted into their fold, with the Dey of Tunis pleading with him to lead his corsairs and promising him riches if he took up the position, instead of returning to England to seek a pardon.[65] Generally, however, this change meant depletion in power for the Atlantic pirates, particularly within the scope of their operations and with the consequential loss of control over markets and market prices.

As established in Chapter 1, legitimate relationships predicated on socio-economic and political associations, had been in place between Britain and Barbary since the time of Elizabeth I. Indeed, English traders were living in Morocco by the latter part of the sixteenth century and Morocco was identified as an important commercial centre.[66] The ruling North African élite welcomed English traders, tradesmen, mariners and pirates alike, embracing their knowledge and technology with a view to advancing and expanding their own. Captain John Smith, in 1604, provides a vivid description of both the natural and cultural world of Morocco, with interesting insights into the interplay between European and North African communities. He observes that there was, at that time, English goldsmiths, 'plummers', carvers, stonemasons and watchmakers working in Barbary. So impressed was the ruling king Mullah Hamet with their skill and abilities that he was paying them ten shillings a day and providing them with food, clothes and lodging. He also allowed them to trade freely for whatever they needed.[67] It encouraged migration from England to these port cities and towns in North Africa, which in turn stimulated trade, legitimate or otherwise. With English tradesmen embraced by the ruling powers, English pirates, along with their goods and their knowledge, were similarly accepted into North African social and economic life.

Newfoundland provided the pirates with ready supplies of fish, bread, wine and cider and in return they supplied plundered goods to the settlers there.[68] Migratory fishing communities were located around Harbour Grace and Ferryland, and this coincided with the developing Grand Banks fishing industry at St John's, which was to become a thriving business from 1615 onwards, worth an estimated £120,000 to England for the fish catch alone in that year. The figures are given by Richard Whitbourne as part of his survey of Newfoundland in the 1620s:

> The burthens and Tunnage of them all one with another, so neere as I could take notice, allowing euery ship to be at least threescore tunne (for as some of them contained lesse, so many of them held more) amounted to more then 15000. tunnes. Now for euery threescore tunne burthen, according to the vsuall manning of Ships in those voyages, agreeing with the note I then tooke, there are to be set down twenty men and boyes: by which computation in these 250. saile, there were no lesse then fiue thousand persons. Now euery one of these ships, so neere as I could guesse, had about 120000. fish, and fiue tunne of Traine oyle one with another.
>
> So that the totall of the fish in these 250. saile, when it was brought into *England, France* or *Spaine* (being sold after the rate of foure pound, for euery thousand of fish, sixe score fishes to the hundred, which is not a penny a fish, and if it yeeld lesse, it was ill sold), amounted in money to 120000. pound.[69]

As Easton's primary base until he moved to Villafranca, he stored and exchanged goods at Harbour Grace but at times would also target the fishing fleets. This point is teased out in more detail below when considering the economic impact of the pirates' presence in Newfoundland but their activities coincided with and were directly tied into the setting up of the many English New World merchant venture companies. These included the Virginia Company in 1606, the London and Bristol Company, also referred to as the Newfoundland Company, in 1610 and the Bermuda Company, 1611–12.[70] The English East India Company had already been established since 1600, and nearer home the Ulster plantation began in 1609–10. The latter scheme drew investment from many of the London companies, including the Mercers' Company, Merchant Taylors' Company and Skinners' Company.[71] Many individuals involved in these companies were also invested in other joint-stock companies overseas, and the plantation of Ulster was regarded as competing with expansion in overseas colonial interests. Fifty-five of the fifty-six companies involved in the Virginia Plantation, for example, became involved in the Ulster Plantation scheme, compelled to do so by the king.[72] At Dundaniel in west Cork, the East India Company invested £7,000 or more in purchasing woods, building a dock and constructing two ships, one of 400 and the other 500 tons, along with building offices, houses, forges and other storehouses. These supported the iron works that were established there and employed 300 workers.[73] Ships therefore could be found loaded with rich and diverse cargoes sailing between the Old and New World; critically they also held information and knowledge of new speculative opportunities at home and abroad.[74] Such opportunities could be exploited by pirates and officials, to enrich and empower themselves.

BLURRED LINES AND OFFICIAL CRIMES

Specific individuals can be identified as being involved in legitimate speculative ventures but with questionable activity also taking place. Vice-Admiral Humphrey Jobson was invested in overseas pursuits including that of the Jamestown colony in Virginia. His name is recorded on a list of adventurers on the charters of 1606, 1609 and 1612.[75] A proposition was put forward by lord president of Munster Sir Richard Moryson in 1609, to pardon and then transport pirates from Munster to the emerging plantation settlements in Virginia:

> Should his Lordship please allow of their [the pirates] employment in the intended plantation of Virginia, which I have not yet mentioned unto them, before I resolve of your pleasure, I think good use might be made of them for the present there, both in defending them now in the beginning, if they shall be disturbed by any in their first settling, in relieving their wants from tyme to tyme, and in easing the charge of the journey coming so good cheap. Besides, being active men and good marryners, hereafter when time shall wear out their former offences, with better desert in other countryes not troubled so near at hand with their spoiling, they may return and prove necessary instruments of His Majesty's service.[76]

Moryson's proposal seeks to solve the pirate problem while at the same time augment colonial efforts overseas. It is indicative of the government's view that, for the most part, the pirates in Munster were still Englishmen who could assist the plantation process on both sides of the Atlantic and over time, their previous offences could be forgotten. Humphrey Jobson's dealings with the pirates could, in turn, be used for his own speculative ventures. It would be an irony indeed if such ill-gotten profits were in turn put to use re-settling pirates in colonies abroad, perhaps to establish similar trading habits there and ensure a continued mutual link across the ocean between the southwest of Munster and the colonies in the New World. On the same list of investors in the Virginia colony is James Duppa.[77] Then living in Leghorn (now Livorno) in Italy under the auspices of the duchy of Tuscany, Duppa too was a noted pirate from the southwest coast of England, who patrolled the Mediterranean and traded extensively with the Atlantic pirates in Mamora.[78] He and his brother Michael were active around North Africa during the time period 1612–14.

Michael had bought a Spanish vessel from fellow English pirate William Baugh when in Mamora and was listed as a member of Captain Henry Mainwaring's pirate crew at Mamora in 1614, manning his own Flemish ship of 160 tons in consort with known Atlantic pirates, among them captains John Ellis and Robert Walsingham. There also at the same time was Irish pirate Captain Patrick Myagh.[79] This last account is noteworthy, as the Dutch fleet, led by Captain Moy Lambert, during their attack on the pirate and settler community in Crookhaven killed Myagh and many of his crew in March of that year.[80] Though the account of Myagh in Mamora is dated to August 1614, it refers to January and February of that year when the pirates were in Mamora, as Edward Davenant's report states that Myagh's ship, of 160 tons, had arrived into Crookhaven three or four days before 4 March 1614.[81]

A case that reveals the extent of collusion, malpractice and official piracy that was taking place with admiralty officials and speculators in ventures both in Ireland and overseas is that of a ship called the *Pearl*. After it was wrecked in 1613 near Dursey Island in Bantry Bay, the *Pearl* became part of a protracted dispute between the English East India Company, admiralty officials, the captain and crew of the ship, the Spanish ambassador Diego Sarmiento de Acuña, first count of Gondomar, and the king himself.[82] A deposition of Walter Rockwell, a mariner of Bristol, deposed that the ship was 'casually run aground', suggesting it was a deliberate act. Other contemporary sources suggest otherwise, reporting that the ship was in danger of total loss and the cargo near destruction: 'the *Pearl* was so much distressed with a Storm at the place where she arrived, that her Bulk is broken or made altogether unprofitable as I hear, but the goods are saved with small loss'.[83]

The *Pearl* was on its way back to England from a 'privateering' venture to Sumatra, then part of the Dutch East Indies, under the command of Captain Samuel Castleton of London, and where it had spent two years targeting ships and their cargoes. Though heading for a port in England, there is no surviving account to explain why the ship ended up on the Irish coast, but as suggested in Chichester's letter, the ship may have been blown off-course by bad weather. It is also the case that, as an interloper, Castleton may have preferred to land the goods in Ireland rather than in a port in England, and may have had prior knowledge of the potential ready markets available along the coastline of Munster.[84] The cargo was saved by Sir Richard Bingley, then captain of the king's ship *Dreadnought*. He arranged to have the cargo removed, with three local fishermen in Castletownbere hired to assist with the unloading of the goods, using their fishing vessels and receiving payment of twenty marks a month for the work. According to depositions of some of the crew of the *Pearl*, the fishermen were engaged over several months in the transport of cargo from the stranded vessel. During this time the stricken shipment was taken to Berehaven, in advance of transport to England, though it seems that at least one of the fishing vessels brought some part of the goods to Dingle.[85]

The cargo was reputedly of great value, though this was revised as the judicial case progressed, and there were very many parties who had vested interests in acquiring them for themselves.[86] Indeed, in December 1613, when directed to bring the 'bark *Pearl*' from Ireland to London (supposedly it is the cargo on board that is being referred to here), Henry Howard, the earl of Northampton, states that 'this course is the safest both for the Ambassadors and the proprietors, but the Lord Admiral [Nottingham] thinks that by his patent, all those matters belong to his jurisdiction'. As the cargo made its way back to England, much of it was siphoned off. Bingley loaded the goods into a number of ships and sent the vessels to various ports in England.[87] Northampton, agitated at the potential loss of all the cargo, requested Sir William Monson, admiral of the Narrow Seas fleet, to bring the remainder of the goods from Ireland himself to ensure its safe arrival. He was sent to take command of the *Dreadnought* and he brought it and another ship back to London in March 1614. At this point the owner of the *Pearl*, John Morris, originally leased by the East India Company, was looking to have his goods returned. So too was the Spanish ambassador, Gondomar, who regarded the goods as rightfully Portuguese, as they had been taken off a Portuguese ship in the east.[88]

Nottingham argued jurisdiction over the goods, as lord high admiral. King James, who saw the opportunity to seize a valuable cargo to bolster the coffers of his dwindling exchequer, thwarted Nottingham's effort, but he also had an ulterior motive – he wished to reward a favoured courtier, Robert Carr, Viscount Rochester, whom he had made 1st earl of Somerset in November 1613. As suggested by Calvin Senning, in his detailed account of the whole affair, there were rumours at that time that Northampton and Somerset were planning to embezzle the entire prize and share the profits. The conclusion of the legal wrangling was that the crown sold the cargo, with Sir Lionel Cranfield and Sir Arthur Ingram, London merchants, handling the sale for the king.[89]

The involvement of these two individuals, business partners in both financial and political endeavours, was not a chance occurrence. Cranfield, who during his career was a merchant, financier and member of parliament, had been knighted in 1613 and appointed surveyor-general of the customs. At the time of the loss of the *Pearl*, he was a successful and very rich export merchant and speculator in maritime ventures. Cranfield's speculations in overseas trade and political affairs brought him into contact with Ingram, who himself was involved in money-lending as a young man. Ingram rose rapidly in the political ranks, with support from key government players such as the earl of Northampton and Thomas Howard, the earl of Suffolk.[90] The potential profit that was to be made from the cargo of the *Pearl* was enticement enough for both men to become involved. A 1621 petition by the owners of the goods looking for restitution specifically mentions Cranfield and Ingram selling the goods from the *Pearl* as a prize, when the cargo was supposed to be in Westminster under lock and key pending the results of the admiralty court case. The crew of the ship too looked to be paid for the voyage, petitioning for back pay as late as 1625, and eventually given cursory payments in 1629. Conspicuous by their absence, there is no specific mention of pirate involvement, apart from attempts to suggest that the owners of the ship were, themselves, pirates.

Sir Lionel Cranfield and Sir Arthur Ingram were also participants in an earlier 1609 case relating to goods from a ship of the same name – the *Pearl*, which had been laden in St Lucar in Spain in 1607 with 'a great quantity of … hides, cochineal, indigo, ginger, … leather, pearls and … Spanish money'. When on its way to Calais, it was captured by English pirates, Captain Alexander Vaughan and Captain Blanch. They took the ship to Larache near Tangiers in northern Morocco where some of the goods were offloaded onto an English ship, the *Jonathan*, and when off southern Spain some eleven barrels of indigo, seven and a half barrels of cochineal and £542 worth of Spanish realls of eight were place on board the *Peter* of London, a ship hired by Lionel Cranfield, Arthur Ingram and another colleague, William Massam. When it reached London, the goods were confiscated by the lord high admiral and sold at a very low price to Cranfield, Ingram and Massam. They then resold them at a substantial profit. The owners of the *Pearl* sought recompense from Cranfield and his cohorts, but to no avail. Other of the goods from the *Pearl* were transported to Ireland, where pirate captains Richard Robinson and Vaughan sold some of them to Paul De Cuper, the agent commissioned by the admiralty to recover the goods from the pirates. A deposition by Humphrey Jobson, whose brother Deputy Vice-Admiral Richard Jobson was liaising with De Cuper, provides an account of events surrounding the cargo of the *Pearl* and its many stakeholders. Frustration is discernible in the protracted examination by Humphrey Jobson because of the purchase by Cranfield and Ingram of the goods and Jobson's apparent inability to control such matters. The owners fared no better, with the seals removed from the goods, they were unable to prove that they owned them.[91]

Senning states, as a fitting conclusion to his account of the later *Pearl*: 'The need and greed of the king, his courtiers, and officials seemingly being a stronger force than their sense of justice, the way was made clear for those whose position of power and influence gave them licence to take what they wanted, to commit an act of piracy of their own and plunder the plunderers.'[92] The cases of both ships named *Pearl* provide clear evidence for decisions made that were self-motivated, involving many of the same players and going all the way to the lord high admiral and the king himself, to prosper from and control maritime affairs, and illustrates the lengths to which they were willing to go to fulfil their needs. Such was the eagerness of individuals to profit from the cargo on ships that it is fully understandable why piracy flourished.

Individuals like the Duppa brothers successfully navigated the thin line between being a legitimate merchant adventurer and outright pirate – they were involved directly with the pirates in North Africa but also invested in overseas adventures alongside government officials such as Humphrey Jobson and Thomas Crooke. Other men like Cranfield and Ingram appear to have done the same. Senior's account of James Duppa shows him to have been considered a 'tufted taffeta captaine' by fellow English pirates, who regarded him more as a merchant and trader than a pirate.[93] James Duppa went on to become financially involved in the Guiana Company, set up by Robert Rich, second earl of Warwick, who himself was noted for private maritime ventures that often crossed into the bounds of piracy. The company looked to colonial ventures in the Amazon from the late 1620s.[94].

Lauren Benton, in her studies of the seventeenth-century legal geography of the oceans, discusses the application of legislative admiralty controls on the high seas and how they were regularly influenced by the applied commercial strategies of mariners, merchants and pirates: 'The creation of a colonial admiralty court system extended English legal authority through the empire at the same time that it opened new avenues for the avoiding of courts in England [and by extension Ireland] and in particular the colonies.'[95] In many cases, therefore, the commercial gains of merchant venture expeditions justified the means by which such economic returns were achieved.[96]

THE COST OF PLUNDER AND IMPACT ON TRADE

A number of the ships captured by the pirates were significantly rich, and certain nations, France in particular, began complaining vehemently to James of their mounting losses and the impact it was having on trade. During an eighteen-month period from 1608 fifteen ships were captured, with their French owners signalling that two of them were particularly valuable. The *St Anne* of Giles, captured off Cape St Vincent, was carrying gold and silver valued at 36,000 livres (*c.* £3,600), and the *Hunter* of Le Havre was taken in the harbour at Safi with a cargo of cotton and barley, worth 50,000 livres

(c. £5,000). These figures vary somewhat from those provided by the admiralty, who carried out its own assessment of the loss. According to its valuation the *St Anne* was carrying gold doubloons and Spanish silver reales worth only £1,150, though they neglected to include the rest of its cargo, including 1,870 hides, thirty-seven bags of ginger, cochineal and sugar, which would certainly have increased the value of the loss. The loss of the *Hunter* was assessed as carrying cotton, barley and other goods worth in the region of £4,550.

The impact of principally English-dominated piracies was not felt just in the Atlantic, but within the Mediterranean too. As early in James' reign as 1604, the duke of Florence sent bitter representations about his losses in the Levant amounting to some 200,000 crowns. The trading routes dominated by the Venetians at that time were also seriously interrupted by the pirates, with it estimated that thousands of pounds worth of trade was lost. As Clive Senior concluded, 'it was the rapaciousness of the [English] corsairs which made the Senate decide to open diplomatic relations with England with a view to receiving compensation for the losses of Venetian merchants'.[97] The pirates based in northern waters under Bishop, as already noted, networked with John Ward and Simon Danseker within the Mediterranean. From 1609 Danseker had moved his base to Marseilles in France, and with Ward operating out of Algiers, and, from 1613, with Easton based in Villafranca, legitimate shipping within the Mediterranean or moving through the straits of Gibraltar had to run the gauntlet of piratical attack on all sides.[98]

The range and scale of the pirates' operations by 1610 and throughout successive years resulted in James receiving representations from both French and Spanish ambassadors insisting he consider issuing pardons to the pirates in the hope of resolving the problem. A French remonstrance sent to the lords of the Privy Council in London showing losses covering 1610 and 1611 named several pirate captains, but singled out Thomas Francke in particular. He had taken five ships as prizes and was causing the most damage at that stage to their merchants.[99] The document discusses shipping from the port of La Rochelle, with losses from seventeen vessels given as 362,000 French francs (livres). Senior correctly indicates that these figures may include all shipping out of La Rochelle, not just French ships, but in any event, losses were substantial. Cargoes looted included sugar, wine, cochineal, Campeche wood and money. Even if conservative values on numbers are taken as given in the contemporary sources, a French vessel to the value of £1,000 or more was captured by English-dominated pirate activity every month.[100] It was not without its risks, however, and Francke encountered harsh treatment too as a pirate. When competing Flemish pirates captured him in 1611, for example, he was subjected to torture that included burning the ends of his fingers.[101] While the rewards could be substantial, they could often come with a personal price.

In Newfoundland, at times, the impact was even more acute. In 1612 Easton reportedly took one fifth of all provisions landed and every fifth man from the fishing boats there to replenish his crews.[102] The latter was not wholly by force, however, and by June of 1613 Easton had constructed his own fort in Harbour Grace equipped with sixteen guns. By then too he had allegedly recruited up to 500 English fishermen from the fishing crews and had augmented his fleet from four vessels to nine, to a total proposed value of £10,400. The damage caused to the French fishing fleet was estimated to be around £6,000 and that to the Portuguese at £3,000. Easton and his fleet also captured a large Dutch vessel valued at £1,000. It is estimated that the overall damage done in financial terms at Newfoundland was in the region of £21,400. D.W. Prowse perhaps observed correctly, in his *History of Newfoundland*, when he notes that 'The Colony [in Harbour Grace] was practically without law or government; there was no civil or military force to maintain order amongst a floating population of fifteen to twenty thousand turbulent fishermen. No wonder there were disorders and crimes.'[103] The focus for such attacks was also to supplement their diet rather than acquire marketable produce, as cargoes of fish were cumbersome and not easily transported.[104] Easton did seem to have in place a type of protection racket, with the colonists paying for security in either money or goods, including the requirement to revictual the pirates' ships.[105]

Easton moved from Harbour Grace to Ferryland, some 78km southeast of Harbour Grace, where he is said to have had a 'great house'.[106] To date, there has been no identified cultural evidence for warehouses or similar safe storage facilities for the pirates' goods, at either Harbour Grace or Ferryland; but other archaeological objects at least hint at the links between Ireland and Newfoundland from that period. The discovery of an Irish silver shilling during excavations at Ferryland, within the lower layers of the defensive ditch, provides evidence for contact via transatlantic traffic and probable trade during the reign of James VI/I, from the earliest phases of occupation at the Colony of Avalon.[107] It is an example of a coin dating from the second issue of 1604–7 during the king's reign, and one can ponder if the pirates

FIGURE 40: View across harbour at Ferryland, Newfoundland, where vice-admiral of the pirates of the alliance, Captain Peter Easton, established his fortification and main base.
IMAGE: DR JAMES LYTTLETON

themselves, or perhaps even Peter Easton, may have brought it from one of the harbours in Ireland only to lose it while in Newfoundland.

Certainly, it was Iberian shipping that was most impacted by the pirates' predations. From 1606 to 1608, James received repeated complaints through Spanish ambassadors of damage to their ships and trade by English pirates, though Dutch renegades were also among those who attacked Spanish ships at this point. The king of Spain, Philip III, estimated that his exchequer lost '20,000 ducates' in custom duties in just one year. There was thus an impact not just on trade and merchant interests but on the royal revenue of Spain itself. Overall figures are not available for Spain's losses, but James, in an audience with the Spanish ambassador in 1612, was told that the pirates had done '... more damage since the conclusion of the peace [with England in 1604] than before in time of war. Even the Dutch do not do so much.' The fact that the majority of the pirates chose not to target merchant ships of their own country provided immediate advantage to English trade, and though not all English ships escaped attack, the collective impact on foreign shipping led to increased market opportunities for English merchants.

The issue of English merchants dealing with the pirates, including buying plundered goods at knock-down prices through foreign ports and then reselling them at inflated prices, added to the anger of other affected nations. In 1610, for example, the English agent John Harrison in Morocco, reported that the pirates had so much plundered goods for sale 'At Mamora, a harbour of pyrates upon the coast of Barbarie', and at such reasonable prices, that legitimate merchants could not compete in the market place.[108] The Dutch too were suffering huge losses of goods and ships, to the reputed value of about 600,000 ducats, an extraordinary amount. The Dutch were intent on sending ships of their own to North Africa to try to tackle the pirates directly, though with the dual purpose of attempting to open trade with the Turks, 'as the pirates were able to buy goods there at very low prices'.[109]

There were reciprocal impacts too, with the wine trade seriously obstructed by French reprisals on English traders and was regarded as piracy on the legitimate trade of another country. This counter-action spread and traditional tensions with countries such as Spain began to mount, with James fearing a breakdown in peaceful relations. The Dutch too began formulating plans to tackle the pirates head-on in Irish waters, and sought commissions from James to enter the harbours of southwest Munster. The situation was compounded by James' refusal to grant letters of marque or reprisal to his own merchants to allow them seek their own restitution:

> … as for L'res of Marke, if it be impartially considered, whether … it will be profitable or not; it may be feared, considering the quantity of our stock there, and the resolve of our ships and men thether, that whilst wee goe about to right one, wee shall prejudice another in a greater quantity; for it must be supposed, if any such L'res of Marke be granted here and expedited upon Spaine, Spaine will revenge himself upon such as he shall find there, of which what can be the [result] but a breach of peace …[110]

While James was not about to allow merchants take reprisal and run the risk of collapsing the agreements between states, relationships between England and its fellow European coastal nations were close to breaking point. James came under increasing pressure from within and without to consider all options to solve the problem of piracy. The business being done by the pirates near home as well as abroad was closely scrutinised on several levels, not just with regard to damage inflicted. The wider political and socio-economic implications began to influence actions taken against the pirates by the crown from 1611 onwards, which in turn affected the operations of the pirates themselves and influenced decisions on their future.

Before reflecting on the measures taken to suppress the impact of the alliance, which is dealt with in Chapter 7, the social lives of individuals is worth considering and their engagement with each other on an everyday basis. Some businesses linked both social and economic elements of the pirates' lives, like that of alehouses, safehouses and prostitution, and while they became key components in the business of piracy, they are far more difficult to quantify. The actions of certain pirates, such as captains William Baugh and Peter Easton discussed above, give us a sense of what business life was like for the leading lights within the hierarchy of the alliance. Where possible, it is worth delving deeper into the 'ordinary' lives of others around them, not just the captains and members of the general crew, but the wives, children or other women mentioned in the sources. Such individuals are even more imperceptible than their pirate counterparts, but are no less important to the cultural history of the time.

CHAPTER 6

The Social World of Amphibious Lives

For many of them [the pirates] have their wyves and children in these parts about Limcolme [Leamcon], where and among whom is thought to be store of money.[1]

Tracing the everyday lives of the pirates and their families in the southwest of Munster is difficult, as the sources contain limited information specific to routine or daily events. Cultural evidence remains speculative, though some sites associated with contemporary English officials and crown agents are identifiable. There is a similar paucity of information about the social landscape of Munster into which the pirates arrived, with Gaelic-Irish social norms just as difficult to assess, particularly for tenants within a given lordship. As discussed in the opening chapter, some elements of the native élite remained, with members of the O'Driscoll sept engaging with the arriving undertakers, admiralty officers and settlers during the first decade or so of the seventeenth century. Less is known about members of the O'Mahony sept, though the record of their involvement in the attack on William Hull's holdings in the 1640s confirms their continued presence in the area. Even less is known of those native folk who would have been the tenants of the ruling Gaelic-Irish lords. Certainly many remained within the region, some living in emerging English settlements and demesnes or in more remote badlands, well scattered and dispersed.[2]

For the pirates and their cohorts, being remote ensured discretion and with that the opportunity to do business, live lives and negotiate pardons in a less officially intrusive environment. A contemporary account, in five fire-damaged fragments, contains short but important settlement details at Leamcon in about 1612. Dealing specifically with the method for negotiating pardons, the writer (examinate) recounts that the meetings usually took place in Admiral 'Byshopps house who hath ben a pirott' and who 'came in' or who had stepped down from piracy on the guarantee of the lord deputy, Sir Arthur Chichester and under William Hull's protection. Bishop was then 'dwelling' on Hull's lands as the account states clearly that Hull had '... built each of them [the pirates] houses after the English fation [fashion]'. The 'Company' of pirates had two houses, referring to either members of a specific crew or pirates within the alliance in general, who had two houses at their disposal. The examinate and another pirate were glad to share an 'Irish

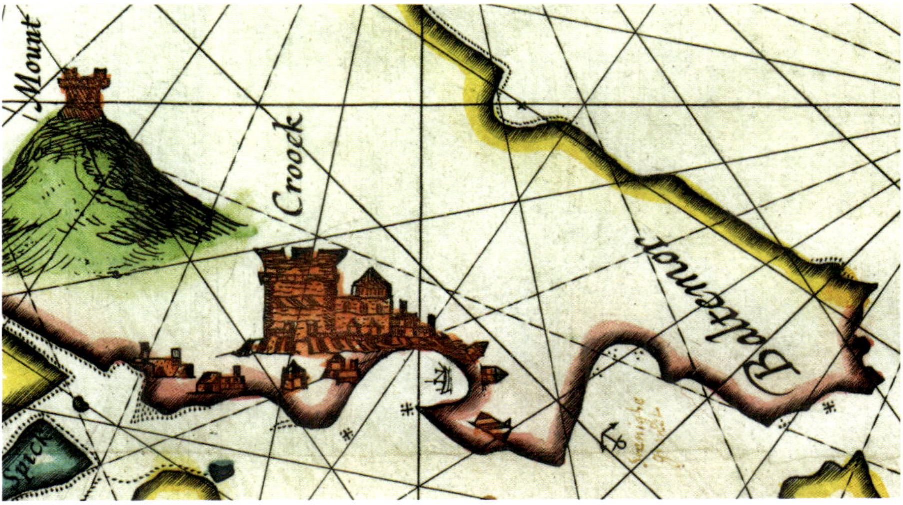

FIGURE 41: Dún na Séad Castle as depicted on the 1612 Dutch chart showing the earlier tower house of the O'Driscoll lords, now gone, and the later fortified house of Thomas Crooke.
SUB GÖTTINGEN, 4 H BRIT P III, 6 RARA, UNIVERSITÄTSBIBLIOTHEK, GÖTTINGEN, GERMANY

cabin'. This suggests residual Irish tenants on Hull's estate in Leamcon, or the cabins where Gaelic-Irish formerly lived. The examinate concludes the passage by stating that all sorts of people were there '... and every man spake his mynd freely'.[3] Certain houses, it would seem, were used as locations for meetings and negotiations for pardons, as communal living spaces for men in the alliance when they came ashore, while others were also the home of 'settled' pirates and their families, like that of Admiral Richard Bishop.

What is clear from the examinate's account is that there was a dedicated settlement of pirates in Leamcon, with accommodation provided by Hull in accordance with provisions for such plantation development, though he did not establish a formal settlement. These new houses were built alongside existing 'Irish cabins', that were either inhabited by the Irish or at that stage vacant but still extant. It is possible that the English settlers, including the pirates and their families who were obviously provided for by William Hull, lived on Hull's estate alongside Irish natives, with all doing so as tenants. This was certainly the case for new English settlers in most other seignories in Cork.[4] The pirates and their families stepped into the role of settlers on emerging English estates in southwest Munster, for their own purposes as well as forming part of the official expansion of settlement; thus did they serve both the process of plantation and the business of piracy.

FIGURE 42: Inverted view of Long Island from the 1612 Dutch chart with settlement cluster focused on the north harbour and other possible industrial buildings indicated on the island.
SUB GÖTTINGEN, 4 H BRIT P III, 6 RARA, UNIVERSITÄTSBIBLIOTHEK, GÖTTINGEN, GERMANY

The latter, discussed in the previous chapter, was multi-layered, and other occupational activities can also be included within the commercial sphere of the pirates' world. Alehouses or taverns became the foci of business both legitimate and illegal, allowing space where deals could be discussed, agreed and executed; safehouses and clearing houses served the critical purpose of ensuring the safe passage of goods and individuals during the course of business. Many of the women in the pirates' lives were engaged in prostitution, often as a necessity during the long absence of their men when at sea. A part of most coastal port towns and harbours through time, the business of sex played a central role, but the records for sex workers from the early seventeenth century in rural Ireland are sparse.[5] Certainly, women were integral to the lives of the men in southwest Munster at that time, with sporadic mention of them within the sources; picking out these records and using them to provide a collective image of their world within the world of men – as wives, sisters, daughters, sex workers or as business associates – adds a crucial layer to understanding the cultural history of southwest Munster at the time. This is discussed in more detail below.

WILLING PARTICIPANTS OR PRESSED PREDATORS?

There is no doubt that the majority of the men who were active in the alliance were there by choice, such were the numbers. Unsurprisingly, men examined by the admiralty under suspicion of piracy are replete with tales of coercion to join the pirate crews and forced to remain on board against their will. Certainly there is a marked similarity across examinations of suspected pirates taken at the time, almost scripted in detail, and reflecting perhaps aligned stories and agreed actions to ensure each man supported the other in the telling of tales. This would have served a number of purposes, and was not just an attempt to infer innocence, but more appropriately, to deflect guilt. Many of the men were family men who would have looked for ways to gain respectability in settled society within the emerging plantation schemes, whose purpose was to contribute legitimately to that society. Their contribution to developing settlements, the plantation policy in Munster and colonial ventures overseas was not lost on parliament or the crown, as already discussed, and indeed could have influenced transcriptions of examinations taken.

Many of these men, like their pirate captains, had served aboard commissioned ships and they too would have considered themselves victims of circumstance. Their accounts sought to distance themselves from the pirates who were there by choice, and to show themselves as partaking in 'honourable crimes', as signified by Henry Mainwaring and discussed in Chapter 3.[6] They sought to bolster their chances of release or, failing that, of obtaining a pardon. While the reality was more than likely different, with many joining the pirate crew willingly with a common goal of advancement and riches, it is in the wider context of the socio-economic and political processes in place at the time that the examinations of these men need to be considered.

PIRATES EXAMINED AND RE-EXAMINED

The High Court of Admiralty series HCA 13/266 contain various examinations, including of twenty-six men in Youghal suspected of piracy; the documents date from February 1608 to March 1613, with the majority dating to May 1610. Some were first taken in Youghal and repeated in England when several of the men were transported for re-examination.[7] Conspiracy on the detail of events is evident within the examinations of the twenty-six men in Youghal and suggests a certain pre-planning, where accounts needed to tally, and where safety in numbers was a strategy not just on the water but on shore as well. Some of the claims of being pressed into service may well have been genuine. In 1612 the lord deputy Sir Arthur Chichester, when writing to the English Privy Council, provided a detailed overview of a man named Latimer, for whom he had provided protection and on whose behalf he had sought a pardon. Latimer had moved with his family to Kerry in Munster as a settler but was pressed into service by Captain Peter Easton. He managed to escape, according to his account, and returned in a ship to the Bay of Tralee. He brought with him 'three Pirate Mariners and 16 ffishermen taken by Easton in the Newfoundland'.[8] Along with another sailor named Sneller who was conscripted by Dutch pirate Peter Johnson, Latimer was subsequently issued with a pardon, with the council finding that '... the King, as in other like cases, considering their purpose to abandon this wicked life, is graciously pleased to take them into mercy, and their pardon will be sent by the first packet [mail ship]'.[9]

In 1614, Richard Bishop admitted that he had taken two members of his crew 'contrarie to their will by force', because he recognised their value, one being a surgeon.[10] Individual talents were thus beneficial to the pirate operations and such men, whether voluntarily or otherwise, served onboard as part of the pirate crews. It is also notable from the accounts that ending up as part of a pirate crew could be cyclical, not just because some men chose to spend time ashore engaged in legitimate employment but also because they could work at sea as ordinary sailors on merchant ships or fishermen within the wider fishing industry. The life of a mariner in those times was transitory, was fraught with dangers and could, within any given season, be concurrently lawful and unlawful depending on the ship within which one served and its maritime objective. Opportunities, when presented, could be the influencing factor in courses taken.

In 1610 mariner John West claimed that he had been serving on a merchant ship that was foundering off Mogador (now the city of Essaouira) on the Moroccan coast; he sought safety on pirate Captain Tibault Suxbridge's ship then anchored in the bay, alongside Captain Peter Easton and his ships. Suxbridge set sail for Baltimore in Munster, whereupon Deputy Vice-Admiral Richard Jobson looked for details of the crew. According to West's deposition, Suxbridge refused to release him at that point because he 'had the French tongue', his ability to speak French an obvious asset to pirate business.[11]

Of the twenty-six men, presumed pirates, a sizeable number formed part of Captain Tibault Suxbridge's crew at some point. Curiously – or perhaps fatefully – Suxbridge had been killed during one of the voyages, losing his life on the way back from Newfoundland to Baltimore in an encounter with a French ship.[12] He was in no position therefore to corroborate (or otherwise) his cohorts' story. Suxbridge, possibly from Ratcliffe in London, was master under pirate Captain Richard Robinson in 1608, at which time he and Peter Easton made off with two of Robinson's prizes, having quarrelled with the veteran captain, and thereafter set out on their own, with Suxbridge in overall command.[13] Referred to as a 'little fellowe', Suxbridge carried out numerous lucrative plundering expeditions. These included taking the *Elizabeth* of London, when off the Canary Islands, the *Brave* of Dieppe off Ushant, and at some point capturing the *Content*, a flyboat that he made his 'admiral'. Based for the most part in Baltimore, he would venture across the Celtic Sea to Torbay and Cawsand Bay in England to recruit men. Suxbridge's final voyage in 1609 led from Morocco via the Azores and the West Indies and northward to Newfoundland. It was when on his way back to Munster that he met his death at sea.[14]

It is noteworthy that Ratcliffe, located on the banks of the River Thames and known as a town for shipbuilding, sailors, and as the point of departure for many of the voyages of exploration in the later sixteenth century, was also known as a place patronised by dissenters. Though the religious beliefs of men like Suxbridge are not known, perhaps Baltimore and the southwest coast of Munster proved to be a place of religious freedom, as noted in Chapter 3, not just for non-conformists like the 'Baltimore Syndicate' of John Winthrop, Thomas Crooke and James Salmon, but as spiritual latibules for ordinary settlers too, including pirates. Suxbridge, like many of the pirates, had a family living onshore, a wife and two daughters, whom we shall discover more of below.

As identified above, several of the men are listed as serving on board Suxbridge's ships at various times, including John Lambert, John West, Edward Higgins, John Lee, Richard Hayman, Robert Dunne, John Baker, John Trevor, John Elliot, John Sares and George Darsely. Darsely's examination recorded him as 'of Suffolk' and recounts that '3 or 4 of the consorts of Suxbridge the pirate that lay in that harbour [Baltimore] came in the night & forcibly took him out of his bed & carried him aboard' and kept him prisoner for some months.[15] This account is remarkably similar to that of Roger Salter, discussed below, who was also taken out of his bed during the night and forced to serve as one of Richard Bishop's crew.[16]

Of those listed, John Baker and John Lambert certainly had careers as pirates in their own right. Baker was active in Ireland by 1610, attempting 'to recover some debts' and as his examination details, '… having a daingerous fall at Baltimore from a cliffe' he went aboard Suxbridge's ship to seek the aid of his surgeon, Edward Higgins. Baker sought his care 'to cure his hurt', whereupon the pirate captain 'sett sayle and putt to sea; and for the coast of Spaine, and after that to Barbary …'. Baker's testimony recounts the voyage taken by Suxbridge's ships, from Barbary to the Indies and onto

Newfoundland, including their encounter with the French ship that led to Suxbridge's death. Baker's figures for the number of men on board the pirate's ship tally with those given in several other examinations taken at that time. Baker goes on to proclaim his innocence: '… during that time, he took not any shippe, nor any other goods …'.[17] He obviously survived his arrest and examination, as he is recorded again as captain of his own Flemish ship from which he plundered two vessels, the *Edmund* and *Francis* of Newhaven off Padstow in July 1614; thereafter he disappears from the sources.[18]

John Lambert similarly had a long career ranging from 1608 to 1613, and was master in one of Captain James Harris' ships. He clearly formed part of Suxbridge's main crew, and was also closely associated with Peter Easton. Lambert claimed that he was part of a merchant crew on board a ship from La Rochelle that came to Baltimore in 1609, whereupon they sold their cargo of salt to a 'Mr Clotworthie of Corke'. While there Richard Bishop sent six of his men to the merchant ship and captured Lambert and brought him on board his own ship. They set sail to the coast of Spain where they met up with Suxbridge. There, Lambert transferred to Suxbridge's ship and took the same journey back to Baltimore as detailed by John West, with Lambert proclaiming the same blamelessness: '… that in all that tyme he was with Capt. Suxbridge shippe they neither took shipps nor any other things from any'.[19] Reminiscent of tales told of archetypal pirates, there is confusion as to whether Lambert was subsequently executed or not, with one account recalling that he successfully bribed the hangman, whereupon he made his escape. If accounts are correct, he was still active in May 1613 when a John Lambert of Southwark was captain of the *Come Again* of twenty-five tons and thirty hands that plundered the *Bennet* of Bristol near Milford Haven.[20]

Fellow crew member Edward Higgins was taken on board Captain Richard Robinson's ship *Bull, Bear and Horse* when in Baltimore in 1607 and forced to work as ship's surgeon when the resident surgeon, named Johnson, chose not to take part in the pirate's next voyage. Higgins' deposition lists the following as among Robinson's crew: 'Arthur Drake, master, Peter Easton. Harvy Williams, Masters mate, Thomas Francke Boatsman [boatswain], ~~Wm Tompson~~ and various others whoe made towards the Coast of Spain'. During the course of their voyage they captured two French ships, one laden with thirty tons of wheat and the other an eighty-ton ship laden with cochinel, indigo and cloves. They carried the ships to Larach in Barbary and sold all the goods, except the cochinel and indigo which were shared out thus:

> Capt. Robinson had 8 shares, Captain Duffold 7, the Mr [Drake] 7, Peter Easton 6, the Master's mate [Williams] 6, Tho. Francke 5, ~~Wm Tompson 8 shares~~, and this examinate 3 shares, each share amounting to 4li – 11s. odd mony after which divided they returned for Ireland and arrived at Baltimore....[21]

What is notable here, both in positions held on board and shares divided, is that in 1607 Peter Easton (though his position is not stated) and Thomas Francke were still serving members of crew under Captain Richard Robinson and his lieutenant, black man Arthur Drake. Race, it seems, was not a factor on board when it came to seniority of command and these men were serving their time as part of the ordinary crew before they split from Suxbridge and led their own fleet of ships.

The value in modern terms of each share mentioned by Higgins would be £536 sterling or €600, quite a return from just one plundered ship. Higgins, upon reaching Baltimore, left the pirates' company and settled on the island of Inishbeg, 'Isle of Spike', in Baltimore Harbour for nine months. In January 1610, Higgins met with Suxbridge '... at Captain Hull's at Limecon' where he was again 'persuaded' to come aboard his ship. He was once more 'carried to sea' on what turned out to be Suxbridge's final voyage.[22] It is clear that Higgins was either somewhat unlucky in his encounters with Suxbridge or was in fact actively and willingly part of the crew, with Higgins' and Suxbridge's attendance at William Hull's house in Leamcon suggesting the latter was most probably the reality.

Another crew member examined was John Lee who, as a fisherman on a ship of Plymouth, spent six weeks catching pilchards in Crookhaven in 1609. Lee stopped over in Baltimore while making his way to Kinsale to seek a voyage on a ship then under construction there and destined for Fowey in Cornwall; a friend of his, John Pearce, was on board Suxbridge's ship in Baltimore and Pearce persuaded Lee to come onboard. Suxbridge, wanting men, set sail and took Lee 'against his will'. The same details are given by him of Suxbridge's voyages and show that when Lee returned to Ireland in March 1610 he turned himself over to Sir William St John and the vice-admiral of Munster, Humphrey Jobson. From then, he declared that he worked as a labourer for 'one Mr Clarke at Lymecon'.[23] Lee's testimony suggests that he formed part of a legitimate fishing venture when he first arrived in Crookhaven but found himself caught between legitimate work and piracy voyages, no doubt reflecting the reality of life in remote coastal areas.

The mention of 'Mr Clarke' is curious here too, as Roger Salter similarly mentions an individual named 'Clarke' in his examination. Salter, from Suffolk, had arrived into Ireland four years previously, in 1606, apparently in the service of one 'Holland' and then 'Maddoxe', though there is no further information as to what Salter was doing or who these men were. In about 1609 he went to Baltimore to visit a friend, 'William Woollmer', a known associate of Richard Bishop. According to Salter, one night three or four of Bishop's men took him by force and carried him on board their ship. There, he says, 'they made me drunke' and 'before he could remember himself' (before he sobered up) they set sail. He spent eight weeks with them, during which time they captured a pink of Dunkirk, into which Bishop placed James Harris as captain and Salter as one of the crew, to sail it back to Munster. They were separated from Bishop in a storm and proceeded to make their own way back to Baltimore. At Easter, Salter explained, 'he stole away' from the pirates and since then 'served one Mr Hexam and then one Clarke'. The examination closes with Salter using a rather rehearsed line, that he 'neither remembered their names [the pirates] nor their places of abode, And for goods by them … to any victuals or munition for he knowth nothing'.[24]

Salter's deposition does not state if Clarke was operating out of Leamcon, but the examination of one John Walker [Walter] again mentions a man named Clarke. Walker, 'a Gloster Shire [Gloucestershire] man', was serving aboard a merchant ship when he was taken by force by Bishop, who held him for two weeks. When they made it back to Baltimore, Walker 'stole away from them' and returned to Bristol. In July 1609 he was again serving on a merchant ship in the Irish Sea and encountered the pirate John Finch, who, as told by Walker, also took him by force. He was to serve as master of one of Finch's ships, replacing the previous master who had drowned while drunk.[25] Finch, from Boxley in Kent, was a sailor out of Plymouth; during a voyage to Safi on the northwest coast of Morocco in 1606 he and several others seized the ship *Hunter* of Normandy and held it to ransom, for 26,000 ounces of Barbary gold. He was arrested for piracy upon returning to Barnstable but negotiated a pardon, though he returned to piracy shortly afterwards.

He is recorded as leading a crew of 'landish men' up the Shannon in Ireland in 1609, during which time Walker was the ship's master. Walker and some of Finch's men were captured on the Shannon but Walker was released on condition that he expose Finch as a pirate, which his examination suggests he did. Walker describes a 'kinsman' of Limerick planter Sir Francis Barkley coming aboard and it was then that Walker took the opportunity to

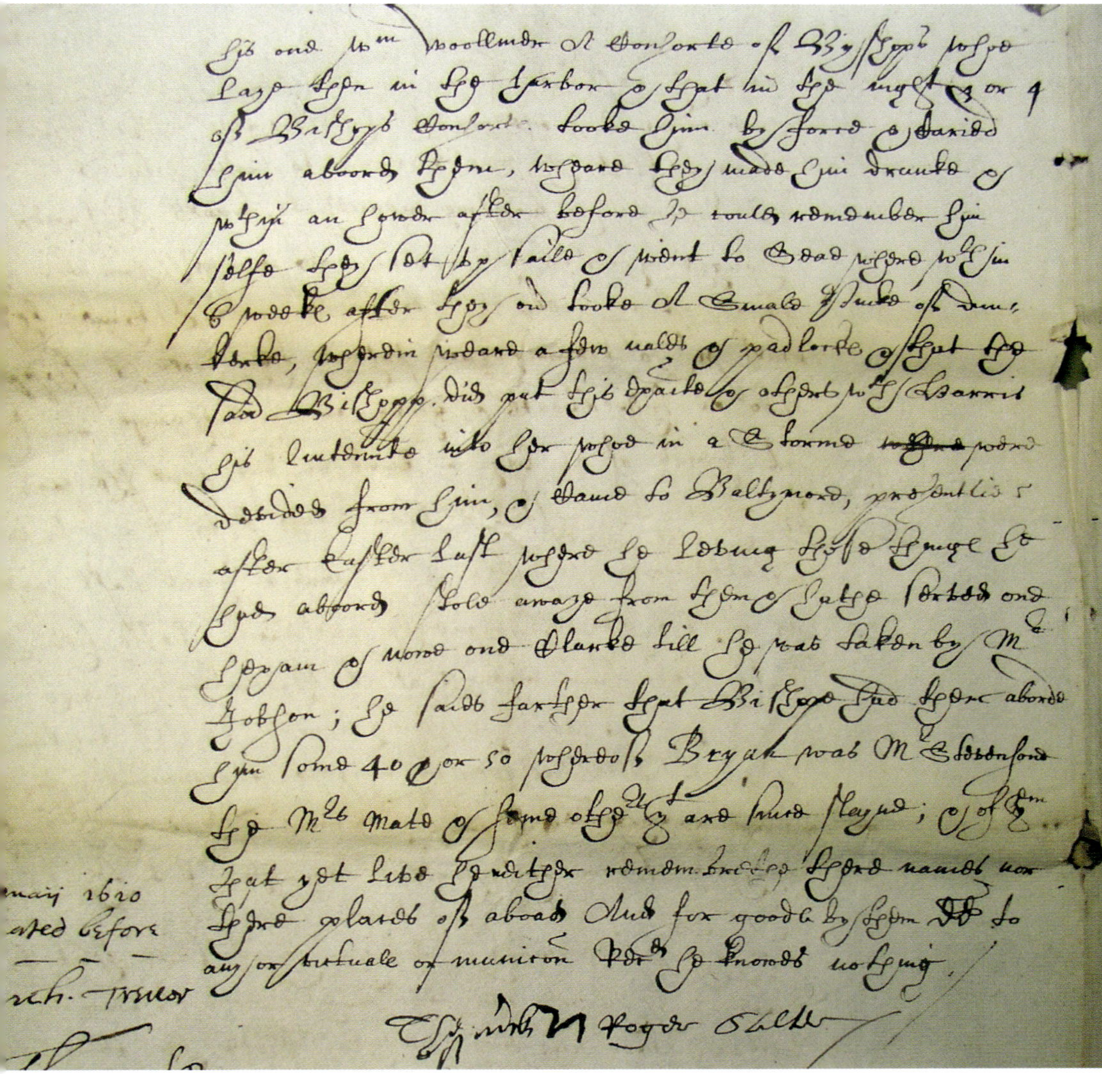

FIGURE 43: Detail from Roger Salter's HCA deposition of 14 May 1610, with his pirate mark as his signature and his full name written beside it by a court clerk.
TNA, HCA EXAMINATION 13/266, FF. 106–106V

leave the ship with him. Vice-Admiral Humphrey Jobson engaged Walker at that stage as a negotiator between him and Finch in order to persuade the pirate captain to accept a pardon. He was unsuccessful, however, and Finch set sail and continued his pirate ways. Walker claimed he, with his wife and family, had settled at 'Bandon Bridge where he was now taken by Mr Jobson's directions'. Three of Finch's crew came ashore in Limerick, 'one his name is

Clarke and the other 2 he knowth not' but Walker adds that he heard they had been taken from a merchant [ship] of Bristol, 'as he was'.[26]

A 'Clarke' is also named as part of Finch's crew. In William Sares' examination we read that Sares escaped when on the Shannon along with the gunner, a Scotsman named Dromble, the master's mate Howard Penny and the boatswain John Clarke, all of whom had formerly been part of a crew on a merchant ship of Bristol – corroborating Walker's deposition. Sares surrendered in Cork and was sent to Youghal by Jobson, where purportedly he was robbed by some of the soldiers in the prison. Sares recalled that they took £23 in gold but gave him £9 16s. recompense in what sounds more like a transaction than theft.[27]

In a later examination of pirate Nicholas Tompson (Thompson), taken in December 1615, mention is again made of a 'Captain Clarcke' of Ratcliffe as part of the crew of a ship under Captain Walshingham and Richard Bishop.[28] Whether these men named Clarke are one and the same cannot be discerned, but it is clear from relationships on a local level between the pirates, admiralty officials and those involved in emerging settlements that individuals active in the alliance also assumed semi-legitimate roles on shore, either through direct engagement by crown officials or by way of involvement in legitimate trades such as fishing.

Kentish man John Sares explained that he was a sailor on a merchant ship of Plymouth, but was also taken by Suxbridge against his will. Sares again gives an almost verbatim account of the route taken by Suxbridge but provides greater insight into the pirate captain's death. Suxbridge's ship had lost its mast and the pirate captain was slain by cannon shot from the French ship when attempting to plunder it; thereafter the rest of the pirates abandoned their attempt to take the ship. Predictably, Sares names the main pirate captains involved – Suxbridge and Harris – but was unable to recall any other detail relating to the crew and their names as 'they prefer not … to bee called by their names but by their office and employment'.[29] It is not known if William Sares and John Sares were connected or what happened to both men following their examinations taken in Youghal.

It is open to discussion whether these apparently aligned accounts reflect adherence to a certain code or fidelity among the men who claimed to be forced into pirate service. Certain accounts suggest that conscripted men were treated with less regard than those who chose to serve. Some of those forced by Peter Easton in 1611 to serve on his ship, for example, sought passage back to Ireland on Captain Roope's ship. When they reached Kinsale, however, they were put ashore without money or means, with some of them dying as a consequence. If Higgins' account is to be believed, such treatment could explain why he received the least amount of shares even though he was surgeon on board, a position usually considered of high importance and reflected in the share amounts divided out. The life of men forced to be pirates was, if such tales be true, often a thankless one.[30]

AMPHIBIOUS PROFESSIONS

The examinations, as established above, can provide suggestions as to the professions of the men when not at sea. Robert Dunne's opens by stating that he arrived into Ireland around 1608 and before being taken against his will by Suxbridge, on whose ship he served as a cook, he 'lived near Baltimore as a labouring man'.[31] Thomas Champion from Surrey was a tailor and had come to Ireland to marry. He was practising his trade in Baltimore and did some work for members of Captain Harris' crew. He went aboard to collect monies owed to him and was carried to sea against his will. When the pirates returned to Baltimore after three weeks they were intercepted by Sir William St John and Vice-Admiral Humphrey Jobson. Upon providing proof of his apprehension, Champion was allowed to return to his trade as a tailor in Baltimore.[32]

Simon Ashdon and Samuel Man have similar accounts of 'conscription'. Ashdon, a Somerset man, was part of the crew of a ship that was charged by Nottingham, the lord high admiral, in 1608 to seek out and prosecute pirate John Ward and his men. The ship sprang a leak off the Straits of Gibraltar and its captain was forced to sell it. Ashdon explained that the captain and some of his crew landed on the 'Christian shore' (European side of the Mediterranean) but left him and the rest of the crew in Tunis. There, he found passage in Captain Richard Bishop's ship for a period of ten weeks; by June 1609 'the first Christian lands they came to was Baltimore in Ireland'. He left them at that point and worked as a shoemaker in Baltimore and Ross (Rosscarbery) for nearly a year. 'Wanting work, he fell into carrying of wood at Ballydehab [Ballydehob] beyond Baltimore' where he was apprehended by Humphrey Jobson. Ashdon pleaded that he did no harm to anyone during the time he was with Bishop; he could not remember any of the ordinary crew's names, claiming that it had been so long since he was with them, apart from '… John Bryan, that was then Master & one Captain Sams [Sammes] & William Kandull'.[33]

Samuel Man from Devonshire lived in Plymouth and worked as a tailor. He was carried off by Peter Easton in 1609 when Easton was at Cawson Bay and spent six months on board, during which time they plundered a Flemish ship and took it as a prize. Man arrived into Leamcon in the prize and persuaded Easton to let him go ashore, with Man declaring in his examination: 'for that he [Man] was not willing to continue that [pirate] kind of life'. He handed himself over to Jobson and lived thereafter in Creagh, outside of Baltimore. He recalled that when at Leamcon, Captain Hull's brother [Henry Hull] and a number of others came aboard the pirate ships, but did not buy any goods or deliver any money. No further details as to their business on board was given.[34]

The onshore professions indicated for the men examined are, for the most part, decidedly working class, comprising tradesmen, fishermen and labourers; the potential for others, perhaps the pirate John Clarke, to step into a junior management role when ashore is therefore interesting. Clearly not all the men who were engaged in piratical ventures at the time were willing participants, and some sought to return to their legitimate work as soon as they could. For those who seized the opportunity to venture on plundering expeditions, and apart from those whose profession was that of mariner, sailor or ordinary seaman, such skills allowed them to integrate and contribute more readily when on shore, with family, friends and other settlers; it helped them to build a life within a developing community and provided choices for men if they elected to stay ashore rather than face the perils of the open ocean.

SHORE CREWS AND COMMERCIAL TIES

The previous chapter disclosed the wealth that could accrue from lawful as well as unlawful business, even when factoring in deliberately inflated returns, inaccuracy of transcription and other agendas affecting the presentment of figures. Business on land, as on the water, required labour, and the plantation schemes demanded diversity in people and trades to support a developing settlement and in turn provided opportunities for those at all levels of society to establish themselves and prosper. Industries such as fishing required crew to man the ships and to fish, but they also needed to draw on other occupations to supplement its activities. Richard Whitbourne, for example, when observing the fishing industry in Newfoundland in the 1620s, set out clearly the range of individuals needed:

> And withall it is to be considered, that the trade thither (as now it is) doth yeerely ser [set] on worke, and relieve many numbers of people, as Bakers, Brewers, Coopers, Ship-Carpenters, Smiths, Net-makers, Rope-makers, Line-makers, Hooke-makers, Pully-makers, and many other trades, which with their families have their best means of maintenance, from these Newfoundland voyages. Add to them the families or servants of divers [various] Owners and Masters of such ships, as goe thither, and mariners with their families, hereby employed and maintained.'[35]

Though not as detailed in specific trades, William Hull's 1641 deposition provides a list of items damaged or stolen from his estates that also gives a sense of what was involved in his fishing industry, and the running of his estates and general household. Listed as attacked, damaged or stolen were sixteen seine boats at Leamcon, a large coasting boat of twelve tons and fish cellars (fish palaces), 'three hundred and sixty bucklers to presse fishe', along with 'prespoles' (press poles) for the extraction of train oil and thousands of staves and hoops for barrel construction, within which the oil was placed or salt was stored. Additional material taken included coopers' twigs, dealboards 'to lay fishe on boats', buckets and bowls, handbarrows, baskets, sticking rods, washing tubs, spare cork for seine boats, stopnets, Turk nets (tucknets), seine nets, tarpolins (taupaulins), along with masts, beams, planks, pitch and resin, anchors, cables (anchor ropes) and bouyropes, for use on or construction of his fishing vessels.

From his general demesne in Leamcon and Clonakilty, and including a number of islands in Roaringwater Bay, cows, sheep, rams and horses were taken; also bags of wool, corn, hay, wheat, coals, and the general pillage and destruction of 'twoo faire houses at Lymcon & Clonakelty with Barnes, stables, malthouses…'.[36] Onshore, able-bodied men would have been needed to build the fish cellars/palaces, fish-holding ponds, quays and landing stages; coopers to construct the barrels for the fish, salt and train oil; men to man the bucklers to press the fish; carpenters to repair boats and sail makers to rig them; fishermen to fish and agents to manage and run the whole operation; these were all central to the industry. The ongoing running of other businesses, like the malthouse for brewing, husbandry for the livestock, tilling of the land and general running of the households all required staff – tenants that included men and women and resources that could be drawn upon. Plantation patents stipulated the employment of English settlers, rather than Old English and Irish, though in reality this rarely worked and among numerous lists of labourers on established settlements, native Irish are regularly recorded and at times out-numbered those from the English settler community.[37]

Whether William Hull was subject to the full rigours of such regulations when establishing his estates, considering he did not develop a settlement in an official capacity, is not clear, but he certainly allowed English pirates to settle on his land under the guise of accepting pardons and working legitimately thereafter. By 1609 several pardoned pirates had settled there. They were more than likely lawfully involved in the pilchard industry with him or within his wider estates, in Leamcon, Clonakilty or Crookhaven, either in business directly or as local workers. Though records for these individuals are scant, the examination of men like John Lee and Roger Salter, as outlined above, imply that they worked as labourers or in some other capacity at Leamcon and elsewhere in west Cork when not at sea plundering ships.[38] The repeated mention of 'Clarke' or 'Mr Clarke', for example, points to specific individuals in place who performed certain tasks, perhaps as clerks, negotiators, estate managers or recruitment agents. Other examples, too, exist. Samuel Cade was living at Leamcon by 1609 and had a long piratical career. The earliest reference to him is in 1603 and he was still active in 1616 in the North Sea. A Barnstaple mariner, he was then serving under Captain William Harvey, who also had a house on William Hull's estate. Cade was engaged by Humphrey Jobson in Leamcon to act as intermediary between him and Cade's fellow pirates. Indeed both Jobson brothers, Humphrey and Richard, used similar tactics, as discussed further below, to 'legitimately' engage with the pirates while at the same time assuring that a steady supply of money and goods found their way into their keeping.

Involved in a similar way to John Walker, Cade boarded the pirates' ships, recovered goods, sold pardons and at certain times arrested individuals on behalf of the admiralty.[39] Officials were thus appointing 'ex-pirates' to engage with active pirates in order to either persuade them to accept pardons or use force to recover goods and capture individuals. This juxtaposition of justice being offered and justice meted out allowed the pirates of the alliance to regulate themselves, while at the same time facilitated officials in maintaining a steady income stream and investors in availing of the service of these men in legitimate industry, or indeed allowed the families of the pirates to reasonably settle in southwest Munster.

Thomas Crooke's rapid establishment of the town of Baltimore included dividing it into tenement lots, with a garden and a plot allocated to each settler for building and grazing their cattle. He accepted tenants as freeholders, with fixed annual rents, as a means of encouraging advancement and permanence in his settlement.[40] This had the added advantage of ensuring there was a return to the admiralty through custom fees. Baltimore and Crookhaven are listed in 1607 among the harbours that had not paid any revenue for many years, claiming exemption under Kinsale's charter.[41] Crooke's investment in the fishing industry in Baltimore generated profit, and, like that of Hull's in Leamcon and Crookhaven, legitimate enterprises may also have fronted for the laundering of monies accrued through pirate business.

The Strafford map of Baltimore shows Crooke's settlement in the early years of its establishment. It is significant in that it provides a view of the town for that early period, including indications of the fishing activity taking place there at that time, both on the water and on land.[42] It is shown as a vibrant maritime harbour, with a variety of vessels, including fully masted ships, fishing boats and smaller tender vessels. The various types of fishing methods that were used in the pilchard industry are also indicated, with 'open seining' and 'fixed engine seine' fishing depicted, and the fishermen themselves. Both methods incorporated the use of a 'hewer' or primary vessel that would deploy the seine nets and follow the shoal. In turn the 'follower' or support vessel that held the other end of the net would gather it around the shoal, essentially ensnaring the fish. The catch was then either hauled into the hewer and landed on shore (open seining) or had one end of the net fixed or anchored to a shore base, where the net could be pulled ashore when the fish had been surrounded (fixed engine seining). Possible fishery-related buildings on the shoreline of the Cove are also depicted, as is settlement and fortified sites immediate to the harbour (Figure 22).

The intensity of activity is illustrated in the manning of the vessels both within and without the harbour, and the smoke coming from the chimneys of what were decidedly settler houses, as specifications under the development of a settlement included the building of houses with chimneys. The scene is one of utilisation of the landscape within the confines of a controlled environment. The activity is focused on the main settlement of Baltimore, where the fortified structure of Dún na Séad Castle surrounded by a large bawn wall is shown, outside of which is also drawn the defined and well laid-out plantation town.

The date of this map is the subject of ongoing discussion but what is certain is that it dates to the first half of the seventeenth century. It could be the map mentioned by Richard Boyle when he wrote to the earl of Dorchester in February 1631 to seek support in fortifying the harbour against pending raids by Algerine pirates:

> A Mapp of the Harbour and Towne of Baltimore, which I had cause to have drawn to present withall, and that your Lordship may observe how the Town and Harbour lyeth and how narrow the entry of the Harbour mouth is and how easily and fitt it is to bee fortified and secured ... I have receaved new intelligence that the Turkes are preparing to land [and] infest those Maritime parts of Munster ...[43]

The map is housed in the Sheffield City Library Archives among the earl of Strafford's papers but Boyle refers to the draughting of a map in his papers housed within the Devonshire Collection in Chatham House in London.[44] The map could easily be older, however, dating to when Crooke's settlement was newly established, which would mean that the map commissioned by Boyle is a separate document that remains yet to be discovered.[45] If the Strafford map is earlier than that referred to in 1631 by Boyle, then it would be an important representational view of Crooke's plantation, showing settlers, industry and maritime activity at a time when Baltimore was the primary northern headquarters for the pirates. It would be tempting indeed to speculate that members of the pirate community were among those depicted in the activities illustrated, including the fishing industry, or that vessels shown could represent some of the ships operated by members of the pirate alliance.

Crooke invested in other resources along the southwestern coast of Munster too for which he would have required labour. He reached a commercial agreement with two gentlemen, Thomas Wilson and Dudley Norton, in 1608, for example, for the purchase of 'certain lands and woods lying upon or about the Bay of Bantry, and for the improvement of the same to the communal interests of all three parties'.[46] Crooke needed to look beyond the confines of Baltimore itself in his acquisition of natural resources, particularly for his fishery industry where timber was needed for barrel-making and press beam construction; it also served as an important asset for fuel, building materials, for boatbuilding and repair and as a trading commodity.[47] In 1608 when Phillip Cottingham was sent over to Ireland to survey the woodlands in

Munster he reported that much of the finest timber had already been used for the manufacture of barrel staves but that farther west, in 'Desmond's country', there were still good woods to be found.[48] Simon Ashdon's employment as a wood carrier in Ballydehob perhaps provides the historical record for an ex-pirate's involvement in this industry.[49] Captain Richard Robinson similarly deposed that since arriving into Baltimore in 1609 and seeking a pardon, he was engaged in fishing and the making of pipestaves.[50] What the sources indicate is that large numbers of those men who were members of the pirate alliance and who operated along the Munster coastline also formed part of the settler community and were engaged in its developing industries.

ILLICIT BEDFELLOWS: PIRATE FAMILIES AND THEIR WORLDS

The families of the pirates receive passing mention within the sources. Many lived in the general southwest Munster area, though others based themselves farther afield in places such as Dublin. According to Roger Middleton, writing to the earl of Salisbury in August 1611, 'many of them [the pirates] have their wyves and children in these parts about Limcolme, where and among whom is thought to be store of money'.[51] Southwest Munster, Leamcon and Baltimore, in particular, became the location of choice for the familial homes of the pirates' kin and extended entourage. Captain Richard Robinson made provision for his family by leaving money with his brother in London to invest for his two children, with the interest sent to his wife to support her in Plymouth. In 1608 Robinson moved his wife and children to Ireland so he could see them more regularly, and they are recorded as living in Leamcon on William Hull's land.[52]

Very often the only way pirates could provide financially for their families was to leave monies with extended family members whom they would have occasion to meet, or with fellow crew, merchants or sailors whom they knew were returning to either England or Ireland. In 1607 pirate Captains John Ward and Anthony Johnson gave the master of the *Husband* £200 worth of Barbary gold to deliver to their wives on his return to England, and Johnson would send presents home to his wife, sister and mother on occasion.[53] Whether an actual mail system used by pirates and their families existed is not clear, though the piracy of the early eighteenth century certainly had one. On Ascension Island, for example, a well-organised mail system was in place, with a post office used by the families of the pirates of that time, including Captain Samuel Burgess, implying a sense of normality within the lives of those involved.[54]

The receipt of such monies and goods was in itself illegal, but mothers and wives particularly came to expect it. Indeed, local admiralty officers tended to turn a blind eye to it, perhaps because it ensured that women and children were provided for but perhaps also due to the fact that some of the officials were intimidated by the pirates' wives and mothers. One account tells of William Smith, marshal of the admiralty court in England, being accosted by several angry wives of pirates who had not received the expected monies sent ashore by their husbands, but which seems to have been retained or pocketed by Smith.[55] Admiralty officers would also charge expenses for engaging with pirate goods, with Richard Jobson arguing that he expended some of his own money in delivering recovered goods to England. These included thirty-two chests of sugar from a pirate captain named Parker, at a personal cost of £138, which seems an enormous amount and was no doubt inflated. Parker, noted as 'a yonge man not having any heare [hair] on his face and of a middle stature', served under Richard Bishop. Jobson kept forty 'loaves' of sugar from another ship, some of which he shared with his brother Humphrey and some with the vice-president of Munster, Richard Moryson. Jobson retained a certain amount for himself, contending it was to cover expenses generated through official duties.[56]

Jobson's transactions with pirate Captain William Thompson, mentioned previously, and his use of pirates in the process of negotiating pardons for each other is telling. Recorded as 'an old man' in 1610 with sources suggesting he had a long pirate career, records show that Thompson was active off the coast of Africa up to 1606, with his activity in Ireland dating from 1607, first under Richard Robinson and then as part of Suxbridge's fleet in 1608.[57] In 1609, after the capture of the two French ships, both Robinson and Suxbridge returned to Ireland. Among their crew was Henry Duffield, who when examined in 1610 in Youghal specifically mentioned Thompson:

> Captn: Tompson, John Pharoe [Farrow] Captn: 'Gennyngs' [Jennings] – to whome Robinson gave the French ship, was brought into Baltimore whereof Gennyngs made [it] a man of warre.

Duffield specifically recounts that Thompson was 'on account of piracy with Suxbridge' and came into Leamcon with the second French ship, the *Brave* of Dieppe, mentioned earlier, and made it his man-of-war.[58] In Thompson's crew too was Philip Harvey, a Plymouth mariner and known pirate, and on completing another voyage together, both returned to Munster: 'he [Thompson] returned to Lymecon with a reasonable good stoare of money, where he hath remained ever since'.[59] Duffield's examinations, and those of his cohort John Pharoe, as listed, both state that they too remained in Leamcon from that time, with Pharoe involved in fishing.[60] Whether these men had any family with them is not recorded.

Thompson was induced by Richard Jobson to hand over the *Brave* to its French owners in lieu of a pardon. Jobson had issued a protection to Thompson and his family who were with him in Leamcon and this had been endorsed by Henry Danvers, lord president of Munster. Jobson again used Thompson as a go-between with the pirates, utilising his experience as a long-term insider. On the face of it, Thompson was prepared to acquiesce, and in his several examinations he provides specific details on ships, crew, provisioning of vessels and details on those active ashore. At Leamcon, for example, Thompson states:

> … one Nathanaell a butcher killed beefes at Captaine Hulls house at Lyme Com and sold 7 or 8 beeves to Captaine Bishoppe and Captaine Parker pirates but whether they were Hulls beefe or the said Nathanaells ownes he cannot saith.

Thompson also mentions that one 'Waye a minister dwelling in Lyme Com did willingly victualle and entertaine all manner of pirates that came in there'.[61] From his examinations it is clear that Thompson was more willing than many of his cohorts to provide details, suggesting that he was confident of Jobson's offer of security. In 1609 Jobson retained a ring with seven small diamonds, which Thompson specified was in return for the vice-admiral's 'promise to give this examinate [Thompson] release from prison'.[62] However, the promise proved hollow when Jobson's successor, Izon Kempe, raided Thompson's house in Leamcon in March 1610. Kempe 'took awaie three barres of golde being some seven or eight ounces'. Sir William St John arrested and transported Thompson to Newgate Prison in London, though the pirate's wife had given St John 'a ring of pearls greater and better than that which Richard Jobson had', on the understanding that it was to secure her husband's release. Sir William St John was not to be trusted, however, and rather than making representations on behalf of Thompson, he allowed the old pirate to be sent for trial; Thompson was sentenced to death in

October 1610 and hanged on the foreshore at Wapping's Execution Dock soon after.[63] Many of Thompson's fellow pirates were watching closely how he was treated, and his betrayal and execution led many of them to think twice about accepting the word of admiralty officials in Ireland. Pirate Captains Easton, Francke and others chose instead to look elsewhere to assure their future.[64] The handling of Thompson illustrates the workings of the admiralty and those in power; even with promises made by those whom the pirates thought were steadfast, such words could well prove worthless when multiple players became involved.

PLACES OF LEISURE

One of the most famous pirate-associated taverns must surely be the Admiral Benbow. Robert Louis Stevenson's description, in the opening pages of his classic pirate tale *Treasure Island*, when ex-pirate Old Billy Bones first enters and orders a bottle of rum, is gripping. Old Bill launched into the song 'Fifteen Men on the Dead Man's Chest – Yo-ho-ho and a Bottle of Rum' which has since been adopted as the traditional pirates' anthem.[65] 'Dead man's chest' certainly conjures up an image of buried treasure and trunks full of booty. Stevenson was referring to Dead Chest Island, however, also called Dead Man's Chest Island, near Deadman's Bay in the British Virgin Islands, which was uninhabited and lacked water or any other resources. Now part of a national park, marooning on the inaccessible and inhospitable island would have guaranteed death. When Old Bill begins to sing, with tankard in hand, the archetypal image of the rum-swilling old seadog comes to mind. So too does the sense that the Admiral Benbow itself afforded sanctuary to pirates, providing shelter, seclusion, entertainment and a place to conduct inconspicuous business. This was, perhaps, the critical constituent in the development of inns and taverns as liminal places that attracted and accepted a diverse social clientele. These hostelries were conducive to government officials and pirate alike, they could double as domestic domiciles, and were often the focus for more furtive undertakings run by the women in the pirates' world.

Peter Pope, in his study of the cultural significance of alcohol and tobacco to the settlers in Newfoundland in the early seventeenth century, suggests that both commodities served as 'little hearths'. They provided warmth and comfort to wayward sailors and maritime travellers, including pirates, at a time when recreational behaviour was moving outside the home to centralised locations such as tippling houses and taverns.[66] These gathering spaces formed a key component of the localised market place, where both native and newcomer were welcome. They were the focus for the diffusion of English tastes within the plantation environment, and the exchange of 'civilised' ideas allowed for like-minded or at least fellow countrymen to gather. Those in accord also saw the opportunity to profit from alcohol, and in 1617 Sir Ralph Bingley and Sir William St John formed a partnership to acquire the patent for the registering or licensing of Irish alehouses for twenty-one years, at a crown rent of £500. It had the backing of Sir Edward Villiers, the duke of Buckingham, with Sir Thomas Roper becoming the major partner in the enterprise.[67]

Alehouses became homes away from home within the plantation landscape, and Prof. Audrey Horning in her study of the cultural role of the alehouse in the Ulster plantation noted: 'The role of alcohol in lubricating cross-cultural interactions, while also exacerbating colonial conflicts, deserves further consideration.'[68] Certainly, there may have been places where drink was served prior to New English settlement and the heyday of piracy along the southwest coast of Munster, but the frequenting of such establishments by the Gaelic-Irish or Old English would not have been commonplace. The native tradition of hosting and feasting did include drinking, but primarily of wine and locally made beverages such as mead and 'uisce beatha' (meaning 'water of life', it was a barley-based whiskey), and was predominantly done in the secure environs of their own seats of power, providing the opportunity to display wealth while at the same time entertain invited guests.[69] The growth in alehouses and taverns in a sense 'professionalised the role of hospitality' and brought individuals outside the confines of their own home to drink, engage and be entertained.[70] This in turn allowed all strata of society to gather, intermingle and share news, discuss common ideas and deliberate on mutual business interests, including overseas ventures, while expanding the local knowledge base.

Contemporary sources record that these 'tippling houses' were often thought of as dens of iniquity with, as Treadwell describes, unregulated alehouses considered nurseries of sedition.[71] There was no regulation of drinking places in Ireland in that early period, and no doubt síbíns and illegal drinking houses existed all along the coast, wherever the demand dictated. The lack of official control did not change until about 1620 with the introduction of the alehouse patents, which regulated the establishment and running of taverns, inns and alehouses in general. In 1612 an effort was made to regulate the consumption of alcohol and the establishment of alehouses with the attempted introduction by Sir John Davies of the 'Act for the erecting of common inns and suppressing the multitude of alehouses'. This proved to be ineffective, however, due to the difficulty in enforcement, particularly in remote areas and because many establishments were set up in private dwellings and thus extremely difficult to identify.[72] The setting up of alehouse patents did raise extra capital through the imposition of licence fees, but it was also an attempt to prevent the gathering of individuals who were involved in dubious ventures and who could, under the cover of such places, conduct their business in relative secrecy and safety.

Captain Skipwith's report of 1611 again confirms the attraction that alehouses and taverns held for the pirate community. The pirates, he wrote

> ... may be enterteyned and kept in those alehouses three moneths or more without payment for anything they take, every pyrate having his factor there for whom hee provideth men and other necessaries against their arrival, and there receveth payment largely for his paynes, soe that it is a perpetuall market for that trafficque.[73]

This centrality of purpose not only facilitated the pirates when onshore but also supported ancillary businesses, most particularly that of boarding house, brothel, or both. In many places, these establishments provided asylum for travellers, among them merchants, sailors and pirates, who enjoyed a degree of safety while they rested, recuperated, enjoyed themselves, carried out business or, like Billy Bones, avoided those they did not want to meet. In turn, the pirates brought welcome income into the small villages and towns along the coast. For others, particularly local women or the wives, children or relatives of the pirates, it ensured that they could make a living when their men were at sea. The 1613 deposition of pirate Edmond Flinte, a real-life pirate who once more brings to mind yet another character from *Treasure Island*, gives an account of meeting a fellow pirate, Henry Orenge, when in a boarding house in Dublin.[74] Flinte admits to knowing Orenge for over twelve months, with Orenge serving as master on board the *Cat*, the vice-admiral in William Baugh's fleet.[75] An earlier account places Orenge in Leamcon around 1610, which means he was an active member of the pirate alliance for a number of years.[76]

The place where Flinte stayed was 'the house of Mistress Suxbitche of Dublin', wife of pirate Captain Tibalt Suxbridge. When indicted in 1613,

FIGURE 44: Red garnets or 'carbuncles' cut 'en cabochon', from India; they have been given a date range of AD 1501–1625 and form part of the Cheapside Hoard collection.

Orenge was listed as a mariner from Plymouth but to have come from Ratcliffe. It is curious that Tibault Suxbridge was also a Ratcliffe man, and perhaps this is where the link between the two began. Orenge, upon arrival at Mrs Suxbridge's house, referred to her as 'sister', suggesting that Orenge and Tibault Suxbridge were related through marriage. Both Edward Flinte and Henry Orenge lodged at the house for about a week. Orenge had gone to Dublin to sell jewels stolen from Baugh's ship in Kinsale. Baugh had captured Orenge and subjected him to torture, including pulling out his nails, in an attempt to induce him to reveal where the jewels were hidden, but Orenge managed to escape.[77] According to Flinte, Orenge told Mrs Suxbridge and her two daughters that he also had diamonds and a 'carbuncle of great prise' hidden within 'the pletes of his hose'. He offered Flinte a jewel worth £100 as an enticement to accompany him to England to sell the others. Both men went to West Chester where Orenge was able to sell one of his precious stones to a goldsmith for £90, but he never paid Flinte what was agreed, and Flinte admitted later that Orenge 'had given him the slipp'. Orenge's heist comprised 611 jewels that included rubies, sapphires, topaz, emeralds, two ounces of marguerite and a number of large carbuncles (garnets) (see Epilogue for a discussion on the Cheapside Hoard from the period).[78]

FIGURE 45: Time piece made from a single cut Colombian emerald crystal, with hinged lid and gold clasp. Time plate is enamelled in green with circular gold suspension loop and button. Part of the Cheapside Hoard and dated to AD 1576–1600. © IMAGE ID: 64941, THE MUSEUM OF LONDON COLLECTION

FIGURE 46:
Wall plaque on Green Street, Dingle showing a wyvern clutching a bird in its claw, with another bird overhead. While anecdotal evidence suggests this has associations with prostitution (as Green Street was the focus of such trade in the sixteenth and seventeenth centuries), the features on the plaque may also indicate Islamic links.
IMAGE: CONNIE KELLEHER

PLACES OF PLEASURE

The diversity and value of just some of Captain William Baugh's cargo and the wealth that could be generated from piracy is again indicated in Flinte's testimony. It also provides written evidence for safe houses run by members of the pirates' families, in this case in Dublin. These also functioned as clearing houses and places where pirates could stay while planning onward journeys, making connections and setting up deals to sell their booty. Other safe houses must surely have existed elsewhere in Ireland; in October 1612 Lord Deputy Chichester, writing to the Privy Council, refers to 'the other Guest houses upon the shore, which are commonly full of Idle Men, which always attend their [the pirates] commings and to run their fortunes'.[79] This wider network of connections both locally and nationally, with potential familial links, presents a picture of the pirate alliance that is seldom shown in the literary sources. Whether established in Dublin or not before the loss of her husband, certainly following the pirate captain's death in 1612 Mrs Suxbridge would have needed to find a way of surviving. From the obvious familiarity between her and the pirates lodging with her, and her sibling links with Henry Orenge, it is reasonable to infer that her boarding house was well established before 1613 when Edmund Flinte was examined. Her daughters' presence also suggests that this was, in fact, the family home or a family-run business, or both. Boarding houses like these frequently fronted as brothels, with Henry Mainwaring describing the scene in Munster as having 'Good store of English, Scottish and Irish wenches which resort unto them, and these are strong attractors to draw the common sort of them hither'.[80]

The presence of sex workers in the harbours of southwest Munster is borne out by a report given to the admiralty in 1609 by a pirate called Gibbs of Salcombe, active in Baltimore, who loaded his ship and set sail. He carried with him 'two of the pyrates and some of their whores, about five in number'.[81] Still another account from December 1615 tells of pirate Nicholas Tompson [Thompson] of Ratcliffe, 'beinge a short man with a little blacke bearde' who was 'very ill of burneinge by whoores and [the] surgeon did dress him'.[82] Though pointing to a deliberate act of burning as perhaps a consequence of Thompson maltreating the women, non-payment for services rendered or other infringement of business rules, it may also infer that the 'burneinge' is that of a sexually transferred disease like syphilis, rife at the time in most harbours and port towns. Archaeological evidence connecting sexually transmitted diseases and the life of a pirate can be gleaned from the remains of pirate Blackbeard's ship the *Queen Anne's Revenge*, lost in 1718 in Beaufort Inlet, North Carolina. Among the thousands of artefacts recovered from the wreck was a urethral syringe used by the surgeon on board to treat syphilis. Chemical analysis revealed that it contained mercury, commonly used to treat the disease, with some positive effect. Perhaps the lesser of two evils, as the adverse side-effects of this liquid element to those who administered or received it were not yet known at the time.[83]

Violence was commonplace, particularly among men who, upon reaching shore after many months at sea, were eager to indulge themselves in places of leisure and pleasure. Excess and the freedom of being back on land frequently led to riotous and aggressive engagement between the pirates themselves or those living and working onshore. Captain John Smith, writing in 1609, observed the pirates' behaviour:

> Many times, they had very good ships, and well manned, but commonly in such factions amongst themselves, and so riotous, quarrelous, treacherous, blasphemous and villanous, it is more than a wonder they could so long continue to doe so much mischieve; and all they got, they basely consumed it amongst Jewes, Turkes, Moores and whores.[84]

Some captains lost men as a consequence of inebriation, Captain Gilbert Roope among them, whose crew ran away when the captain was drunk 'on top of a hill'. Others appear to have engaged in curious activity, with an account of pirates active on the River Thames revealing that when fighting, they '… usuallie hitte one an other in the teeth with theire whoores …'.[85] Whatever this obscure behaviour is actually referring to, it seems to have been primarily confined to shore, with little evidence for any major incidents when at sea, though there are the exceptions. John Nutt, the pirate captain who was active later in the 1620s, captured a bark near Dungarvan Harbour, west of Waterford in Ireland, which was carrying among its passengers some fourteen women. According to Hugh Baker, a sailor of Youghal, examined in May 1623 by Sir Lawrence Parsons, all the women '… were ravished by the pyrates company' and Nutt himself kept a Mrs Jones, wife of a saddler in Cork, in his cabin '… and there had her a week'.[86] Though the account is shocking, such incidences were rare, and generally pirate crews agreed that such behaviour was prohibited on board their ships.

Though not common practice, at times women did accompany pirate captains on board ship, as seen in the example above with Gibbs and discussed by Appleby in his study of *Women and English Piracy*, but it was generally looked upon as bad luck.[87] In 1609, Captain John Jennings, when at Baltimore, persuaded an Irish woman to join him on board during a plundering venture. The loss of up to eleven members of crew during an engagement with a Spanish ship and a narrow escape from one of the king's ships provoked the remaining angry crew to blame the captain for having a women on board; they proclaimed that the ship was '… so out of order, it was a just judgement from God against them, in suffering their Captaine to bring his whore aboard … to wallow in his luxurie'. It was Jennings' fellow captain, Gilbert Roope, who raised the mutiny. Roope declared '… success in their condition was never found, when a woman was more Master of the Captaine, then the Captaine of his men …'. Roope and the crew broke into Jennings' cabin and found him in the embrace of the Irish woman. He was imprisoned in the gun room, and Roope replaced him as captain. The detail of the case is contained in the record of Jennings' trial and execution, along with nineteen other pirates. There is no more mention in the records of the woman. It can be inferred that she was a sex worker, but no further information is provided on the individual – what her name was, how old she was or where she came from; she is simply credited with being the harbinger of bad luck. Neither is her fate known, if she survived the voyage or was 'lost' at sea.[88]

The nature and extent of the alehouse, boarding house or sex trade in the remote parts of southwest Munster may be impossible to gauge. The input of women into the lives and businesses of the pirates during that early period, who they were and what happened to them thereafter must, for the most part, rely on speculation.[89] An example can be drawn from thespian pirate Captain Lording Barry when he brought his ship into Berehaven in August 1615. Among the many 'goods' surrendered to Humphrey Jobson was 'a negro wenche', most probably a slave.[90] From what is known of Barry, at times referred to as Ludowick Barry, he had a colourful piratical career intertwined with his penchant for literary creation. It is because of his writing that we know quite a bit about him. He was a gentleman of London, around thirty years of age in 1616; he sailed with many of the leading pirates of the time, including Richard Bishop and his close colleague Captain James Harris. He was captured as part of Harris' crew in Baltimore in 1609 but was subsequently released. He focused much of his attention on Mediterranean waters, working out of Leghorn, allied with the duke of Tuscany. In 1614 he was lieutenant to pirate James Duppa, whose interest in expeditions to the Amazon were attractive to Barry, who was also keen to invest in ventures overseas.[91]

An informed biography of Barry indicates that he was an educated man, who had received bachelor's and master's degrees from Cambridge. He invested heavily in developing a boys' theatre company in the Whitefriars district of London and wrote several plays, with perhaps the most famous being *Ram-Alley: or Merrie-Trickes. A Comedy Divers Times Here-to-fore Acted by the Children of the Kings Revels*, written in 1607–8 and printed in 1611. Running out of money in 1608 coincided with King James shutting down the London theatres (due to the bubonic plague), and it was this that forced Barry to turn to piracy. His pirating career continued until 1615, when, following a spell in the debtors marshalsea in London, he sailed with Sir Walter Raleigh on an unsuccessful gold-mining venture to Guiana. A will left after his death in 1629 contains no mention of any wife or family.[92]

What his relationship was with the 'negro wenche' he put ashore in Berehaven or what happened to her thereafter remains a mystery. A story steeped in local lore, and that may have evolved from tales of such women carried on board pirate ships, concerns Leamcon House. It recounts, bleakly, an interment within the walls of the house of a female black slave. Who she was or why such an act would have taken place remains unknown, or if indeed there is any truth to the tale. It is not clear if this relates to William Hull's fortified house, when the event may be linked to the time of Barry and the pirate alliance, or if it is associated with the later eighteenth-century house now standing and when the trade in slaves was at its height. Curiously, when part of the existing house – which is a later Georgian successor to the original Hull house, though with original fabric within the later structure – was renovated in the 1950s, human skeletal remains were discovered within the space between the roof and wall. Nothing further is known unfortunately of this discovery or what happened to the remains, whether male or female, and no subsequent archaeological evidence has been found to substantiate the story.[93] Folk tradition also recounts that pirates frequently killed and buried the bodies of slaves where they also buried their treasure, so that the ghost of the slave watched over the booty thereafter. No doubt a tale to act as a deterrent to those who would seek out the buried loot.

Frequently, it was women who became alehouse- and tavern-keepers, and apart from providing sustenance and lodgings, the mistress of the house could also provide loan or pawnbroker services. John Appleby notes that these places became the 'focus of a subculture of crime based on prostitution, theft or receiving stolen goods', and indeed contemporary 'civilised' attitudes to drinking establishments and consumption practices, albeit within an urban setting and underscored by puritanical perspectives, present a picture of these places, and those within them, as dens of iniquity. Preceding the established associations that sought to address loose moral standards and indecent occupations, such as the Society for the Reformation of Manners, established in 1691, certain strata within society were frowned upon as coteries of uncivilised behaviour, and commentators at the time did not restrain themselves in their descriptive pronouncements.[94] Barnaby Rich's proclamations on the multitude of taverns in Dublin in 1610, for example, included: '... it is a rare thing to find a street in Dublin without a tavern, as it is to find a tavern without a strumpet'. And he described the women running the places variously as 'alewives ... the most filthy Queens in the country ... filthy and beastly alehouse keepers ... idle housewives that are very loathsome, filthy and abominable, both in life and manners ... some of them known Harlots'.[95] Such commentary is subjectively tainted, but tavern and alehouses were, in reality, places for individuals from all strata of society to gather, where men and women were present, though generally with specific gender briefs and sexual division of labour.

Women did play a central part in the business of piracy, particularly in assisting with the disposal of goods. Of seventeen individuals examined for aiding and abetting pirates in England, seven were women, including Catherine Shepherd, *alias* Sutton, Dorothy Cooper and Joan Parks, all of whom were indicted in 1619. In 1634, for piracy on a ship named the

Fortune, Jane Francis, Joan Harris, Elizabeth Patrickson and Mary Persival were indicted but later acquitted.[96] The listing of the names of the women provides a tangible link to piracy, giving them a semblance of individuality within the sources. Others, such as the wife of Thomas Barloe, are mentioned in an examination taken in 1609 in connection with a ship carrying beer brought into Baltimore by a Rob Gybbs of Plymouth, possibly the same Gybbs [Gibbs] mentioned above. The beer was offloaded but the vessel continued to Leamcon, where Gybbs and Barloe's wife sold it. It is not clear if Mrs Barloe was at Leamcon and took part in the sale or if she was onboard the vessel itself. What is suggested is that she had direct input into the transactions that took place.[97]

A short but important entry in the examinations of two pirates, held within the Cottonian Manuscripts Collection in the British Library and signed off by Henry Howard, the earl of Northampton, provides an important glimpse into the activities of the women in Baltimore and Leamcon who are directly linked with the pirates of the alliance. The document has been damaged by fire, with the date also missing, but from the pirates mentioned a date range of 1611–12 can be posited.[98] The word 'Women' is clearly written and stands out among the more cursive script; the 'trade' of the women is referred to, as are suggestions on how to curb their activity. The examinate states that of all those who visited the pirate ships in Baltimore, for the most part it was women, and of them, some had 'no husbands' but were friends and others were the wives of the pirates. The women are said to have been involved in the trade of fishing but that they also awaited returning ships, where they found work 'prostituting their own Bodies'. The examinate closes by stating that it was impossible to patrol the area '… because these parts of Baltimore are the continuall resort of Pyrates'. He suggests that first there was a need to drive away '… all corrupt Inhabitants that live upon the trade …' of prostitution and secondly that '… a couple of shippes well manned together by night in Baltimore and Lymecon …' would secure the harbours and force the pirates to be accountable for their activities.[99]

It provides an image of a community of working single or married women onshore in both Baltimore and Leamcon who were engaged in several trades, including that of the sex industry, and who mingled with the pirates on land and on their ships in a mutual meeting of minds, and bodies, for familial reasons, for business or for pleasure. The caveat must be entered that this is just one brief view into the activity of women in Baltimore and Leamcon, detailed by an individual whose motives are not fully known but who, and as discussed in more detail in the next chapter, may well have been influenced by Northampton's own vested interests.[100] It is a provocative glimpse nonetheless, but one where extrapolation is obvious and presumption part of the story. The identification within the examination of the importance of driving away those women, to break the symbiotic flow of business and community, is clear, and in the separation of one there was the perception of an initiated decline in the other.

This approach was not unique to the pirate activity in Munster. In studies of littoral communities elsewhere, including the emerging fishing settlements of Newfoundland, it was remarked: '... soe long as there comes noe women they [the men] are not fixed'. The presence of women brought with it a perception of permanence and establishment, the gender-biased view of 'home builders' and 'temptress' and the concept that a woman could become 'Skipper of the Shore crew'. While women tended to be subordinate to men, their ability to keep order onshore and in some cases to be the ones controlling elements of business there, such as the handling of fish on the quaysides, the running of households or the management of business, as in the case of Mrs Suxbridge, should not be underestimated.[101] While there was a clear division of labour and perceived gender polarity, including sexual divisions, the centrality of women to both the business of piracy and its social workings in Munster at the time deserves far wider consideration.

THE CULTURAL FOOTPRINT OF INVISIBLE THINGS

The location of most of the alehouses, taverns or brothels within the named villages, towns and rural places of Munster may never be identified without archaeological investigation, and even then, as in contemporary times, they may not be readily recognisable. Certainly there was at least one tavern, if not more, within the towns or suburbs, as denoted by Chichester's letter and from the mention of alehouses at Bandonbridge in a proclamation of 1610; in 1612 strict rules were laid down in Coleraine as part of the plantation policy in Ulster that allowed only three taverns and no more than ten alehouses to be established.[102] It is difficult to identify their locations and particularly so in a rural setting outside official plantation areas, though contemporary sources suggest their presence.[103]

It is possible to gain a better understanding of these places of consumption from comparative evidence elsewhere.[104] From investigations carried out in the 1950s, the remains of brewhouses excavated in Jamestown, Virginia, revealed that they were rectangular structures with brick foundation but were wooden-framed buildings, in keeping with colonial building specifications.[105] Extensive ceramic assemblages from a deep pit excavated at Narrow Quay in Bristol in the late 1970s provided evidence for distilling and alcohol use along the Bristol quaysides in the seventeenth century.[106] Evidence for the location of such structures, which were directly associated with the development of the plantation settlements in Ireland, can be gleaned from some plantation maps. Thomas Raven's map of Newtown Limavady shows Thomas Phillips' two-storey inn with associated signage. Unfortunately no such depictions have been found on settlement maps for southwest Munster.[107]

Pottery assemblages are also informative on activities that were taking place in an area at the time, both utilitarian and commercial. It is plausible to suggest at this point, from documentary evidence of cargoes arriving on pirate ships, that there was a thriving domestic scene, including no doubt a drinking place in Leamcon on William Hull's estate, supported by his brewing pursuits, and certainly in Baltimore within the more formal settlement. Archaeological investigations of other coastal sites in west Cork have recovered evidence of transatlantic maritime trade through artefactual assemblages, particularly pottery. Investigations at the castle sites of Dún na Séad and Kilcoe and at Sherkin friary have identified diverse domestic and continental wares denoting extensive maritime trade across the Atlantic from medieval times onwards, but with the sixteenth and seventeenth centuries particularly represented. Pottery from Sherkin Franciscan friary includes examples from Spain, Portugal, France, Holland, Germany, Italy, England, Ireland and China; of the Iberian assemblages, a rich regional typological diversity is represented, with significant quantities of nine different types of wares.[108]

Comparative evidence, though from an urban setting, can be considered from the seventeenth-century maritime site in Limehouse, London, at a time when that part of the port of London was emerging as a mercantile centre and was closely connected with piracy and privately operated vessels. Pottery, glass and other material found in ditches, wells and cess pits originated from Holland, France, Germany, Spain, Italy, Portugal, Turkey and as far away as Iran and China. It is argued that the finds represent the remains of booty from trade and plunder and that 'the discoveries offer a unique opportunity to view a seventeenth-century community of intimately interacting seafaring families from the perspective of their land-based material culture and the remains of their homes'. The finds from Limehouse and the discussion around their variety and origin, particularly the pottery, indicates the nature

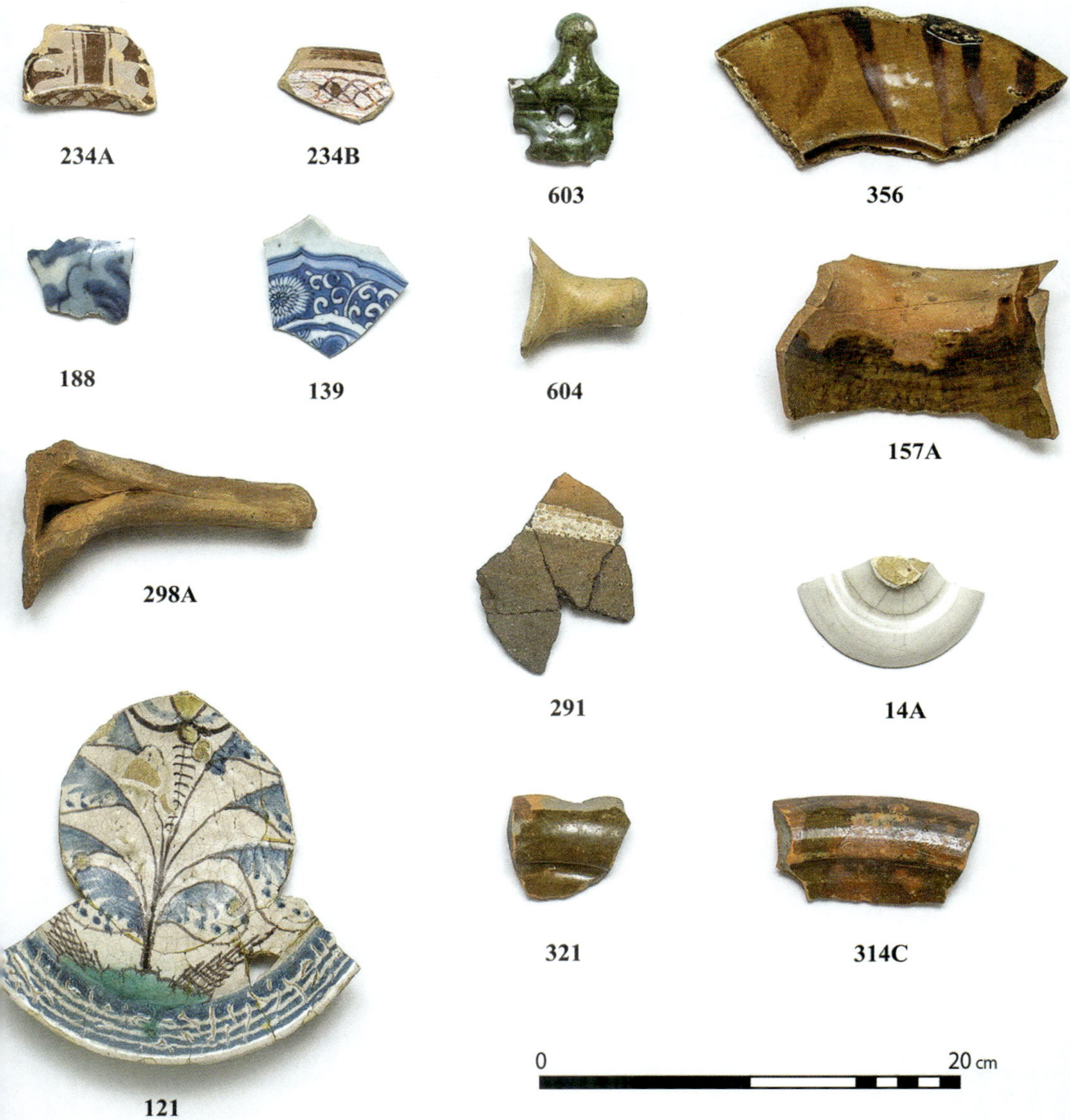

FIGURE 47: Selection of pottery recovered during archaeological excavations at Sherkin Franciscan friary and indicative of transatlantic trade, with the Iberian examples showing rich regional diversity.

and extent of trade, travel and maritime movements of the community there at the time, and where piracy and prostitution played a part. [109]

Identifying the archaeological evidence for prostitution in remote areas such as the coastal harbour towns and villages of Munster is more challenging, however. No such study has been carried out from a historical perspective for the seventeenth century in Ireland and certainly an archaeological one has not been attempted to date. Docks, ports and harbours have always been places of activity for the sex industry across the world, servicing the transient maritime trade, but the activity itself can leave practically no distinguishing cultural evidence. Sadly, sex workers were often invisible when alive and in death they remain so.[110] Contemporary sources certainly confirm sex work was an integral part of social life at the time in ports and harbours. In 1610 Vice-President Edward Harris highlighted the link between pirates, prostitutes and drinking establishments:

> Whereas the kinges most excellent Maiestie having ben enformed of the contynuall relief that Pyratts haue received from tyme to tyme in the western partes of this Province as Baltimore, Inisherkin, and Divers other partes thereabouts aswell by the contynuall supplyes of such Desperat and Dishonest men as resorted thither to Joyne and Combyne themselues with the said Pyrates, as also of such shameless and adulterous women, as Daylie repair vnto them, and especially by the meanes of Divers Taverns, Alehowses and victualling howses, that haue frome tyme to tyme basely and mercenarily intertained both theis kyndes of people ….[111]

Associated relationships and collaboration among coastal communities challenged the political order of the day, undermined the commercial viability of legitimate maritime enterprise across the Atlantic and questioned the perceived 'civilised' social standing of plantation policy. It was no wonder then that central government in England, headed by King James and pressurised by commercial and political interests across Europe, was forced to consider more conciliatory ways to tackle the problem of piracy in Munster. Measures, therefore, were put in place in an effort to suppress a regime, one that accepted and embraced sub-cultural, 'uncivilised' behaviour, but had proven to be too resistant and too corrupt to eradicate. By 1611 the pirate alliance, through its operations across the North Atlantic and farther afield, had built its own virtual maritime empire that necessitated negotiated engagement by the English crown rather than aggression for suppression's sake.

CHAPTER 7

The Beginning of the End: Suppression, commission and execution

I will die a poor labourer in mine own country, if I may, rather than be the richest pirate in the world.[1]

The capture and loss of the *Concord*, as discussed in Chapter 2, forced the Privy Council to write to the lord deputy in Ireland in 1612 and concede, that due to the strength of the Alliance of Pirates in Munster, with '… so formidable and so wicked a course of piracy, with such power of men and means …', the king

> … consented to forego the strict course of justice, and to exercise his clemency, their Lordships signify their approval of his [Chichester] proceeding … [in] negotiation ….[2]

Thus began official dialogues between the pirates and the crown. It was some years earlier, however, from about 1609 that many of the pirate leaders began considering their status. Most by then had successful careers, and with families settled in the southwest and commercial opportunities opening up in the New World, pirates like Richard Bishop and many of his colleagues sought to regain their legitimate lives through the mechanism of reprieve. The colony at Jamestown in Virginia had been established by 1607, and in 1609 John Guy was in the process of setting up the colony in Cuper's Cove, Newfoundland. Colonial ventures like these therefore provided prospects for lawful engagement in maritime commerce and overseas exploitation, and the men in the pirate alliance could consider a return to their respected lives as mariners. The pirates were not the only parties seeking conciliation measures, and both government and admiralty officials similarly sought remediation. It was the assembly of pirates in Munster by that time, with such strength in numbers but also so economically essential to the area, that primarily motivated the crown to look to other ways to suppress their 'illicit' operations, but in a way that did not force them to abandon the region entirely.[3]

Coinciding with the Stuart signal to initiate talks with the pirates, the king correspondingly conceded in 1612 that the States-General in Holland could send a Dutch fleet into the coastal waters of Ireland, to intercept and essentially interrupt the pirates and their activities there. It was a controversial move and one that had a devastating and direct impact on the alliance two years later when the Dutch attacked Crookhaven in 1614. The attack, discussed in detail below, shocked central government in its intensity and callous disregard not just for the terms of the commission agreed but for life itself, attacking pirates, townsfolk and government officials. The Dutch attack coincided with the Act for the Suppression of Pirates in 1613, and its coming into force in 1614, as well as the fall of Mamora in 1614 to the Spanish. This marked a turning point for the alliance.[4] Their Atlantic theatre of operations was forced to change, and vulnerabilities developed when hunting grounds were constricted; the fact that the king allowed ships of a competing nation to enter the harbours of Ireland was a reckoning indeed, and with the enactment of new legislation that allowed for trial and execution on Irish soil, the mindset of many men began to waver and change.

PRESSURE FROM WITHIN AND WITHOUT

King James devised a two-pronged approach to tackling the piracy at that time: directly by force and through negotiation and engagement. Commanding his royal ships to intercept pirate vessels proved ineffectual, primarily because of the prolonged neglect of the navy along with continued collusion between the pirates and serving officials. While the sanctioning of Dutch ships to enter Irish waters was controversial, a more conciliatory approach involved the issuing of pardons to those pirates who agreed to submit. This tactic tallied with government policy and the customary procedure to issue general pardons to criminals at the end of a parliament. In 1610 a general pardon was issued from which many of the pirates in Ireland benefited.[5] Pirates like Richard Bishop and his colleagues may, at that point, have seized the opportunity to look for a pardon though most did not receive their pardons until after 1612, but the process may well have begun with the close of parliament in 1610. Another critical impetus for consideration of acceptance of pardons may have been the elevation of small towns and villages, primarily in the plantation areas of Ulster and Munster, to borough status in 1613. Baltimore and Bandon, for example, were made royal boroughs in that year. The principal reason for this was to achieve a Protestant majority in the Irish parliament, ensuring two individuals from each new borough could attend and could therefore vote for the nine pieces of suggested legislation then going through parliament.[6] One of the laws put forward for debate was the Law to Suppress Piracy.[7] While the ultimate political aim of elevating such places to royal borough status was to achieve the majority in parliament, it also enabled greater control of smaller but strategically placed market towns and harbours by forcing local government officials to become answerable directly to parliament; they were thus under greater scrutiny from central government than had hitherto been the case in remote areas such as west Munster.

Each method had its own diplomatic, political and economic impact, but it was primarily through negotiations, submissions and the issuing of pardons that the alliance itself was eventually dispersed and disbanded.[8] These measures were not founded on central government political intent, however, but rather through a combination of pressure from international representations at court and changes in global economic markets. The Dutch in 1612 had forged official trade agreements with the Ottomans in the Levant, for example, and thus needed to eradicate the pirate predation in the Atlantic to ensure unimpeded access to the waters between Ireland and the Mediterranean.[9] Changes in the composition of pirate crews from 1614, when the North African corsairs began to dominate, may have been another element in making Ireland's pirate scourge, by then, unsustainable.[10]

The weakened state of the king's ships at that point meant outright attack on the pirate bases in Ireland was not a viable option. In 1610 the lord deputy clearly highlighted the need to consider alternative action to address the power of the pirates:

> Upon consideration had of the pyratts … and of the harmes they may do being made desperate and so well furnished and provided, and having here no shipping to curbb or restrayne their access and attempts, the *Lyon's Whelp* being too weake to grapple with them ….[11]

Attempts were therefore made to reach a 'middle course' as a way to curb the impact of the pirates on shipping, trade and local affairs. Henry Danvers, the lord president of Munster, noted that it was unlikely that the pirates could be subdued or 'expulsed' from the area due to the expense that the king's ships would incur, which by necessity had to return to England to be repaired and restocked. This frequently meant the detention of the king's ships for lengthy periods in England's royal dockyards. He put it to the English Privy Council that they should consider pardoning the pirates who showed a willingness to renounce their unlawful ways and submit to the crown.[12]

The lack of naval power was noted as early as 1607 when the Venetian ambassador to England, Nicolo Molin, sent a report home declaring that the full fleet then comprised only about thirty-seven ships, many of them old and rotten and barely fit for service.[13] His concern was that if the king's navy could not keep control of the waters of the North Atlantic and ensure safety for ships from predatory attacks, the Dutch would take control: 'for the Dutch will become masters of these seas, as they keep as a rule upwards of 100 armed ships in commission'.[14] Piracy and its impact on international shipping and political affairs had become a major embarrassment for the king both nationally and internationally. At a time of colonial expansion on a global scale, with the seafaring nations vying for supremacy of the oceans and with Spain ever anxious to ensure that the Dutch were not gaining a nautical hold, representations to James from the courts of Spain as well as on behalf of Spanish and Venetian merchants grew exponentially. The king was conflicted, however, as many of the pirates continued to target England's traditional enemy, Spain, and therefore served the purpose of controlling Iberia's commercial influence.

Not all of the members of the alliance were so inclined. When James outlawed privately operated ships from 1603, many men who subsequently found themselves active in the alliance chose instead to take letters of marque from the Dutch and operate under their flag. Indeed many of the Atlantic pirate leaders began their careers as privately commissioned mariners under Dutch letters of marque, including Richard Bishop in 1604 in the Mediterranean in his ship the *Blessing*. Peter Easton served under a Dutchman, Captain Isaac, in 1607 and John Jennings, who lived in Flushing with his family in 1603, operated a Dutch ship called the *Pied Lion*.[15] Some of the actions of the alliance could be an advantage to English maritime control and expansion, but it was clear the king could not rely on them.

GOVERNING THE PIRATE PROBLEM

The English exchequer at this time was nearing bankruptcy, which meant that James was unable to put money into augmenting his ships even if he had the will to do so. This was compounded by an ongoing investigation into corruption and malpractice in the admiralty, surrounding, among others, the earl of Nottingham, who continued, even in advancing years, to treat the navy as his own private domain to be used to maintain personal income obtainable through the ports of England and Ireland.[16] Examinations of pirates taken at the time highlighted the ineptitude of Nottingham in controlling his deputies and naval captains in their handling of the piracy dilemma. Examinations were used as a means to gain intelligence on the pirate operations and were a vehicle for justifying the pardoning of some of the pirates who were willing to relinquish their errant ways; they were also useful to rival naval commission members when attempting to oust fellow colleagues. In 1608 the king ordered a commission into 'abuses and discords' in the navy. It was first headed by Nottingham, but he was superseded some months later by another commission under the direction of the earl of Northampton, who had a persistent hatred of his cousin, the earl of Nottingham, and seized any opportunity to undermine the lord high admiral. Northampton may have harboured a personal hope of becoming lord treasurer and was determined to find proof of corruption in the navy at all levels, including that of his cousin, his admirals and deputy vice-admirals around the coast, in order to ingratiate himself with the king and secure his own position.[17] An examination of two of the pirates in Munster, Captain John Jennings and Captain James Harris, provides specifics on how the pirates were able to operate successfully with the complicity of naval officers. Captain Williams of the king's pinnace *Tramontane*, patrolling the Irish coast against piracy at the time, was extorting money and goods from the pirates in return for permitting free movement along the coast of Munster. Others complicit with Captain Williams were the earl of Thomond and, not surprisingly, brothers Humphrey and Richard Jobson.[18]

Harris' examination describes Richard Bishop's and Captain Williams' engagement in open business, to the full knowledge of Jobson and fellow admiralty colleagues in Baltimore and Leamcon. The underlining of certain sections by Northampton is indicative of his use of these examinations as a device to emphasise to the king the rampant corruption and collusion within the admiralty, all under Nottingham's watch.[19] An additional examination of Captain Harris, which gave the full complement of pirate captains by name, explained their movements and the payments they made to officials in the ports and harbours used as pirate bases. The earl of Northampton and men like him began to accumulate evidence on the pirates' operations and the level of complicity involved. It allowed for some form of determination to be made on the best way to tackle the piracy problem.[20]

No single action was viable, however, due to the relationships that existed between local officials and individual pirates. As several commissions were issued to individuals to negotiate on behalf of central government, confusion reigned, and this is no more clearly illustrated than with William Hull. In March 1610 vice-president of Munster Sir Richard Moryson was ordered to arrest Hull for his suspected complicity but at the same time Hull was in

England receiving a commission that authorised him to negotiate with pirates on behalf of the government.[21] It was no surprise then that the pirates were able to continue to operate freely and take their time to consider pardons or other courses of action. It is equally understandable why foreign powers such as the Dutch were growing ever more frustrated with such a protracted and conflicting situation – an issue clearly highlighted by Moryson, who said that 'much confusion is daily bred by the multiplicity of inferior persons, authorized under others to parley with them [the pirates]'.[22]

INTERNAL CONFLICT AND CONTROVERSIAL ACTIONS

The pirates' relationship with local officials, and the acquiescence of those officials in higher office, were all part of the social commerce that was part of rural life in remote coastal communities. In a sense the pirates 'legitimately' controlled the area along the coast of Munster in as much as this was an accepted way of life in those areas: they operated openly, with the support of officials, and the king and his officers seemed powerless to do anything about it. As piracy in Munster was part of a wider process and central to expanding commercial and political networks within the Atlantic, these networks had the vested interests of individuals linked to them and the economic foundations of emerging merchant empires at their core. The fact that admiralty officials such as Nottingham and Northampton were working against each other in a power struggle also meant that hidden agendas influenced actions: Northampton, for example, sent the examination of pirates Jennings and Harris to Secretary Thomas Lake seeking permission to reprieve them as he feared that their testimonies were so damning that Nottingham would have them executed, 'because they tell tales'.[23] Though Harris and Jennings were given reprieves at that point by the king, both were hanged shortly afterwards at Execution Dock in London.[24] Jennings had voiced his distrust of the king's pardons in 1608 and was ultimately proven correct.[25]

Alternative approaches had to be taken if the pirates were to be controlled and suppressed, even if such measures meant bowing to external political pressure and tolerating actions that would be personally objectionable to the king and his court. One suggestion was to depopulate areas, specifically the islands around Baltimore and Roaringwater Bay, to eliminate physically the pirate strongholds there. The case was made that:

> … wee can fynde no other assured meanes left for the securities of those Lewde and wicked Pyrattes but the vnpeopling and Layeing wast certaine Ilands in those borders and other places open vnto their arrival which they haue and yet Do hitherto most comonly frequent.

It was quickly ruled out as an option, however, being considered that such a move:

> … would haue ben grevious vnto some particular persons and if peradventure vnavailable to prevent the said mischeefe, there being a great number of ports in those partes as commodious and of as easie and salfe access as those wee intended to Displant, And for that we hold it [hold off on it].[26]

Essentially, it ran the risk of undermining the English settlements there, while in addition, the existence of other areas along the same coastline where the pirates could find safe harbour meant that the problem would just become more mobile. As well as this initiative, a commission was set up to oversee the closure of all but a few taverns and alehouses, and to put in place a licensing system for those that would remain open, again in an attempt to control the victualling places of pirates.[27]

A radical but strategic move saw consent being given to Dutch access to the territorial waters of the English crown, specifically the harbours in Ireland, as already referred to above. In 1611 the Dutch ambassador in London, Sir Noel de Caron, protested that such was the impact of the pirates on Dutch shipping, it was becoming unprofitable for them to go to sea. He petitioned the king to allow Dutch ships access to the harbours of Ireland as 'they desire Licence to enter into the Ports and Harbours when there is cause'.[28]

These complaints formed part of the impetus to acquiesce to the Dutch, but more embarrassingly, James had to concede that his ships were having no impact on the pirates in Ireland. This was made clear when it emerged that a number of captains of the king's ships operating in Ireland were in fact part of the problem, as outlined by Captain Williams' collaborations with Bishop, and this was compounded by James' unwillingness to invest money from his ever-dwindling exchequer funds in the navy to properly arm and upgrade his ships. Though James agreed to allow the Dutch enter ports and harbours in Ireland, it was not without conditions: 'with the restriction before they enter his ports they shall give notice to his officers, and that they shall leave the goods they find in the pirates' possession in the custody of his ministers, to be restored to the true proprietors'.[29]

The Dutch were already making forays into the harbours of the southwest in search of the pirates even before officially petitioning the king for a commission to do so. In April 1611, two Dutch ships had attacked Richard Bishop and his crew off Baltimore, capturing Bishop's ship, with the pirate admiral barely escaping with his life.[30] Writing from the harbour at Long Island, outside Leamcon, Roger Middleton, who was there to negotiate individual pardons, wrote that the pirates had left the area as 'fear [of the Dutch] drove them hence', also forcing Middleton to go to Mamora to entreat with Bishop and his fellow pirates there.[31]

The following October, Skipwith wrote to Chichester informing the lord deputy that the pirates were willing to submit but they were not prepared to remain in Ireland to negotiate as they would not risk being surprised again by 'the Hollanders'. The pirates had left for the coast of Spain but Skipwith confirmed that they had agreed to submit upon their return.[32] While the Dutch sought to deal with the pirates to prevent attacks on their merchant ships, particularly the large, heavily armed Dutch East India merchantmen that were frequently intercepted on their homeward journeys from the Indies, there was also a retributive element to the rivalry between the two. In April of 1611, some of the leading pirate captains, including Rear-Admiral Thomas Francke, Thomas Hussy, William Baugh, Lewis Plumley and Captain Parker, were in Mamora. There they attacked the Dutch fleet, under the command of Captains Stoute, Jacques and Johnson. The battle at sea went on for three days, with the Dutch eventually defeated and Captains Stoute and Jacques slain and only Johnson managing to escape; the English pirates too suffered heavy losses, with Baugh and Francke the only pirate captains to survive. In further justification for the attack at Mamora, the Dutch had previously captured and tortured Captain Francke, and no doubt, revenge was also part of Captain Francke's motivation during the attack.[33]

'BUSIED IN THEIR MASSACRE': THE DUTCH ATTACK AT CROOKHAVEN

At this point, the king consented and granted permission to the States-Generals in Holland to allow a Dutch fleet to enter Irish and also Welsh harbours to engage with the pirates by force and take them prisoner.[34] The idea of allowing the Dutch such access was discussed in July 1611 by Antonio

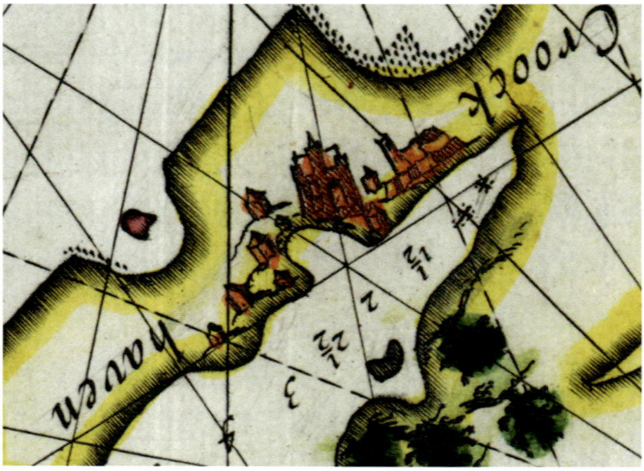

FIGURE 48: Inverted detail from 1612 chart of Crookhaven harbour and settlement, with depths and anchorages indicated; the information assisted the Dutch in their successful attack on the pirates there in 1614. 4 H BRIT P III, 6 RARA, UNIVERSITÄTSBIBLIOTHEK, GÖTTINGEN, GERMANY

Foscarini, Venetian ambassador in England. On completion of discussions between the king and his council, full permission was granted, with obvious support from Venice, as Foscarini reported:

> Dutch ships may in future chastise pirates in all ports of the Kingdom of Ireland, both following them up in the act of flying or going on purpose to attack them in the harbours except such as are fortified, inside which of course the pirates cannot find shelter. This shows that the idea of the King and Council is to extirpate the pirates by force rather than in any other way, and it is thought a matter of moment that his Majesty should oblige the States in so important an affair.[35]

The Dutch wasted no time in preparing a fleet, and part of the preparation was to map the coastline of Ireland, with the commissioning of detailed charts and the drafting of a set of sailing instructions to provide first-hand knowledge of the areas they intended to target. The Dutch, at that stage, did not have the required information to navigate their vessels safely into the small bays and havens around Ireland, particularly along the southwest coast, as evidenced by the fact that they sought pilots from the local officials in Munster. Thomas Crooke refused, as noted earlier, and the Dutch were once again forced to complain to James. In September of that year an order was issued to all the vice-admirals in Munster that 'the States shipping are to be furnished with pilots to follow the pirates'.[36]

FIGURE 49: Elevated view of Crookhaven from the west, with remains of early quay on foreshore and the wider view of the harbour in the distance. IMAGE: CONNIE KELLEHER

In 1612 Hessel Gerritszoon, chief hydrographer with the Dutch East Indies Company, engaged English cartographer John Hunt to draught a chart. As discussed in the Introduction, Gerritszoon was acting on behalf of the States-General and engaged Hunt to sail around Ireland starting at Crookhaven, which seems to have been the primary focus for the Dutch, and to map and describe the coastline as he proceeded.[37] The anti-pirate chart of the southwest coast certainly highlights Crookhaven as a harbour of note, with depth ranges included in the detail and the main settlement within the town indicated. The Dutch augmented their existing fleet of ships, numbering eight and already at sea under the command of Captain Moy Lambert, with a further eight ships.[38] The entire fleet was under the overall command of lieutenant-admiral for Zeeland, Guillaume de Zoete de Laecke, Lord of Houthain (Haultain), and indeed it is to him that Hessel Gerritszoon directs his report in the opening pages of the 1612 document.[39] Gerritszoon explained that it was a 'William Lery [possibly Leary] of Wexford, one of the best pilots in Ireland' who accompanied him and John Hunt during the mapping of the Irish coast.[40] The full Dutch fleet was in Falmouth in early 1612, where it took on enough supplies for six months at sea. While the Dutch attacked some pirate ships in the intervening period, they did not attack Crookhaven until August 1614, at which time the agreement between

James and the States-General may have lapsed and this could explain why their unprovoked and unannounced attack on the harbour went beyond all bounds of any commission agreement.[41]

Edward Davenant, a Cork merchant living on Whiddy Island in Bantry, was in Crookhaven to liaise with the pirates for the restoration of stolen goods to London merchant Thomas Boothby. The lord deputy had given Irish Captain Patrick Myagh, who was commanding the pirates in Crookhaven, protection on condition that he return the goods to Boothby. Myagh had acquired the goods from a fellow pirate captain, a Dutchman named Peeters, who had plundered the goods off Cape Finisterre in January 1613. When in Ireland seeking a pardon, Peeters had given the goods to Myagh.[42] It is Davenant's first-hand account of the events that provide the most vivid overview of what took place at the time. Though the scroll containing the examination has been damaged on one edge by fire, the full account of the attack can nevertheless be discerned.[43] Upon arriving at Crookhaven on 4 March 1614, Davenant was shown the protection granted to Myagh; it also contained the provision that the pirates give satisfaction to Boothby. The Cork merchant explained that he spoke with several of the pirates and all indicated that they were willing to accept a pardon, had left their ships and were then on land. Admiralty officers, including the deputy vice-admiral Charles Hargill, were present and Myagh brought a Robert Grymes on board his ship to show him Boothby's cargo and confirm that all was there. It 'had in her, Satin, grograine, Holland [cloth], canvas and sundry other goods and moneyes of the said Myaghe & his companie'.

On the same day, Davenant reported, Dutch captain Moy Lambert arrived into the harbour with four man-of-war. Hargill took a boat out to Lambert's ship to speak with him and confirm that the pirates had protection. In an effort to gain their attention, Hargill shouted at the Dutch, but was ignored. Lambert put three of the ships' boats into the water and he and his crew, all armed, rowed to Myagh's ship. One of Lambert's captains, Jacob Johnson, went aboard the pirate captain's ship, which was at the time, as Davenant describes, 'being on ground' and may have been beached either for careening purposes or for repairs, or was just in shallow water awaiting a rising tide. In any event, Myagh's ship was 'close to shore' and vulnerable.[44] Davenant's report continues that Johnson '… without demanding any question did promptly with his ordnance shoote Myagh's ship through and through'. Johnson's shot ignited gunpowder on the ship and it exploded, with the 'powder blast' nearly killing Myagh's crew who remained on board, with 'many scorched and wounded'.[45] If Davenant's report is true, the Dutch then proceeded to carry out what can only be described as murderous acts. Johnson and his men:

> ... stripped naked & murdered in most savage manner sundry of Captain Myagh's company, & in like sort murdered there one called – Erle, a land man & no pirate, & also one – Morgan, who attended Captain Hargill. Then and there they wounded also most grievously whom many named Thomas Smith, & Richard Conway, gentlemen, who came to Crookhaven to accompany Captain Hargill, by his own appointment.[46]

This may well have been the same Captain Johnson who was the only surviving captain after the attack by the English pirates on the Dutch fleet in Mamora in 1611, and would explain Johnson's extreme actions when attacking Myagh and his fleet in Crookhaven – with revenge the driving force behind his deadly attack. Smith [also written 'Smyth' in some accounts], who was wounded, was also burnt during the explosion, and a companion of his, John Tregiddell, also received numerous wounds during the attack. While this was taking place, Captain Myagh, his two sons and fellow crew jumped overboard but upon reaching shore were captured by the Dutch and killed. Myagh's third son survived but was seriously injured. Of those murdered, the Dutch stripped them, and Davenant said that he saw some of the Dutch wearing 'some of Captain Myagh's apparel'. A young cabin boy of Lambert's was accredited with killing Captain Myagh, whereupon he also stripped naked the pirate captain. Seventeen corpses were recorded as being on the shore, with many more lying dead elsewhere. Residents from the town tried to assist those who attempted to make it ashore from the ship but the Dutch fired at them; fearing for their own lives, they returned to the town. The following day, when Davenant and some of Hargill's men went aboard the Dutch captain's ship to seek restitution, Lambert threatened to burn the town. Davenant's account recalls the events unfolding

> ... in view and hearing of the townsmen, and various others of his Majesty's subjects, who cried out continually to the Hollanders that Myagh and his company were protected.

With Myagh's ship in the shallows, along with reports that settlers offered assistance to those coming ashore, it suggests that the place was close to the present-day village of Crookhaven.[47] Certainly, there was a thriving community within the main town area of Crookhaven, as is indicated on the 1612 Dutch chart, where houses and the main O'Mahony castle are drawn, and therefore the events of the attack would have taken place in full view of the townsfolk.

Thomas Smith later petitioned the ambassador to Holland seeking recourse, and his account suggests that he too was a government agent in Crookhaven:

> … how uncivill a manner one Moy Lambert, a commaunder of certaine of the States' men of war, hath demeaned himself in one of his Majesty's havens in Ireland (under coullor of prosecuting pyrattes), farr beyond the favourable commission which the States had to that purpose obtained from his Majestie, and contrary to the rules both of equity and humanity. The which outrage, extending not only to the spoyle of our marchantes' goods, but to the slaughter of many of his Majesty's subjects, and the cruell wounding and burning of Thomas Smyth, this peticioner, being his Majesty's officer, whilst he was honestly occupied in doeinge the dutyes of his charge, hath moved us seriously to recomend to your lordship this affaire, praying yow to deale effectually with the States ….[48]

In October 1617, after many representations to the States-General in Holland seeking redress, both Thomas Boothby and Thomas Smith were awarded compensation; Boothby received 10,000 guilders to cover the cost of losing his goods to Captain Lambert, and Thomas Smith 2,000 gilders, 'amountinge in all to 1,200 li sterling … on the condicion that the said Boothbie, his sonne, and servants, and likewise the said Smyth, doe rest contented and fully satisfied …'.[49] The compensation paid to both parties was considerable; Smith, for example, received the equivalent of £157,824 sterling or €180,486 in current value. It is not known if anyone else who suffered at the hands of the Dutch at that time in Crookhaven received any recourse from the States thereafter.

VISUALISING AN ATROCITY AND LAYING THE OUTCOME TO REST

English officials, settlers and the men in the pirate alliance were shocked by the unrestrained viciousness of the Dutch attack. When looking out the harbour from the tranquil village of Crookhaven today, it is difficult to imagine the horror of the events that unfolded in August 1614. The potential for cultural material as a result of the attack to remain undiscovered on the seabed in Crookhaven, whether wreck or artefactual evidence, was discussed in Chapter 3. In attempting to visualise where in Crookhaven the events took place some four hundred years ago, however, it is all the more affecting when we consider some of the names of those who died, who they were and where they were buried; then a sense of the true tragedy and atrocity of the Dutch attack can be more fully reflected upon. Among those who were killed, along with Myagh and his sons, were Thomas James, boatswain in Myagh's ship; Nicholas Gorte (or Goyte), sailor, and his wife Eleanor; Richard Tailor, sailor; John Thomas, who was a passenger and had been made master in Myagh's ship; Edmond Fortescue, a gentleman of Devon and also a passenger on board; Roger, a butcher, possibly from the town; Morgan, servant to Captain Hargill; an Irishman named Donnell, a servant to Peregrine Banester (Banister), no doubt a settler, and Henry Harte, servant to John Hoskins (Hesking).[50] Harte had been examined the previous August, in 1613, in relation to Captain William Baugh's arrival into Leamcon. He was a mariner of Plymouth and about forty-five years of age; whether his involvement with or knowledge of the two pirate captains – Myagh and Baugh – reflects a career as a pirate or legitimate sailor remains undetermined.[51]

It is presumed that settlers and officers were buried with due diligence in dedicated burial grounds or family plots, but whether the pirates who died were buried locally or indeed in unmarked ground also remains a mystery. The latter was often the case for shipwrecked sailors, unknown mariners and pirates, the tradition being to bury deceased sailors on the foreshore where their graves would be washed over by the tides, or on the edge of sea cliffs, overlooking the open ocean. This is not to be confused with those men who were executed on charges of piracy and who were treated somewhat differently, as discussed below.

Local folklore has tales of several possible graves intermittently visible when sand levels change on White Strand at Ballyrisode, to the east of Crookhaven.[52] Certainly, stone settings and a series of upright stones on the upper foreshore are visible there at low tide. The two uprights, not unlike markers or headstones, lie about one metre apart at slight angles to each other and parallel to the shore. Nearby is a sub-rectangular stone box-like setting, comprising three flagstones set on edge, with the open side facing the sea. Tradition recounts a battle taking place in the seventeenth century

FIGURE 50: Archaeological site on Ballyrisode strand, Toormore Bay, with stone settings and upright slabs. These may represent the remains of a prehistoric or later site, but tradition also tells of the burial of pirates on the beach following a pirate battle there in the 1600s.
IMAGE: CONNIE KELLEHER

on the beach at Ballyrisode between English ships and pirates, in which members of the Canty clan, from Canty's Cove, were involved. The pirates were victorious, though with some casualties, who were laid to rest on the strand. If there is any truth in the tale, perhaps the stone uprights could be evidence of the battle. In the absence of archaeological excavation, however, it is not possible to state what this site is or if the upright stones and box-like feature are one or two distinct features.

It could, however, also be a much earlier site, suggested by comparative archaeological evidence elsewhere. Similar stone settings were discovered on the foreshore of Coney Island, off the coast of Sligo, in 2014 and subsequent archaeological excavation and geophysical survey established that it was a prehistoric Bronze Age cooking site, a *fulacht fiadh*.[53] Other such submerged or inundated prehistoric sites have also been investigated elsewhere, and as climate change impacts the coastal fringes of remote areas, more of these sites are being discovered.[54] It is more probable that tradition and folklore have grown up around these ancient sites, with stories of the sea adapted and the presence of upright stones retrospectively considered to be the remains of drowned sailors or pirates, with their deeds forming part of an emerging verbal mythology embellished with time.

Many burial places of individuals in a coastal location remain unknown, particularly for those washed ashore or who were killed and buried hastily.[55] In Crookhaven the local burial ground in the seventeenth century was to the immediate west of the town, in the old church of St Mullagh or Molloga.[56] The chapel was in a ruined state by 1699 when Bishop Dive Downes visited the area, and in 1700 a new parochial church, dedicated to St Brendan, was built on the site of the earlier church. Dr Brown, bishop of Cork, financed the erection of the new church for the accommodation of sailors frequenting the port of Crookhaven.[57] Attached to the church is a graveyard, and it is plausible that those who died as a result of the Dutch attack in 1614 may have been placed in this burial ground. Only the inscriptions on late eighteenth- and nineteenth-century gravestones are now readable, with a number commemorating losses by drowning of local individuals. The majority are unmarked headstones that bear no inscription but may be indicative of those lost or killed locally and buried in the older section of the graveyard prior to the construction of the new Church of St Brendan.

The burial places for pirates have always been elusive, as has any official documentation for their death. Some graveyards and burial sites have associations with piracy, including St Paul's in Harbour Grace, Newfoundland, the hilltop cemetery on Ile Sainte-Marie in Madagascar and the recently discovered possible resting place of pirate Captain Samuel Bellamy and several of his men in a secluded area near Cape Cod, Massachusetts.[58] In Ireland only one grave site is tied directly with a pirate from the sixteenth–seventeenth centuries, that of Grace O'Malley, who is reputed to be buried in the O'Malley tomb in the Cistercian Abbey on Clare Island in County Mayo.[59]

To date only one known burial place for a pirate who was directly involved in the alliance in Munster is identifiable. Pirate captain Richard Robinson (Roberts), who settled his family in Munster after receiving a pardon in 1609, was on a list of prisoners sent to England on suspicion of piracy in 1610. Whether this was a mistake or he continued to pirate after being pardoned is uncertain, but he was subsequently released. He died shortly afterwards and a death notice is held in the parish register in St James' Church, Garlickhithe

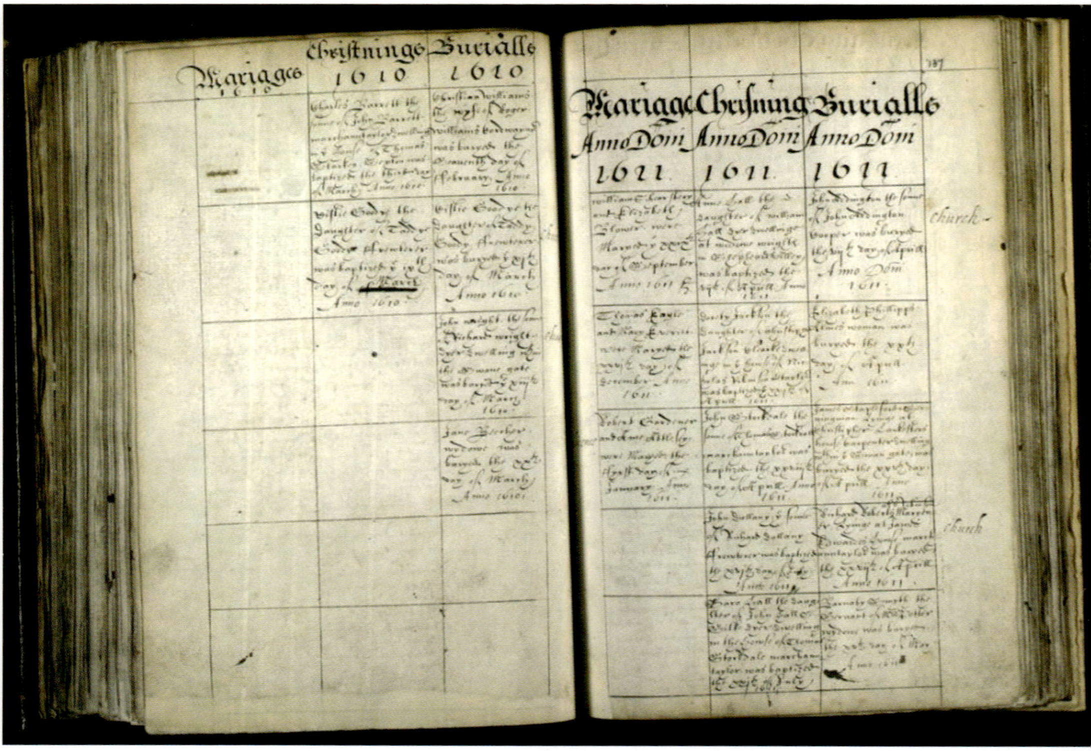

FIGURE 51: Death notice of pardoned pirate Captain Richard Robinson/Roberts from 1611. The notice is on right page, fourth box down and records his burial in April of that year in the parish register of St James' Church, Garlickhithe, City of London. P69/JS2/001/MS09138, LONDON METROPOLITAN ARCHIVES, CITY OF LONDON COLLECTION

in London. He was buried in St James' cemetery, next to the church in Garlickhithe, on 27 April 1611.[60] One can only ponder on the final resting places of the other pirates who died during their time in the alliance or thereafter when not at sea.

A jury of admiralty officials and local townspeople was immediately convened in Crookhaven subsequent to the 1614 attack and unanimously found that the action of the Dutch commander and his crew was wilful murder. The compensation paid to Thomas Boothby and Thomas Smith came with a further condition attached to it, and one that must have been hard to accept. It decreed that Moy Lambert and his crew would be exonerated and no further claims could be brought against them.[61] Of the varied accounts of Moy Lambert's career in historical documents, little mention is made of the commission issued by King James to the Dutch or the stipulations attached to it; indeed in a Dutch pamphlet celebrating the victory against the pirates in Ireland, Moy Lambert and his crew are hailed as champions.[62]

TRACES OF TRIALS AND PLACES OF EXECUTION

The coming into force of the Act Against Piracy in Ireland in 1614, as the 'Act for the Punishing of Pirates and Robbers at Sea' (Act 11, 12 and 13 Jas. 1, c. 2), provided the means for officials to apprehend, hold trials against and send for execution within Ireland those found guilty of piracy.[63] It essentially closed the loophole that had existed in the Irish legislative process, and in theory this should have had a visible impact on curbing piracy in the region.[64] In practice, however, it had little effect, primarily due to the deep-rooted corruption that existed within these remote areas on the edge of empire, and the fact that, by then, piracy was acceptable both on a social and on an economic level.

While the HCA examinations record the trials and executions of numerous pirates for the period, as discussed previously, they also can include reference to places of execution, though these tend to be general in nature.[65] As with burial sites, the physical location of hanging places or associated spaces is of interest in that the placement of gallows or gibbets was just as important in suppressing piracy as was the act of execution itself. An account is given of three individuals, John Morris, Peter Hilliard and Hugh Rogers, with others unnamed, who had taken a ship in Dalkey in Dublin but who sailed north to seek safe anchorage in Lough Swilly; they were captured and transported back to Dublin. Arraigned under Sir Adam Loftus, they were found guilty and hanged on 30 May 1614. What is particularly interesting about this account is that it specifically states that the three pirates were 'executed upon the strand, at low-water mark, by Dublin'.[66] This secured admiralty jurisdiction as the foreshore was outside the ambit of the common courts of law. The same was the case in England, where at Wapping, on the River Thames, and best known as Execution Dock, pirates were hanged. The marshalsea prison in Southwark, London, on the banks of the Thames was the traditional admiralty prison where pirates were held pending being marched, as a public spectacle, to Execution Dock. In Scotland, pirates were hanged on a gibbet at the Sands of Leith near Edinburgh, on the foreshore, with an account from 1610 specifically recording that nine pirates were hanged upon 'the sandis of Leyth, within the floddis-mark'.[67]

The same year the 'Trial of thirty English Pirates, before the Vice-Admiral of Scotland, his Deputes, and certain Lords of the Privy Council' was held. Listed are the thirty pirates who were said to have been at 'Long Iland, in Ireland, ane [a] plaice of resort of all Pirates and opin Roberis [robbers]'. The thirty pirates and their ship were in west Cork in July 1609, under the command of Captain William Randell. Of the others named, some are clearly English but more are possibly Dutch or Scandinavian. While Captain Randell and his men were at Long Island, the transcript also mentions several of the pirates who formed the alliance, including Captains Bishop, Easton, Harvey and Coward. The trial transcript is extensive and covers the movements of the pirates throughout 1609 from the coast of Munster, north to Norway and their predations around the Western Isles. They were captured off Kirkwall Castle and when tried were found guilty and sentenced thus:

> … to be tane [taken] to the Peir [pier] and schoir [shore] of Leith, within the Sie-flood and mark thairof, and their to be Hangit upoune one gibbet till they be deid.[68]

Of the thirty listed, one Richard Robinson is named but is also recorded as having an alias, Dik Couper or Dik de Hoyser. It may be presumed then, and considering that all thirty pirates were executed, that this refers to a different Robinson from the captain who frequented the Munster coast and who was eventually interred in St James' cemetery in Garlickhithe in London. The potential that they were related, however, cannot be ruled out. The tradition of hanging continued at Leith until 1822 and it is clear that such liminal places were favoured for pirate execution in particular.

In Dublin, Old Newgate prison seems to have served this official purpose. It stood where the Cornmarket is now located and was originally one of the city gates in an area that was not too distant from the tidal River Liffey within the medieval confines of the Viking quarter of Wood Quay, Winetavern Street and St Audoen's.[69] Perhaps pirates were also marched from Old Newgate to the river's edge to be hanged 'on the strand'. Reclamation of the area from the nineteenth century onwards, in conjunction with extensive modernisation in the early twenty-first century, now leaves a populated area removed from the water with no sense of riverine or indeed estuarine attachment.

There are a number of recorded places of execution in Dublin where gallows were located. One was at the northeast corner of St Stephen's Green, where pirates are recorded as executed in 1766.[70] The bodies of the pirates were hung up in irons on either the South Wall or on a gibbet at MacCarrell's wharf, near Ringsend, or at the piles below the Pigeon House.[71] During the twelfth century, the Anglo-Normans had a gallows erected on the north shore of the River Liffey, possibly near the present intersection of Parkgate Street and Infirmary Road. The approach to this would have been via Old Bridge (now Fr Mathew Bridge) and Hangman's Lane (now Hammond's Lane), the original name for the latter lane an obvious indication. Another gallows in use up to the seventeenth century, the gallows at Gibbet's Mead or Meadow, was mentioned regularly in various correspondences to do with the city. Shortly after the restoration in 1660, the gallows was moved across the river to Kilmainham, where the jail was then located.[72]

In Cork City, Gallows Green (now renamed Greenmount, on the southern approach to the city) was the location of the city's gallows, though it is not clear if this is where pirates were also hanged.[73] Outside the city, in the more rural areas of Munster, the marshalsea prison in Bandon is the most probable location where petty criminals and pirates were detained, along with debtors, as previously surmised in relation to pirate Captain William Baugh in 1619.[74] Gallows Hill in Bandon is where the town gallows was located, but no records have been found for the execution of pirates in Bandon from the time of the alliance. From an archaeological perspective, the potential for cultural remains of hanging places or gallows to survive in the intertidal zone on beaches or strands is minimal, with many of these places now developed or reclaimed over time. Indeed, if evidence has been or were to be found in such areas, perhaps in the form of wooden structures or wooden piles, they may well be misinterpreted as representing the remains of quays, wharves, old jetties or simply mooring posts. The probability that such remains may have been a gallows would not readily come to mind. Archaeological evidence relating to the execution of pirates could, therefore, have been and may continue to be easily missed or misunderstood in the cultural record.

Finding evidence for either the execution structures or the human remains is again fraught with difficulty. Structures were often temporary, leaving little or no cultural footprint. Monson brought a gallows with him in his ship, which he set up on the foreshore to hang offenders when caught. He did exactly that when in Broadhaven in Mayo, during the time when he impersonated pirate Captain Henry Mainwaring.[75] To compound the problem further, many individuals executed were either removed after hanging to other locations – as previously discussed in relation to the pirates that were executed in Dublin – and their remains displayed, or were buried in mass graves.[76] Other bodies were frequently suspended from gallows or gibbets at the entrance to harbours or on headlands, as a deterrent to pirates who intended to enter the waterways. A reference to one such act comes from an account of services rendered by Sir Thomas Button between 1614 and 1621. During that period he was commander of the Irish coast fleet, including the ships the *Phoenix* and the *Moon*. In 1618 he captured a pirate named Captain Austin and his crew at Oysterhaven near Kinsale, where both parties fought each other for a full day, with the pirates finally defeated. Austin lost his ship and many of his crew. Six of the 'Chiefest' of the captured crew were condemned to Cork jail and executed there but the master of the ship, as recorded in Button's log, '… for example sake (on the head lande nearest the place I tooke them att) was hangd in Chaynes [chains] in November 1618'.[77]

The term 'hanged in chains' specifically refers to being hanged on or in a gibbet or iron cage, as opposed to doing the 'sheriff's dance' on the gallows. The heads of the dead could then be spiked or their bodies placed in a gibbet and displayed in conspicuous locations.[78] The thirty pirates hanged at Leith in 1610 were thus displayed, and certainly the most infamous hanging and gibbet execution was that of pirate William Kidd. He was hanged at Execution Dock, at Wapping Quay in London in 1701, and then placed inside the iron cage located at Tilbury Point for all to see.[79]

Toponymic evidence, like that of Hangman's Lane, as well as geographical locations can give clues as to hanging places. The setting used by Button for the execution of Captain Austin may have been the headland at the eastern tip of the entrance into Kinsale Harbour. Now called Pregane Point, up until the mid-nineteenth century it was called Hangman's Point.[80] Oysterhaven lies immediately to the east and the headland would have provided a clear view for anyone entering or leaving both harbours. It is here that hangings were carried out at the time of the Irish Rebellion, when in 1649 Prince Rupert reputedly hanged a number of would-be deserters from the royalist side on the headland in full view of the parliamentary fleet.[81] While this may have been a singular event, it is possible that the site was a traditional hanging place, as the placename suggests. It may thus have been the scene of many other, now unrecorded, executions of brigands, thieves and no doubt pirates in the past.

It is only in recent times that cultural evidence has been found for these execution places, with historical and folkloric evidence among the primary sources for their locations, at least on a documentary and oral level.[82] Cartographic sources can similarly be invaluable, and maps like that of Bantry and Beara can illustrate the location of a hanging place, in this case a gallows near the area known as Blackrock, the early landing place in Bantry town.[83] While no doubt at times the limb of a tree could be used as an on-the-spot solution, for formal hangings, structures tended to be in centrally placed locations that made it a socio-political spectacle, with the gathering of the masses to witness the event. While records show that certain numbers of pirates were captured and executed, the strength of the pirate alliance and the wealth generated by their business meant they had forged their own society, which required alternative approaches if it were to be brought into the fold.

INDIRECT ACTION, PARDONS AND PERSONAL ASSURANCES

Prior to the coming into force of the Piracy Act in 1614, many of the leading pirates captured in the southwest were extradited to England, though this was in some instances considered a formality, with pardons for some already assured. It did not always turn out as planned, however, as discussed earlier in relation to pirate captains John Jennings and James Harris, as assurances of pardons and protections by one could be overturned by the vested interests of another.[84] Northampton may have had ulterior motives in wanting to keep the two pirates alive, but what this case highlights is the difficulty of tackling the pirate problem on the ground. The ingrained nature of piracy within the communities in Munster, as elsewhere in remote coastal areas, and the corruption of the admiralty officers there, meant dealing with any issue remotely was almost impossible.[85] The closing line of Harris' examination, when he reflects on the reality, underlines perfectly how trust was a subjective thing. Harris refers to 'the readiness of Officers to discharge them [execute them] upon takinge their money'.[86] By January 1610, however, both pirates had been hanged at Wapping having spent over ten months in prison, and though their reprieve was issued from the highest office of the crown, they still did not escape the hangman's noose.[87]

Consideration of pardons – and their acceptance – by many members of the alliance began to increase from about 1608.[88] While some took advantage of the offer by the English crown of a general pardon, others called the bluff of the government with threats of heightened attacks if pardons were not forthcoming.[89] Thomas Coward opted for the latter approach when captured and transported to England in 1610; he proclaimed that the pirates would attack the fishing fleets in Newfoundland the following spring if pardons were not forthcoming immediately: 'his advice is to receive them to mercy, otherwise they are resolved to prey upon the subject as well as the stranger'.[90] It was shown just a short time later that Coward had returned to his old ways, even after his petition had been given favourable consideration, thus supporting the suspicion by the crown that the issuing of pardons may not have actually solved the pirate problem: '… Coward, to whom favour was lately shown in a similar case, has returned to his former courses, and is now a dangerous pirate'.[91]

Over the next four years, up to 1614, the majority of pirates within the Atlantic alliance sought, at one time or another, a pardon from the crown but most of these, if not returning outright, continued to dabble in piracy when the opportunity allowed. Attempts at direct action continued, with orders issued in 1609 to Sir William Monson to send out three king's ships to Baltimore, with Lord Deputy Chichester providing the mariners to man the ships, which were to engage with the pirate fleets there.[92] Individual naval ships, under the command of Sir William St John, continued to frequent the waters in search of pirates, but though there were some captures, it had little if any significant impact on the pirate activity.[93] It was no doubt complicated by St John's history of proclivity for double-dealing and treachery, as was clearly seen when he intercepted pirate Captain William Baugh in Kinsale and embezzled part of the plundered cargo for his own gain.[94] A general pardon then seemed to be the best option. Official negotiations were thus sanctioned, with certain officers tasked with liaising with the pirates to discuss terms and requirements, though this too was open to flagrant abuse. Roger Middleton arrived into Ireland in 1611, accompanied by Humphrey Curson and William Perpointe, to begin parlaying with the pirates. Well before that, however, there were attempts at unofficial negotiations, with general instructions issued to tease out the sensibilities of the pirates and their terms if they indicated that they were willing to come in to discuss reforming their ways.[95]

Henry Skipwith too was tasked with negotiating with the pirates. In August 1611 he had returned from London with warrants to protect the pirates from attack by the king's ships if they were willing to submit. He did state that the pirates were disinclined to remain on the southwest coast at that point, as they were concerned about the Dutch, whom they knew were at sea with a fleet intent on attacking them, which ultimately proved to be the case. Skipwith noted that the pirates headed for the safety of the coast of Spain (and then presumably onto Mamora in North Africa) but had given

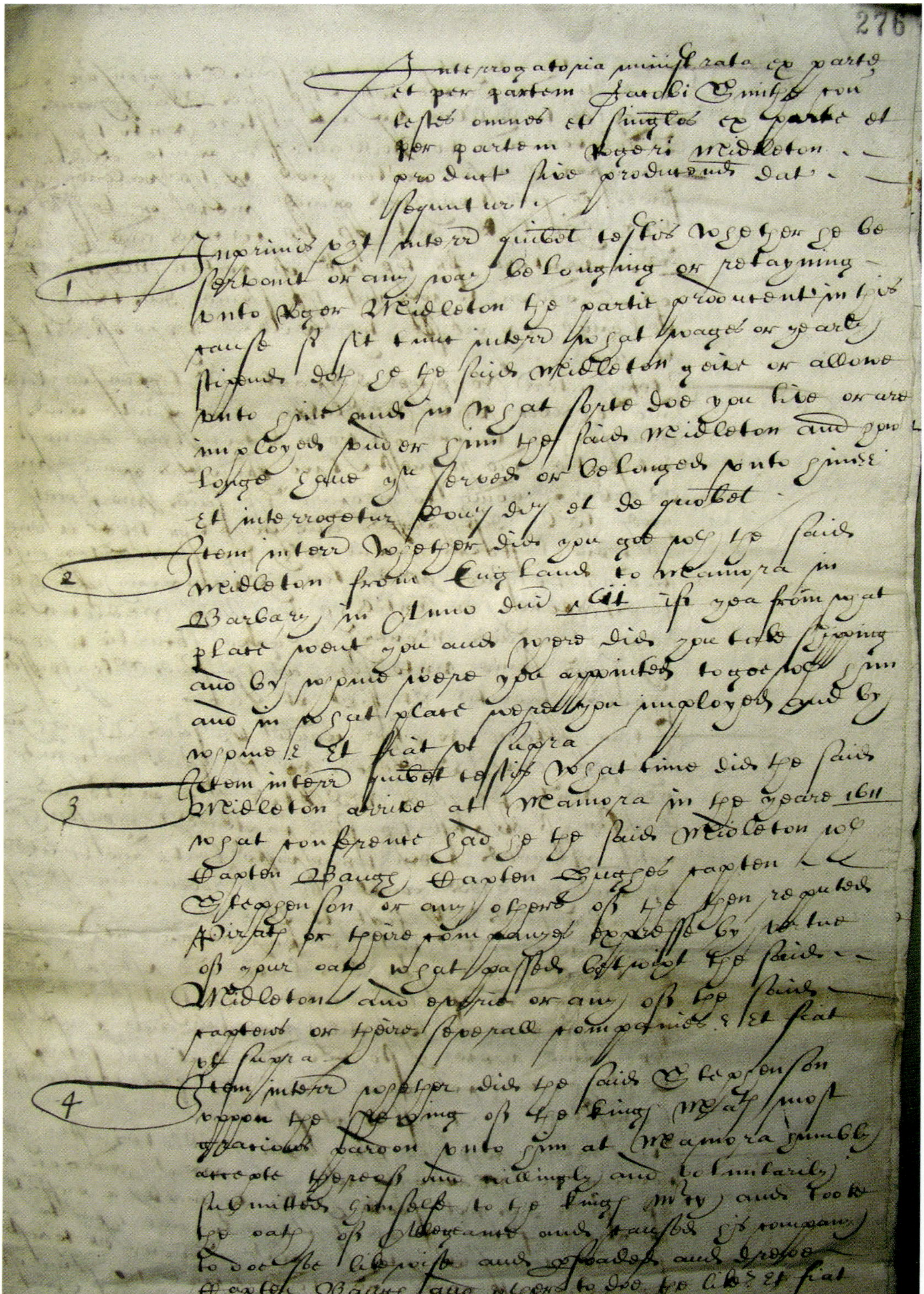

276

Interrogatoria ministrata ex parte et per partem Jacobi Smith con[tra] testes omnes et singulos ex parte et per partem Rogeri Middleton product[os] sive producend[os] dat[a] sequuntur.

1 Imprimis ... interr[ogetur] quilibet testis whether he be servant or any way belonging or pertayning unto Roger Middleton the partie producent in this cause ... what wages or yearly stipend doth the said Middleton give or allowe unto him and in what sorte doe you live or are imployed under him the said Middleton and how longe have you served or belonged unto him. Et interrogetur ... de quolibet.

2 Item interr[ogetur] whether did you goe with the said Middleton from England to Mamora in Barbary in Anno domini 1611 ... from what place went you and where did you take shipping and by whome were you appointed to goe with him and in what place were you imployed and by whome. Et fiat ut supra.

3 Item interr[ogetur] quilibet testis what time did the said Middleton arrive at Mamora in the yeare 1611 what conference had he the said Middleton with Capten Baugh Capten Hughes Capten Stephenson or any others of the then reputed Pirats or their companyes ... by vertue of your oath what passed betwixt the said Middleton and them or any of the said captens or their severall companies. Et fiat ut supra.

4 Item interr[ogetur] whether did the said Stephenson upon the hearing of the Kings Maties most gracious pardon unto him at Mamora humbly accepte thereof ... willingly and voluntarily submitted himself to the Kings Matie and tooke the oath of allegiance and caused his company to doe the likewise and persuaded and [illegible] Capten Baugh and others to doe the like. Et fiat

FIGURE 52: Account from 1613 of Roger Middleton's negotiations in 1611 with pirate captains, including William Baugh, William Hughs and others, when arranging pardons for the pirates in the alliance. TNA, HCA EXAMINATIONS 13/226, F. 276

promises to return. By that stage Middleton and Curson had arrived into west Cork with the pardons for the pirates, and Skipwith reported to the lord deputy that 'all the pirates are resolved to receive their pardon upon the conditions therein offered'. What is curious about Skipwith's account to Chichester is that he concludes by suggesting what can only be construed as a double-cross: he proposed that garrisons be placed in the harbours most favoured by the pirates and upon their return they could then be 'assaulted by such forces as shall be sent against them'.[96] Some years earlier Skipwith had negotiated directly with Richard Bishop in an attempt to persuade the pirate admiral to act as an intermediary between the crown and the men active in the alliance. In July 1611, Skipwith provided a report to Chichester from Leamcon giving details of the pirates and their operations, when considering their pardons. Easton, having captured the *Concord*, brought the ship to Leamcon, whereupon Skipwith attempted to persuade him to deliver the ship and its cargo back to the owners. It fell on deaf ears, due primarily to the fact that Easton did not like Skipwith. The vice-admiral wrote:

> ... I conceded that my persuasions would not prevaile much with him [Easton], in respect of his former distaste of me, I thought good to sende Bishop, to use his best meanes w'th al he had interest in, to prepare Easton to that motion, who did proceede accordingly.[97]

Skipwith was using Bishop as the intermediary at that point to exert influence on his fellow pirates. Bishop, in turn, wished to be looked upon favourably by the lord deputy:

> I am entreated by Bishop to be a suiter to your Ld to remember him, who hath now againe in my knowledge refused these pirates offer of giving him their best ship and a good share of their wealth, and to make him general to his greater grace wth The Duke of Florence but his answer was I will dye a poor labourer in mine owne country if I may, rather than be the richest pirate in the world.[98]

Skipwith suggests, tentatively, to Chichester that better use could be made of the men but qualifies it later by saying that if he has overstepped the mark it is down to his poor judgment:

> All the rest of the Pirates doe with all humility begge his majesty's mercy, upon which condition they make offer to surrender up all their shippes and goods likewise, and to renounce the Duke of Florences protection. The ships are all good and well provided. This company is almost all of our nation that are pirates now, amongst whom are many good mariners of whom necessary use may be made. Howsoever the knott beinge broken, it will be a longetime ere such a force be gathered together againe.[99]

As with Sir Richard Moryson's correspondence to the earl of Salisbury two years earlier in August 1609, when he suggested that these men could become settlers in Virginia, Skipwith similarly made the case to Chichester to look beyond their crimes because they were Englishmen and could still serve the cause for empire.[100]

No sooner had Roger Middleton and Humphrey Curson landed in North Africa in 1611 than Middleton 'busied himself with extracting personal gratuity from the pirates' rather than offering the terms of the pardons that he had with him. Indeed, he seems to have encouraged Captain William Baugh to take more ships as prizes in advance of receiving his official pardon.[101] When he returned to Ireland, Middleton continued to extort money from the pirates, including from Captain Stephenson upon his arrival back into west Cork in 1612, though the pirate captain had agreed when in Mamora to take the offer of a pardon.[102] Middleton and Curson's handling of the negotiations was severely compromised by self-interest, a point not missed by Skipwith when he complained of both men's behaviour.[103]

Fresh pardons were offered to all the pirates in 1612, with the intention of inducing the return of goods and, if possible, ships to merchant owners, and to lessen the increasing representations to the crown from international interests. Instead, and primarily as a consequence of Middleton's duplicitous actions, extremely generous terms were offered whereby the pirates were allowed to keep their booty when issued with the newly extended pardons.[104] Skipwith once more noted the conniving conduct of Middleton in the offering of such generous terms but he was very soon thereafter called before the admiralty himself on suspicion of receiving pirate goods during the course of his own negotiations with them. These were not isolated events. Hull sold some of the booty in his keeping for his own gain, while Skipwith was ordered to pay for the goods he was found to have taken from German merchant Harman Holtsho, whose ship had been plundered and its goods placed in Skipwith's care in Castlepark in Kinsale.[105]

By the end of 1612 the majority of the leading men of the alliance had surrendered, either in England, Ireland or Mamora, and had received pardons. Insider dealings by the negotiators and deputy vice-admirals, along with double-crossing of colleagues across the board, pirates and officials alike, heightened the suspicions of a number of the pirates, with many by then distrusting the intentions of the crown, both on a local and central level. Peter Easton, Thomas Francke and Gilbert Roope left Ireland in advance of receiving their pardons, worried that they would be swindled and executed should they surrender. By that time they had also received a tempting offer from the duke of Florence to serve under his protection, one that Easton was considering accepting. In an apparent testimony given to Skipwith, the pirate captain stated: '… now in respect of the Duke of Florence's offer and the greatness of this [potential] wealth, I am otherwise resolved' (to accept).[106] Though a pardon was finally granted for the three in 1612, they took the offer and voyaged to Tuscany, where they remained under the protection of the duke for a time. By 1613 Easton had moved his operations, and loyalty, to Villafranca in Italy and there he remained for the rest of his days, serving under the protection of the duke of Savoy.[107] Captain Francke may have returned, however, or his family and relatives remained on in west Cork, as records list a 'Thomas Francke' living in a house in Clonakilty in 1631, in a property comprising three houses all leased by Richard Boyle to a man named Daniel Howard.[108] Whether this Thomas Francke was the aged pirate, who would probably have been in his fifties or older by then, or was a relative is not known, but certainly those with the surname 'Francke' remained on in Munster after the demise of the alliance.

This should have seen the end of the piracy issue in the southwest, but through a combination of reneged terms, involving non-receipt of their agreed share of booty, or being given pay-offs rather than their pardons, many of the pirates returned to a life of plunder. This included most of the crews belonging to Easton and Francke who had voyaged to Villafranca with their captains, but who were treated so badly that they returned to Mamora and served under Henry Mainwaring there. By 1614 there was, however, a very dramatic change in the command structure of the pirate alliance; the main players including Bishop, Easton, Francke, Robinson, Stephenson and Jennings were either pardoned, relocated elsewhere, settled in west Cork or executed, and a new captaincy was in place. There were at least sixteen independent pirate captains commanding their own vessels, most of whom had not been prominent within the fleets of what comprised the alliance when in its heyday in Munster. Some names still appeared, such as Robert Walsingham, for instance, but on a more independent, self-reliant level than before. They were not supported by an alliance of men but operated more as an opportunistic marauding pirate presence in the Atlantic.[109]

THE FALL OF MAMORA AND ITS IMPACT

In 1614 the Spanish sent a fleet of ships across the Straits of Gibraltar and attacked Mamora – in part because of sporadic assaults on its coastline by the Moriscos since their expulsion began in 1609, but also because of the constant attacks on its merchant shipping by pirates.[110] Various attempts had been made over the preceding years to prevent Mamora from being used by the pirates and essentially becoming a pirate port. In 1611, for example, Spain attempted to block the harbour by sinking ships 'filled with stones and bound together by mortar', and it was noted that:

> Don Pedro di Toledo succeeded in closing the entrance to the harbour of Ma'amura, in spite of the Moors. He sank eight ships in the mouth of the harbour.[111]

In August 1611 the Venetian ambassador to England, Antonio Foscarini, reported that the Spanish had 'seized the port of Ma'amura with a view to fortifying it and so to command the Straits'.[112] Though not fully successful, it did discourage some of the pirates from using the port and so they began to look elsewhere in North Africa. With the fall of Mamora to Spain, many of the pirates shifted their theatre of operations farther south to Rabat, but the loss of their main, independent pirate base in Africa essentially spelled the end of free trade and seasonal settlement for the members of the alliance.[113] It is interesting to note that just before Mamora fell to the Spanish, the pirate captains there were still predominantly English, primarily under the command of Captain Henry Mainwaring, and remained a force to be reckoned with. Serving under Mainwaring were several captains who in turn commanded their own ships but with new or lesser-known pirates. These included: '… Vice-Admiral Capt. Knightlye, rear-admiral Capt. John Collins, … Robert Walsingham in a ship of a hundred tons, Capt Jollife, … Capt Woodland …' and also Captains John Fleming, 'Richard' Myagh and Christopher Thickpenny in ships of their own.[114] This was the last time Myagh (most probably the same man as 'Patrick' Myagh of Crookhaven)

FIGURE 53: Kasbah Mahdiyya (Mehdia) and harbour, with River Sebu and wider Atlantic in view. The Moroccan entrepôt fell to the Spanish in 1614. © PROF. RICHARD PENNELL

would sail the warm waters off Africa. Soon after, he voyaged back to Ireland, where the attack by Moy Lambert's men on his base in Crookhaven ended his pirate ways.

Utilising the pirates' skills as mariners rather than executing them was clearly considered in the case of Captain Henry Mainwaring, whose prowess as a commander and knowledge of the workings of the alliance was ultimately used against the pirates themselves.[115] Similar approaches were taken elsewhere: in the 1620s, for example, Chinese officials dealing with their own pirate troubles also engaged the pirates active in those waters in an effort to curb their activity. The pirates operating in the South China Sea at the time were given powerful posts to persuade them to abandon piracy; this was much to the annoyance of the Dutch East India Company, which was eager to dominate the trade routes to China and which itself looked to liaise with the pirates to monopolise trade in the region.[116] It is perhaps noteworthy in this context, though not surprising, that it was the Dutch in 1614 who had taken the most direct action to tackle the pirate problem in Ireland.

From a social perspective, and considering the strength of the pirates in Munster, where they had essentially developed their own independent coastal state, the idea of looking beyond their crimes in order to justify their reprieve was central to the crown's approach. The concept of 'forgiveness' for offences like piracy, where expressions of regret for such crimes committed, if thought to be genuine, could lead to reprieves, was applied elsewhere in later times.[117] Mainwaring's applied view of *pulchrum scelus*, or 'noble crimes', being of a lesser offence when a certain code of practice was followed, such as not attacking fellow Englishmen, certainly made the decision to pardon individual pirates more palatable and easier to justify.[118] Pardoning the pirates in the southwest ensured that the emerging population in the remote areas of Munster retained its sense of Protestantism and 'Britishness', with the pardoned pirates then regarded as an integral part of the local population and their settlement viewed as 'belonging to household and local community'.[119] The 'forgiving' of these individuals by the crown, where 'clemency went to the desperate and contrite or to those with something to offer', was vindicated by arguing that these now 'British' subjects could advance plantation and commercial objectives not alone in Munster but across the Atlantic as well, expanding empire and enterprise. In claiming to have protected homeland trade and assisted with the repatriation of captives, and having shown contrition for their crimes by offering service to the crown, the pardoned pirates ingratiated themselves and made the issuing of pardons easier and more acceptable.

Captain Robert Walsingham, who becomes more prominent in the later time of the alliance, then serving under Mainwaring in North Africa, is a good example of this. As one of a group of men considered for a time as social outcasts, even serving as part of an Ottoman fleet at one point, he still ended up serving in the king's ships under Robert Mansell and became one of the main players on the expedition to Algiers in 1620–1 to attack the Turkish pirate fleet there.[120] It was Walsingham's protests that he had been forced into piracy in the first instance and then pressured into serving aboard the Ottoman fleet thereafter that supported his pardon, in that he appeared contrite in his affirmations and honourable in his actions towards his fellow Englishmen. No doubt in reality it was Walsingham's specialised knowledge of the Algerine defences that was considered essential for the expedition in 1620 and it was this that justified his pardoning and inclusion in the official fleet.[121]

Henry Mainwaring, perhaps the quintessential pirate-hunter turned pirate turned pirate-hunter, published his proposed 'remedy' in 1618 for defeating the pirates, which put forth the premise that

> … those which are now out may be cut off, and those that are not yet may be prevented, which were both an honourable thing for the State, an acceptable thing to God, and a great benefit to all Christian Merchants.[122]

Mainwaring's proposed handling of the alliance was predicated on his first-hand knowledge of the pirates themselves, many of whom, once pardoned, returned to piracy or at least, like Bishop, were later known to provide safe houses for active pirates when required.[123] Essentially, Mainwaring advised that any discussions with the pirates in the form of negotiations or deal-making would prove useless, and he proposed looking at the pirate problem as a whole. He sought to address piracy at all levels, beginning with deterring individuals from taking up piracy in the first instance. To stem the number of unemployed mariners entering into piracy, he suggested empowering all admiralty officers in the ports of England and Ireland so that they could enquire as to the business of all mariners whom they encountered, including those who were known ex-pirates. He proposed more stringent measures for Ireland due to its remoteness, and suggested that all those who were known to have been pirates, and their families, should be relocated to live inland from the coast, in an effort to completely cut the pirates off from their coastal activity and maritime links – a depopulation of the coastline, in a sense. He argued that it would ensure they no longer held bases there and thus could no longer rely on local aiders and abettors.[124] Mainwaring's *Discourse* was a useful guide, but its practical applicability was certainly influenced – and hampered – by prevailing circumstances and individual agendas on a local level. In that respect, little had changed.

CONTINUITY AND CHANGE

The enactment of legislation in Ireland and the capture of key pirate harbours such as Mamora in 1614 by Spain forced the centre of pirate power to move elsewhere. To most northern European citizens the name Turk was synonymous with pirate and the ports and harbours of North Africa were places where renegades from society could find refuge and protection. Throughout the heyday of the pirate alliance, however, political links with the North African and Mediterranean states continued, sustaining diplomatic relations from the time of Elizabeth I, though James was less inclined to address military and diplomatic agreements with Islamic rulers. With Mansell's unsuccessful Algiers expedition in 1620, James was forced to agree a treaty with the Barbary ports to protect trading interests.[125] With the shift, in the early part of the seventeenth century, of the commercial maritime economic centre from the Mediterranean region to the Atlantic, European and North African states had to change their focus and allegiances. Similarly, from 1612 the Dutch and Ottoman Empires had in place trade agreements, building on contacts through merchants over the preceding decade.[126] As New World opportunities continued to expand and merchant empires vied to acquire a piece of the lucrative spice trade, new ways of doing business developed, new covenants were made, and pirates and their ways changed accordingly.

A greater change was to hit Ireland's shores, however, with the arrival into Atlantic waters of ships belonging to North African and Ottoman Turks, better known perhaps by the more frightening term of 'Barbary corsairs'. The second decade of the seventeenth century was a notable turning point in pirate predation. The change came on the coat tails of pardons issued to the main pirate leaders, while others chose to serve out their time under the protection of foreign powers. Piracy continued, but under the command of Muslim captains or under converts to Islam – those who had 'turned Turk'. These pirates now looked to human captives as the cargo of choice. English merchants too saw the value in human cargoes and engaged in reciprocal trade in Islamic slaves sold in European markets.[127] Pirates persisted in targeting ships on the high seas but extended tactics to include terrestrial attacks on coastal communities. Predation on the open ocean took on a heightened and more frightening aspect that was to become a far greater menace to trade, shipping and human survival than any previous piratical activity in the North Atlantic.

CHAPTER 8

Decline and Transformations

The Turks have also taken Englishmen, Frenchmen, Spaniards, and Portingales. The ships are now hovering off the coast [of Ireland], their crews consisting of several different nations.[1]

While many of the men of the alliance returned to piracy, exonerations facilitated the elevation of lesser captains to fill the void created when senior figures chose to retire or relocate. Many who settled continued to assist other pirates by providing safe refuge, accommodation and access to a ready black market.[2] Bishop continued to be implicated in piracy, as confirmed by Lord Deputy Sir Oliver St John in 1617:

> This day I am advertised [by] letters from himself and from my Lord Boyle, [that] Sir Thomas Roper hath apprehended a notable pirate, one Fleaming, of the birth of this country. He took him in th' house of one Cap[t.] Bishopp an old pardoned pirate, that lives suspiciously near Limcon and Scull Haven, ever plotting with and relieving of pirates, [not] withstanding that I have given often … to the governors of these part[s] … an eye upon him.[3]

Piracy thus continued, as did corruption by those on land. But this was no longer within a framework of an association of pirates, with captains, crews and fleets sailing in unison under an agreed command structure.[4] Piracy now re-emerged on a more individual, opportunistic basis, where pirate captains – whether English, Dutch, Flemish or Irish, or those who served under the Muslim flag – did so with a small group of fellow pirates or as single ships plundering and then trading their booty. The harbours of southwest Munster thereafter were not acknowledged bases, but did continue as viable trading posts and re-victualling stations throughout the year and, when required, places of refuge provided by then-retired pirates. This persistence in piracy was assisted in no small measure by government officials remaining in office in the area, with most of the leading players continuing their tenure from the heyday of the alliance. Networks were thus maintained, symbiotically, between ex-pirates now settled in the area, corrupt admiralty officers still in place and new faces entering the scene.

PIRATE CAREERS AND CAREER PIRATES

By 1611 many Atlantic pirates who had operated primarily out of Ireland had been pardoned, executed or killed. Among them was Cornish captain Peter Boniton, another of Bishop's leading captains; captured off the coast of Spain, he was taken to France and executed in Marseille in 1609. Boniton was one of the pirate captains who openly traded with Thomas Crooke in Baltimore, and for which Crooke was called to England. Boniton may have been the information-gatherer among those in the alliance as he was noted to be 'One of the Ireland Pirates, whose purpose it was to goe unto the Straits to learn newes', and perhaps this indicates part of the strength of the alliance overall, where certain pirates were either tasked with, or dedicated themselves to, acquiring relevant maritime knowledge to inform the alliance's operations. During one of these information-gathering voyages, however, in 1609, Boniton lost his freedom and subsequently his life.[5] Others, as previously noted, such as Tibault Suxbridge, died during engagements at sea,[6] while more again succumbed to the gallows. Many, including captains Jennings and Harris, had their fates dictated by the competing political and personal agendas of the earls of Nottingham and Northampton.[7] A 'Captaine Flemming', captured by Sir Thomas Button in July of 1616 in the royal naval

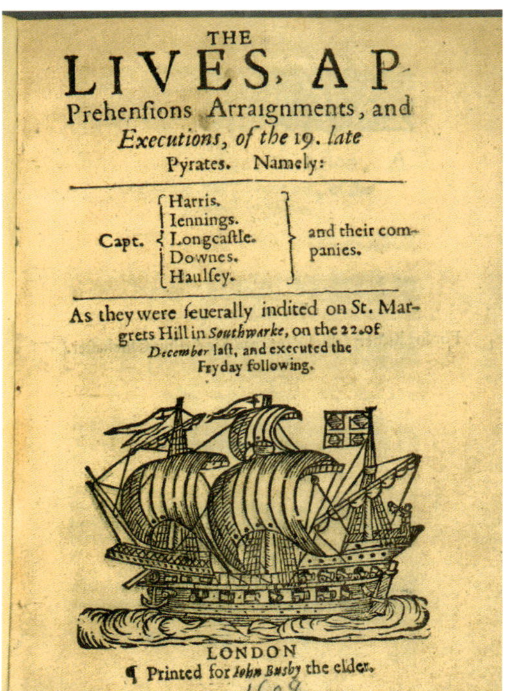
THE
LIVES, AP-
Prehenſions Arraignments, and
Executions, of the 19. late
Pyrates. Namely:

Capt. { Harris. Iennings. Longcaſtle. Downes. Haulſey. } and their companies.

As they were ſeuerally indited on St. Margrets Hill in *Southwarke*, on the 22. of *December* laſt, and executed the Fryday following.

LONDON
¶ Printed for *Iohn Busby* the elder.
1609

FIGURE 54: Image of front cover of *The Lives, Apprehensions, Arraignments and Executions of the 19 Late Pyrates*, containing an account of the trial and final days of the lives of pirate Captain John Jennings and his companions, published by E. Allde in 1609.
STC/725:21; HENRY E. HUNTINGTON LIBRARY AND ART GALLERY, SAN MARINO, CALIFORNIA

ship the *Moon*, was also executed 'in Chaines' in Youghal, while most of his crew were hanged at the same time in Cork.[8] This would seem to be a different Captain Fleming to the Fleming mentioned as captured in Richard Bishop's house in Leamcon, if the dates of apprehension of both men are correct. Fleming was taken from Richard Bishop's place and was en route to England for trial, but was recalled by the lord president of Munster, the earl of Thomond, who chose to deal with him in Ireland under the newly enacted legislation on piracy.[9]

Thomas Salkeld or Sockwell, '... that pettie reable and pirate' and at one time self-proclaimed king of Lundy Island off Wales, operated on occasion out of Ireland. Injured during a revolt by prisoners whom he was holding on Lundy Island, he sailed for Munster. Salkeld served first under Bishop and Jennings, finally becoming one of Peter Easton's captains.[10] It was while serving on board Easton's ship that he seems to have fallen out with the captain and was summarily thrown overboard. This may have been done in an attempt by Easton to curry favour with the crown, with the report on Easton's actions containing letters from the pirate captain to the chief justice and baron; in them he sought assurances of a pardon, with supporting letters by Thomas Roper and Richard Boyle. The details of the protection given can be understood from the lord deputy's letter:

> I have thought it not amiss to temporasise with them for a tyme, and have signed a protection for them for the space of forty days, in which among other provisions I have restrained them from comminge ashore other than two or three att once, and those to be only just as the vice president shall allow of to make provision for their moves of free access for their eating from day to day while they stand prohibited and not for store or to carry out of the harbour, and that they shall not permitt any man to come aboard to trade or trafick with them ...[11]

The pirates did not abide by the letter of protection, however, and were quickly noted as frequenting their base ashore. In any event, Easton chose not to submit and instead took up a legitimate commission elsewhere. Indeed, such was Easton's success serving under the duke of Savoy, he later queried why he should have considered a pardon from one king, when he was king of 'his own domain' in Italy. Such was the power and wealth of some of the pirates following a career of successful plunder, individual men regarded themselves as being on a par with royalty. Arch pirate John Ward famously declared of King James, 'If he reign king of all the land, I will reign king at sea.'[12] While arrogance prevailed, knowledge and experience often counted as much as power and strength. Easton's expertise in ordnance, for example, was a competency that the duke of Savoy readily identified. In serving as part of the duke's siege train, Easton is reported to have 'covered himself in glory'.[13] It is curious to note that in 1579 an engineer by the name of John Easton arrived into Waterford with munitions for the garrison there. By 1589, under a fiaunt of Elizabeth I, he had been granted a pension of £40 sterling a year for life in consideration of his skill as an engineer, and in particular as a skilled cannon founder. Whether proficient as a gun maker or gun operator, it is interesting to consider if both men were related and if a tradition of handling ordnance was part of the Easton family lineage.[14] Certainly, Peter Easton's pedigree suggests that he came from a seafaring family who were directly involved in maritime expeditions during the reign of Elizabeth I. One member was master of a ship named the *Sunshine* that formed part of the Davis expedition in 1585 in search of the Northwest Passage and another was involved in the fight against the Spanish Armada in 1588.[15] Easton's knowledge and skills therefore may have been inherent and applied in their best capacity when he became leader of the alliance in 1611.

Though the majority of the men in the alliance were amphibious in their lifestyles, many maintained a long career in piracy. Five years of activity for a pirate was considered lengthy, given that in the golden age of the early eighteenth century in the Caribbean, eighteen months was considered a very successful career.[16] Of all the pirates operating at the time, Captain John Jennings and Captain Thomas Tucker perhaps had among the longest careers, stemming from at least 1603 to when both men were executed – Jennings in 1610 in London and Tucker in 1616 in Denmark.

Thomas Tucker is a constant in the High Court of Admiralty papers from that early period. His career on the high seas certainly falls within the sphere of archetypal pirate and provides a valuable and colourful insight into the nature and extent of piratical activity and the diversity of terrain involved. A Newcastle mariner, he was described by naval commander Sir William Monson as 'a seaman bred from his youth, and continual practice made him excellent in his art and profession'.[17] He is first mentioned in the HCA indictments in 1605 when he captured the ship *William* of Leith at Portland and robbed it of its cargo of Gascony wine belonging to London merchants. During his time in the alliance in Ireland, Tucker served predominantly under Peter Easton, though when indicted he argued that as an ordinary sailor on board the trader *Daisy* of Sandwich, he had been pressed into service by Easton in 1611 when the pirate captain attacked the ship. He became master's mate in Easton's captured *Concord* of London, but by 1613 Tucker was seeking a pardon. He did not receive one and, like Easton, chose instead to serve in Savoy. In the year that followed he earned a wage of twenty-five crowns a month as a soldier in the service of the duke in Villafranca but then returned to his life as a pirate on the high seas, joining Captain John Woodland in Mamora. Woodland was arrested in Ireland and Tucker took over his ship as captain.[18]

For the next year Tucker successfully captured vessels off Flamborough Head, off the Yorkshire coast, plundered the *Thomas* of Newcastle, captured the *Holy Lamb*, a Flemish ship, and sailed down the English Channel where he harassed the Newfoundland fishing boats, before returning to the Azores. His marauding continued, taking a ship from Brazil carrying sugar, green ginger and specie. In October 1614, he looted a Spanish West Indiaman of its cargo of hides, wood and tobacco worth £1,000; after robbing a French ship, he returned to Ireland. In his time as captain of his ship *Fortune* he amassed a sizeable treasure trove of goods and monies, but from 1614 he once again began making representations for a pardon. In 1615 Lord Deputy Chichester sought instruction on how he was to deal with Tucker. With no pardon forthcoming, Tucker once again set sail, this time for Russia via Broadhaven in Mayo to seek his continued fortune as a pirate in northern waters.

As with so many of Tucker's associates, chief among them being Henry Mainwaring, Tucker was entertained by Gaelic-Irish chief Michael Cormack in Broadhaven who had an open house for pirates. The admiralty records of the time state that 'Cormocht kept a gold chain and 400 dubloons in safe keeping for Captain Tucker'. Tucker's ship was wrecked in a storm off the Faroe Islands, but he managed to survive with some of his crew in one of the ship's boats and made it to Iceland. While there, the pirates captured an English fishing vessel but Tucker's tenure as captain of the ship was brief as his crew mutinied, turned on their captain and brought him back to Yarmouth where they handed him over to the admiralty. Sent to London for trial in July 1615, he spent nearly a year in jail. Through the intercession of his fellow pirate Henry Mainwaring, he was released. Mainwaring, who had by 1616 received his pardon from the crown, argued that Tucker and his men had been part of his crew so the pardon should cover all of them equally. Part of the conditions of Tucker's pardon, like all other pardons, was that he return to 'civilian' life, and Tucker took up employment in a merchant ship on a trading expedition to Denmark. During the voyage, however, Tucker's luck finally ran out as a Danish ferryman recognised him for his past piracies. On reaching Danish shores, he was arrested, tried and executed in Denmark in 1616.[19] The tale of Tucker would no doubt be reflective of many other pirates throughout that period and later. It illustrates the 'adventurous' exploits of the men involved and the wide geographic extent of their activities, and goes some way to confirming our imagined impressions of pirates, showing that at times fact can indeed mirror fiction.

A select number of other pirate captains who were prominent in the alliance went on to forge legitimate maritime careers after they received their pardons. Henry Mainwaring was perhaps the most successful. In 1614 he was in the northwest of Ireland awaiting his pardon, no doubt at Broadhaven Bay.[20] When he eventually received it in 1616 he went on to write his *Discourse*, which he presented to the king in 1618 and he was knighted in that year. He was on active service as commander in the king's navy, lieutenant of Dover Castle and was a member of parliament in 1621. In 1637 he was appointed rear-admiral in the navy, elevated to vice-admiral in 1639 and received his doctorate in physics from Oxford University in 1643. Throughout his naval career he was involved in numerous expeditions until his death at the age of sixty-six in 1653.[21]

Robert Walsingham, discussed in the previous chapter, another of the leading captains of the alliance, also alleged he had been pressed into service when captured by Easton off the Guinea coast out of the merchant ship the *Daisy* of London in 1611, in union with his fellow pirate Thomas Tucker. Walsingham chose to remain on with Easton and became an accomplished pirate in his own right. He served for a time under Bishop before becoming one of Easton's senior captains, when Easton became admiral of the alliance. By 1614 Walsingham is listed as one of Mainwaring's captains in a ship of 100 tons based out of Mamora.[22] He arrived into Berehaven sometime after 1617 seeking a pardon, but not before he had spent time pirating with a Turkish fleet.[23] He had joined the pirates in Algiers in 1614, after the fall of Mamora, and by late 1616 he was commanding a Turkish fleet of six ships, along with fellow English pirates James Haggerston, William Clark, Thomas Kelly and a man named Browne of Limehouse, London, three of whom had been active in the alliance. By 1618 he was on trial in England for piracy and, though found guilty, was not executed. Due to the part he played in the 1620 Algiers expedition, he was subsequently engaged as a commander in the king's navy. It was not to last, however. In 1622 he was a prisoner in the

Tower of London on suspicion of returning to his pirating ways. Whether he was executed or not thereafter is not recorded.[24]

THE PROCESS OF SUPPRESSION

Among the letters of the earl of Cork, Sir Richard Boyle, is found the following, from 8 June 1625:

> I also held a goale delivery at Corke …, where were executed 8 pirates, viz Cap'n Nathanyell Smyth als Squarye, Matheu Gunter, Alphonsus Theker, Richard Tross, Samuell Boucher (Butcher), Richard Dalby, William Gilbyns, and Wm Knott: all 8 archpirates were executed.[25]

In another letter Boyle explains why he executed the men:

> … first, that they are a gang of notorious pirates and be good pilots upon this coast, … that they would spoyle the subjects trading thither, and generally hinder the king's customs, having already robbed English, Scotch, Irish and French, and housed themselves in several ships: secondly, if they should goe serve under foreign princes as they have done, and are so inclined, they might prove mischievous instruments to infest these coasts, knowing the harbors thereof, and most of them being also seamen: thirdly, we fynd that their intent was to victual at Long Island, And then to goe into the River of Kilmare [Kenmare], and take the ordnance out of the *Robe of Skeen* lying moored there, as also the powder belonging to that ship, and stowed in Sir Thomas Ropers seller there and then to sea in the pram they took from English and laden only with … canon shot of Mountesbay, being a strong warlike ship of 200 ton with only … ordnance and munitions, whereof shipped, then to go to sea again and make purchase of all that came to hand.

Boyle executed the men to prevent any further mischief to his majesty's 'subjects and dominions' and he offered a fourth reason – to prevent their escape:

> … as they be able and desperate men, as we counted reason to fear their escape, and then their skill and mallace might prove mischievous,

> revenges, and especially Sir William Hull is very fearful of their revenge if they should in any sort escape, because he took their ship.[26]

In February of that year, the crew of the *Hope* under Dutch captain Hugh Williams, acting under commission from the States-Generals in Holland, captured pirates Gunter and Trosse off the coast of Ireland. Williams delivered the pirates to Sir William Hull in Leamcon and in return the Dutch captain and crew received £20.[27] Hull by then was paying commissioned ships to apprehend pirates and deliver them to him. It is understandable why he would be somewhat concerned if the same pirates had escaped the clutches of the earl of Cork and returned to seek recompense from Hull in Leamcon.

Boyle's description of the pirates is informative too, in that he acknowledges their skills but again fears their intent, though the fact that he recognised them as Catholic sympathisers was perhaps one of the primary mitigating reasons for their execution: 'Nathaniel Smith, is an insolent man, and thought to be a good navigator, an obstinate Papist, and lives with his family in Donkirk.' Of Gunter and Tross [Trosse] he states that '… they are noted arch-pirates these may years. … The general report was that Gunter has been in prison for piracies xix [19] tymes and that Tross hath by some piracies betrayed as many ships. And for Theaker, he is also a notorious papist ….'[28]

From about 1615 there was a concerted effort by central government to clamp down on those who were assisting the pirates and enabling a continued ready market for their goods locally. In 1616, for example, the lord president the earl of Thomond received a set of sixteen instructions, part of which involved

> … the apprehention of releevers of Pyrattes and to punishe seuerally anie that shall vpon anie pretence haue conference with them and to remoue all those that Dwell in places where Pyrattes Doe usually resorte or where they maye resorte.[29]

The newly invigorated approach to tackling piracy, and which included aiders and abettors, applied to all government officials in the Munster area; instructions were issued to admiralty officers accordingly. Those who were involved in direct dealings with the pirates came under more intensive scrutiny. William Hull retained his position as deputy vice-admiral, ensuring Leamcon continued as a hub for trade and contraband. His lawful business interests were expanding by then too, and his links with investors, with some of whom he had familial ties, meant that he had a vested interest in remaining in west Cork and therefore needed to retain the crown's favour. By 1620 he was serving as rent collector for Richard Boyle for the southwest of Munster and such relationships, as correctly identified by John Appleby in his study of Hull, meant that he could turn 'the illegitimate, irregular and increasingly tenuous business of piracy into more legitimate forms of enterprise, revealing clearly the enduring importance of the relationships between family and fortune in seventeenth-century Ireland'.[30]

As Hull sought to legitimise his affairs, pirates continued to frequent the southwest coast, and at times Hull was, once again, under suspicion of complicity; in addition he also came under scrutiny for under-paying revenue returns to Lord High Admiral George Villiers, first duke of Buckingham, who had succeeded Nottingham in 1618. Hull was not alone in this, and familiar names come up, again with strong business and familial ties. These include Thomas Crooke's brother-in-law James Salmon, who was then stationed in Castlehaven and who continued to reap rewards, both personal and official, in his capacity as deputy vice-admiral there. Sir Lawrence Parsons, who by the 1620s had acquired the estate of Birr in County Offaly, continued to be involved in Admiralty affairs in Munster, along with handling leases for his cousin Sir Richard Boyle and absentee speculator Thomas Roper. Parsons died suddenly in 1628. Sir Thomas Roper, created first Viscount Baltinglass and baron of Bantry in 1627, was, unsurprisingly, also under suspicion of withholding funds. Though he had extensive business investments by that time in Munster, Leinster and Ulster, many of them had proven unprofitable.[31] It was with his holding of the patent for the registering or licensing of alehouses, received through his close ties with Viscount Villiers, that helped him recoup some of his losses, and it was this connection that allowed him such leeway in administering the monies that he collected.[32]

PRIVATE COMMISSIONS AND MARITIME ECONOMIC WARFARE

Hull's links with the earl of Cork were vital to his successful progress from proscribed middleman to legitimate operator. His piratical liaisons proved to be extremely lucrative but changing times necessitated changing focus. Hull began to use his early commercial rewards to advance his landholdings in coastal Munster, and though he had acquired the town of Crookhaven in the early 1600s and established Leamcon as his primary demesne from that time, the main expansion of his estates date from the 1620s. These included extensive tracts of land from the O'Mahony Gaelic lords and rent from tenants, many of whom were retired pirates and pirate families. Though biased to reflect his own agendas, Hull's deposition shows that by the time of the 1641 Rebellion he had amassed substantial wealth stemming from landed interests, livestock, commercial ventures and maritime infrastructure.[33]

Hull's actions did not take place in isolation, however, and the wider impetus for change was reflected in new opportunities opening up following the death of King James in 1625. A series of conflicts commencing from that year, including the war between England and Spain from 1625 to 1630, coinciding with the war between England and France from 1627 to 1629, witnessed an influx of privately operated foreign vessels into the waters around Ireland and England, among them French men-of-war, Dunkirkers and Biscayners. English ships were attacked and trade was threatened, but men like Hull recognised the opportunity for commissioning their own private ships to legitimately attack Spanish and French shipping.[34] Commissioned ships once more began to support maritime affairs by supplementing the king's ships; unlike his predecessor, Charles I supported the naval fleet and sought to augment it. James' depletion of the navy enabled an escalation in foreign attacks with no effective naval force to counter them. The outbreak of war with Spain and later France placed additional strain on naval resources. Though England had strong merchantmen by this time engaged in trans-oceanic trade, the combined threat from privately commissioned foreign marauders and Islamic corsair attacks, as discussed below, focused the new king's attention on rebuilding the royal and merchant fleets. George Villiers, the duke of Buckingham, had, since his coming to office in 1618, sought to commission dedicated privately owned men-of-war, but it was clear by 1625 that there was a need for large-scale assistance from the merchant marine if England was to retain control of its trade, waters and empire.[35]

With the crown now willing to reissue letters of marque in Britain and Ireland and with greater investment in the navy, opportunities re-emerged for men of the sea to gain rightful employment. The rejuvenating of the naval fleet, however, required greater service, and press-ganging again came to the fore. By 1635, for example, plans were in place to increase the number of crown ships to fifteen and press 4,000 men to serve on board.[36] Large numbers of mariners, primarily English in nationality and including those who were still active as pirates (those not retired or pardoned), saw a chance to return to their lawful professions as officers, sailors, merchants, ship's carpenters, surgeons, gunners, trumpeters, soldiers or ordinary seamen.[37] For men like Henry Mainwaring this welcome return to official naval and merchant seafaring meant a return to a respectful life. Others, however, such as Robert Walsingham, who availed of opportunities to command under a legitimate flag, could not shake off their former ways and continued to serve both masters.[38]

By 1627 Hull had three commissioned ships: the *Fortune* of Leamcon, 100 tons with twelve ordnance and sixty men; the *Talbot* of Leamcon, 200 tons, twenty-four guns and 150 men; and the *Phoenix*, a forty-ton ship which Hull may have captained himself. Indeed, Hull expanded his private maritime interests, partnering in a merchant syndicate in Bristol and setting out the ships *Dolphin* and *Elizabeth* from there. He became an eager promoter of privately commissioned vessels from the 1620s in what later became known as 'privateering' in the true sense from the 1640s.[39] In Ireland the commissioning of private vessels was tightly controlled by the High Court of Admiralty in England, including the requirement to send all prizes and goods to London. As was to be expected, this was a bone of contention for those investors in Ireland who complained that agents in England were in a perfect position to swindle them out of the true value of goods.[40] As a consequence, those like Hull continued to serve their own purposes – his privately commissioned ships formed part of his legitimate affairs but he also helped himself to shares of the prize goods before sending the remainder with the ship to England.

As old habits die hard, he also continued to contract with pirates, and his direct business dealings at Leamcon with pirate Claes Compaen are a good example. The 'great pirat Campaan' was recognised as perhaps the most famous of the Dutch pirates, with books and poems written about him and his misdeeds retold as heroic tales.[41] He possessed two ships, referred to in the sources as the 'Admiral' of 400 tons, with thirty-five pieces of ordnance and a crew of eighty men, and the 'Vice-Admiral' of 220 tons, carrying twenty-six guns and with a complement of forty men, most of whom were Dutch and Germans, but with about a third made up of English and Irish.[42] An account from 1625 describes that 'where he has a rendezvous is in Ireland betweene the Long Iland and the mayne [mainland] there he is greatly favoured by one Sir William Hull'.[43] While the same account lists Compaen's extensive seasonal plundering routes, which ranged from the coast of Barbary, Spain, the Straits, France, England, Ireland, and back to Barbary, it advocates for a continuation of a semi-formal gathering place at Leamcon, at least where he was concerned, and survival of piratical networks and markets. This would further verify Hull's continued efforts as a 'fence' or receiver, known to deal in plundered goods and to launder cargoes at agreed prices to interested local parties, with Leamcon serving as the collection point.[44] Following one plundering expedition, Compaen had in the hold of his ship, and no doubt readily dispersed in west Cork,

> ... seaven hundreth and tenn pound weights of Barbary gold in ducats, barres and grayne [dust] betweene five and six hundreth weighte of silver and much monies besides of English coyne.[45]

Hull carried on business as usual, though perhaps with a greater emphasis on his private investments in commissioned ships and the returns that could be had from prize-taking. This continued until Hull and some of his plantation colleagues were the focus of attack and clearance during the 1641 Irish Rebellion. A greater threat loomed, however, and the menace of North African corsairs was to strike in the dark hours of a June morning and send shockwaves along the southwest coast of Munster.

THE ALGERINE RAID ON BALTIMORE RECONSIDERED

The most fundamental change in piracy from about 1615 was that the North Atlantic scene was no longer dominated by Englishmen. Slowly, predation became more international in character. The economic incentives prevailed but the focus for many of those now involved shifted to include human cargo as part of the piratical trade. As time passed, piratical activity intensified, with the growing magnitude of the problem acknowledged in a report sent from Madrid by Sir Francis Cottington in October 1616:

> The strength and boldness of the pyrats (or rather of the Turks) is now grown to that height, both in the Ocean, and *Mediterranean* Seas, as I have never known anything to have wrought a greater sadness and distraction in the Court, then the daily advice thereof. Their whole fleet consists of 40 Sail of tall Ships, of between 200 and 400, Tuns apiece; Their Admiral has 500 Tuns. They are divided into 2 squadrons, the one of 18 Sail, remaining before *Malaga* (in sight of the City), the other about the *Cape St. Marie*, which is between *Lisbone* and *Sevil*.[46]

Through communications and contact with pirates like John Ward, Richard Bishop, Henry Mainwaring and Robert Walsingham, the North African corsairs augmented their existing knowledge of ship construction, seamanship and warfare. Barbary merchants and traders had contact with mainland Europe and Britain throughout the previous century and would have been familiar with European ship design, elements of which they would have integrated with their own, allowing for longer and farther voyaging; by the second decade of the seventeenth century, however, the character of North African piracy had altered and evolved dramatically. Together with this transformation in technology and seafaring capabilities, North African pirates now set their predatory eyes beyond the Mediterranean to the coastal settlements of the North Atlantic.[47]

In the summer of 1627 the people of the Westman Islands in Iceland were suddenly subjected to a horrifying raid by North African corsairs; three dozen citizens were killed and close to four hundred taken captive to be sold thereafter in the slave markets of northern Africa. Though this would not be the last time that Iceland and its neighbouring Faroe Islands would be attacked by Turkish corsairs, the first-hand account from one of the captives of the 1627 attack, Reverend Ólafur Egilsson, records a harrowing tale of fear, loss and grief. One interesting entry may contain a clue to continued links with the piracy of the previous few decades:

> … while the people were still unprepared, the evil pirates lowered three boats overboard and very quickly put three hundred into them and rushed ashore. In the boats were English pilots who had guided the pirates to Iceland, where none had ever before managed to come ashore.[48]

No names are given for the pilots but it is possible that they were North Atlantic pirates who were then in the service of the North African corsairs. What is important about this is that while the pirates were now specifically targeting coastal settlements irrespective of how remote they were in the Atlantic, those who assisted, in this case the English pilots, had first-hand knowledge of the waters and routeways taken. Tucker's voyages north and his plundering of Danish and other vessels there confirms the broad knowledge held by the pirates of the alliance of the waters of the northern seas. North African corsairs had thus armed themselves with more appropriate ships, armaments, men and knowledge to expand their horizons for plunder into colder climes and darker waters.[49] Another slightly later retelling of the events, written in the form of a saga and dating to 1643, mentions Danish pilots, one in particular who was a captive slave but who used his knowledge of the northern waters to procure his release.[50] The Danish connection here again suggests cross-cultural links between North Atlantic mariners and Ottoman Turks who were now expanding their horizons northwards. Of course, some captains within the North African pirate collective were themselves European renegades, as we will see when discussing the raid on Baltimore below, which allowed for first-hand knowledge of the waters of the North Atlantic.

In 1626 the economic impact for Ireland from Turkish pirate raids on merchant ships was raised by the mayor of Limerick when in a letter to lord deputy Falkland he stated that '… the townsmen … are very poor, owing [to] pirates, Turks, Dunkirkers, and Spaniards, who have taken six of their ships at sea …'. The impoverished townspeople suffered such loss of goods and income that they could not afford to pay for the redemption of the captives.[51] In January 1631 Richard Boyle, the earl of Cork, wrote to Lord Dorchester to report that the mayor of Waterford had received communications from Waterford merchants. They had returned from the coast of Spain with news that thirty-six sail of 'Turks' (Ottoman Turks) had been pirating along Spain's coast and they feared that the ships would soon reach Ireland.[52] It was in February of that year that Boyle relayed his own concerns about a possible pirate raid occurring along the Munster coastline and he sought assistance with fortifying Baltimore, but his pleas fell on deaf ears.[53]

Skirting the coast of Cork at that time were two warships under the command of Dutchman Jan Janszoon (variously spelled Jansz, Janszoon or Johnson in the sources) van Haarlem, then known as Murad Reis, in charge of the sultan's fleet in Salé. Janszoon was a seasoned sailor, who began his career in charge of a privately commissioned Dutch ship but eventually abandoned his loyalty to his own country and joined the fleets of the corsairs in North Africa. He adopted the moniker 'Murad Reis', signifying that he had converted to Islam, and was accepted fully by the North African rulers, rising to the rank of admiral. He led an illustrious and exceptionally successful career, on a par with his compatriot Claes Compaen, and their pirating operations; Dutch piracy and how Dutch officials dealt with it provides interesting contemporary and comparative reading to that of the alliance (see Epilogue).[54]

Just four months after Boyle's letter, on 20 June 1631, the North African pirates attacked Baltimore, killing two and taking 107 settlers captive, though some sources suggest the number was higher.[55] Murad Reis had captured a fishermen named Hacket in Dungarvan, who then piloted the pirates from there, around via Kinsale and on to Baltimore.[56] Reis moored his ships to the east of Baltimore Harbour and attacked the settlers in the part of the town known as the Cove. The day after the attack, Hull wrote to Boyle from Leamcon: 'The [Turkish] ships are plying off and on near Mizen Head.' The corsair vessels had been there for nearly a week and a worried Hull reported that if the pirates were not driven off, they would ruin trade and the people would be unable to pay their debts.[57] Hull then received a letter from Joseph Carter, sovereign of Baltimore, on 20 June, informing him that

> … this last night just before day two Turke men-of-war … have carried away men, women and children – one hundred & eleven, and 2 more they slayed … the ships are going to the west, … they will put in about Leamcon or Crookhaven.[58]

Hull's follow-up letter to Boyle suggested that there were other pirate ships plying the waters around Crookhaven and Mizen and perhaps Murad Reis' two vessels joined them after his raid on Baltimore. On 25 June, just days after the attack, the full account of the raid was relayed to the king.[59] A full list of those taken captive was also sent to the English Privy Council in July and included another, shorter account of the raid.[60] From the correspondence sent back and forth the shock and alarm was discernible, with an escalating sense of fear of further attacks. It is interesting to note that one of the captives listed was a William Gunter, along with his wife, maid and seven sons, and one can ponder if he was related to pirate Captain Mathew Gunter, discussed above (in Chapter 4) and listed as executed by Boyle in 1625. William Gunter was certainly a settler, but whether he resided in Baltimore as a consequence of legitimate plantation or as the extended family of one of the alliance's captains remains unknown. It would be an irony indeed if the latter were true and they found themselves victims of the new wave of North African pirate predation.[61]

The traditionally identified landing place of the North African pirates when they raided Baltimore was at the Cove, to the southeast of the main plantation settlement. From there, the pirates are said to have attacked the houses in the Cove directly from the strand. Similarly, the houses in the Cove are described variously as thatched, possibly of plaster and wood, and as 'cabins', representative of what the native Irish would have lived in prior to the development of the plantation settlement.[62] A more plausible

FIGURE 55: Detail from Strafford Folio map of Baltimore showing houses on the hill overlooking the Cove; the main harbour is seen, with fishing and boats at anchor, at the small cove of Tramadroum. Two fully-masted ships are shown outside the harbour.
WWM/STR P 20/100 WENTWORTH WOODHOUSE MUNIMENTS, SHEFFIELD CITY LIBRARY ARCHIVES

landing location, however, was into the little cove of Tramadroum ('the bay of the ridges'), south of the Cove area itself, around the small headland of Coney Island and located on the north side of the main entrance to the harbour.[63] As discussed briefly in Chapter 3, recently revealed archaeological evidence in the form of an old slipway and basal remains of a stone quay suggest infrastructure was in place, at some point, that would have facilitated the mooring of boats and easy access to and from the area. Whether these features were in place at the time of the Algerine raid remains to be confirmed. When considered in connection with Thomas Crooke's industrial complex immediately inland from Tramadroum, including the recorded monument of a fish palace, there is the potential that this early quay and slipway were directly associated with the fishing industry, and would no doubt have been readily known and in use.[64]

In respect of the houses mentioned, from the list of captives from Baltimore, most would appear to have been either New English settler or Old English surnames. This points to the probability that settlers were living in the Cove area, with the Cove very much part of Thomas Crooke's plantation settlement at that stage. It was the location of the earlier settlement in Baltimore and therefore it is probable that remaining indigenous were also living there.[65] The diversity of natives and newcomers would tie in with Crooke's fishing complex, as well as the more substantial domestic dwellings adhering to plantation construction regulations 'in the English fashion'.

While some structures would have been industrial (Crooke's fishing industry) or for agricultural/domestic animal usage, and thus may have been thatched, the majority of the settlers' houses would have adhered to plantation standards. This is borne out by their representations on the two contemporary cartographic sources, the Dutch John Hunt chart of 1612 and the Strafford map of Baltimore.[66] Both show the settlement in the Cove comprised of houses of one-and-a-half or two storeys, roofs that have a high pitch and thus most probably slated, and with most having chimneys. These would certainly be representative of settler houses rather than the lesser, thatched cabins of the Irish.

It is known from the contemporary accounts of the raid that Murad Reis moored his two ships to the east of the harbour entrance, perhaps at the entrance or outer limits to Eastern Hole Bay. From here the pirates, once they had lowered their 'long boats', could come ashore directly to the immediate north of Eastern Hole Bay, where there is a narrow shingle strand and a small river running into the sea and where it would be a short climb over the hill to the Cove. Alternatively, with Tramadroum the more probable landing place, the pirates would have rowed (as is referred to in the accounts) around the headland upon which the beacon is now located at the entrance to Baltimore Harbour, and 'along all the shoare'.[67] The strand there leads right into the Cove, past the fish palace site into the town proper. To land in either of those locations would have allowed for a rapid, sudden surprise attack and, by extension, efficient escape and return to their ships thereafter. If the pirates had used the main strand at the Cove itself, just below the main settlement at Baltimore, it would have required extensive rowing around the full headland at the entrance to the harbour, around Coney Island and then navigating between moored fishing boats. The reciprocal journey would have been the same but with their boats laden with captives.[68] The stealth by which the raid was carried out, the rapidity of the event and the speed at which the Algerines made their escape with their human cargo points to an access known in advance, used previously by some of the men, and which afforded ease of movement in the dark of night.

EVIDENCE BENEATH THE WAVES?

At the time of the emerging Algerine threat in the Atlantic, there were a number of pirates whose names became synonymous with the piracies of that era. One of those names was Nutt.[69] There were allegedly two pirates

FIGURE 56: Baltimore Harbour entrance looking from Tramadroum Cove. This was the cove most likely used by the Algerine pirates when carrying out their raid in 1631. IMAGE: CONNIE KELLEHER

with the same surname, John and Robert Nutt, both English and more than likely brothers. John Nutt had reputedly received a pardon by 1623 and thereafter commanded privateers, but he remained active around Ireland up to 1632. It is not known if Thomas Wentworth, earl of Strafford and newly appointed lord lieutenant of Ireland, had him executed or not.[70] Nutt had close links with George Calvert, later Lord Baltimore, and his settlement in Newfoundland.[71]

Robert Nutt was also active about the same time around the southwest coast of Munster, visiting Long Island and Crookhaven in April 1632.[72] A similar, slightly later account also refers to a pirate named Nutt sailing in consort with 'Turks' when surveying the Irish harbours in 1632, when another attack was mooted.[73] For this period, there are numerous entries in the High Court of Admiralty papers that refer to Robert Nutt's exploits around the southwest corner of Ireland, from Ballinskelligs to Kinsale.[74] It would appear, from the contemporary accounts, that Robert Nutt was more active in Ireland than his sibling John Nutt, who is more readily associated with Newfoundland and the southern coast of England, though no doubt crossing paths and collaborating when needed. In the 1620s, as we have already read in Chapter 6, according to the examination of Hugh Baker,

FIGURE 57: National Monuments Service's (UAU) diver surveying two cannon at the Dunworley Bay wreck site in 2009. © CONNIE KELLEHER, NATIONAL MONUMENTS SERVICE

John Nutt captured a bark when off the Waterford coast and then proceeded to Long Island. This stretch of water along the southern passage seems to have been favoured by Nutt, with Baker's account detailing that he would lie between 'Ireland and the port of Torbay, near Dartmouth, for a fortnight'.[75]

Around this time a ship associated with the Algerine Turks, and possibly that of the pirate 'Nutt' (though it is not clarified which Nutt is referred to) was lost in Dunworley Bay in County Cork. Accounts vary as to the name of the ship, with both *Rover* and *Black Mary* suggested.[76] Dunworley is a smaller harbour within the southeastern corner of the larger bay of Clonakilty on the southern coast of Cork, with Kinsale Harbour to its southeast.

South-facing, the entrance to Dunworley is marked by a continuous reef system that reveals itself through two pinnacles, the larger Cow Rock and the smaller Horse Rock, with the latter covered at high tide and a hidden hazard to shipping over the centuries. The Dunworley Bay wreck site lies at the base of the western side of Horse Rock.[77] *In situ* lower hull timbers are visible on the seabed, along with seven iron cannon, two of which – a swivel gun and an iron gun were recovered; two iron anchors – a large bower and a small kedge – are also recorded from the wreck site.

Of the guns, collectively they are of variable sizes and calibres and distinguishing features suggest they are English.[78] One, a small-calibre falcon or falconet, has a much-eroded maker's mark on the breech end near the touchhole that has been positively identified as belonging to John Browne, of the famous Browne family of Horsmonden, royal gun founders through four generations, from the 1590s to the 1670s. The Browne family marks varied with each generation, with those on the Dunworley wreck gun attributed to the early to mid-seventeenth century and potentially placing the wreck within the time period of the Algerine raid on Baltimore.[79] Recorded results of the excavated hull timbers point to a well-built, medium-sized ship when fully constructed. The mixture of iron ordnance on board suggests it may have been a merchant vessel that would have acquired guns from numerous sources. There were ready markets in Europe for the sale of cannon at that time and such merchantmen would not have been particular as to the type of guns used once the size and price were right.[80]

At that time along the south coast of Ireland, large numbers of merchant ships were trading out of the many harbours and ports, and the ship could have been one of those merchant vessels. The guns too could be earlier guns on a later ship, as guns had a long use life. But the wreck remains may also point to a ship that was used by pirates, as they too would have acquired guns from whatever source opportunity presented – from ships captured, from ready markets or through interchange between ships – leading to a mixture of gun types on board. An example is the swivel gun, favoured by pirates as it could be moved easily from one part of a ship to another or from one ship to another. Generally, they were used for close-up engagement and as anti-personnel weapons. Pirates particularly sought them as they were mounted on the gunwales and assisted with the boarding of other vessels during the course of a capture. The archaeological investigations at the wreck site, frustratingly, did not recover definitive evidence as to the identity or exact date of the wreck. The true origins of the Dunworley Bay shipwreck, and

FIGURE 58: Ballinskelligs Castle, County Kerry, the McCarthy Mór towerhouse built in the sixteenth century to control shipping in the bay. By 1620 it was occupied by Christopher Sigersen, sheriff and collector of duties on ships. The bay was used as a base by pirate Captains John and Robert Nutt and their fleet of ships during that period. IMAGE: CONNIE KELLEHER

whether or not it provides a direct link to the pirates Nutt and the North African raid on Baltimore, for now at least remain a mystery.

By 1622 James had ratified, albeit begrudgingly, the treaty between the North African ports of Algiers, Tunis and others; the ongoing war between England and Spain meant that he could not continue to tackle the problem of piracy, including its impact on trade, while also engaging Spanish forces on land and in the water. Essentially, he could not afford to have an adversary on both sides of the straits.[81] Though this helped in 'decriminalising' the activities of the North African pirates, as they then concentrated on attacking Iberian shipping, it also prohibited English ships from attacking those of the Barbary States. Though diplomatic relations with the ports of Morocco, Tunis and Algiers had been in place since the latter part of the sixteenth century, the treaty opened the ports in North Africa to legitimate trade by English ships, but also allowed pirated goods to enter the ports and harbours of Ireland and England more easily, where they continued to find ready markets. The raids by North African corsairs did not end with the treaty, however, and the Barbary threat increased, culminating in Ireland with the raid on Baltimore in 1631. Piracy remained a constant wherever trade ships plied the oceans and opportunity presented itself. This was a period too, with the advent of the Caroline administration, when privateering was once again used as a legitimate mechanism for maritime predation on the high seas. As the seventeenth century progressed, piracy and privateering became indivisible once more.

PER SIMPLICEM DESINENTIAM – THE END OF THE ALLIANCE

In reality, the pirates who formed the alliance were engaged in socio-economic warfare. The changing face of empire at that time also meant that politics was intricately associated with maritime matters. The reasons for the success of the alliance are many; they involve timing, expanding global opportunities, the opening up of new territory, and expansion of existing markets in remote regions to avail of those changing times, which in turn allowed men who were pirates to capitalise on their actions. Whether these men were *hostis humani generis* ('enemies of mankind'), victims of circumstance or tactical opportunists, pirates continue to fascinate.[82] One of the key ingredients was familiarity and the pirates in many instances knew in advance the places they used and the people they dealt with. As N.A.M. Rodger correctly observed:

> Real pirates always had friends, who did not call them pirates but some politer word. Enemies were called pirates, not necessarily with legal justification.[83]

And so it is. Certainly the agreement that was in place – be it a code or guidelines, written or verbal – and that was followed by the majority of the men of the alliance in refusing to attack any ship apart from those that were the traditional enemies of England, would suggest men of circumstance and men who were decidedly discriminate.

Mainwaring, in his *Discourse* in 1616, suggested clearance of the coast and selective separation of settlement to prevent symbiotic relationships developing or continuing. He advised that the tradition of piracy in the remote coastal areas needed to be severed, and in part this took place. Above all, however, time and tide overcame the alliance. Men tired of their piratical ways, and identified new opportunities to lead legitimate lives, albeit, for some, on the proceeds of their ill-gotten gains. Others chose to go it alone and join other disparate bands of marauders. The Alliance of Pirates ceased to operate as a cohesive force from about 1615 and the southwest coast of Munster was no longer to serve as a safe haven for pirate nests. Mainwaring's suggestions, though only partly implemented, still impacted the pirates of the alliance. Over the course of the next five years new pirates arrived on the scene, and while keeping the tradition of piracy in southwest Ireland alive, they did not operate on a par with those of the alliance. Mainwaring put it simply to the king: if the Alliance of Pirates were tackled as suggested, they would *Per simplicem desinentiam* – simply cease to exist.[84]

Although the age of the alliance was over, piracy was to persist, and indeed flourish, as trade routes continued to expand across the globe. The perceived heyday of pirates is considered to be the early eighteenth century when those infamous buccaneers were based in places like Tortuga in the Caribbean or Port Royal, Jamaica.[85] A century earlier, when the Alliance of Pirates had their heyday around the coast of Munster and throughout the North Atlantic, should now properly be seen as Ireland's golden age of piracy.

Epilogue

Penaſer
Roſbren
Aſa
Down
Spick
Cove
Copenger
Rosbren
Spain
13. voet
Sken
Hare
Flats
Hoge
Il sherke
Clere

And in Ireland because there is little or no shipping belonging to the Country, to command strictly that no seafaring man, especially that hath been a Pirat shall come within 10 or 12 miles of the seaco[a]st.[1]

Piracy prevailed in the seas off Ireland, with changing players and changing circumstances dictating actions and targets. The pirate nests in coastal southwest Munster, and west Cork in particular, diminished but did not disappear altogether. Willing local populations continued to engage with pirates and smugglers, handling contraband goods and trading in provisions, accommodation and entertainment in return for commodities from other realms. The face of piracy may have altered, with the North African corsairs dominating from the 1620s onwards, but the actuality of pirate life and smuggled goods within the context of remote coastal communities remained the norm.[2]

The Alliance of Pirates in the North Atlantic can be considered as a singular event not alone specific to Ireland but also within the wider history of piracy. It cannot, however, be viewed in isolation. It mirrored other nations' pirates, including the Dutch renegades and pirates in Mamora in 1611, for example, who were also seeking pardons from their respective governments during the same period.[3] A comparative analysis of both piratical groups, their scope of operations and eventual decline would certainly inform more fully on the nature and extent of piratical activity from the northern hemisphere in that period. The parallels are clear, and these piratical powers availed of the opportunities that emerged when evolving states were challenging the hold of the traditional maritime powers on the ocean highways. Competing powers sought control of the seas, of new lands, new goods and new markets, through maritime warfare, on a military, private and piratical level. Depending on which side of the divide a player was positioned, their actions could on the one hand be regarded as legitimate, respectable and indeed honourable or on the other as wholly criminal, uncivilised or as the 'enemy of mankind'.

The alliance evolved due to a variety of mitigating circumstances. The outlawing of privately commissioned ships allied with the depletion of not just the king's ships but also the merchant fleet as a whole under King James VI and I provided ample opportunities for piracy to flourish. The clamping down on officials' autonomy within the pirate ports and harbours in southwest England necessitated the transfer of territorial opportunities to Ireland; the final stages of land acquisition under the Munster Plantation paved the way for the men of the alliance to land and settle and admiralty officials and other men of means to continue their involvement with underground trade. The fall of the Gaelic Order after the Battle of Kinsale in 1601–2 and the ousting of native power in the southwest heralded the era of piracy in Munster. Pirates and their co-conspiratorial government officials rapidly filled the vacuum. The opening up of world trade markets with the establishment of settlements and trading posts in the New World and beyond provided the pirates with a perfectly located nest in Munster that linked their other bases in Newfoundland and northwest Africa in a seasonal parade of ships; they could control and patrol the shipping within the whole of the North Atlantic while at the same time looking across the Atlantic to new lands of opportunity.

The alliance sustained in Ireland for so long because the legal mechanisms to tackle it head-on were not enacted until 1614. Until then, willing land-based partners linked the pirates of the sea to smugglers, businessmen, gentry, officials and locals on land. The men of the alliance generally, though not always, abided by a certain honour code to target only the common enemies of the crown. This approach certainly assisted in making their actions less egregious. Pardons were more easily sought and, for some, more easily argued at official level. More than anything, the piracy that evolved from that time in the early seventeenth century was, as identified by other authors on the subject, tolerated because it was economically and militarily advantageous to the English colonial vision throughout the Atlantic. This proved to be the case with later piracy in the Caribbean too but is no less relevant for the North Atlantic Alliance of Pirates.[4] On a separate though related level, apart from national offences within disputed territorial waters, the pirates were also integral to the growth in global maritime crimes, then an inherent element of colonial expansion. Aiders and abettors on land, serving their own intrinsic agendas that included political struggles with other officials; pressure from merchant interests; personal burdens as a consequence of overseas investments – all influenced and encouraged a synergetic relationship between pirates and landed élites. One could not function or survive without the other. The story of the alliance, as with other eras of piratical activity, tells us as much about those on the land as those on the sea.[5]

THERE STILL BE TALES TO TELL

This is by no means the full story of piracy at that time in Munster or the North Atlantic; rather it is but an introduction to the lives, lifestyles and landscape of the main characters in the alliance, their associates, families and adversaries. There were many other individuals – among them settlers, officials and pirates – and there are many more links to be investigated before the tale can be told in its entirety. Men of all nations continued to touch the coast of Ireland with acts of piracy, individually, including Irishmen. One, a Captain David Burke, for example, is noteworthy, due to his plunderings in the 1620s off the southwest coast, particularly around Valentia in Kerry and Cape Clear near Baltimore.[6] The alliance, however, acted as a coalition of men, who responded to political upheaval at home in England by availing of prospects overseas and rich pickings on the high seas. A complex set of characters were involved in what became a commercial industry in plundered goods in southwest Ireland, and such complicated relationships were commonplace in government circles and certainly in daily life in remote coastal regions. What seems to emerge from the depositions of those examined, combined with the geographic extent of the pirates' hunting grounds and the cultural evidence revealing itself within this pirate landscape, is that a network of communication – predominantly oral – existed that ensured the successful operation of a lucrative underground market.[7]

As discussed in Chapter 2, no evidence has come to light on whether the pirates in the alliance had any written code, agreements or 'articles' that directed their actions. Their modus operandi when at sea, however, suggests that they had some mechanism of governance, but how formalised this was remains a mystery. Mainwaring told of agreed signals for giving chase or to indicate who was who at a distance, to aid recognition. A more thorough assessment of early pirate governance could provide more clarity on whether such formal instruments existed. It is obvious that such systems had evolved by the latter part of the seventeenth century though that in itself does not infer that similar procedures were adhered to at the time of the alliance, or indeed in earlier periods. Exquemelin's account, as discussed, taken in tandem with other sources, including the 'articles' associated with contemporary pirates Bartholomew 'Black Bart' Roberts and Samuel 'Pirate Prince' Bellamy, are indicative of how order was maintained in what could often be a very disorderly world.[8] While the captain, for example, was duly elected by the vote of the crew, so too was the master or quartermaster. He was also judged by his previous successes, particularly his ability to maintain discipline on board ship. He needed to be trustworthy as one of his primary responsibilities was that of treasurer, overseeing the safe keeping of captured booty and its subsequent equitable distribution. Generally, the captain, master, quartermaster and other men of position on board (which included the surgeon, carpenter and gunners) would receive a higher share of the spoils than ordinary crew, with such detail covered in the articles as agreed. The system included pirates who had been injured, shares owing to their families, or compensation provided to loved ones in the event that a pirate was killed during his time at sea. It was clear from accounts that the wives or widows of some of the pirates active in the early seventeenth century went as far as to harass the local admiralty officers to seek out their expected shares or monies sent ashore for them by their men.[9] More detailed analysis of sources that look in particular for evidence of pirate governance during the sixteenth and early seventeenth centuries in the North Atlantic may shed important light on their operations when at sea but also on their lives on shore and responsibilities to family and kin.

The motivations behind the decisions taken by the men and their families following the demise of the alliance could perhaps be ascertained by delving deeper into the history of other ruling states or the archives of places where the alliance had its bases. Exploring the background to the Duchy of Savoy and its political power-grabs within the wider context of European and Mediterranean rivalries may reveal why Peter Easton and others chose to relocate to Villafranca, for instance. The expertise provided by these men, in this case Easton's prowess with ordnance to the Savoyard cause, would make an interesting study of the later lives of those pirates and their influence on the maritime capabilities of contemporary ruling states like Savoy in Western Europe. The Moroccan and other North African archives could hold yet-to-be-discovered details on some of the men, their operations and where they may have ended their days, if focused research were applied to their interrogation. It is not clear if Richard Bishop remained in west Cork, for instance, though some sources, as discussed, suggest that he did, while others chose to settle in the hotter climes of North Africa. Similarly, tracing the men who may have resettled in places like Virginia, whether they were successful, raised families, carried on clandestine lives or died there would continue to connect the story of Atlantic piracy across the oceans into later times; it would inform on the continued movement of material culture and expand our knowledge of colonialism in the New World.

Connections, both economic and familial, between resident officials in west Cork, with William Hull the obvious example, helped to safeguard the pirates from official government scrutiny. Lesser associates could be similarly linked in other ways that fed into the pirate machine. Strategic commercial connections elevated the business of piracy to the level of a well-run profitable enterprise where illegal goods and monies could be laundered.[10] Exploring the workings of such networks provides vital insight into the intricacies of pirate business itself. For the goldsmiths of Cheapside, for example, including the longstanding Company of Goldsmiths still in place today but whose origins lie in the twelfth-century guilds of London, piracy would have been just a part of their wider trading operations and business transactions.[11] The early seventeenth century proved to be the most challenging period for the Company of Goldsmiths, under the Stuart King, where compulsory loans and gifts became a fundamental part of his royal policy, and his royal purse; this too perhaps necessitated looking outside the realm of legitimate business when opportunities presented, with members of the goldsmith community providing clearing houses for pirated goods.[12]

The astonishing late sixteenth- and early seventeenth-century Cheapside Hoard, discovered by workmen in 1912 when digging the cellar of a Jacobean goldsmith's premises, strikingly reveals the variety and range of international trade in gems and jewellery, particularly emeralds, that was taking place during that period. The hoard comprises gemstones from across the oceans, including emeralds from Colombia, topaz from Brazil, diamonds from India, rubies from Burma, lapis lazuli from Afghanistan, turquoise from Persia, pearls from Bahrain and opals, garnets and amethysts from Hungary. As rightly stated by Hazel Forsyth of the Museum of London where most of the collection is housed, this was 'a trade both highly organized and necessarily secretive; a trade that offered tempting opportunities for the smuggler, factor, gem dealer, merchant and jeweller'.[13] The discovery, with the hoard, of a red intaglio stone seal bearing the arms of William Howard, 1st viscount Stafford, dates the deposition in the cellar to a period between his ennoblement in 1640 and the Great Fire of London in 1666, when the Cheapside building itself was destroyed. As to when the hoard arrived into Cheapside, this is still open to debate.[14] Members of the pirate alliance, like so many others, sought to clear their stolen merchandise through London's goldsmiths, as confirmed by the engagement that took place between pirates Henry Orenge and Edmunde Flinte in 1613.[15] The splendour of the Cheapside Hoard reveals in graphic detail the global nature of the trade in jewellery and the sheer

FIGURE 59: Gold and pearl single-masted ship pin from the Cheapside Hoard. A pink-white baroque pearl forms the hull of the ship and the rigging, mast and rotating pennant are made of gold, dated to the sixteenth century.

diversity and wealth that such transactions could reap for individuals, and suggests why loyalty was so fickle when fortunes could be made through the plunder of precious gems.

The concept of a 'pirate landscape', no more so than a 'pirate ship', warrants more considered thought and investigation. Both were integral to the success of piracy.[16] For trade networks to exist on the ground, ships had to dock and cargo had to be landed. Pirates needed to access the coast and in turn those waiting on land needed to rendezvous at the arranged time. The rugged seaboard of Munster was more than conducive to pirate business, to safe passage, to the mooring of ships and even the settlement of families. Indeed, little has changed, apart from the nature of contraband, with smuggling attempts still taking place in modern times along parts of that same coast.[17] Hand-carved steps and platforms, for example, acted as coastal access points, many with associated natural caves and caverns to accommodate the temporary storage of goods. Quays, docks and landing stages in established estates and harbours, like that at Leamcon, point to legitimate usage. When considered together with the intensity of piracy at William Hull's estate, however, their placement within this maritime landscape takes on heightened and enlightened meaning and interpretation. Certain places are almost beyond refuting as pirate/smuggler sites, the precipitous steps at Streek Head/Gokane Point in Crookhaven or the steps, platforms and light niches at Dutchman's Cove in Castlehaven perhaps the most striking examples identified to date. Both sites whisper loudly of secret usage, with the dead of night, as ex-pirate Captain Henry Mainwaring wrote, being the preferred time.[18] The cultural links between sites like these and past piratical activity again warrants more expansive assessment and perhaps in time such features may become the fingerprints of pirates and smugglers within hidden landscapes.[19]

No definitive 'pirate ship' or 'pirate shipwreck' has been identified or confirmed in Ireland, yet. There are certainly historical records for numerous ships lost during the heyday of the alliance, including those during the Crookhaven attack when Captain Patrick Myagh lost his ships in the harbour.[20] There are possibilities, however, with the Coconut wreck and the Dunworley Bay wreck potentially linked to two piratical events – Claes Compaen's trading in Leamcon in 1625 and the Algerine raid on Baltimore in 1631. The dating evidence from both wrecks is contemporary with both events and the material cultural evidence also lends credence to the possibility, particularly with the Coconut wreck. Positively proving that both are pirate-associated wrecks continues to be the issue in the absence of extensive underwater archaeological excavation. Even then the complete story and identity of the wrecks may remain frustratingly inconclusive and disputed, as has been the case with other wrecks discovered around the world. Only for those remains where specific artefacts have provided the key to its identity or when material cultural evidence and historical sources align to argue positive identification has it been possible to definitively call the discovery a 'pirate wreck'.[21]

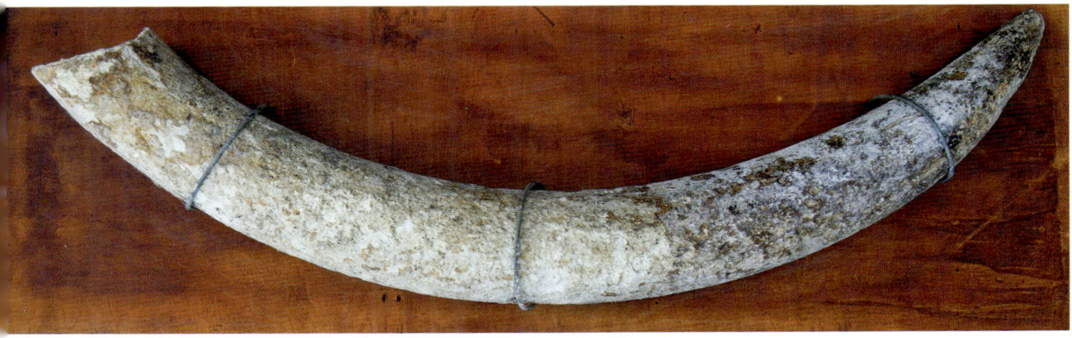

FIGURE 60: Tusk recovered from Baltimore represents evidence for trade in ivory and is possibly indicative of the remains of a wreck in the harbour.
IMAGE: CATHAL TWOMEY; © BUSHE'S BAR, BALTIMORE

PERSONAL TALES IN AN IMPERSONAL WORLD

Those individual pirates who were active either wholly or occasionally in the alliance have more extensive tales to tell. Characters central to events, and those on the periphery, deserve much greater scrutiny. It is known that 'Irishman' Captain Patrick Myagh was considered a pirate, but he may have had legitimate links to some of the leading merchant and landowning families in Cork and Limerick, which may better explain his capabilities as a mariner and perhaps his wider links within the west Cork community. Variously spelled as Meage, Myagh and Meage, the name is generally considered to be a corruption of the same surname, with other variants including Mewagh and Meade.[22] The Myagh family (and all its variations) are believed to have come from Bristol after the Anglo-Norman invasion in the twelfth century. They settled in Cork and Kinsale, and records show, filled every public office.[23] In various documents relating to deeds of land pertaining to acquisition and leases in and around Cork, several individuals with the surname Myagh/Meage are found regularly among the signatories. Though Captain Patrick Myagh was killed in 1614 during the Dutch attack, familial connections may have sustained, with names including Ann Meade, Christopher Meagh, Thomas Meagh, Garreth Myagh, Robert Meagh (Constable) and David Meaghe listed alongside familiar names like Coppinger and Crooke in a collection of Cork deeds.[24] In 1601 a letter from the lord deputy mentions the late mayor of Cork John Meade and in 1603 a David Miaghe was serving as sheriff's bailiff in West Carbery. In that year too Dominic, George and David Meagh are listed as merchants of Cork, while Robert Meaghe is referred to as sovereign in Kinsale.[25]

Undoubtedly the Meade lineage and their connections with the sea continued into later periods, including a Thomas Meade appointed as deputy judge for the admiralty in Kinsale in 1677, with a commission entitling him to jurisdiction from Kinsale and 'all the coast of Cork to the west thereof'.[26] More considered research into merchant family archives and other collections could provide definitive connections that would certainly shed more light on men like Patrick Myagh and his position as a leading captain and ship owner in Crookhaven. It may also reveal why the Dutch under Captain Moy Lambert chose to target Crookhaven in 1614, with perhaps Myagh's potential merchant links a deciding factor?

The Dutch, as expected, presented an alternative version of events. Captain Moy Lambert was hailed a hero for his actions against pirates around the Irish coast, and pamphlets were issued in Holland in celebration; one was titled *On the Glorious Victory Obtained Against the Pirates*. As discussed by Virginia Lunsford in her excellent study of Dutch piracy and privateering, the pamphlet provides valuable details on the Dutch attack on the 'Anglo-Irish pirates'. It provokes sympathy for the Dutch merchants who were victims of their plunderings, it inspires admiration for Moy Lambert and his men who conquered the pirates, and portrays the men of the alliance as 'wicked', 'merciless', 'cruel', 'disgraceful' and 'godless'.[27] The complexity of characters involved in warfare at sea at that time was matched only by the complexity of agendas served in any given jurisdiction.

Arthur Drake was one of the only black men recorded as holding a rank on a pirate ship in the North Atlantic at that time, though later accounts from the eighteenth century of pirates such as Captain Black Caesar, who captained his own ship and also served under the famous Edward Teach (Blackbeard), were also notable.[28] Drake was no doubt as complex a character as his fellow members of the alliance. With a name that was quite probably adopted, tracing where men such as Drake came from, how he rose up the ranks and what his background was would give a wider perspective on the ethos within the pirate crews, known, for the most part, for their democratic and equitable system when on board ship. Whether Drake was of African, New World or Islamic origin, whether he had been a fugitive slave or indeed ordinary sailor from his own land remains a mystery. With the diversity of encounters and magnitude of voyages taking place at the time, it is not surprising that men like Drake were frequenting the ports and harbours of the North Atlantic. Crews were drawn from all elements of society and from all quarters of the globe, and for the most part tended

FIGURE 61: Salter's Bar, now Bushe's Bar, in Baltimore, in early 20th century. The name Salter may have arrived into the area in 1609 with pirate Roger Salter. IMAGE: THE SCOTTISH PHOTOGRAPHIC TOURING & PICTORIAL POSTCARD CO. 1909; CATHAL TWOMEY; © BUSHE'S BAR

to be 'truly cosmopolitan'.[29] Drake represents this multicultural quality, and the apparent equality that was in place within an organisation comprised of so-called 'godless' and 'cruel' men.[30] The 'civilised' worlds of those nations who chose to pillory the actions of desperate men were generally far less egalitarian in their societal and demographic governance than was the world of pirates at the time.

The social life of some of the pirates and their associates in Munster can be traced to a certain degree, but for others, anonymity and invisibility remains part of their story. Tracing the lineage of the men who settled in west Cork or the general Munster area would add another dimension to the pirate story. Names like Myagh have already been discussed, but others, such as Salter, for instance, have different strands to the family. Under the Ulster Plantation the Salter Company received its first grant of lands in 1618 in Derry, so the name can be traced in that region to the period of settlement of that time.[31] There is a chance, however, that some resident Salters now living in Munster could be direct descendants of Roger Salter, who arrived into Baltimore around 1606. He is mentioned in several entries in the High

Court of Admiralty records as an active pirate, though he did, like many others, claim to have been pressed into service by Admiral Richard Bishop's men.[32] This is one of the earliest records for the Salter line in Ireland, and of the examples of the name still extant in the Republic of Ireland several members are to be found in the Munster area.[33] In Baltimore today one of the local establishments, Bushe's Bar, was formerly named Salter's Bar up to the 1970s, and perhaps the foundations of such tippling houses may also date back, if only anecdotally, to the time of the alliance itself.

Certainly, taverns and alehouses within small communities in ports and harbours became central to the everyday lives of the inhabitants in those remote places, both native and newcomer. The establishment of these gathering places along the southwest coast of Ireland was a material element within the wider colonial considerations for Munster and soon formed part of the regular lives of those living there. Though one could consider these places as 'the ready receptacle for malefactors', facilitating career criminals and fronting as brothels, this is not so easily defined and in fact distorts the reality. Certainly more recent studies have shown that in dealing with 'careers' like prostitution and piracy, both of which formed part of the custom of provincial society, public houses provided equity of clientele in any given settlement. Such establishments, first and foremost, provided entertainment, and allowed for socio-political encounters where 'locals' could keep an eye on strangers and where alcohol could be accessed, legally.[34] The nature of such encounters was multifarious and no doubt did draw the criminal mind. They were places where all customers, including pirates, could spend their disposable income when ashore but also where the families of pirates could live or meet, could make a living, could provide safe accommodation and could operate quasi-legal businesses. Where these tippling houses and meeting places were located in rural southwest Munster awaits discovery but if identified could provide greater understanding of the public world of those who patronised them.

The women in this rural world were integral to all elements of the pirates' lives in Munster. Determining their specific role and who these women were as individuals is almost impossible.[35] Many were the wives, siblings and children of the men who had settled in the west Cork area and they too made it their pirate nest. Most of these women to date remain nameless and invisible, both historically and archaeologically, apart from a select few whose surnames are given, with the wife and daughters of pirate Captain Tibault Suxbridge the most recognisable. Others are referred to in connection with the men of

FIGURE 62: There still be pirates in Baltimore! IMAGE: JULIANNA O'DONOGHUE

the alliance – merely as their wives or widows, for example, but with no further details that would ensure uniqueness and individuality. Other female agency included prostitution, functioning as pirate cohorts or employment in local commerce, including the fishing industry. It is a fact, however, that the lives of these women was hard, not only because they were linked with criminal activity but also because many had to fend for themselves over long periods when their men folk were away at sea. They were members of the terrestrial crew of coastal and maritime communities who needed to engage with commerce on land and from the sea and as a consequence could also be victims of violence and harassment, though accounts of violence against women by pirates in the area for the period in question are rare or simply were not recorded.[36]

Most women of the time needed to be self-reliant, entrepreneurial in their approach to life in order to survive, and many used sex work to supplement their income. More than anything, they needed to be capable of adapting to change in what were undoubtedly ever-changing times. Rather than being insular, most would have been culturally aware, with full knowledge of the transatlantic world and their opportunities as relayed by the men of the sea they met or lived with. The sea was a fundamental part of these women's lives as it was for the men, whether they chose to sail aboard the pirate ships or remain ashore to maintain homes or run businesses. The story of the Alliance of Pirates is as much about the women in their lives as it is about the business of piracy or the landscape within which the pirates operated. The invisibility of these women, on all levels, leaves the most glaring void in that tale and one that deserves greater attention and further exploration if a gender balance is to be brought to the maritime story of these coastal communities.

The historical view of pirates and their associates was of 'uncivilised' beings, existing outside cultured and enlightened society; a subculture set apart and therefore to be shunned, abhorred and feared. The men of the alliance, however, were not separate individuals removed from the rest of the coastal communities in Munster but were in fact members of the same communities engaged in activities that formed part of the everyday lives of coastal settlements everywhere. The men and women of the alliance, and those 'legitimate' officials who supported them, were comprised of local Gaelic-Irish, resident Old English and newly arrived speculators and settlers under the Munster Plantation. The Alliance of Pirates that emerged and prevailed during a complex, changing period was made up of a variety of characters. The amphibious nature of these pirates illustrates the pluralistic, culturally rich world of early seventeenth-century southwest Munster, which connected Ireland across the Atlantic to Newfoundland, North Africa and the New World. The story of the Alliance of Pirates, their families and cohorts underscores the importance of linking land and sea.

NOTES

INTRODUCTION

1. Mainwaring to the King, 'A Discourse in Four Fragments', *Cottonian MSS Collection*, no date, Otho E VIII, Discourse, f. 341v; Mainwaring, 'Discourse – Of the Beginnings, Practices and Suppression of Pirates', p. 41.

2. M. Rediker, 'Life under the Jolly Roger', *The Wilson Quarterly*, vol. 12, no. 3, 1988, p. 156; C.R. Pennell (ed.), *Bandits at Sea* (New York: New York University Press, 2001), pp. 3–19.

3. J.C. Appleby, *Under the Bloody Flag: Pirates of the Tudor age* (Stroud: The History Press, 2009), p. 13.

4. S. Percy and A. Shortland, 'The Business of Piracy in Somalia', *Journal of Strategic Studies*, vol. 36, no. 4, 2013, pp. 541–78; N.A.M. Rodger, 'The Law and Language of Private Naval Warfare', *The Mariner's Mirror*, vol. 100, no. 1, 2014, pp. 5–16.

5. J.C. Appleby, *Women and English Piracy, 1540–1720: Partners and victims of crime* (Woodbridge: The Boydell Press, 2013); D.P. Geanacopoulos, *The Pirate Next Door: The untold story of eighteenth-century pirates' wives, families and communities* (Durham, NC: Carolina Academic Press, 2017); Edward T. Fox, 'Piratical Schemes and Contracts': Pirate articles and their society, 1660–1730', PhD thesis, University of Exeter, 2013.

6. E. Hobsbawm, *Bandits* (London: Abacus Publishing, 2000).

7. M. Rediker, *Villains of All Nations: Atlantic pirates in the golden age* (London and New York: Verso Publishing, 2004), p. 101.

8. P. Lehr, *Pirates: A new history, from the Vikings to Somali raiders* (New Haven: Yale University Press, 2019), p. 8.

9. J. Ohlmeyer, *Making Ireland English: The Irish aristocracy in the seventeenth century* (New Haven and London: Yale University Press, 2012), pp. 101–25.

10. James VI & I (James Charles Stuart) reigned from 24 July 1567 to 27 March 1625. He reigned as King James VI of Scotland but with the joining of the crowns in March 1603 following the death of Elizabeth I, he then also assumed the title James I of England, Wales and Ireland. His mother was Mary Queen of Scots and his father was Henry Stuart, Lord Darnley. James ruled until his death in 1625.

11. M. MacCarthy-Morrough, *The Munster Plantation: English migration to southern Ireland, 1583–1641* (Oxford: Clarendon Press, 1986), pp. 171–90; C. Senior, *A Nation of Pirates: English piracy in its heyday* (London, Vancouver and New York: David & Charles Publishers, 1976), pp. 48–77, 195–6 and Appendix III.

12. Sir Ric. Hawkins to the Council, 18 September 1608, SP 14/36, f. 21, ff. 25r–26v (TNA, State Papers Online, Gale Document No. MC4323586683); Hawkins

explains his work in dealing with the pirates in Devon and along the southern coast of England and admits that the king's actions were partly responsible for encouraging the pirates to move their base of operations to the southwestern coast of Ireland.

13. D. Mathew, 'Cornish and Welsh Pirates in the Reign of Elizabeth', *The English Historical Review*, vol. 39, no. 155, 1924, pp. 337–48; C. L'Estrange Ewen, 'Organised Piracy around England in the Sixteenth Century', *The Mariner's Mirror*, vol. 35, no. 1, 1949, pp. 29–42.

14. This point is argued by both MacCarthy-Morrogh, *The Munster Plantation*, pp. 221–2 and Appleby, 'The Problem with Piracy in Ireland, 1570–1630', in C. Jowitt (ed.), *Pirates? The politics of plunder, 1550–1650* (New York: Palgrave Macmillan, 2007), p. 43, and J.C. Appleby, 'Settlers and Pirates in Early Seventeenth Ireland: A profile of Sir William Hull', *Studia Hibernica*, vol. 25, 1990, p. 104; see also Rediker, *Villains of All Nations*, pp. 38–82, and J. Acosta, 'Piracy's Influence in the Atlantic World', master's thesis, University of Florida, 2005, pp. 39–57, both of which discuss the motivations behind men turning to piracy and the social set-up on board a pirate vessel.

15. B. Fuchs, 'Spanish Lessons: Spenser and the Irish Moriscos', *Studies in English Literature, 1500–1700*, vol. 42, no. 1, 2002, p. 45.

16. Sir Richard Moryson to Salisbury, 22 August 1609, SP 63/227, f. 91v (TNA, State Papers Online, Gale Document No. MC4347580473); Appleby, *Under the Bloody Flag*, pp. 13–14; P. Earle, *The Pirate Wars* (London: Methuen Press, 2004), p. 93.

17. Appleby, *Under the Bloody Flag*, pp. 21–54.

18. J. de Courcy Ireland, *Ireland and the Irish in Maritime History* (Dublin: Glendale Press, 1986); T. O'Neill, *Merchants and Mariners in Medieval Ireland* (Dublin: Irish Academic Press, 1987); M. McCaughan and J. Appleby (eds), *The Irish Sea: Aspects of maritime history* (Belfast: Institute of Irish Studies, 1989); A. O'Sullivan and C. Breen, *Maritime Ireland: An archaeology of coastal communities* (Stroud: Tempus Publishing Ltd., 2007).

19. C. Breen, 'The Gaelic Maritime Lordship of O'Sullivan Beara', *Journal of the Cork Historical and Archaeological Society*, vol. 106, 2001, pp. 21–36 and *The Gaelic Lordship of the O'Sullivan Beare: A landscape cultural history* (Dublin: Four Courts Press, 2005).

20. O'Neill, *Merchants and Mariners*, p. 126.

21. A. Chambers, *Granuaile: The life and times of Grace O'Malley* (Dublin: Wolfhound Press, 1979 and 1983); Appleby, *Women and English Piracy*, pp. 197–202.

22. C. Kelleher, 'The Gaelic O'Driscoll Lords of Baltimore, Co. Cork: Settlement, economy and conflict in a "maritime" cultural landscape', in L. Doran and J. Lyttleton (eds), *Gaelic Ireland: Lordship in medieval and early modern Ireland* (Dublin: Four Courts Press, 2007), p. 145; P. Naessens, 'Gaelic Lords of the Sea: The coastal

tower houses of south Connemara', in Doran and Lyttleton (eds), *Gaelic Ireland* (Dublin: Four Courts Press 2007), pp. 217–35.

23. Kelleher, 'The Gaelic O'Driscoll Lords of Baltimore', p. 138.

24. Peter Carew to the Privy Council, 2 November 1568, *Cal. S.P. Ire. 1509–1573*, p. 392; Lord Deputy Fytzwylliam to Burghley, 30 March 1573, SP 63/39 f. 131 (TNA, State Papers Online, Gale Document No. MC4309504927); Petition of Fineen O'Driscoll, 7 September 1573, SP 63/42 f. 70 (TNA, State Papers Online, Gale Document No. MC4309585216).

25. Sir Warham Sentleger to Lord Burghley, 25 May 1582, SP 63/92 f. 176 (TNA, State Papers Online, Gale Document No. MC4309604139); Sir Warham Sentleger to Walsyngham, 15 August 1583, 63/104 f. 44 (TNA, State Papers Online, Gale Document No. MC4309605287).

26. Deposition of Morrys Wise of Waterford, aged about 45 or 46, 29 March 1582, in J.C. Appleby (ed.), *A Calendar of Material Relating to Ireland from the High Court of Admiralty Examinations, 1536–1641* (Dublin: Irish Manuscripts Commission, 1992), pp. 48–9.

27. R.D. Edwards (ed.), 'Letter-Book of Sir Arthur Chichester, 1612–14', *Analecta Hibernica*, vol. 62, no. 8, 1938, pp. 20–1.

28. M. Caball, 'Culture, Continuity and Change in Early Seventeenth-century South-West Munster', *Studia Hibernica*, vol. 38, 2012, pp. 39–42.

29. Rodger, 'The Law and Language of Private Naval Warfare', pp. 5–16.

30. VOC: Vereenigde Oostindische Compagnie; Dutch East India Company; WIC: West-Indische Compagnie; Dutch West India Company.

31. Ibid., pp. 6–7.

32. J.L. Anderson, 'Piracy and World History: An economic perspective on maritime predation', *Journal of World History*, vol. 6, no. 2, 1995, pp. 183–4.

33. R.C. Ritchie, *Captain Kidd and the War Against the Pirates* (New York: Barnes & Noble, 2006), pp. 17–26.

34. Ibid., pp. 11–18; W.J.H. Taylor, 'Investigation of the Evolving Relationship of Pirate, Buccaneer and Privateer Between the English State, and the Ways in Which They Contributed to Laying the Foundations of the British Empire in the Caribbean During the Period 1650–1725', BA degree thesis, University of Wales, 2010, pp. 7–10.

35. Ritchie, *Captain Kidd and the War Against the Pirates*, p. 19.

36. S. Willis, 'The Archaeology of Smuggling and the Falmouth King's Pipe', *Journal of Maritime Archaeology*, vol. 4, 2009, pp. 51–65.

37. P. Galvin, *Patterns of Pillage: A geography of Caribbean-based piracy in Spanish America, 1536–1718* (New York: Peter Lang Publishing, 1999), pp. 11, 90–3.

38. E.T. Jones, 'Illicit Business: Accounting for smuggling in mid-sixteenth-century Bristol', *Economic History Review*, vol. 54, no. 1, 2001, pp. 17–38.

39. Mainwaring, 'Discourse – Of the Beginnings, Practices and Suppression of Pirates', p. 17.

40. Mayor and aldermen of Bristol to Sir Daniel Dun, judge of the high court of admiralty, 20 September 1610, HCA 13/226, f. 137r; pirate Thomas Coward and his 'confederates' are discussed.

41. Senior, *A Nation of Pirates*, pp. 48–77.

42. G. Bak, *Barbary Pirate: The life and times of John Ward, the most infamous privateer of his time* (Stroud: Sutton Publishing, 2006), pp. 175–86.

43. Generally, 1608–14 would be the main active period for the alliance, with Bishop serving as its admiral from about 1609 to 1612.

44. See Appendix 2 of C.M. Senior, 'An Investigation of the Activities and Importance of English Pirates, 1603–40', PhD thesis, Bristol University, 1972; Appendix 1 of C. Kelleher, 'The Confederacy of Pirates in Southwest Cork in the Early Seventeenth Century: Trade, plunder and settlement, a historical and archaeological study', PhD thesis, Trinity College Dublin, 2013.

45. Sir Ferdinando Gorges, Governor of Plymouth, to Salisbury, 5 July 1611, SP 14/65 f. 29r (TNA, State Papers Online, Gale Document No. MC4323680717).

46. P. Gosse, *The History of Piracy* (New Mexico: Rio Grande Press Inc., 1932 and 1990 reprint), pp. 1–2.

47. Anderson, 'Piracy and World History'; T. Andrade, 'The Company's Chinese Pirates: How the Dutch East India Company tried to lead a coalition of pirates to war against China, 1621–1662', *Journal of World History*, vol. 15, no. 4, 2005, p. 417.

48. Gosse, *History of Piracy*, p. 107.

49. Mathew, 'Cornish and Welsh Pirates', pp. 337–8.

50. Anderson, 'Piracy and World History', p. 187; Galvin, *Patterns of Pillage*, pp. 3–4.

51. A.O. Exquemelin, *The Buccaneers of America* (New York: Dover Publications Inc., 1893 and 1969); Geanacopoulos, *The Pirate Next Door*, pp. 9–10, 31–4.

52. For an interesting discussion on the concept of pirate codes and property rights, see C.M. North, 'Not Just Guidelines: Pirate codes and the emergence of property rights in *The Invisible Hook*', *Review of Austrian Economics*, vol. 23, 2010, pp. 307–13; see also P. Leeson, *The Invisible Hook: The hidden economics of pirates* (Princeton, NJ: Princeton University Press, 2009), pp. 45–82.

53. Anderson, 'Piracy and World History', pp. 185–6.

54. Mainwaring, 'Discourse – Of the Beginnings, Practices and Suppression of Pirates', pp. 26–9; Mainwaring particularly mentions the Greek Islands as having an open welcome for the pirates; 'The Straits' was a generic term used at the time to mean the Mediterranean.

55. The area of North Africa that lies west of Egypt and which is today known as the Maghrib.

56. SUB Göttingen, 4 H BRIT P III, 6 RARA: Hessel Gerritszoon, *Beschrijvinghe van de Zeecusten ende Havenen van Yerlandt/Description of the Seacoasts and Ports of Ireland*. Universitätsbibliothek, Göttingen. Germany, ff. 1–17; W. Voorbeijtel Cannenburg, 'An Unknown "Pilot" by Hessel Gerritsz, Dating from 1612', *Imago Mundi*, vol. I, 1935, pp. 49–51; J. Keuning, 'Hessel Gerritsz', *Imago Mundi*, vol. 6, 1949, p. 53; C. Kelleher, 'Depicting a Pirate Landscape: The anti-pirate chart from 1612 and archaeological footprints on the ground', *Journal of Irish Archaeology*, vol. 23, 2013, pp. 77–92.

57. Kelleher, 'Depicting a Pirate Landscape', pp. 81–3.

58. The National Archives Currency Converter 1270–2017, http://www.national archives.gov.uk/education/resources/currency-converter-1270- 2017

59. XE Currency Converter, https://www.xe.com/currencyconverter/

60. Senior, 'An Investigation of the Activities and Importance of English Pirates, 1603–40', pp. 246–7.

61. Examination of Edward Higgins, 5 May 1610, HCA Examinations 13/266 ff. 98v–99r.

62. Deposition of Edmunde Flinte, 3 September 1613, HCA Examinations 13/42, ff. 223v–224r; Appleby (ed.), *A Calendar of Material*, p. 138; Senior, 'An Investigation of the Activities and Importance of English Pirates, 1603–40', p. 253.

63. R. Oresko, 'Bastards as Clients: The House of Savoy and its illegitimate children', in R. Mettam and C. Giry-Deloison (eds), *Patronages et Clientélismes, 1550–1750 (France, Angleterre, Espagne, Italie)* (Lille: Institut de Recherches Historiques due Septemtrion, 1995), pp. 36–67; C. Jowitt, *The Culture of Piracy* (London and New York: Routledge Publishing, 2016), pp. 157–9; see Glossary.

64. Senior, 'An Investigation of the Activities and Importance of English Pirates, 1603–40', pp. 92, 435–6.

65. Vincenzo Gussoni, Venetian Ambassador in Savoy, to the Doge and Senate, 30 March 1613, *Cal S.P. Ven. 1610–1613*, 'The Corsair [Easton] is on the point of acquiring Marquisate and other fiefs', entry 804, p. 516.

CHAPTER 1
Deeds and Misdeeds: The beginnings

1. Mainwaring, 'Discourse – Of the Beginnings, Practices and Suppression of Pirates', p. 16.

2. M.G. Hanna, *Pirate Nests and the Rise of the British Empire, 1570–1740* (Williamsburg, NC: University of North Carolina Press, 2015), p. 6.

3. J. Brotton, *This Orient Isle: Elizabethan England and the Islamic world* (London: Penguin Books, 2017), pp. 61–86.

4. Hanna, *Pirate Nests and the Rise of the British Empire*, pp. 21–57.

5. C.D. Penn, *The Navy Under the Early Stuarts* (London: John Hogg, 1920), p. 1; N.A.M. Rodger, *The Safeguard of the Sea: A naval history of Britain*, vol. 1 (London: Harper Collins, 1997), p. 327.

6. Hanna, *Pirate Nests and the Rise of the British Empire*, pp. 44–5.

7. Ibid., pp. 36–7; D.O. Flynn and A. Giráldez, 'Born with a "Silver Spoon": The origin of world trade in 1571', *Journal of World History*, vol. 6, no. 2, 1995, pp. 209–10.

8. P. Frankopan, *The Silk Roads: A new history of the world* (London: Bloomsbury, 2015), pp. 218–19.

9. Appleby, *Under the Bloody Flag*, pp. 67–77, 104–8.

10. Hanna, *Pirate Nests and the Rise of the British Empire*, pp. 42–52.

11. Ibid.

12. Brotton, *This Orient Isle*, pp. 8–9.

13. Ibid., pp. 61–71.

14. Mainwaring to the King, 'A Discourse in Four Fragments', *Cottonian MSS Collection*, Otho E VIII, Discourse, ff. 336rv–337v; Mainwaring, 'Discourse – Of the Beginnings, Practices and Suppression of Pirates', pp. 30–1.

15. J.C. Appleby, 'War, Politics, and Colonization, 1558–1625', in N. Canny (ed.) *The Origins of Empire* (Oxford: Oxford University Press, 1998), pp. 62–3.

16. K. MacMillan, 'Discourse on History, Geography, and the Law: John Dee and the limits of the British Empire, 1576–80', *Canadian Journal of History*, vol. 36, no. 1, 2001, pp. 1–26; K. MacMillan, 'John Dee's "Brytanici Imperii Limites"', *Huntington Library Quarterly, Notes and Documents*, vol. 64, nos. 1 & 2, 2001, pp. 151–9; G. Parry, 'John Dee and the Elizabethan British Empire in Its European Context', *The Historical Journal*, vol. 49, no. 3, 2006, pp. 643–75; Appleby, 'War, Politics and Colonization', p. 62.

17. Appleby, *Under the Bloody Flag*, pp. 211–46.

18. MacCarthy-Morrogh, *The Munster Plantation*; Appleby, 'The Problem with Piracy in Ireland', pp. 41–55.

19. W.H. Hardinge, 'On Manuscript Mapped Townland Surveys in Ireland of a Public Character, from Their Introduction to 23rd October 1641', *Proceedings of the Royal Irish Academy*, vol. VIII, 1861–1864, pp. 39–55.

20. MacCarthy-Morrogh, *The Munster Plantation*, pp. 144–8; J. O'Donovan, *Miscellany of the Celtic Society* (Dublin: Goodwin, Son & Nethercott, 1849), pp. 99–105 deals specifically with James' inquisition of 1609 for the southwest of Ireland and provides valuable insight into the holdings of the Gaelic-Irish in the area, with a detailed discussion on the wealth of the O'Driscoll lords: see in particular pp. 99–105.

21. O'Donovan, *Miscellany of the Celtic Society*, p. 105 details that the lords (O'Driscoll) had their own bailiffs who levied duties on those using the harbours, with orders given that the 'Lord's Bailiff ought to be assisted in the execution of their offices by all the strengths in the Harbough or Country'; Breen, *The Gaelic Lordship of the O'Sullivan Beare*; Kelleher, 'The Gaelic O'Driscoll Lords of Baltimore', p. 134.

22. D.B. Quinn and K. Nicholls, 'Ireland in 1534', in T.W. Moody, F.X. Martin and F.J. Byrne (eds), *A New History of Ireland. Vol III: Modern Ireland, 1534–1691* (Oxford: Oxford University Press, 1976, 2003 reprint), pp. 9–12; For a detailed discussion on spatial distribution of sites and uses of their harbours by the O'Donnells of Donegal, see Máire Ní Loingsigh, 'An Assessment of Castles and Landownership in Late Medieval North Donegal', *Ulster Journal of Archaeology*, vol. 57, 1994, pp. 145–58.

23. Lords such as the O'Driscolls did not remain in total isolation following the defeat of the Anglo-Normans in the southwest at the Battle of Callan in 1261, but were influenced by and no doubt selectively adopted strategic ways from the new arrivals in order to govern more judiciously: Kelleher, 'The Gaelic O'Driscoll Lords of Baltimore', pp. 134–5; K. Nicholls, 'The Development of Lordships in County Cork, 1300–1600', in P. Flanagan and C. Buttimer (eds), *Cork History and Society* (Dublin: Geography Publications, 1993), pp. 157–210.

24. J. O'Mahony, 'A History of the O'Mahony Septs of Kinelmeky and Ivagha, *Journal of the Cork Historical and Archaeological Society*, vol. 15, no. 84, 1909, p. 192.

25. L. Price, 'Armed Forces of the Irish Chiefs in the Early 16th Century', *Journal of the Royal Society of Antiquaries*, vol. 62, 1932, p. 303.

26. O'Mahony, 'A History of the O'Mahony Septs', pp. 192–3.

27. C. Breen, 'Galley-Castles in Gaelic Medieval Ireland?', in P. Martin (ed.), *Castles and Galleys: A reassessment of the historic galley-castles of the Norse-Gaelic seaways* (Barra: Islands Book Trust, 2017), p. 214.

28. C. Breen, 'The Post-medieval Coastal Landscape of Bantry and Beara', in A. Horning, R. Ó Baoill, C. Donnelly and P. Logue (eds), *The Post-Medieval Archaeology of Ireland, 1550–1850*, Irish Post-Medieval Archaeology Group Proceedings I (Wicklow: Wordwell Ltd., 2007), pp. 206–9; Kelleher, 'The Gaelic O'Driscoll Lords of Baltimore', pp. 134–58.

29. Kelleher, 'The Gaelic O'Driscoll Lords of Baltimore', pp. 139–42; Breen, *The Gaelic Lordship*, pp. 113–21; E. O'Mahony, 'The O'Driscolls and Their Revenues from Fishing – the 1609 Inquisition', *Mizen Journal*, vol. 8, 2000, pp. 128–30; E. O'Mahony, 'Baltimore, the O'Driscolls and the End of Gaelic Civilisation', *Mizen Journal*, vol. 8, 2000, pp. 110–27.

30. J.C. Appleby, 'Women and Piracy in Ireland: From Gráinne O'Malley to Anne Bonny', in Pennell (ed.), *Bandits at Sea*, pp. 286–8.

31. Appleby, *Women and English Piracy*, pp. 197–202.

32. Chambers, *Granuaile*, pp. 76–96; J. Cook, *Pirate Queen: The life of Grace O'Malley, 1530–1603* (Cork: Mercier Press, 2004).

33. Appleby, *Women and English Piracy*.

34. O'Donovan, *Miscellany*, pp. 99–107; O'Mahony, 'The O'Driscolls and Their Revenues', pp. 128–30; F.W. Harris, 'The Commission of 1609: Legal aspects', *Studia Hibernica*, vol. 20, 1980, pp. 31–55; this is a good overview of the 1609 commission, primarily dealing with the plantation of Ulster, but includes a discussion on those involved and the course taken to carry out the commission; addresses Munster in the context of earlier failures with the attempted plantation there; MacCarthy-Morrogh, *Munster Plantation*, pp. 73, 81, 151–64.

35. O'Donovan, *Miscellany*, pp. 103–4.

36. Ibid., p. 105; Kelleher, 'The Gaelic O'Driscoll Lords of Baltimore', p. 137, 142–50.

37. M. O'Dowd, 'Gaelic Economy and Society', in C. Brady and R. Gillespie (eds), *Natives and Newcomers: The making of the Irish colonial society, 1534–1641* (Dublin: Irish Academic Press, 1986), pp 120–1; K. Nicholls, *Gaelic and Gaelicized Ireland in the Middle Ages* (Dublin: The Lilliput Press, 2003), pp. 186–96; O'Donovan, *Miscellany*, pp. 105–6.

38. M. MacCarthy-Morrogh, 'English Presence in Munster', in Brady and Gillespie (eds), *Natives and Newcomers*, pp. 170–1.

39. C. Breen, 'Famine and Displacement in Plantation-period Munster', in J. Lyttleton and C. Rynne (eds), *Plantation Ireland: Settlement and material culture, c. 1550–c. 1700* (Dublin: Four Courts Press, 2009), pp. 132–9.

40. MacCarthy-Morrogh, 'English Presence in Munster', pp. 173–80; D. Power, 'The Archaeology of the Munster Plantation', in Horning et al. (eds), *The Post-Medieval Archaeology of Ireland*, p. 27.

41. O'Mahony, 'A History of the O'Mahony Septs', pp. 9–24.

42. C. Kelleher, 'Pirate Ports and Harbours of West Cork in the Early Seventeenth Century', *Journal of Maritime Archaeology, Special Edition: The Social Archaeology of Ports and Harbours*, vol. 8, no. 2, 2013, pp. 348–51.

43. Appleby, *Women and English Piracy*.

44. Mathew, 'Cornish and Welsh Pirates', pp. 337–48; L'Estrange Ewen, 'Organised Piracy around England', pp. 29–42; Rodger, *The Safeguard of the Sea*, pp. 344–52; S. Murdoch, 'Peacetime and Piracy, 1560–1618', in *The Terror of the Seas? Scottish maritime warfare 1513–1713* (Leiden and Boston: Brill Publications, 2011), pp. 111–52.

45. R. Steele, *Tudor and Stuart Proclamations, 1485–1714*, 2 vols, 1910, in particular vol. 2, Part 1 deals with Scotland and Ireland in general but not specific to piracy from the period; Steele, *A Proclamation Against the Maintenaunce of Pirates*, 3rd August 1569, no. 641 (Bodleian Library: STC 2nd Ed. /8017/455:82); D.G.E. Hurd, 'Some Aspects of the Attempts of the Government to Suppress Piracy During the Reign of Elizabeth I', unpublished MA thesis, London University, 1961; L. de Lisle, *After Elizabeth: The death of Elizabeth and the coming of King James* (London: Harper Perennial, 2005), p. 94; see Martin (ed.), *Castles and Galleys* for a selection of papers that discuss Gaelic-Scottish and Gaelic-Irish use of galleys, seafaring and piracy during the period of Elizabeth I and in earlier times.

46. M. Oppenheim, 'The Royal Navy under James I', *The English Historical Review*, vol. 7, no. 27, 1892, pp. 471–96; Penn, *The Navy Under the Early Stuarts*; Rodger, *The Safeguard of the Sea*, pp. 347–78.

47. Penn, *The Navy Under the Early Stuarts*, pp. 1–12.

48. 'Charles Howard, second Baron Howard of Effingham and first earl of Nottingham, 1536–1624', *Dictionary of National Biography* (Oxford: Oxford University Press, 2004–7), http://www.oxforddnb.com/view/article/13885

49. Robert W. Kenny, *Elizabeth's Admiral: The political career of Charles Howard, earl of Nottingham, 1536–1624* (Baltimore & London: The Johns Hopkins University Press), pp. 33–63.

50. In 1610, for example, a commission was issued to the earl of Nottingham, lord high admiral, to try piracy in the courts, though it is not known to have been in any way effective. The commission stated that pirate numbers were on the increase and needed to be suppressed. Twelve commissioners were appointed to try cases both of piracy itself and anyone suspected of assisting them. It is interesting to note that the commission further indicated that procedures for such trials were to accord with the civil and maritime laws and all other judges and courts were forbidden to deal with such cases; see Reginald G. Marsden, *Documents Relating to Law and Custom of the Sea, 1205–1767* (London: Navy Records Society, 1915–16), pp. 381–2.

51. D.D. Hebb, *Piracy and the English Government, 1616–1642* (London: Scolar Press, 1994), pp. 10–11; Senior, 'An Investigation of the Activities and Importance of English Pirates, 1603–40', p. 11. Senior notes that all commissions issued between 1604 and 1625 were solely for the capture of pirates.

52. R.G. Marsden, 'The High Court of Admiralty in Relation to National History, Commerce and the Colonisation of America, AD 1550–1650', *Transactions of the Royal Historical Society*, New Series, vol. 16, 1902, pp. 76–8.

53. Steele, *Proclamations*.

54. Senior, *A Nation of Pirates*, p. 10.

55. Steele, *Proclamations*, 8 July 1605, no. 1014.

56. W. Frank Craven, 'The Earl of Warwick, a Speculator in Piracy', *The Hispanic American Historical Review*, vol. 10, no. 4, 1930, pp. 457–60; Senior, *A Nation of Pirates*, p. 9.

57. Kenny, *Elizabeth's Admiral*, pp. 260–86.

58. Giovanni Carlo Scaramelli, Venetian Secretary in England, to the Doge and Senate, 5 October 1603, *Cal. S.P. Ven. 1603–1607*, p. 100; Hebb, *Piracy and the English Government*, pp. 8–9; This is part of a protracted complaint by Scaramelli and the Venetian government over the capture of several of their ships, including two large merchantmen, the *Balbiana* and the *Geopandita*; Scaramelli's complaints of English-dominated piracy dated back to the reign of Elizabeth I and continued into James' time; for a full account of Venetian economic losses through pirate attacks, see Alberto Tenenti, *Piracy and the Decline of Venice, 1580–1615* (London: Longmans, Green & Co., 1967).

59. Senior, *A Nation of Pirates*, pp. 9–10.

60. M. Oppenheim, *A History of the Administration of the Royal Navy from 1509 to 1660* (London: Gower Publishing Co., 1896 and 1988).

61. Senior, *A Nation of Pirates*, p. 10

62. MacCarthy-Morrogh, *Munster Plantation*, pp. 215–16, points out that one of the primary intentions of the initial but unsuccessful attempted plantation of Munster in 1569 was to build towns at Baltimore and Berehaven to discourage pirates who frequented the area; such activity was closely interwoven with the legitimate business of privately owned vessels that also operated out of Munster at that time, and with which individuals like the vice-president Sir Thomas Norris were closely linked.

63. Craven, 'The Earl of Warwick', p. 457; Lord Deputy Chichester to the Lords of the Council, 26 June 1613, 'his Majesty was driven to make reparation of their [pirates] misdeeds dayly, and yet Piracy increased or continued nevertheless', Edwards (ed.), 'Letter-Book of Sir Arthur Chichester', p. 12.

64. Kevin Costello, 'The Court of Admiralty in Ireland, 1580–1877', PhD thesis, University College Dublin, 2005, pp. 1–17, 23–6 and *The Court of Admiralty of Ireland, 1575–1893* (Dublin: Four Courts Press, 2011), p. 78; Senior, 'An Investigation', p. 114; J.C. Appleby and M. O'Dowd, 'The Irish Admiralty: Its organization and development, c. 1570–1640', *Irish Historical Studies*, vol. 24, no. 96, 1985, pp. 301, 305.

65. The Lord Deputy to the Lords of the Council, 25 July 1612, Edwards, 'Letter-Book', p. 36; Lords of the Council to Sir Arthur Chichester, 30 November 1608, *Cal. S.P. Ire. Jas 1. 1608–1610*, pp. 105–6: Chichester was instructed to send over pirates the following January to Barnstaple, Bristol or Chester to stand trial; R.O. Moore,

'Some Aspects of the Origin and Nature of English Piracy, 1603–1625', PhD thesis, University of Virginia, 1960, pp. 56–79, 98–107. Moore devotes a full chapter to piracy in Ireland, pp. 181–213.

66. Appleby and O'Dowd, 'The Irish Admiralty', pp. 299–301; Costello, 'The Court of Admiralty in Ireland', pp. 41–2 and *The Court of Admiralty of Ireland*, pp. 15–17.

67. Sir Arthur Chichester to the Earl of Devonshire, Lord Lieutenant of Ireland, 2 January 1606, *Cal. S.P. Ire. 1603–1606*, p. 382; Chichester to Salisbury, 27 June 1610, *Cal. S.P. Ire. 1603–1606*, p. 473.

68. Piracy Act 1613 (11, 12 and 13 Jas I, c. 2, 1613–15); Costello, 'The Court of Admiralty', p. 81.

69. Appleby and O'Dowd, 'The Irish Admiralty', p. 302.

70. D.E.C. Yale, 'A Historical Note on the Jurisdiction of the Admiralty in Ireland', *The Irish Jurist*, vol. III, new series, 1968, pp. 146, 149; Senior, 'An Investigation', p. 24; Marsden, *Documents Relating to Law and Custom*, pp. xv–xxx; Jon Neufeld, 'The Evolution of the Legal Concept of Piracy in Early Modern England', *Journal of World History*, 2011, pp. 1–13.

71. Yale, 'A Historical Note on the Jurisdiction of the Admiralty in Ireland', p. 149, n. 22; Yale refers to HCA 1/32/1, no. 68 as the abortive commission.

72. Appleby, *Under the Bloody Flag*, pp. 158–67.

73. Ibid., pp. 13–20.

74. Appleby and O'Dowd, 'The Irish Admiralty', p. 299.

75. R.G. Marsden, 'Early Prize Jurisdiction and Prize Law in England', *English Historical Review*, vol. 24, 1909, pp. 243–55.

76. Appleby (ed.), *A Calendar of Material*, p. ix.

77. L.H. Laing 'Historic Origins of Admiralty Jurisdiction in England', *Michigan Law Review*, vol. 45, no. 2, 1946, p. 164.

78. W.G. Perrin, 'The Lord High Admiral and the Board of Admiralty', *The Mariner's Mirror*, vol. 12, no. 2, 1926, p. 117.

79. Laing, 'Historic Origins', p. 165; Appleby and O'Dowd, 'The Irish Admiralty', pp. 299–302.

80. Costello, 'The Court of Admiralty', pp. 16–17.

81. Lords of the Privy Council to Sir John Perrot, 7 February 1572, 'French claim to certain goods of a ship detained in Youghal', *APC 1571–1575*, p. 81; Lords of the Privy Council to Sir John Perrot, 30 March 1753, ibid., p. 93; Lords of the Privy Council to Sir John Perrot, 25 April 1753, ibid., p. 100; Lords of the Privy Council to Sir John Perrot, 23 June 1573, 'send originals of the billes of lading … of the shippe of Marcelles staied at Corke', ibid., p. 119; Lords of the Privy Council to John Perrot,

27 June 1573, 'to make restitucion of a certain shipp', ibid., p. 121; Lords of the Privy Council to Sir John Perrot, 3 July 1573, ibid., p. 125; Appleby and O'Dowd, 'The Irish Admiralty', pp. 302–3.

82. J. Mathiasen, 'Some Problems of Admiralty Jurisdiction in the Seventeenth Century', *The American Journal of Legal History*, vol. 2, no. 3, 1958, pp. 215–36; Marsden, *Law and Custom*, pp. 359–60; Marsden, 'Early Prize Jurisdiction and Prize Law in England', p. 245; G.F. Steckley, 'Merchants and the Admiralty Court During the English Revolution', *The American Journal of Legal History*, vol. 22, no. 2, 1978, pp. 137–75 provides a good discussion on the disputes between the common law courts and those of admiralty civil law jurisdiction in England.

83. *Certain Select Cases in Law, reported: by Sir Edward Coke, knight, late Lord Chief Justice of England And one of His Majesties Council of State. Part XIII: XXI Trinity Term, anno 7 Jacobi Regis. The Case of the Admiralty* (London: The Second Edition, Printed by the Assigns of R. and E. Atkins, Esquires, for H. Twyford, T. Basset, and B. Sherley, 1677); this provides a good insight, albeit in a very legalistic way, of Coke's reasonings in regard to common law jurisdiction and that of admiralty authority, prior to the Henrician act, including discussing whether individuals who pirated goods on the high seas could be tried in England under the common law or if they could only be attainted by an act of parliament, pp. 52–4.

84. Appleby and O'Dowd, 'The Irish Admiralty', pp. 299–301.

85. Appleby (ed.), *A Calendar of Material*, p. xi; K.R. Andrews, *Elizabethan Privateering during the Spanish War, 1585–1603* (Cambridge: Cambridge University Press, 1964). The Admiralty received a tenth of all prizes taken by commissioned private vessels; insight into the extent of such wealth that was obtainable is given by Andrews, pp. 129–31.

86. Appleby (ed.), *A Calendar of Material*, p. xiii.

87. Costello, 'The Court of Admiralty', p. 4.

88. Appleby (ed.), *A Calendar of Material*, p. xiv.

89. Costello, 'The Court of Admiralty', p. 4.

90. Letter to the Lord Justice of Ireland from Lords of the Council, 23 November 1579, *APC 1578–1580*, p. 318.

91. Appleby and O'Dowd, 'The Irish Admiralty', p. 303.

92. Ambrose Forth to Walsyngham, 6 August 1579, Dublin; he reports on the 'dangerous state of Ireland', *Cal. S.P. Ire. 1574–1585*, p. 179; Appleby and O'Dowd, 'The Irish Admiralty'.

93. Costello, *Court of Admiralty*, pp. 15–17.

94. Ambrose Forth to Lord High Admiral Howard, 25 February 1587, *Cal. S.P. Ire. 1586–1588*, p. 269.

95. K.R. Andrews, *Trade, Plunder and Settlement: Maritime enterprise and the genesis of the British Empire 1480–1630* (Cambridge: Cambridge University Press, 1984), p. 28.

96. MacCarthy-Morrogh, *Munster Plantation*, pp. 177–222.

97. Instructions given by the Privy Council to Sir William Winter, 17 March 1580, *Cal. Carew MSS 1575–1588*, p. 233–5.

98. Ambrose Forth to Sir Julius Caesar, 25 February 1586, *Lansdowne* MSS 145, f. 37 (London: British Library).

99. J. Hardiman, *History of the Town and County of Galway*, Appendix III, Charter of Elizabeth to the town of Galway (Dublin: W. Folds & Sons, 1820), p. xxiii.

100. J.T. Gilbert (ed.), *Calendar of the Ancient Records of Dublin in the Possession of the Municipal Corporation*, vol. I (Dublin: Joseph Dollard Publishers, 1889–95), pp. 36–7.

101. Reading of the charters of Youghal, at Dublin, 2 December 1609–10, Annals of Youghal, R. Caulfield (ed.), *The Council Book of the Corporation of Youghal from 1610 to 1659, from 1666 to 1687, and from 1690 to 1800* (Guildford: J. Billing & Sons, 1878), p. xxxi.

102. See *Cal. Carew MSS 1515–74*, p. 436 and *Cal. Carew MSS 1575–88*, p. 214; in 1585 the great woodland in Munster is mentioned with a good store of timber available in Youghal for shipbuilding, with local shipwrights and mariners on hand and where two ruined abbeys were in use as storehouses; A.K. Longfield, 'Anglo-Irish Trade in the Sixteenth Century as Illustrated by the English Customs Accounts and Port Books', in *Proceedings of the Royal Irish Academy, Section C: Archaeology, Celtic Studies, History, Linguistics, Literature*, vol. 36, 1921–4, pp. 326–7; in 1591 the export of timber from the southern harbours in Ireland, including from Youghal to the ports of Milford, Cardiff, Bristol, Bridgewater, Barnstaple, Padstow, St Ives and Fowey is mentioned; see also MacCarthy-Morrogh, 'English Presence in Munster', pp. 175–81.

103. A.F. O'Brien, 'The Royal Boroughs, the Seaport Towns and Royal Revenue in Medieval Ireland', *Journal of the Royal Society of Antiquaries of Ireland*, vol. 118, 1988, pp. 13–26.

104. V. Treadwell, 'The Establishment of the Farm of the Irish Customs, 1603–1613', *The English Historical Review*, vol. 93, no. 368, 1978, pp. 580–602.

105. N. Canny, *Making Ireland British, 1580–1650* (Oxford: Oxford University Press, 2001), pp. 311–13.

106. 1612, Heads or titles of the Acts concerning the Common Weal, no. 7: An Act against pirates, *Cal. S.P. Ire. 1611–1614*, p. 250; Sir John Davys to the Earl of Somerset, 31 October 1614, passing of the Act against pirates, ibid., p. 516; Piracy Act 1613: 11, 12, and 13 Jas, 1, c. 2 (Irish Statute Book); V. Treadwell, 'House of Lords in the Irish Parliament, 1613–1615', *English Historical Review*, vol. 80, no.

314, 1965, p. 101; T.W. Moody, 'The Irish Parliament under Elizabeth and James I: A General Survey', *Proceedings of the Royal Irish Academy, Section C: Archaeology, Celtic Studies, History, Linguistics, Literature*, vol. 45, 1939/40, pp. 52, 60.

107. Costello, *The Court of Admiralty*, p. 15; Appleby and O'Dowd, 'Irish Admiralty', pp. 303 and 308; R.G. Marsden, 'The Vice-Admirals of the Coast', *English Historical Review*, vol. 22, 1907, pp. 753–5.

108. Costello, *The Court of Admiralty*, pp. 15–17.

109. Appleby and O'Dowd, 'The Irish Admiralty', p. 308.

110. Marsden, 'The Vice-Admirals of the Coast', p. 755, n. 153.

111. The Lord Deputy to Secretary Nicholas, 11 June (misdated)/5 July 1627, *Cal. S.P. Ire. Charles I, 1625–1632*, p. 249.

112. Appleby and O'Dowd, 'The Irish Admiralty', pp. 307–8.

113. O'Donnell, 'Excavations at James Fort, Kinsale', p. 1.

114. J.N. Healy, *The Castles of County Cork* (Cork: Mercier Press, 1988), p. 247.

115. See www.heritageireland.ie/en/south-west/desmondcastle/RegisteredMonument (RMP) no. C0112-034006 and National Monument no. 360 + Registered Monument (RMP) no. C0112-036 & 083 and National Monument no. 525 Castlepark/Old Fort/James Fort; www.archaeology.ie

116. M. O'Donnell, 'Excavations at James Fort, Kinsale, 1974–1998, *Journal of the Cork Historical and Archaeological Society*, vol. 107, 2002, pp. 1–70; Paul Kerrigan, *Castles and Fortifications in Ireland, 1485–1945* (Cork: The Collins Press, 1995), p. 64.

117. J.C. Appleby, 'The Affairs of Pirates: The surrender and submission of Captain William Baugh at Kinsale, 1611–1612', *Journal of the Cork Historical and Archaeological Society*, vol. 91, 1986, pp. 68–84.

118. Wards [undated] 1607, SP 63/221 f. 23r (TNA, State Papers Online, Gale Document No. MC4347480115); 'Captain Henry Skipwith, Constable of Castle Park, himself at 5s., lieutenant, 18d., gunner, 12d., and 20 soldiers at 8d. the piece'.

119. D. Woodward, 'Sir Thomas Button, the *Phoenix* and the Defence of the Irish Coast, 1614–1622', *The Mariner's Mirror*, vol. 59, no. 3, 1973, pp. 343–4.

CHAPTER 2
A Piratical Alliance

1. Translation from Irish (Gaelic) to English: 'There is no strength without unity.'

2. Senior, 'An Investigation of the Activities and Importance of English Pirates, 1603–40', p. 362. Senior identified the problem when attempting to calculate actual numbers for his study of English piracy.

3. Sir Richard Moryson to Salisbury, 22 August 1609, *Cal. S.P. Ire. 1608–1611*, p. 277; Senior, 'An Investigation of the Activities and Importance of English Pirates, 1603–40', p. 362.

4. Sir Arthur Chichester to Salisbury, 17 August 1609, *Cal. S.P. Ire. 1608–1611*, p. 273; '... under the command of Byshope, their admiral', Sir Arthur Chichester to Salisbury, 17 August 1609, SP 63/227, ff. 81r–82v (TNA, State Papers Online, Gale Document No. MC4347580466).

5. Moryson was made acting president by Henry Danvers in 1607, following the death of Sir Henry Brouncker, but this was only temporary; he resumed his official role as vice-president of Munster from 1609.

6. Sir Richard Moryson to Salisbury, 22 August 1609, *Cal. S.P. Ire. 1608–1611*, p. 277.

7. Senior, 'An Investigation of the Activities and Importance of English Pirates, 1603–40', see Appendix 2, pp. 374–443 for biographical details of pirates including those who frequented Irish waters; see also Appendix 1 of Kelleher, 'The Confederacy of Pirates in Southwest Cork in the Early Seventeenth Century', for an inventorised listing of the pirates.

8. HCA 13 in general and HCA 13/226 in particular; HCA/227 also provides important information on piracy along the coast of Munster, several involving William Hull, but these essentially post-date the main period of the alliance; Senior, 'An Investigation of the Activities and Importance of English Pirates, 1603–40', pp. 345–69; Mainwaring, 'Discourse – Of the Beginnings, Practices and Suppression of Pirates', pp. 9–52.

9. Mainwaring, 'Discourse – Of the Beginnings, Practices and Suppression of Pirates', pp. 15–16.

10. Senior, 'An Investigation of the Activities and Importance of English Pirates, 1603–40', p. 362.

11. Marc' Antonio Correr and Zorzi Giustinian, Venetian ambassadors in England, to the Doge and Senate, 20 November 1608, in H.F. Brown (ed.), *Cal. S.P. Ven. 1607–1610*, vol. XI (London: His Majesty's Stationery Office, p. 192.

12. Report from Richard Kerry, 27 January 1610, HCA 1/47, ff 78–79r. Report from Richard Kerry, undated (but c. 1610), HCA 1/47, f. 105.

13. Ibid.; Senior, 'An Investigation of the Activities and Importance of English Pirates, 1603–40', pp. 136, 400.

14. MacCarthy-Morrogh, 'English Presence in Munster', in Brady and Gillespie (eds), *Natives and Newcomers*, pp. 189–90.

15. J. Ohlmeyer, 'Civilizing of Those Rude Partes': Colonization within Britain and Ireland, 1580s–1640s', in Canny (ed.), *The Origins of Empire*, pp. 124–47.

16. N. Canny, 'The Munster Plantation: Theory and practice', in Canny, *Making Ireland British*, pp. 150–3; N, Canny, 'The Permissive Frontier: The problem of social control in English settlements in Ireland and Virginia 1550–1650', in K.R. Andrews, N. Canny and P.E.H. Hair (eds), *The Westward Enterprise: English activities in Ireland, the Atlantic and America, 1480–1650* (Detroit: Wayne State University Press, 1979), pp. 17–44.

17. Senior, 'An Investigation of the Activities and Importance of English Pirates, 1603–40', Appendix 1, pp. 345–69: a list of some of the main names involved, taken from the HCA 1 Indictments relevant to pirates, covering the years 1603–40. Senior evaluates the operational details of the pirates and analyses the figures, providing critical information on these men, their ships and their movements.

18. Sir Arthur Chichester to the Earl of Devonshire, Lord Lieutenant of Ireland, 2 January 1606, *Cal. S.P. Ire. 1603–1606*, p. 383; Senior, 'An Investigation of the Activities and Importance of English Pirates, 1603–40', p. 385, notes that Connello and his crew were captured in 1605, which may be correct as the date of Chichester's letter was 2 January; this would make Senior's date correct in that the new year would have commenced in March.

19. Sir Arthur Chichester to Earl of Devonshire, Lord Lieutenant of Ireland, 2 January 1606, *Cal. S.P. 1603–1616*, pp 382–83; Benefit of clergy: see Glossary.

20. First verse of Psalm 51, also known as the 'neck verse', as those who read it, claimed benefit of clergy and received a reprieve, avoided hanging by the neck from the gallows.

21. Sir Arthur Chichester to the Earl of Devonshire, Lord Lieutenant of Ireland, 2 January 1606, *Cal. S.P. Ire. 1603–1606*, pp. 382–3.

22. Senior, 'An Investigation of the Activities and Importance of English Pirates, 1603–40', pp. 385–6.

23. The mayor and alderman of Bristol to Sir Daniel Dun, judge of the High Court of Admiralty, 20 September 1610, HCA13/226, f. 137r; Deputy Chichester to the Privy Council, 16 July 1607, SP 63/222, ff. 21v–22r (TNA, State Papers Online, Gale Document Number MC4347480293); Senior, 'An Investigation of the Activities and Importance of English Pirates, 1603–40'.

24. Deputy Chichester to the Privy Council, 16 July 1607, SP 63/222, ff. 21v–22r (TNA, State Papers Online, Gale Document Number MC4347480293).

25. Sir Arthur Chichester to the Privy Council, 30 March 1608, SP 63/223, ff. 137r–138v (TNA, State Papers Online, Gale Document No. MC4347480622); Senior, 'An Investigation of the Activities and Importance of English Pirates, 1603–40', p. 386.

26. From Lord Chiefe Barron [Winch] concerning Coward and his companions, 2 April 1608, SP 63/223, f. 150r (TNA, State Papers Online, Gale Document No. MC4347480628).

27. Sir Arthur Chichester to the Privy Council, 11 April 1608, SP 63/223, f. 184v (TNA, State Papers Online, Gale Document No. MC4347480646).

28. Mayor and aldermen of Bristol to Sir Daniel Dun, judge of the High Court of Admiralty, 20 September 1610, HCA 13/226, f. 137r.

29. Senior, 'An Investigation of the Activities and Importance of English Pirates, 1603–40', p. 400.

30. Before the mayor and aldermen of Bristol, 8 June 1610, HCA 13/226, f. 222r.

31. Senior, 'An Investigation of the Activities and Importance of English Pirates, 1603–40', p. 257; the primary source for this comes from HCA 13/97, f. 202, 19 December 1608.

32. Senior, 'An Investigation of the Activities and Importance of English Pirates, 1603–40', Appendix 2.

33. A petition of Rich. Bishop and Wil. Wollman, on behalf of themselves and others living in piracy, *Cottonian* MSS Otho E/VIII, f. 170, no date.

34. Sir Richard Moryson to Salisbury, 22 August 1609, *Cal. S.P. Ire. 1608–1610*, pp. 277–8.

35. Rich Bushopps of Skull in Ireland, aged about 52 years, 17 August, 1614, HCA 13/98, f 213, Criminal Examinations.

36. Senior, 'An Investigation of the Activities and Importance of English Pirates, 1603–40', p. 378.

37. Bak, *Barbary Pirate*, pp. 175–86.

38. Ibid., pp. 13–46.

39. Ibid., pp. 54–5, 110–11.

40. Senior, *A Nation of Pirates*, p. 97.

41. A. Nixon, *Newes from Sea of two notorious Pyrats Ward the Englishman and Danseker the Dutchman. With a true relation of all or the most piracies by them committed unto the sixt of Aprill 1609* (London: for N. Butter, and sold at his shop, at the signe of the pide Bull, 1609; Th/74:E.462[29], EEBO – Early English Book Online).

42. Senior, *A Nation of Pirates*, p. 96.

43. Deposition of Wm. Young of Pembroke, taken prisoner by Capt. Thomas Salkeld, a pirate, April 17, 1610, *Cal. S.P. Dom. Jas. I 1603–1610* (1857), pp. 590–605.

44. Lord Admiral Nottingham to Salisbury, 8 August 1609, , *Cal. S.P. Dom. Jas. I 1603–1610* (1857), pp. 524–40; Bak, *Barbary Pirate*, p. 154.

45. The English ambassador to the cabinet, 23 June 1608, *Cal. S.P. Venice*, entry 268. This refers to Larache, the harbour town in north-west Morocco and which, in Ward's time, was a free port for pirates. It fell to the Spanish in 1610.

46. Bak, *Barbary Pirate*, pp. 111–12.

47. Marc' Antonio Correr, Venetian Ambassador in England, to the Doge and Senate, Venice, 12 November 1609, *Cal. S.P. Ven. 11: 1607–1610* (1904), pp. 376–91; http://www.british-history.ac.uk/report.aspx?compid=96965&strquery=Ward

48. Exquemelin, *The Buccaneers of America*, pp. 70–85.

49. Mainwaring to the King, 'A Discourse in Four Fragments', *Cottonian MSS Collection* Otho E VIII, Discourse, ff. 334v–334r; Mainwaring, 'Discourse – Of the Beginnings, Practices and Suppression of Pirates', pp. 23–5; see Glossary for terminology.

50. Examination of Richard Millington, 21 August 1613, HCA Examinations 13/42, ff. 214v–214r & f. 216v.

51. Geanacopoulos, *The Pirate Next Door*; Appleby, *Women and English Piracy*.

52. Senior, 'An Investigation of the Activities and Importance of English Pirates, 1603–40', Appendix 2.

53. Vice-president and Councell of Mounster, Mogeely, September 1611, signed Rich. Moryson, Edw. Harrys, Tho. Roper, Par Lane, H. Gosnold, *Harl. MS. 37r*, in M. Curtis Clayton (ed.), *Council Book for the Province of Munster, c. 1599–1649* (Dublin: Irish Manuscripts Commission, 2008), p. 73.

54. Sir Richard Moryson to Salisbury, 22 August 1609, SP 63/227, f. 90 (TNA, State Papers Online, MC4347580473).

55. M. Oppenheim, 'Piracy in Ireland', in *The Naval Tracts of Sir William Monson in Six Books* (London: Navy Records Society, 1902–14), p. 74.

56. Senior, *A Nation of Pirates*, p. 31.

57. Sir Arthur Chichester and Lord Carew to the Privy Council, 29 July 1611, SP 63/231, f. 164r (TNA, State Papers Online, MC4347680207).

58. Senior, 'An Investigation of the Activities and Importance of English Pirates, 1603–40', p. 88; Harbour Grace is a town in Conception Bay on the Avalon Peninsula in the province of Newfoundland and Labrador, Canada. Its earlier spelling of Harbor Grace denotes its origins as a migratory fishing and pirate base in the sixteenth century, when it was first founded as a settlement by the French in 1517, its original name probably derived from Harve de Grace (Grace Harbour); http://www.hrgrace.ca/site/

59. Senior, 'An Investigation of the Activities and Importance of English Pirates, 1603–40', p. 137.

60. Deposition of Thomas Hunt of Ratcliffe, mariner, aged about 33, 24 July 1610, HCA 13/41, f. 59; Deposition of John Keld of Plymouth and Newcombe, mariner, aged about 37 years, 7 May 1611, HCA 1/47, f. 188; Senior, 'An Investigation of the Activities and Importance of English Pirates, 1603–40', p. 138.

61. Deposition of Richard Hunt, of Wapping, mariner, 19 June 1611, sailor, HCA 1/47, ff 201r–202v; Deposition of Jacques Henriques of Rotterdam in Holland, merchant, 28 February, 1611, HCA 1/47, ff. 265–6.

62. Senior, 'An Investigation of the Activities and Importance of English Pirates, 1603–40', p. 137.

63. Senior, 'An Investigation of the Activities and Importance of English Pirates, 1603–40', pp. 373, 394–5.

64. Report from Richard Kerry, 27 January 1610, HCA 1/47, ff 78–79r.

65. Examination of Anthony Bull, 8 January 1611, HCA 13/226, f. 95.

66. Senior, 'An Investigation of the Activities and Importance of English Pirates, 1603–40', p. 139.

67. Sir Ferdinando Gorges and the examination of various captains, 4 July 1611, SP 14/65, f. 16 (30).

68. Senior, 'An Investigation of the Activities and Importance of English Pirates, 1603–40', pp. 140 and 191.

69. 'Mainwaring, Sir Henry (1586/7–1653)', *Dictionary of National Biography* (Oxford: Oxford University Press, 2004), http://www.oxforddnb.com/view/article/38733

70. Grant to Hen. Mainwaring, on surrender of Robt. Gosnold […] Captain of St Andrew's Castle, 10 June 1611, *Cal. S.P. Dom. Jas I*, 1611–18, p. 41.

71. Mainwaring and Perrin, *The Life and Works of Sir Henry Mainwaring*, pp. 3–34, 50; the Venetian ambassador, Antonio Donato, cited this as the reason for Mainwaring's entrance into piracy, referring to him as 'Manerino'; see Antonio Donato, Venetian Ambassador in England, to the Council of Ten, 17 January 1618, *Cal. S.P. Ven. 1617–1619*, entry 695; https://www-british-history-ac-uk.elib.tcd.ie/cal-state-papers/venice/vol15/pp430-436

72. Mainwaring and Perrin, *The Life and Works of Sir Henry Mainwaring*, p. 59.

73. H. Horwood and E. Butts, *Pirates & Outlaws of Canada, 1610–1932* (Toronto: Doubleday Publications, 1984), pp. 25–34. Certain inaccuracies exist in the detail provided, and while interesting information is given on Mainwaring, lack of due referencing of sources needs to be taken into account.

74. 'Mainwaring', Sir Henry', *Dictionary of Canadian Biography* (Toronto: University of Toronto Press, 2000), http://www.biographi.ca; 'Mainwaring, Sir Henry (1586/7–1653)', *Dictionary of National Biography*, http://www.oxforddnb.com.elib.tcd.ie/

75. Gosse, *The History of Piracy*, pp. 118–19; J.D. Rogers, *A Historical Geography of the British Colonies: Newfoundland*, vol. 5, part IV (Oxford: The Clarendon Press, 1861), p. 58; Horwood and Butts, *Pirates & Outlaws of Canada*, pp. 11–34.

76. Vincenzo Gussoni, Venetian Ambassador in Savoy, to the Doge and Senate, 3 March 1613, *Cal. S.P Ven. 1610–1613*, entry 780; 'enclosed in preceding Despatch':

'The Conditions on which Nice and Villafranca were declared Free Ports', 3 March 1613, *Cal. S.P Ven. 1610–1613*, entry 781 (accessed via British History Online).

77. 'Mainwaring, Sir Henry (1586/7–1653)', *Dictionary of National Biography*; W.A. Shaw, *Knights of England: A complete record from the earliest of times to the present day of all the orders of chivalry in England, Scotland and Ireland, and the Knights Bachelors*, vol. II (London: Central Chancery of the Orders of Knighthood, Sherratt & Hughes, 1906).

78. B. Willis, *Notitia Parliamentaria: Containing an account of the first returns and incorporations of the cities, towns, and boroughs, in England and Wales, from 1542 to 1660, that send members to Parliament* (London: Browne Willis LLD, 1750), p. 185

79. MacCarthy-Morrogh, 'The Munster Plantation, 1583–1641', p. 362; R. Dunlop and G. O'Brien, 'An Unpublished Survey of the Plantation of Munster in 1622', *Journal of the Royal Society of Antiquaries of Ireland*, vol. 14, no. 2, 1924, p. 131; Mainwaring and Perrin, *The Life and Works of Sir Henry Mainwaring*, pp. 2–5; Mainwaring, *Discourse*, vol. II, p. 284.

80. 'Jean Chevalier's sketch of Sir Henry Mainwaring, c. 1646–47', in Mainwaring and Perrin, *The Life and Works of Sir Henry Mainwaring*, pp. 276–7.

81. Mainwaring, 'Discourse – Of the Beginnings, Practices and Suppression of Pirates'.

82. Lord Danvers to the Earl of Salisbury, 3 June 1608, SP 63/224 f. 108v (TNA, State Papers Online, Gale Document No. MC4347480748). In reference to aiders and abettors, Danvers distinguished between them and the pirates with the use of the terms 'land pirates' and 'sea sharkers'.

CHAPTER 3
Honourable Crimes and Corrupt Times

1. The Lord Deputy to the Lords of the Council, 25 July 1612, Edwards (ed.), 'Letter-Book of Sir Arthur Chichester', p. 36.

2. Hanna, *Pirate Nests and the Rise of the British Empire*, pp. 4, 73.

3. Mainwaring, 'A Discourse in Four Fragments', *Cottonian* MSS Otho E/VIII, ff. 329–344r (TNA, State Papers Online, Gale Document No. MC4318815326, 2012); Mainwaring, 'Discourse – Of the Beginnings, Practices and Suppression of Pirates', p. 11.

4. Lord Danvers to the Earl of Salisbury, 3 June 1608, *Cal. S.P. Ire. 1606–1608*, pp. 395, 549–50.

5. *By the King. A Proclamation Against Pirats, 1608* (Imprinted at London by the Deputies of Robert Barker, Printer to the Kings most Excellent Majestie), http://eebo.chadwyck.com.elib.tcd.ie/search/

6. Senior, 'An Investigation of the Activities and Importance of English Pirates, 1603–40', p. 26.

7. The Lord Deputy to the Lords of the Council, 31 October, 1612, Edwards, 'Letter-Book', p. 61.

8. Mainwaring, 'Discourse – Of the Beginnings, Practices and Suppression of Pirates', p. 48; see opening paragraph.

9. Appleby and O'Dowd, 'The Irish Admiralty', p. 317.

10. Senior, 'An Investigation of the Activities and Importance of English Pirates, 1603–40', p. 289.

11. Kenny, *Elizabeth's Admiral*, p. 76.

12. MacCarthy-Morrogh, *The Munster Plantation*, pp. 217–18.

13. Andrews, *Trade, Plunder and Settlement*, pp. 18–28.

14. Appleby, 'Settlers and Pirates', p. 83.

15. Lord Danvers to [the Lords of the Privy Council or the Lord Salisbury], 19 January 1609, SP 83/226, f. 14 (TNA, State Papers Online, Gale Document no. MC4347680236); Lord Danvers to [the Lords of the Privy Council or the Lord Salisbury], 19 January 1609, *Cal. S.P. Ire. 1608–1610*, p. 130; Senior, 'An Investigation of the Activities and Importance of English Pirates, 1603–40', pp. 289, 379, 421, 426, 431.

16. Richard Jobson of Windsor, 21 April 1610, HCA Examinations 1/47 f. 107v.

17. Andrews, *Trade, Plunder and Settlement*, p. 28.

18. It is unclear if this is the same ship as the *Pearl* (*Pearle*) allegedly run aground in 1613 near Dursey; see Chapter 5 for a more detailed discussion on the *Pearl* affair; C.F. Senning, 'Piracy, Politics and Plunder under James I: The voyage of the *Pearl* and its aftermath', *The Huntington Library Quarterly*, vol. 46, 3, 1983, pp. 187–222; the name 'Pearl' was a common one for ships throughout this period, see R.G. Marsden, 'English ships under the Reign of James I', *Transactions of the Royal Historical Society*, new series, vol. 19, 1905, p. 328.

19. Deposition of Gionisius Gallot of Calais, aged about 35, 16 June 1609 HCA Examinations 13/40, f 161r–162r; Deposition of Humfrey Jobson, aged about 36, 15 July 1609, HCA Examinations 13/40, f 197v–198r; Appleby (ed.), *A Calendar of Material*, pp. 121–2.

20. MacCarthy-Morrogh, *The Munster Plantation*, p. 217.

21. Dr David Heffernan, *pers. comm.*, 24 May 2017 with sources quoted NLI, MS 6,139, p. 10 and NLI, MS 6,142, p. 104; the author is very grateful to Dr Heffernan for his insights and access to his work.

22. Appleby (ed.), *A Calendar of Material*, pp. 78–9.

23. *By the King a proclamation for the search and apprehension of certaine pirates, giuen at our Pallace of Westminster the xij day of Nouember 1604* (Robert Barker, Printer; 1604, Society of Antiquaries, STC, 2nd ed. / 8363, STC / 1875:25; http://eebo.chadwyck.com.elib.tcd.ie/search; one page; Lord Deputy Falkland to Secretary Nicholas, 29 April 1627, *Cal. S.P. Ire. 1625–1632*, p. 227.

24. See Senior's thesis 'An Investigation of the Activities and Importance of English Pirates, 1603–40', pp. 26, 51, 156, 274, 444, where he debates if this is indeed one and the same William Hull; Examination of William Hull, age 37 or thereabouts, 14 July 1609, HCA Examinations, 1/47, ff. 24v–26v, in which he is again examined for his possible dubious dealings with pirates.

25. Appleby (ed.), *A Calendar of Material*, pp. 78–80; Appleby's research indicates that no evidence has come to light for transactions for either the leasing of the lands at Leamcon or the granting of Crookhaven to Hull by the church authorities.

26. W. Maziere Brady, *Clerical and Parochial Records of Cork, Cloyne and Ross*, I (London: Alexander Thom, 1863), pp. xliii, xlvii, lviii, lviv, 170, 172, 173; Brady provides information extracted from *Books of Survey and Distribution for Cork*, with lists of the lands owned or leased by Hull.

27. J. Nunan, 'The Planting of Munster, 1580–1640', Public Outreach Series (published online 2012), pp. 67–72, http://www.jpnunan.com/sitebuildercontent/sitebuilderfiles/josephnunanmunsterplantation.pdf

28. Ohlmeyer, *Making Ireland English*, pp. 64, 104; J. Nunan, 'The Planting of Munster, 1580–1640', pp. 67–68.

29. MacCarthy-Morrogh, *The Munster Plantation*, pp. 153–4, 236–7; A. Horning, 'The Cultural Role of the Alehouse in the Ulster Plantation', in Lyttleton and Rynne (eds), *Plantation Ireland*, pp. 124–5.

30. Deposition of William Weare of Leith, 6 April 1625, HCA Examinations, 13/41 ff. 476v–477v and Testimony of Robert Perey, taken and examined 28 June 1625; Appleby (ed.), *A Calendar of Material*, pp. 153, 305–6.

31. Deposition of William Weare of Leith.

32. Appleby, 'Settlers and Pirates', pp. 78–81; Sir William Hull knight & one of his Maiesties Councell of Mounster, 22 October 1642, Deposition of William Hull (MS 824, ff. 253r–259v, TCD, 1641 Depositions Project, online transcript January 1970); A.E.J. Went, 'Sir William Hull's Losses in 1641', *Journal of the Cork Historical and Archaeological Society*, vol. 52, 1947, pp. 55–68.

33. Appleby, 'Pirates and Settlers', pp. 85–8.

34. D. Townsend, *The Life and Letters of the Earl of Cork* (London: Duckworth & Company, 1904), p. 67.

35. Appleby, 'Pirates and Settlers', p. 87; J. Lodge and M. Archdall, *The Peerage of Ireland Or a Genealogical history of the Present Nobility of that Kingdom with Engravings*

of their Paternal Coat of Arms collected from Public Records, Authentic Manuscripts, Approved Historians, Well Attested Pedigrees and Personal Information, vol. 1 (Dublin: James Moore, College Green, 1789), pp. 144–5, http://archive.org

36. Appleby, 'Pirates and Settlers', p. 87.

37. Deposition of Rich Kerry, 29 January 1610, HCA Examinations,1/47, ff. 79v–83.

38. Sir Arthur Chichester to the Lords of the Privy Council, 26 January 1610, *Cal. S. P. 1608–1610*, pp. 353–4.

39. Sir Richard Morrison to Salisbury, 4 March 1610, *Cal. S.P. Ire. 1608–1610*, pp. 397–8.

40. Appleby, 'Pirates and Settlers', pp. 83–4; see next chapter for a discussion on the sites on Hull's lands.

41. Deposition of William Hull of Leamcon, gentleman, 13 May 1613, HCA Examinations 13/42, ff. 153v–155r; Appleby (ed.), *A Calendar of Material*, p. 131.

42. Appleby (ed.), *A Calendar of Material*, p. 77; Deposition of John Hoskins of Plymouth, mariner, 19 August 1613, HCA Examinations 13/42, ff. 210v–212r; Appleby (ed.), *A Calendar of Material*, p. 135; see Chapter 6 for a broader discussion on this.

43. See D.W. Prowse, *A History of Newfoundland* (London: Eyre & Spottiswoode, 1896), p. 102 for when, in 1612, Easton is accused of forcing fishermen to join his crew, though it is noted that 'many [are] volunteers'; HCA Examinations 13/226 also contains numerous references to pirates, or those 'forced' into piracy in west Cork, who in turn worked legitimately or returned to their old trades once they came ashore.

44. Lords of the Council to Sir Arthur Chichester, 18 November 1612, *Cal. S.P. Ire. 1611–1614*, pp. 301–2.

45. MacCarthy-Morrogh, *The Munster Plantation*, pp. 129–65; Power, 'The Archaeology of the Munster Plantation', pp. 23–33.

46. Five fragments concerning admiralty cases, no date [c. 1616], *Cottonian MSS* Otho E/VIII, ff. 378–379r (TNA, State Papers Online, Gale Document No. MC4318815336, 2012).

47. B. McCarthy, *Dún na Séad: The history of Baltimore castle* (Skibbereen: Baltimore Castle Publications, 2012), pp. 18–31; B. McCarthy, *Pirates of Baltimore: From the middle ages to the seventeenth century* (Skibbereen: Baltimore Castle Publications, 2012), p. 22.

48. O'Donovan, *Miscellany of the Celtic Society*, p. 107; O'Mahony, 'Baltimore, the O'Driscolls and the end of Gaelic Civilisation', p. 126; MacCarthy-Morrogh, *The Munster Plantation*, pp. 151–3.

49. Sir Finie O'Driscoll's Petition, 22 Oct. 1606; Carte Papers, 61, p. 225 (TNA, State Papers Online; Gale Document no. MC4347400016); Sir Finie O'Driscoll's Petition, 22 October 1606, *Cal. S.P. Ire. 1606–1608*, pp. 6–7.

50. MacCarthy-Morrogh, *The Munster Plantation*, p. 151; J. Keay, *The Honourable Company: A history of the English East India Company* (London: Harper Collins Publishers, 1993), p. 10–23, provides a history of Lancaster's command of the company's fleet.

51. O'Donovan, *Miscellany of the Celtic Society*, pp. 106–7.

52. M. MacCarthy-Morrogh, 'The Munster Plantation, 1583–1641', PhD thesis, London University, 1983, pp. 222–3.

53. Curtis Clayton (ed.), *Council Book for the Province of Munster*, pp. 73–4.

54. SUB Göttingen, 4 H BRIT P III, 6 RARA: Hessel Gerritzsoon, *Beschrijvinghe van de Zeecusten ende Havenen van Yerlandt/Description of the Seacoasts and Ports of Ireland*. Universitätsbibliothek, Göttingen. Germany, ff 1–17; WWM/Str P 20/100 Map of Baltimore: Wentworth Woodhouse Muniments, Strafford Folio (Sheffield City Library Archives).

55. E. Cotter, 'Dún na Séad Castle, an early 17th century house in Baltimore, Co. Cork', *Journal of the Cork Historical and Archaeological Society*, vol. 115, 2010, pp. 45–7.

56. C. Kelleher, 'In a Harbour Long Ago', in J. Fenwick (ed.), *Lost and Found: Discovering Ireland's past* (Wicklow: Wordwell Ltd., 2003), pp. 273–86; Kelleher, 'Depicting a Pirate Landscape', pp. 77–92.

57. RMP number CO:150:049: *fish palace*, Record of Monuments and Places (Dublin: Archaeological Survey of Ireland data, National Monuments Service; www.archaeology.ie); Kelleher, 'Depicting a Pirate Landscape'.

58. H. Kelleher, 'The Archaeology of Fish Palaces in West Cork', MA thesis, University College Cork, 1995, p. 29; D. Power, *Archaeological Inventory of County Cork: West Cork*, vol. I (Dublin: Government Stationery Office, 1992), site number 3652, p. 410; C. Kelleher, 'The Maritime Archaeological Landscape of Baltimore, Co. Cork', MA thesis, University College Cork, 1998, p. 27; Kelleher, 'In a Harbour Long Ago'.

59. Thanks are due to Dr Brian Marten for bringing the new sites to the attention of the author. The sites have now been added to the Sites and Monuments Record (SMR): CO150-098 *Quay*; CO150-099 *Slipway*; CO150-100 *road/trackway*; www. archaeology.

60. To the right honourable Lord Deputy, 23 November 1610, *Harleian MSS*, ff. 95r–95v; Richard Moryson to the Vice President and Council of Munster, 24 May 1610; from Curtis Clayton (ed.), *Council Book for the Province of Munster*, pp. 192–9.

61. Petition of James Spenser and other English Inhabitants of a Plantation in Carbrie, county Cork, to the Privy Council, April 1618, *Cal. S.P. Ire. 1615–1625*, pp. 190–1.

62. E. McCracken, 'Charcoal-burning Ironworks in Seventeenth- and Eighteenth-Century Ireland', *Ulster Journal of Archaeology*, vol. 20, 1957, p. 128.

63. The Lord Deputy to the Attorney-General, 20 October 1612, *Cal. S.P. Ire. 1611–1612*, p. 292; MacCarthy-Morrogh, *Munster Plantation*, p. 152; E.J. Priestley, 'An Early 17th Century Map of Baltimore', *Journal of the Cork Historical and Archaeological Society*, vol. 89, 248, 1984, p. 55; H. Barnby, 'The Sack of Baltimore', *Journal of the Cork Historical and Archaeological Society*, vol. 74, 1969, pp. 106–7.

64. O'Donovan, *Celtic Miscellany*, p. 108; Cotter, 'Dún na Séad Castle', pp. 31–47.

65. Lords of Council to Sir Arthur Chichester, 8 March 1608, *Cal. S.P. Ire. 1606–1608*, p. 433.

66. By the Lord President of Mounster, 23 June 1608, Curtis Clayton (ed.), *Council Book for the Province of Munster*, p. 367.

67. Sir Arthur Chichester to the Privy Council, 20 March 1608, *Cal. S. P. Ire. 1606–1608*, p. 447.

68. Copy of a letter from the Lord Bishop of Cork to the Lords of the Council in England, August 1608, *Cal, S.P. Ire. 1608–1610*, pp. 100–1.

69. The Privy Council to Lord Danvers, 20 November 1608, *Cal. S.P. Ire. 1608–1610*, p. 101.

70. Senior, 'An Investigation of the Activities and Importance of English Pirates, 1603–40', pp. 117 and 120; List of names of the undertakers of Ireland, December 1610, *Cal. S.P. Ire. 1608–1610*, p. 548; D.B. Quinn, 'The Voyage of the *Triall*, 1606–1607', in *Explorers and Colonies: America, 1500–1625* (London: Bloomsbury Publishers, 1990), pp. 363–81.

71. Deposition of Roger Bamford, servant to William Angell, 3 September 1607, HCA Examinations 13/19, ff. 18v–21; Appleby (ed.), *A Calendar of Material*, pp. 116–17.

72. Andrews et al. (eds), *The Westward Enterprise*, p. 38.

73. Appleby (ed.), *A Calendar of Material*, p. 298; D.B. Quinn, 'The Voyage of the *Triall*, 1606–1607', in *Explorers and Colonies: America, 1500–1625* (London: Bloomsbury Publishers, 1990), pp. 363–81.

74. Senior, 'An Investigation of the Activities and Importance of English Pirates, 1603–40', p. 117.

75. Lords of the Council to Sir Arthur Chichester, 9 September 1611, *Cal. S.P. Ire. 1611–1614*, p. 101; James' commission to the Dutch and its repercussions is discussed in detail in Chapter 7.

76. Petition of Thomas Crooke to the Lord High Treasurer Salisbury, Undated (*c.* 1612), SP 63/232, f. 43 (TNA, State Papers Online, Gale Document No. MC4347600477); G. Bennett, *The History of Bandon and the Principal Towns in the West* (Cork: Francis Guy Printers & Publishers, 1869), p. 86.

77. 'Sir Thomas Crooke, first baronet (*c.* 1574–1630)', *Dictionary of National Biography* (Oxford: Oxford University Press, 2004), http://www.oxforddnb.com/view/article/6777

78. MacCarthy-Morrogh, 'The Munster Plantation', p. 223.

79. James Salmon to Thomas Crooke, 23 June 1608, SP 63/224 f. 146 (TNA, State Papers Online; Gale Document No. MC4247480782).

80. The author is grateful to Ms Mary Rose Jennings-Hegarty of Oldcourt House for this information and allowing access to her home.

81. Senior, 'An Investigation of the Activities and Importance of English Pirates, 1603–40', p. 106.

82. Appleby (ed.), *A Calendar of Material*, p. 302.

83. John C. Appleby, 'The Defence of Ireland: A naval journal of 1627', *Analecta Hibernica*, vol. 37, 1988, p. 246.

84. Sir Richard Aldworth (to the Lord Deputy), 16 February 1627, at Newmarket, Co. Cork, SP 63/244 ff. 94r–95v, enclosed with letter of Lord Falkland to the Privy Council, 22 February 1627, SP 63/244 f. 93 (TNA, State Papers Online, Gale Document No. MC4347800593).

85. C. Kelleher, '*Santa Ana Maria*: 1628 wreck of the Capitana of La Flota de la Nueva España', in J. Henderson (ed.), *Beyond Boundaries: Proceedings of the 3rd International Congress on Underwater Archaeology* (London: IKUWA3, 2008), pp. 175–82; C. Kelleher, 'Death by Disgrace: Juan de Benevides y Bazán, the 1628 capture of the Spanish treasure fleet and the wreck of *Santa Ana Maria*', in D.M. Downey and I. Pérez Tostado (eds), *Commerce, Culture, Politics and Warfare: Studies in Spanish–Irish connections* (Valencia: Albatross Press, 2019), Chapter 23; *An Inventory of the principall goods taken up, saved and brought into the hands of me James Salmon that came out of the Spanish ship called the St Anna Maria brought into the harbour of Castlehaven by Capten Peter Fransey of Amsterdam, and there cast away and broke to peeces*, 17 January, 1628, SP 63/148, ff. 70r–72r (TNA, State Papers Online; Gale Document No. MC4347881307).

86. List of Names of the Undertakers in Ireland, 1610, *Cal. S.P. Ire. 1608–1610*, p. 547.

87. Sir Finie O'Driscoll's Petition, 22 October 1606; Carte Papers, 61, p. 225 (TNA, State Papers Online, Gale Document no. MC4347400016); Sir Finie O'Driscoll's Petition, 22 October 1606, *Cal. S.P. Ire. 1606–1608*, pp. 6–7.

88. Lords of Council to Sir Arthur Chichester, 31 December 1607, *Cal. S.P. Ire. 1603–1625*, p. 384 (TNA, State Papers Online, Gale Document no. MC4347400512);

Petition of Florence M'Carthy to the Privy Council [undated] prob. 1607, *Cal. S.P. Ire. 1603–1625*, p. 385 (TNA, State Papers Online, Gale Document no. MC4347400513); Florence McCarthy had leased Carriganassig and Ringrone Castles to Herbert Pelham for twenty-one years; Deposition of Richard Thorne of London, 19 August 1613, HCA Examinations 13/42, ff. 204v–205r; Appleby (ed.), *A Calendar of Material*, pp 135–6; Thorne refers to 'captain Skipwith's house at Carginasse' in his deposition.

89. Appleby and O'Dowd, 'The Irish Admiralty', p. 323.

90. Appleby, 'Settlers and Pirates', p. 93.

91. Examination of John Huskins [Hoskins], 19 August 1613, HCA Examinations 13/42, ff. 203v–204r; Examination of Richard Millington, 21 August 1613, HCA Examinations 13/42, ff. 214–17.

92. A.K.W. Malcomson, *Calendar of the Rosse Papers* (Dublin: Irish Manuscripts Commission, 2008), p. iv; K. Costello, *The Court of Admiralty of Ireland, 1575–1893* (Dublin: Four Courts Press, 2011), pp. 4–7, 14–16, 19; Costello, 'The Court of Admiralty in Ireland', pp. 1–17, 23–6.

93. Costello, 'Sir Adam Loftus' First Period as Judge (1612–1619)', and 'The Court of Admiralty, 1628–38, Loftus Second Period', in Costello, *The Court of Admiralty of Ireland*, pp. 4–5, 8–11, 15–16.

94. N. Canny, *The Upstart Earl: A study of the social and mental world of Richard Boyle, first earl of Cork 1566–1643* (New York: Cambridge University Press, 1982), p. 123; Appleby, 'Settlers and Pirates', p. 86.

95. Costello, 'The Court of Admiralty in Ireland', pp. 24–5; Lord Deputy to Secretary Nicholas, 11 June (misdated)/ 5 July, *Cal. S.P. Ire. Charles I, 1625–1632*, p. 249.

96. Appleby, *A Calendar of Material*, p. 148.

97. Sir G. Fenton to Salisbury, 7 June 1607, *Cal. S.P. Ire. 1606–1608*, pp. 191–2; MacCarthy-Morrogh, 'The Munster Plantation, 1583–1641', p. 297.

98. Canny, *Making Ireland British*, p. 330.

99. The Principal Heads of Captain (Barnaby) Riche's Treatise Delivered to My Lord Salisbury, undated, c. 1610, SP 63/229, f. 206v (TNA, State Papers Online; Gale Document MC4347500949); The Principal Heads of Captain (Barnaby) Riche's Treatise Delivered to My Lord Salisbury, undated, 1610, *Cal. S.P. Ire. 1608–1610*, pp. 551–2.

100. Earl of Thomond to Salisbury, 28/29/30 June 1607, *Cal. S.P Ire. 1606–1608*, pp. 206–7.

101. Lords of the Council to Sir Arthur Chichester, 8 March 1608, *Cal. S.P. Ire. 1603–1625*, pp. 433–4.

102. Ohlmeyer, *Making Ireland English*, p. 374.

103. Sir Arthur Chichester to the Privy Council, 30 March 1608, *Cal. S.P. Ire. 1606–1608*, pp. 445–6.

104. The King to Sir Arthur Chichester, 9 June 1608, *Cal. S.P. Ire. 1606–1608*, pp. 552–3.

105. Sir Arthur Chichester to the Privy Council, 5 February 1609, *Cal. S.P. Ire. 1608–1610*, p. 142.

106. Lord Danvers to Salisbury, 24 February 1609, *Cal. S.P. Ire. 1608–1610*, p. 151; Earl of Thomond to Salisbury, 10 March 1609, *Cal. S.P. Ire. 1608–1610*, p. 162.

107. Canny, *Making Ireland British*, p. 330.

108. Lord Danvers to the [Lords of the Privy Council or the Lord Salisbury], 19 January 1609, *Cal. S.P. Ire. 1608–1610*, p. 130.

109. Sir Arthur Chichester to the Privy Council, 5 February 1609, *Cal. S.P. Ire. 1608–1610*, p. 188.

110. Rich. Kerry, servant to Mr Humphrey Jobson, also signed by Daniel Dun and Rich Trevor, 27 January 1609, HCA Examinations 1/47 f. 78r.

111. Sir G. Fenton to Salisbury, 7 June 1607, *Cal. S.P. Ire. 1606–1608*, pp. 191–2; V. Treadwell, *Buckingham and Ireland, 1616–1628: A study in Anglo-Irish politics* (Dublin: Four Courts Press, 1998), pp. 99–100; Ohlmeyer, *Making Ireland English*, pp. 220–1.

112. In May 1916 Thomond made an official but unsuccessful application for the vice-admiralty in Munster, no doubt to gain wider control of maritime affairs; Treadwell, *Buckingham and Ireland*, p. 100; Singleton was principal from 1595 to 1614; https://www.bnc.ox.ac.uk/about-brasenose/history/216-brasenose-people/413-principals-list-of-past-and-present

113. Dr Thomas Singleton to Earl of Thomond, 1 August 1607, *Cal. S.P. Ire. 1606–1608*, p. 234.

114. Mainwaring and Perrin, *The Life and Works of Sir Henry Mainwaring*, pp. 4–5.

CHAPTER 4
Pirate Places and Pirate Traces

1. 'Follow the chart of the pirate havens near Cape Clear', from SUB Göttingen, 4 H BRIT P III, 6 RARA: Hessel Gerritszoon, *Beschrijvinghe van de Zeecusten ende Havenen van Yerlandt/Description of the Seacoasts and Ports of Ireland* (Amsterdam, 1612), p. 19; translated by Dr Edda Frankot; Kelleher, 'Depicting a Pirate Landscape', pp. 77–92.

2. The seminal works of Stanley Lane-Poole, *The Story of the Barbary Corsairs* (New York: G.P. Putnam's Sons, 1890), and B. Fuller and R. Leslie-Melville, *Pirate Harbours*

and Their Secrets (London: Stanley Paul & Co. Ltd., 1935) stand out, though they are not without their prejudicial undertones in places; Fuller & Leslie-Melville include the pirate harbours in Ireland, pp. 92, 167–93.

3. Oppenheim, 'Piracy in Ireland', pp. 59–63; Mainwaring, 'A Discourse in Four Fragments', *Cottonian* MSS Otho E/VIII f. 339r (TNA, State Papers Online, Gale Document No. MC4318895326); Mainwaring, 'Discourse – Of the Beginnings, Practices and Suppression of Pirates', pp. 16–17; Senior, 'An Investigation of the Activities and Importance of English Pirates, 1603–40', p. 397; The Lord Deputy to the Duke of Buckingham, 13 March 1626, SP 63/242 f. 184r (TNA, State Papers Online, Gale Document No. MC434788267).

4. Sir Richard Moryson to Salisbury, 22 August 1609, *Cal. S.P. Ire. 1608–1610*, p. 277.

5. Mathew, 'Cornish and Welsh Pirates', pp. 337–48; C. L'Estrange Ewen, 'Organised Piracy Round England in the Sixteenth Century', *The Mariner's Mirror*, vol. 35, no. 1, 1949, pp. 29–42.

6. Gosse, *The History of Piracy*, pp. 118–19; Rogers, *A Historical Geography of the British Colonies*, p. 58; Horwood and Butts, *Pirates & Outlaws of Canada*, pp. 11–34.

7. 'Easton, Peter (fl. c. 1570–1620)', *Dictionary of Canadian Biography*; D. Whittlesey, *The Earth and the State* (New York: Henry Holt & Company, 1939, reprinted with maps 1944), pp. 59–70.

8. Senior, 'An Investigation of the Activities and Importance of English Pirates, 1603–40', pp. 55–6, 75–7, 82–3, 86–87, 88 n. 1, 133–4.

9. Mainwaring, 'Discourse – Of the Beginnings, Practices and Suppression of Pirates', pp. 15–33; Appleby, 'Settlers and Pirates', pp. 1–2.

10. Chichester to the Lord Admiral, 4 August 1613, in Edwards (ed.), 'Letter-Book of Sir Arthur Chichester', p. 120.

11. Sir Arthur Chichester to the Privy Council, 30 March 1608, SP 63/223, ff. 137r–140r (TNA, State Papers Online, Gale Document No. MC4347480622).

12. T. Stafford, *Pacata Hibernia or a History of the Wars in Ireland during the Reign of Queen Elizabeth 1602*, S. O'Grady (ed.), vol. II (London: Downey & Co., Ltd., 1896), pp. 215–16.

13. Instructions to Sir Anthony Sentleger, Deputy, and the Council (?) July 1550, *Calendar of Carew Manuscripts, 1515–74, Preserved in the Archiepiscopal Library at Lambeth*, J.S. Brewer and W. Bullen (eds) (London: Longmans, Green, Reader & Dyer, 1867), p. 228.

14. Appleby (ed), *A Calendar of Material*, p. 47.

15. Perrot's Project, December (?) 1585, *Cal. Carew MSS 1575–88, Preserved in the Archiepiscopal Library at Lambeth*, p. 416.

16. Examination of John Lee, 5 May 1610, HCA Examinations 13/266, f 99v–100.

17. P/49 (16), Chart of Kinsale Harbour by John Mansell showing the 'dock' on the shoreline below Castlepark, *c*. 1649, Dartmouth Mss Collection (London: National Maritime Museum, Greenwich); an earlier *c*. 1601 chart of Kinsale, anonymously drawn, P/49 (17), shows no such facilities in the area and may indicate that the facilities could have been built after 1601, though lack of representation on the earlier chart is not definitive evidence for later construction; the author is grateful to Dr Elaine Murphy for bring this map to my attention.

18. M.P. Goelet, 'The Careening and Bottom Maintenance of Wooden Sailing Vessels', master's thesis, Texas A&M University, 1986, pp. 6–10, 23–36; R. Barker, 'Careening: Art and anecdote', *Mare Liberum*, vol. 2, 1991, pp. 177–207; Henry Mainwaring, 'The Seaman's Dictionary', in Mainwaring and Perrin, *The Life and Works of Sir Henry Mainwaring*, pp. 118–19.

19. R. Bagwell, *Ireland under the Stuarts and during the Interregnum, 1603–1642*, vol. I (London: Longmans, Green & Co., 1909), p. 104.

20. G. Boate, *Ireland's Naturall History* (London: Imprinted for John Wright, 1652), pp. 12–14, 20–2.

21. C. Kelleher, 'Connections and Conflict by Sea', in Horning et al. (eds), *The Post-Medieval Archaeology of Ireland*, pp. 67–8, 80–2.

22. Sir George Carew to the Privy Council, 28 June 1602, *Calendar of Carew Manuscripts, 1601–1603, Preserved in the Archiepiscopal Library at Lambeth*, p. 255.

23. Sir Arthur Chichester to the Privy Council, 30 March 1608, SP 63/223, f. 139v (TNA, State Papers Online, Gale Document No. MC4347480622).

24. Capt. Henry Skipwith to the Lord Deputy, 2 October 1611, *Carew MSS 629*, f. 178, James I, vol. 6, *Calendar of Carew Manuscripts, 1603–1628, Preserved in the Archiepiscopal Library at Lambeth*, p. 255.

25. Examination of Henry Skipwith, Esq., taken at Kinsale, 23 September 1612, regarding the proceedings with the pirates, *Cal. SP Ire. 1611–1614* (TNA, State Papers Online, Gale Document no. MC4347600525), p. 285.

26. Sir Ferdinando Gorges and the examination of various captains, 4 July 1611, SP 14/65, f. 16 (30); N. Matar, *Turks, Moors and Englishmen in the Age of Discovery* (New York: Columbia University Press, 1999), pp. 57–8.

27. Mainwaring, 'Discourse – Of the Beginnings, Practices and Suppression of Pirates', p. 34. Mehdya is now generally shown on maps in reference to the larger port city of Kenitra, which lies farther inland, along the course of the River Sebou.

28. Mainwaring to the King, 'A Discourse in Four Fragments', *Cottonian MSS Collection* Otho E-VIII, Discourse, f. 339v; Mainwaring, 'Discourse – Of the Beginnings, Practices and Suppression of Pirates', p. 36.

29. E. Erbati and A. Trakadas, *The Moroccan Maritime Survey: An archaeological contribution to the history of the Tangier peninsula*, BAR International Series 1890 (Oxford: Archaeopress Publications, 2008), pp. 23–6.

30. Mainwaring, 'Discourse – Of the Beginnings, Practices and Suppression of Pirates', p. 36, n. 4; M. Newitt, *A History of Portuguese Overseas Expansion, 1400–1668* (London & New York: Routledge, 2005), p. 11.

31. D.S. Ponasik, 'The System of Administered Trade as a Defense Mechanism in Pre-protectorate Morocco', *International Journal of Middle East Studies*, vol. 8, no. 2, 1977, pp. 195–207.

32. 'Bona' or 'Bône' was a fortified coastal town in Mainwaring's time, but is now called Annaba and is a seaport city, in the northwestern corner of Algeria, near the Tunisian border; 'Bougie' or 'Bogee' as it was then known is now named Béjaïa, the Mediterranean port city on the Gulf of Béjaïa in Algeria; Mainwaring, 'Discourse – Of the Beginnings, Practices and Suppression of Pirates', pp. 27–39.

33. C.R. Pennell, 'The Geography of Piracy: Northern Morocco in the mid-nineteenth century', *Journal of Historical Geography*, vol. 20, no. 3, 1994, p. 94; see also J. Bookin-Weiner, 'The "Salé Rovers": Morocco and its corsairs in the seventeenth century', in R.S. Simon and J.C. Hurewitz (eds), *The Middle East and North Africa: Essays in honor of J.C. Hurewitz* (New York: Columbia University Press, 1990), pp. 151–98 and J. Bookin-Weiner, 'The Moroccan Corsairs of Rabat-Salé', in A. Bencherifa and K. Zemrag (eds), *Le Maroc et l'Atlantique* (Rabat: Publications de la Faculté des Lettres et des Sciences humaines, 1992), pp. 163–91.

34. Matar, *Turks, Moors and Englishmen in the Age of Discovery*, pp. 58, 61–2; Bak, *Barbary Pirate*, in particular see Chapter 11, pp. 171–89 for an interesting discussion on the impetus for Ward's conversion; see also N. Matar, 'The Renegade in English Seventeenth-Century Imagination', *Studies in English Literature, 1500–1900, Restoration and Eighteenth Century*, vol. 33, no. 3, 1993, pp. 489–505, which provides an insightful discussion on how such conversions were viewed in England, and includes Ward within the study.

35. F.M. Taleb Al-Olaqi, 'The Fear of Conversion to Islam in Daborne's *A Christian Turn'd Turk* (1609)', *Studies in Literature and Language*, vol. 14, 3, 2017, pp. 2–3; Brotton, *This Orient Isle*, pp. 137–41; D. Vitkus, 'Turning Turk in Othello: The conversion and damnation of the Moor', *Shakespeare Quarterly*, vol. 48, no. 2, 1997, pp. 145–76; D. Vitkus, *Three Turk Plays from Early Modern England* (New York: Columbia University Press, 2000).

36. Matar, *Turks, Moors and Englishmen*, p. 58; Ellen Friedman, 'North African Piracy on the Coasts of Spain in the Seventeenth Century: A new perspective on the expulsion of the Moriscos', *The International History Review*, vol. 1, 1979, pp. 2, 11–14; M. Carr, *Blood & Faith: The purging of Muslim Spain, 1492–1614* (London: Hurst & Co., 2017).

37. K. Parker, 'Reading "Barbary" in Early Modern England, 1550–1685', in M. Birchwood and M. Dimmock (eds), *Cultural encounters between East and West, 1453–1699* (Newcastle-Upon-Tyne: Cambridge Scholars Press, 2005), pp. 93–5; Antonio Foscarini, Venetian Ambassador in France, to the Doge and Senate, 20 October 1609, *Cal. S.P. Ven. 1607–1610*, H.F. Brown (ed.) (London: Mackie & Co. Ltd, 1904), p. 871; Brotton, *This Orient Isle*, pp. 273–5.

38. Mainwaring, 'Discourse – Of the Beginnings, Practices and Suppression of Pirates', pp. 15, 25–40; E. Semple, 'Pirate Coasts of the Mediterranean Sea', *Geographical Review*, vol. 2, 2, 1916, pp. 134–51; Pennell, 'The Geography of Piracy', pp. 272–82; Galvin, *Patterns of Pillage*, pp. 8–19, 75–108.

39. Semple, 'Pirate Coasts of the Mediterranean Sea', p. 153.

40. Bagwell, *Ireland under the Stuarts*.

41. Mainwaring, 'Discourse – Of the Beginnings, Practices and Suppression of Pirates', p. 16; Lane-Poole, *The Story of the Barbary Corsairs*, pp. 14–27.

42. Oppenheim, *The Naval Tracts of Sir William Monson in Six Books*, p. 74.

43. Senior, 'An Investigation of the Activities and Importance of English Pirates, 1603–40', p. 114; A. Tinniswood, *Pirates of Barbary: Corsairs, conquests and captivity in the 17th century Mediterranean* (London: Jonathan Cape Publishers, 2010), p. 69. This is an interesting point; see in relation to the concept of a 'frontier' zone, Ohlmeyer, 'Civilizing of Those Rude Partes': Colonization within Britain and Ireland, 1580s–1640s', in Canny (ed.), *The Origins of Empire*, pp. 125–7; Canny, 'Origins of Empire: An Introduction', in Canny (ed.), *The Origins of Empire*, pp. 2–13; J.C. Appleby, 'War, Politics and Colonization, 1558–1625', in Canny (ed.), *The Origins of Empire*, pp. 70–6.

44. Mainwaring, 'Discourse – Of the Beginnings, Practices and Suppression of Pirates', p. 22.

45. Kelleher, 'Depicting a Pirate Landscape', pp. 77–92.

46. A 'floaty ship' was a ship that drew little water, as described by Sir Henry Mainwaring in 1616 in his 'The Seaman's Dictionary', p. 149; the old Dutch word here is difficult to translate and it is thus interpreted as referring to a ship of shallow draft that could pass in ten or eleven feet of water.

47. H. Gerritszoon, SUB Göttingen, 4 H BRIT P III, 6 RARA, p. 19; the author is grateful to Dr Edda Frankot for translating the document from old Dutch.

48. MPyD58/051: Simancus: Guerra y Ma Leg. 3145: Sketch map of Baltimore, 1600? The author is grateful to Dr Anneleigh Margay for highlighting this source and supplying a copy of the map; 1612 John Hunt chart, in Gerritszoon, SUB Göttingen, 4 H BRIT P III, 6 RARA, p. 14; Map of Baltimore, *c.* 1610–20, WWM/Str P 20/100: Wentworth Woodhouse Muniments, Sheffield Library Archives, UK.

49. Gerritszoon, SUB Göttingen, 4 H BRIT P III, 6 RARA; 1612 John Hunt chart.

50. Capt. M. White, R.N., *Sailing directions for the English Channel, including a general description of the south coasts of England and Ireland, and a detailed account of the Channel Islands* (London: William Clowes & Sons, 1835), pp. 170–4.

51. Inquiries to be made relative to certain Rewards for Connivance taken by Sir Laurence Parsons, Vice-Admiral of Minister [Munster] and Sir William Hull, without making any account to the Lord High Admiral Buckingham [undated], *c.* 1627, SP 63/268, ff. 118v–119v (TNA, State Papers Online, Gale Document No. MC4348000227).

52. Recorded Monument CO:148:02703 *fish palace*, Register of Monuments and Places; Site no. 3654; D. Power, *Archaeological Inventory of County Cork, Volume 1, West Cork* (Dublin: Government Stationery Office, 1992), p. 360; www.archaeology.ie

53. Sir William Hull knight & one of his Maiesties Councell of Mounster, 22 October 1642, Deposition of William Hull, MS 824, ff. 253r–259v (TCD, 1641 Depositions Project online).

54. The author is grateful to Ms Rosanne Meehan and Ms Clare McCutcheon for their expertise and insights on the pottery remains.

55. Recorded Monument CO:148:02602 *Battery*, Register of Monuments and Places; Site no. 3304, in Power, *Archaeological Inventory, West Cork*, p. 411; www.archaeology.ie

56. Lords of the Council to Sir Arthur Chichester, 22 July 1612, *Cal. S.P. Ire. 1611–1614*, pp. 276–7.

57. Order of Council, dated 24 February 1613, written at Whitehall, *Cal. S.P. Ire. 1611–1614*, pp 325–6 (TNA, State Papers Online, Gale Document No. MC4347600630); the accompanying note refers to Baugh as 'late a pirate, pardoned'; Captain Baugh, 10 November 1615, in F. Devon, *Issues of the Exchequer: Being payments made out of his Majesty's Revenue during the reign of James I* (London: John Rodwell Publishing, 1836), pp. 178–9.

58. Deposition of William Hull of Leamcon, gentleman, aged 40, 13 May 1613, HCA examinations, 13/42, ff. 153v–155; Appleby, *A Calendar of Material*, p. 131.

59. Recorded Monument CO:148:016002: *Country House*, Seafort; Archaeological Survey of Ireland (ASI) site notes, National Monuments Service, Department of Culture, Heritage and the Gaeltacht, Custom House, Dublin 1.

60. Seafort: Landed Estates Database, Moore Institute, National University of Ireland, Galway; see http://www.landedestates.ie/LandedEstates/jsp/property-show.jsp?id=2692

61. Whittlesey, *The Earth and the State*, pp. 59–70; Galvin, *Patterns of Pillage*, pp. 16–18.

62. Mainwaring, 'A Discourse in Four Fragments', *Cottonian* MSS Otho E VIII, f. 335v; Mainwaring, 'Discourse – Of the Beginnings, Practices and Suppression of Pirates', p. 25–39; Galvin, *Pattern of Pillage*, pp. 11–12.

63. Senior, 'An Investigation of the Activities and Importance of English Pirates, 1603–40', pp. 126–7.

64. Rev. C.B. Gibson, *The History of the County and City of Cork*, vol. II (London: Thomas C. Newby Publishers, 1861), p. 522.

65. Whittlesey, *The Earth and the State*, pp. 60–5.

66. MPyD58/051: Simancus: Guerra y Ma Leg. 3145; 1612 John Hunt chart, in Gerritszoon, SUB Göttingen, 4 H BRIT P III, 6 RARA, p. 14; Map of Baltimore, c. 1610–20, WWM/Str P 20/100: Wentworth Woodhouse Muniments (Sheffield City Library Archives, UK).

67. Kelleher, 'The Confederacy of Pirates in Southwest Cork in the Early Seventeenth Century', pp. 157–77.

68. Mainwaring, 'A Discourse in Four Fragments', *Cottonian* MSS Otho E VIII, f. 336v; Mainwaring, 'Discourse – Of the Beginnings, Practices and Suppression of Pirates', pp. 28–9.

69. Chart 833: 'Crookhaven' by Capt. White, 1817 (Taunton: Admiralty Office, 1817); White, *Sailing Directions for the English Channel*, p. 170.

70. J. Hawke, 'Canty's Cove: Legend and history', *The Mizen Journal*, vol. 5, 1997, pp. 292–302; P. McCarthy and R. Hawkes, *North Side of the Mizen* (Cork: Mizen Productions, 1999), pp. 100–4.

71. Sir William Hull knight & one of his Maiesties Councell of Mounster, 22 October 1642, Deposition of William Hull, MS 824, f. 253r (TCD, 1641 Depositions Project, online).

72. Hawke, 'Canty's Cove'; McCarthy and Hawkes, *North Side of the Mizen*; Canty's first name is not recorded in the local information but in the 1659 Census in the barony of Kilnalmeaky for west Cork a William Canty is listed as a tenant, with a further ten Cantys also living in the general area at that time; S. Pender, *A Census of Ireland, circa 1659* (Dublin: Irish Manuscripts Commission, The Stationery Office, 1939), pp. 207 and 218, http://www.irishmanuscripts.ie/digital/censusofireland1659/files/html5/index.html

73. Semple, 'Pirate Coasts', p. 136.

74. Kelleher, 'The Confederacy of Pirates'; The author would like to thank Mr P. MacCarthy for relaying the tales of Canty and his lazy pirate ways and for providing an overview of works done at the pier in modern times.

75. McCarthy and Hawkes, *North Side of the Mizen*, pp. 123–33.

76. C. Marangou, 'Carved Rocks, Functional and Symbolic (Lemnos Island, Greece)', in L. Oosterbeek, M. Otte, L. Remacle and D. Seglie (eds), *Prehistoric Art: Signs, symbols, myth, ideology*, XV UISPP World Congress (Lisbon: BAR S2029, 2006 and 2009), pp. 95–7; the early prehistoric residents of Lemnos were known to be pirates and raiders and archaeological survey has shown that several of the rock-cut steps and platforms on the island were directly associated with them; see also M.G. Marten, 'Spatial and Temporal Analyses of the Harbor at Antiochia ad Cragum', MA thesis, Florida State University, 2005, for an interesting study of piracy in the remote harbour of Rough Cilicia in the Mediterranean.

77. NM no. 61, RMP KE104-001: *Skellig Michael* & NM no. 168, RMP KE097-036: *Ballinskelligs Abbey*, Record of Monuments and Places (Archaeological Survey of Ireland data, National Monuments Service; www.archaeology.ie; E. Bourke, A. Hayden and A. Lynch, *Skellig Michael, Co. Kerry: Archaeological stratigraphic report: excavations 1986–2010* (Dublin: Government of Ireland, 2011), pp. 22–4, 469; *Skellig Michael World Heritage Site Management Plan 2008–2018* (Dublin: Department of Culture, Heritage and the Gaeltacht and the Office of Public Works Report, 2008), pp. 13–21.

78. Mainwaring, 'Discourse – Of the Beginnings, Practices and Suppression of Pirates', p. 17.

79. R. Roche and O. Merne, *Saltees: Islands of birds and legends* (Dublin: The O'Brien Press, 1977), pp. 38–9.

80. The author is grateful to Tom and Jane Somerville of Drishane House, Castletownshend, for bringing this site to light and allowing access to it.

81. Timothy Chavasse, *Past Speech of the Sea: A maritime history of Castlehaven* (Cork: Galley Head Press, 2003), p. 29.

82. RMP CO147-090: Coastal Promontory Fort; Record of Monuments and Places (Archaeological Survey of Ireland data, National Monuments Service; www.archaeology.ie)

83. Oppenheim, 'The Royal Navy under James I', pp. 471–96; Penn, *The Navy Under the Early Stuarts*, pp. 84–5; Kenny, *Elizabeth's Admiral*, pp. 162–5, 264–71.

84. Oppenheim, 'The Royal Navy under James I', p. 475; Rodger, *The Safeguard of the Sea*, pp. 347–78.

85. Lord Danvers to the Earl of Salisbury, 3 June 1608, *Cal. S.P. Ire. 1606–1608*, p. 551.

86. Woodward, 'Sir Thomas Button', pp. 343–4.

87. Oppenheim, 'The Royal Navy under James I', p. 121; Oppenheim is cautious of the term 'rebuilt', clarifying that without actual details of what was done to the ship, the term could also refer to repair rather than a complete rebuild, p. 202; Rodger, *Safeguard of the Seas*, p. 329, explains that 'rebuilds' were essentially new ships but built with the timbers from the old ship.

88. Rodger, *Safeguard of the Seas*, p. 219.

89. Kelleher, 'The Gaelic O'Driscoll Lords of Baltimore', p. 147.

90. David Cordingly, *Life Among the Pirates: The romance and the reality* (London: Little, Brown & Co., 1995), p. 186; Mainwaring, 'Discourse – Of the Beginnings, Practices and Suppression of Pirates', p. 15.

91. Deposition of William Jackson, 9 August 1614, HCA Examinations, 13/98. ff. 211r–212v; Mainwaring, 'Discourse – Of the Beginnings, Practices and Suppression of Pirates', pp. 15, 25, 149.

92. Examination of Rich. Kerry, 29 January 1609, HCA Examinations, 1/47, ff. 79v–84r.

93. K.E. Lane, *Pillaging the Empire: Piracy in the Americas, 1500–1750* (New York: M.E. Sharpe Inc., 1998), p. 94; while these two vessel types were distinct in ship design, the term 'flyboat' was used interchangeably in the documents during this early period, with the word 'flyboat' or 'flyboate' often used for both vessel types and with the Dutch fluyt having its equivalent with, for example, the French 'flûte' and Spanish 'felibote'; care must therefore be taken with nomenclature in the contemporary sources; O.H.K. Spate, *The Spanish Lake* (Canberra: Australia National University Press, 2004), p. 19.

94. The author is grateful to Dr Wendy Duivenvoorde of Flinders University, Adelaide, Western Australia, for her insight into the ship types and to her colleague, Dr Willem Van Ham, for information on the possible provenance of the Dutch flags as depicted on the ships.

95. Deputy Chichester to the Privy Council, 16 July 1607, SP 63/222, ff. 21r–22v (TNA, State Papers Online, Gale Document No. 4347480293).

96. Examination of William Hughes of London, 12 August 1612, HCA Examinations, 1/47, ff. 308r–309v.

97. Senior, 'An Investigation of the Activities and Importance of English Pirates, 1603–40', p. 404.

98. Sir Arthur Chichester and Lord Carew to the Privy Council, SP 63/231, f. 164r (TNA, State Papers Online, Gale Document no. 4347680207); Capt. Skipwith to the Lord Deputy, 25 July 1611, SP 63/231, ff. 166r–167r (TNA, State Papers Online, Gale Document no. 4347680208); Deposition of Richard Hunt, of Wapping, mariner, 19 June 1611, sailor, HCA Examinations 1/47, ff 201r–202v; Deposition of Jacques Henriques of Rotterdam in Holland, merchant, 28 February 1611, HCA Examinations, 1/47, ff. 265–266.

99. Capt. Skipwith to the Lord Deputy, 25 July 1611; Foscarini to Doge and Senate, 11 August 1611, *Cal. S.P. Ven. 1610–1613*, p. 195; Senior, 'An Investigation of the Activities and Importance of English Pirates, 1603–40', p. 404; Deposition of William Poulter, 26 April 1611, HCA Examinations, 1/47, ff. 186r–186v; Senior,

'An Investigation of the Activities and Importance of English Pirates, 1603–40', p. 237; ordnance varied greatly throughout the ages and pirates were not choosy when it came to acquiring all makes and sizes of guns.

100. Mainwaring, 'Discourse – Of the Beginnings, Practices and Suppression of Pirates', p. 43.

101. Kelleher, 'The Confederacy of Pirates', pp. 424–9; C. Ewen, 'Introduction', in R.K. Skowronek and C.R. Ewen, *X Marks the Spot: The archaeology of piracy* (Gainesville: University Press of Florida, 2006), pp. 7–8.

102. Mainwaring, 'Discourse – Of the Beginnings, Practices and Suppression of Pirates', p. 149.

103. See for instance: Deposition of Edward Davenant of Whiddy Island, 1 October 1614, HCA Examinations, 13/226 f. 338; loss of Captain Patrick Myagh's ship in Crookhaven: Examination of Rich. Kerry, 29 January 1610, HCA Examinations, 1/47 ff 82v–83r; loss of pirate captain Sammes' ship in Berehaven: Examination of Rich. Kerry, 29 January 1610, HCA Examinations, 1/47 ff 82v–83r.

104. Wreck Inventory of Ireland Database (WIID), wrecks of County Cork shortlist for pirate vessels (National Monuments Service) the reference here to nine wrecks does not include records for privateers lost in the same area.

105. Senior, 'An Investigation of the Activities and Importance of English Pirates, 1603–40', p. 426; Examination of Rich. Kerry, 29 January 1610.

106. V. Lunsford, *Piracy and Privateering in the Golden Age Netherlands* (New York: Palgrave Macmillan, 2005), pp. 129, 289 n. 233 and n. 237.

107. SUB Göttingen, 4 H BRIT P III, 6 RARA: Hessel Gerritszoon, *Beschrijvinghe van de Zeecusten ende Havenen van Yerlandt/Description of the Seacoasts and Ports of Ireland*, pp. 19–20.

108. Appleby, *A Calendar of Material*, pp. 285–9; Deposition of Edward Davenant, 1 October 1614.

109. C. Kelleher, 'The Dunworley Bay Shipwreck: 17th century evidence for piracy and slavery in Ireland?', in C. Horrell and M. Damour (eds), *ACUA Archaeology Conference Proceedings* (US: Advisory Council on Underwater Archaeology, 2010), pp. 138–45; C. Kelleher, 'The 17th-century Dunworley Bay Shipwreck: Illegal activity, archaeological investigations and possible identity', *Skibbereen and District Historical Society Journal*, vol. 10, 2014, pp. 130–9.

110. J. O'Donoghue, 'The Coconut (Colla) Wreck, Schull, Co. Cork, Archaeological Investigations', unpublished interim report, Mizen Archaeology Ltd., 2012, pp. 1–65; the author is grateful to Ms O'Donoghue for allowing access to material and information from the wreck and for permission to publish imagery of artefacts from the site.

111. J. Carter, 'Spanish Olive Jars From Fermeuse Harbour, Newfoundland', *Material History Bulletin: Ceramics in Canada*, vol. 16, 1982, pp. 99–108; C. Kelleher, '*Santa Ana Maria*: 1628 wreck of the Capitana of La Flota de la Nueva España', in J. Henderson (ed.), *Beyond Boundaries: Proceedings of the 3rd International Congress on Underwater Archaeology* (London: IKUWA3, 2008), pp. 175–82; Kelleher, 'Death by Disgrace'.

112. M.W. Marken, *Pottery from Spanish Shipwrecks, 1500–1800* (Gainesville, University of Florida Press, 1994), Chapter 4, pp. 41–138, particularly 134–5.

113. The Names of those who bought Goods of the Pirate Campane at Lymecon, in the West of Ireland [?], 1625, *Cal S.P. Ireland, 1603–1625* (TNA, State Papers Online, Gale Document No. MC4347701417).

CHAPTER 5
The Business of Piracy

1. Roger Myddleton to Salisbury, 23 August, 1611, SP 63/231, ff. 182–182v (TNA London, State Papers Online, Gale Document No. MC4347680227).

2. HCA Indictments, 1603–40, various volumes; Calendared by the *List and Index Society*, vol. 45, 1969 (TNA, London), pp. 20–42; a more comprehensive list is provided by Senior, 'An Investigation of the Activities and Importance of English Pirates, 1603–40', pp. 345–61.

3. Senior, 'An Investigation of the Activities and Importance of English Pirates, 1603–40', p. 63 and n. 5, p. 389; Tenenti, *Piracy and the Decline of Venice*, pp. 76–8, 174, n. 29; Bak, *Barbary Pirate*, pp. 118–24.

4. Deposition of Sir William Hull knight & one of his Maiesties Councell of Mounster, 22 October 1642, Depositions 1641, MS 824, ff. 253r–259v.

5. Ohlmeyer, *Making Ireland English*, pp. 365–6; D. Dickson, *Old World Colony: Cork and south Munster 1630–1830* (Cork, Cork University Press, 2005), pp. 10–28.

6. Vincenzo Gussoni, Venetian Ambassador in Savoy, to the Doge and Senate, 30 March 1613, *Cal. S.P. Ven. 1610–1613*: 'The Corsair [Easton] is on the point of acquiring Marquisate and other fiefs', entry 804, p. 516; Vincenzo Gussoni, Venetian Ambassador in Savoy, to the Doge and Senate, 26 April 1613, *Cal S.P. Ven. 1610–1613*: 'The Englishman [Easton] has covered himself with glory', entry 824, p. 528; Vincenzo Gussoni, Venetian Ambassador in Savoy, to the Doge and Senate, 30 March 1613, *Cal S.P. Ven. 1610–1613*, entry 784, p. 505.

7. Appleby, 'The Affairs of Pirates', pp. 68–84.

8. Examination of Richard Millington, 17 December 1612, HCA Examinations 13/42, f. 114r; see Glossary for definitions of items listed.

9. Examination of Richard Millington, 17 December 1612; Appleby (ed.), *A Calendar of Material*, pp. 128–9.

10. Examination of Richard Millington, 21 August 1613, HCA Examinations 13/42, ff. 214v–214r & f. 216v; Appleby, 'The Affairs of Pirates'.

11. Examination of John Huskins [Hoskins], 19 August 1613, HCA Examinations 13/42, ff. 203v–204r.

12. Examination of Thomas Morris, 19 August 1613, 13/42, ff. 201v–202r; Appleby, 'The Affairs of Pirates', pp. 73–4; Appleby, 'Settlers and Pirates', p. 83.

13. Examination of John Huskins, f. 203v.

14. Examination of Philip Walker, 20 August 1613, HCA Examinations 13/42, ff. 205v–207; Examination of Richard Millington, 21 August 1613; Appleby, 'The Affairs of Pirates', p. 80.

15. Appleby, 'The Affairs of Pirates', p. 75.

16. Deposition of William Weston, 19 August 1613, HCA Examinations 13/42, ff. 199–201r; Deposition of Richard Thorne, 19 August 1613, HCA Examinations 13/42, ff. 204v–205r; Appleby (ed.), *A Calendar of Material*, pp. 135–6; Appleby, *A Calendar of Material*, pp. 134–6.

17. Examination of Richard Millington, 21 August 1613; Appleby, 'The Affairs of Pirates', pp. 74–6.

18. Appleby, 'The Affairs of Pirates', pp. 79–80.

19. Examination of Richard Millington, 21 August 1613.

20. The Lord Deputy to the Lords of the Council, 25 July 1612 in Edwards (ed.), 'Letter-Book of Sir Arthur Chichester', pp. 3–178.

21. Examination of John Huskins [Hoskins], 19 August 1613.

22. Note of payments made to Capt. Baugh, a pirate, since December 1613, in part of sum of 2,586*l.* 16*s.* 8*d.*, March 1616 (TNA London, SP 14/198 f. 20; Gale Document No. MC4323785487); the entry in the exchequer payments list of July 1615 specifically states the amount to have been 2,310*l.* 16*s.* 8*d.* (*c.* £303,900 / €346,130), F. Devon, *Issues of the Exchequer: Being payments made out of his Majesty's Revenue during the reign of James I* (London: John Rodwell Publishing, 1836), pp. 178–9.

23. Examination of William Baugh of Inishoon in Ireland, gent aged 25 years or thereabouts, 23 July 1613, HCA Examinations 13/98, ff. 82r–83v; Appleby, 'Settlers and Pirates', p. 77; Appleby, 'The Affairs of Pirates', p. 81.

24. Sir John Finet to the earl of Salisbury, 27–29 October 1619, *Cal. of MSS of the most Hon. Marquis of Salisbury, 1612–1668*, 22 (TNA London, State Papers Online, Gale Document No. MC4332200202), p. 96. This is an extensive document dealing with various finances but refers to Ralph Bingley's dealings with the pirates and handling of monies; in it Baugh was to receive £1,100 (*c.* £147,505 / €168,000) from Bingley out of a sum of £2,800 (*c.* £375,500 / €427,680) for the pirates, but only

received about £40 (*c*. £5,350 / €6,094) at most. After his death, Baugh's brother attempted to obtain the pirate's share but seems to have been done out of it by Bingley, whereupon Baugh's brother was pursued by Captain Baugh's creditors for outstanding amounts.

25. Appleby, 'The Affairs of Pirates', pp. 79–80.

26. Lord Danvers to the [Lords of the Privy Council or the Lord Salisbury], 19 January 1609, *Cal. S.P. Ire. 1608–1610*, p. 130; Senior, 'An Investigation of the Activities and Importance of English Pirates, 1603–40', p. 407.

27. Examination of John Jennings, a pirate, before the court of admiralty, no date, *Cottonian* MSS Otho E/VIII, f. 360 (TNA London, State Papers Online, Gale Document No. MC4318815332).

28. Ibid.; Deposition of Gionisius Gallot of Calais, sailor, aged about 35, 16 June 1609, HCA Examinations 13/40, ff. 161r–162r. Arthur Drake is one of the only black pirates recorded from this period as a member of the Atlantic pirate crews, though many more must have gone unrecorded at the time; there were others mentioned in later pirate times who made up significant numbers of crews; see for example K. Kinkor, 'Black Men under a Black Flag', in Pennell (ed.), *Bandits at Sea*, pp. 195–210; Leeson, *The Invisible Hook*, pp. 156–71; for Arthur Drake see Senior, 'An Investigation of the Activities and Importance of English Pirates, 1603–40', pp. 387–8; see also D. Leigh, 'Ghost of the Gallows: The historical record of Black Caesar', *Creating Knowledge: The LAS student research journal* (DePaul University), vol. 5, 2012, pp. 28–32.

29. Senior, 'An Investigation of the Activities and Importance of English Pirates, 1603–40', pp. 387–8.

30. C. Corn, *The Scents of Eden* (New York: Kodansha International, 1998).

31. For a history of both companies, see C.R. Boxer, *The Dutch Seaborne Empire 1600–1800* (New York: Harmondsworth Penguin Books, 1965) and *The Portuguese Seaborne Empire, 1415–1825* (London: Hutchinson & Co., 1969); Keay, *The Honourable Company*; see also chapters 11–14 in Andrews, *Trade, Plunder and Settlement*; East Indies are often referred to as the Spice Islands, equivalent to the Malaku Archipelago (the Moluccas) in modern-day northern Indonesia; in contemporary times, the term also included other islands, including nearby Sulawesi (Celebes); the West Indies comprise the Caribbean, Greater and Lesser Antilles and Cuba.

32. Andrews, *Trade, Plunder and Settlement*, p. 4.

33. 'The full note of all the goods I hadd laden aboard my ship as followeth' [?], February 1624, SP 63/239 f. 33 (TNA London, State Papers Online, Gale Document No. MC4347781353); Compaen may have arrived in late January as a letter from the lord deputy dated 1 February mentions that the pirate was at that point in Leamcon: Lord deputy to Sir William Hull, 1 February 1624, SP 63/239 f. 27 (TNA London, State Papers Online, Gale Document No. MC4347781350); Lunsford, *Piracy and Privateering in the Golden Age Netherlands*.

34. The full note of all the goods I hadd laden aboard my ship as followeth' [?], February 1625, SP 63/239 f. 33; Lunsford, *Piracy and Privateering in the Golden Age Netherlands*.

35. The Names of those who bought Goods of the Pirate Campane at Lymecon, in the West of Ireland [?], 1625, *Cal S.P. Ireland, 1603–1625* (TNA London, State Papers Online, Gale Document No. MC4347701417).

36. This may mean massive pieces of gold (ingots or bars) or could also refer to gold from Massa in western Morocco.

37. The Names of those who bought Goods of the Pirate Campane.

38. Ibid.; Ohlmeyer, *Making Ireland English*, p. 528, n. 89.

39. Appleby (ed.), *A Calendar of Material*, p. 306.

40. Inquiries to be made relative to certain Rewards for Connivance taken by Sir Laurence Parsons, Vice-Admiral of Minister [Munster] and Sir William Hull, without taking any account to the Lord High Admiral Buckingham [undated] 1627, SP 63/268 f. 118 (TNA London, State Papers Online, Gage Manuscript no. MC4348000227).

41. Sir Ambrose Heal, *The London Goldsmiths, 1200–1800: A record of the names and addresses of the craftsman, their shop-signs and trade-cards* (Newton Abbot: David & Charles, 1972).

42. Lord deputy to Sir William Hull, 1 February 1624, SP 63/239 f. 27 (TNA London, State Papers Online, Gale Document No. MC4347781350).

43. The Conditions on which Nice and Villafranca were declared Free Ports, 3 March 1613, *Cal. S.P. Ven. 1610–1613*; Vincenzo Gussoni, Venetian Ambassador in Savoy, to the Doge and Senate, 10 March 1613, *Cal. S.P. Ven. 1610–1613*, British History Online, entry 784.

44. Roger Myddleton to Salisbury, 23 August, 1611, SP 63/231, ff. 182–182v (TNA London, State Papers Online, Gale Document No. MC4347680227).

45. Sir Arthur Chichester to Salisbury, 20 January 1611 (1612), *Cal. S.P. Ire. 1611–1614*, pp. 5–6; Chichester was complaining that the 'treasure' allotted from the exchequer for Ireland to pay soldiers, officers, and his own expenses, was both inadequate to cover all necessaries and did not arrive on time, in which case the soldiers had to be paid out of borrowed funds.

46. HCA 30/858, bundle E. 1612–20; these contain papers reporting on how the pirates had to go to the High Court of Admiralty in London to claim their booty; it is a source that deserves far more scrutiny.

47. The Names of those who bought Goods of the Pirate Campane at Lymecon.

48. Senior, 'An Investigation of the Activities and Importance of English Pirates, 1603–40', p. 117.

49. Examination of John Jennings, pirate, before the court of admiralty, ff. 360–4: this document is badly damaged by fire but probably dates to 1609 or 1610; Lord Deputy to the Lords of the Council, 31 October 1612, Edwards (ed.). 'Letter-book', p. 62.

50. Mainwaring, 'Discourse – Of the Beginnings, Practices and Suppression of Pirates', p. 17.

51. Captain Henry Skipwith to Sir Arthur Chichester, October 1611 (NLI, *Carew MSS*, 629, f. 178).

52. Corn, *The Scents of Eden*, pp. 202–3.

53. A. Phillips and J.C. Sharman, *International Order in Diversity: War, trade and rule in the Indian Ocean* (Cambridge: Cambridge University Press, 2015), pp. 130–2.

54. A. Dalby, *Dangerous Tastes: The story of spices* (Berkeley: University of California Press, 2000), pp. 42–3.

55. Corn, *The Scents of Eden*, pp. 246–7.

56. E.A. Weiss, *Spice Crops* (Wallingford and New York: CABI Publishing, 2002), pp. 154–5.

57. R. Findlay and K.H. O'Rourke, 'Commodity Market Integration, 1500–2000', in M.D. Bordo, A.M. Taylor and J.G. Williamson (eds), *Globalization in Historical Perspective* (Chicago: University of Chicago Press, 2003), pp. 6–7, 44.

58. Weiss, *Spice Crops*, p. 156.

59. F. Vieira de Castro, *The Pepper Wreck: A Portuguese Indiaman at the mouth of the Tagus River* (College Station, TX: A&M University Press, 2005), pp.14–15.

60. The Names of those who bought Goods of the Pirate Campane.

61. de Castro, *The Pepper Wreck*, https://www.bbc.com/news/world-europe-45630260

62. O'Donoghue, 'The Coconut Wreck', pp. 1–65.

63. Brotton, *This Orient Isle*, p. 62.

64. Senior, 'An Investigation of the Activities and Importance of English Pirates, 1603–40', p. iii; G. Fisher, *Barbary Legend: War, trade and piracy in North Africa, 1415–1830* (Oxford: Clarendon Press, 1957).

65. Mainwaring, 'Discourse – Of the Beginnings, Practices and Suppression of Pirates', p. 11, 25; for a detailed and informative discussion on the history and ideology of the Ottoman Turks, which also provides a better understanding of how the Algerine Turkish pirates operated, see T. Shuval, 'The Ottoman Algerian Élite and Its Ideology', *International Journal of Middle Eastern Studies*, vol. 32, 2000, pp. 323–44.

66. Matar, *Turks, Moors and Englishmen*, pp. 63–4.

67. E. Arber, 'The Travels and Observations of Captaine Smith', vol. II, from *Capt. John Smith, of Willoughby by Alford, Lincolnshire; President of Virginia, and Admiral of New England. Works, 1608–1631* (Birmingham: John Connor Publishers, 1884), p. 871.

68. Mainwaring, 'A Discourse in Four Fragments', *Cottonian* MSS Otho E/VIII f. 339 (TNA London, State Papers Online, Gale Document No. MC4318895326); Mainwaring, 'Discourse – Of the Beginnings, Practices and Suppression of Pirates', p. 37.

69. R. Whitbourne, A *Discourse and Discovery of Newfoundland* (London: Felix Kingston, 1620), pp. 11–12; (Early English Books Online; STC (2nd ed.) / 25372, Henry E. Huntington Library and Art Gallery, image 16).

70. Other venture companies had been set up to carry out voyages of speculation and exploration to different parts of the globe, including the North West Passage Company, The Muscovy Company and the South Sea Company; these companies had been established under the auspices of the Company of Merchant Adventurers of London; see T. Rabb, 'Investment in English Overseas Enterprise, 1575–1630', *The Economic History Review*, vol. 19, no. 1, 1966, pp. 70–81; D.B. Quinn, 'Advice for Investors in Virginia, Bermuda, and Newfoundland, 1611', *The William and Mary Quarterly*, vol. 23, no. 1, 1966, p. 138.

71. J. Stevens Curl, 'The City of London and the Plantation of Ulster' (London: British Broadcasting Corporation, British History Online, 2001), pp. 1–11.

72. A. Horning, *Ireland in the Virginian Sea: Colonialism in the British Atlantic* (Williamsburg: University of North Carolina Press, 2013), pp. 276–81.

73. Petition of the Merchants trading to the East Indies and of William Burrell [undated] 1613, *Cal. S.P. Ire. of the Reign of James I, 1603–1614* (TNA London, State Papers Online, Gale Document No. MC4347600708).

74. N. Canny, 'The Origins of Empire: An Introduction', in *The Origins of Empire*, p. 28.

75. Jamestown Society, *Qualifying Ancestors: Stockholders in the Virginia Company* (Ancestor Register, 2007), p. 2, http://www.jamestowne.org

76. Sir Richard Moryson to Salisbury, 22 August 1609, Youghall, SP 63/227, f. 90 (TNA London, State Papers Online, Gale Document No. MC4347580473).

77. Jamestown Society, *Qualifying Ancestors*.

78. Senior, 'An Investigation of the Activities and Importance of English Pirates, 1603–40', p. 93; The various grand dukes of Tuscany had been criticised from the sixteenth century onwards by English officials for enticing English sailors and shipbuilders into their service, to serve in their navy and bring knowledge of shipbuilding and seafaring with them to enhance the Duchy's warships. Several high-profile individuals took up residence there, with the lure of living in luxury and becoming wealthy through serving the duke, trading within the Mediterranean

and investing in colonial ventures. In 1607, for example, Sir Robert Dudley, once suitor to Elizabeth I, arrived in Leghorn and quickly established himself within the shipyards and encouraged more of his fellow Englishmen to join him. It was noted at the time that 'The Grand Duke [Ferdinand I] continues to entice English mariners and shipwrights into his service, has brought ordnance from English ships, and taken English Pirates under his protection'; J. Lorimer, *English and Irish Settlement on the River Amazon, 1550–1646* (London: Hakluyt Society, 1989), p. 30. Similar enticements were traditionally made by the dukes of Florence and Savoy, with perhaps Peter Easton the most noted of the Atlantic pirates to eventually settle in Savoy; see also A. Gwynn, 'Early Irish Emigration to the West Indies, 1612–1643', *Studies: An Irish Quarterly Review*, vol. 18, no. 71, 1929, pp. 377–93.

79. Senior, 'An Investigation of the Activities and Importance of English Pirates, 1603–40', pp. 107, 151, 388–9.

80. Examination of Edward Davenant of the island of Whiddy, county of Cork, merchant, aged 45, 1 October 1614, HCA Examinations 13/226, f. 338.

81. Ibid.; Appleby (ed.), *A Calendar of Material*, p. 285.

82. Gondomar was in London representing Portuguese interests, as Portugal was at that time under Spanish dominion; Senning, 'Piracy, Politics, and Plunder', pp. 187–222; this is the most comprehensive account written to date of the voyage, loss and subsequent legal wranglings surrounding the ship *Pearl*.

83. Senning, 'Piracy, Politics, and Plunder', p. 195; The Lord Deputy [Chichester] to the Lords of the Council, 3 November and 6 November 1613; Edwards, 'Letter-book', pp. 132, 140.

84. Senning, 'Piracy, Politics and Plunder', p. 195.

85. Deposition of Walter Rockwell of Bristol, mariner, 7 June 1614, HCA Examinations, 13/42, f 307v [304v–305?]; Deposition of James Stonehouse of London, mariner, 7 June, 1614, HCA Examinations, 13/42, f 305v–306r in Appleby (ed.), *A Calendar of Material*, p. 140; Edwards, 'Letter-book', pp. 132, 140.

86. Senning, 'Piracy, Politics, and Plunder', pp. 196, 199.

87. Ibid., pp. 195–200; Quinn, 'The Voyage of the *Triall*', pp. 363–81, in particular see pp. 379–82.

88. 'Howard, Henry, earl of Northampton (1540–1614)', *Dictionary of National Biography*; Sir Henry Howard was made earl of Northampton by James in 1604, who held him in high favour in his court. The same year he jointly held the office of commissioner of the earl marshal, which afforded him control of merchant activity; he spoke openly in favour of freedom of trade with the Indies, which tied in closely to his own private interests overseas, including the granting of estates in Newfoundland and ingratiating himself with the Spanish court. It may be this latter fact that influenced his dealings in the 'Pearl Affair', as so emphatically stated by Spanish Ambassador Gondomar; Northampton to [Lake], 2 December 1613, *Cal. SP Dom. James I, 1611–18*, pp. 213–19.

89. Senning, 'Piracy, Politics, and Plunder', p. 205.

90. 'Cranfield, Lionel, first earl of Middlesex (1575–1645)', *Dictionary of National Biography*; 'Ingram, Sir Arthur (*b.* before 1571, *d.* 1642)', *Dictionary of National Biography*.

91. Deposition of Gionisius Galliot of Calais in the region of France, 19 June 1609, HCA Examinations, 13/40, ff. 161r–162v; Deposition of Humfridue Jobson of Westminster, gentleman, 15 July 1609, HCA Examinations, 13/40, 197v–198v; Senior, 'An Investigation of the Activities and Importance of English Pirates, 1603–40', pp. 327–8; Appleby, *A Calendar of Material*, pp. 121–2.

92. Senning, 'Piracy, Politics and Plunder', pp. 202–11.

93. Senior, 'An Investigation of the Activities and Importance of English Pirates, 1603–40', p. 388.

94. Duppa went on to command several ships, including the *Seahorse*, *Amity* and ill-fated *Sea-Nymph*, and had a long career as an adventurer, with investments in several companies involved in colonial pursuits in South and Central America, under Charles I; in 1642 he is recorded as an 'Englishman, now elderly, called James Dupay, who years ago was a pirate, afterwards captain of some of the king of England's ships, and now he is very wealthy and has shares in ships'; for a full and excellent account of these colonial ventures see Lorimer, *English and Irish Settlement on the River Amazon*, and for Duppa's involvement in particular pp. 98–9, 101–3, 116–17, 353, 439–45; Hanna, *Pirate Nests and the Rise of the British Empire*, pp. 70–7; W.F. Craven, 'The Earl of Warwick: A speculator in piracy', *Hispanic American Historical Review*, vol. 30, 1930, pp. 457–97.

95. L. Benton, 'Oceans of Law: The legal geography of the seventeenth-century seas', *Proceedings of the Seascapes, Littoral Cultures, and Trans-Oceanic Exchanges Conference*, 2003 (Washington DC: Library of Congress, 2003); see too Benton, 'Legal Spaces of Empire: Piracy and the origins of ocean regionalism', *Journal of Comparative Study of Society and History*, vol. 47, no. 4, 2005, pp. 700–24, http://cssh.lsa.umich.edu/

96. Ritchie, *Captain Kidd and the War Against the Pirates*, pp. 11–20.

97. Senior, 'An Investigation of the Activities and Importance of English Pirates, 1603–40', p. 323; Tenenti, *Piracy and the Decline of Venice*, pp. 56–86.

98. Tenenti, *Piracy and the Decline of Venice*, pp. 85–6.

99. Remonstrance to the Lordships of the English Piracyes in 1610 and 1611 against ye marchants of Rochelle only, *c.* 1612 (specific date not given), SP 78/60, ff. 281–282r (TNA London, State Papers Online, Gale Document No. MC4375 380084): the remonstrance is written in French; Senior, *A Nation of Pirates*, p. 61.

100. Senior, 'An Investigation of the Activities and Importance of English Pirates, 1603–40', pp. 325–6; Senior, *A Nation of Pirates*, p. 61.

101. Examination of James Bell of Ratcliffe, merchant, 9 April 1611, HCA 1/47, f. 177; Senior, *A Nation of Pirates*, p. 25.

102. Antonio Foscarini, Venetian Ambassador in England, to the Doge and Senate, 15 October 1612, *Cal. S.P. Ven. 1610–1613*, H.F. Brown (ed.) (London: His Majesty's Stationery Office, Mackie & Co., 1905), p. 434.

103. Senior, 'An Investigation of the Activities and Importance of English Pirates, 1603–40', p. 142; A letter to the Judge of the Admiraltie, [July?] 1613, *APC of England, 1613–1614* (London: His Majesty's Stationery Office, 1921), pp. 145–6; D.W. Prowse, *A History of Newfoundland from the English, Colonial and Foreign Records* (London: Eyre & Spottiswoode, 1896), pp. 102–3.

104. T. Whitburn, *Westward Hoe for Avalon: In the New-found-land, as described by Captain Richard Whitbourne, of Exmouth, Devon, 1622* (London: Sampson Low, Son & Marston, 1870), pp. 12, 42; Horwood and Butts, *Pirates & Outlaws of Canada*, pp. 11–34; S. Purchas, *Hakluytus Posthumus; or Purchas his Pilgrims: Contayning a history of the world in sea voyages and lande travells by Englishmen and others in 1626*, vol. XIX (Glasgow: Reprinted as *Purchas his Pilgrims* by James MacLehose & Sons, Glasgow, 1907), p. 416.

105. P. Pope, *Fish into Wine: The Newfoundland plantation in the seventeenth century* (Chapel Hill and London: University of North Carolina Press, 2004), p. 50; A.F. Williams, *John Guy of Bristol and Newfoundland* (St John's, Newfoundland: Flankers Press Ltd., 2010).

106. Horwood and Butts, *Pirates and Outlaws*, p. 19.

107. B. Gaulton and J.A. Tuck, 'The Archaeology of Ferryland, Newfoundland until 1696', *Avalon Chronicles: The English in America, 1497–1696*, vol. 8, 2003, pp. 187–8; http://www.colonyofavalon.ca/index.php?option=com_content&view=article&id=54:avalon-defenses

108. Senior, 'An Investigation of the Activities and Importance of English Pirates, 1603–40', p. 328; John Harrison to Salisbury, at Saphia, 10 June, 1610, SP 71/12, f. 82 (TNA London, State Papers Online, Gale Document No. MC4364380042).

109. Marc' Antonio Correr, Venetian Ambassador in England, to the Doge and Senate, 6 August 1609, *Cal. S.P. Ven. 1607–1610*, entry 575, www.british-history.ac.uk.elib.tcd.ie/

110. Arguments against the petition of merchants trading into Spain, complaining of grievances inflicted by the Spaniards, and requesting letters of marque [13 May], 1607, SP 14/27, f. 52 (TNA London, State Papers Online, Gale Document No. MC4323585230).

CHAPTER 6
The Social World of Amphibious Lives

1. Roger Myddleton to Salisbury, 23 August, 1611, SP 63/231, ff. 182–182v (TNA London, State Papers Online, Gale Document No. MC4347680227).

2. Caball, 'Culture, Continuity and Change', p. 41.

3. Five fragments concerning admiralty cases, no date [c. 1616], *Cottonian MSS* Otho E/VIII, ff. 378–379r (TNA London, State Papers Online, Gale Document No. MC4318815336).

4. Caball, 'Culture, Continuity and Change', pp. 37–56; Dickson, *Old World Colony*, pp. 10–28; MacCarthy-Morrogh, *The Munster Plantation*, pp. 137–176, 225–243.

5. For a valuable discussion on the context, role and influence of women during the sixteenth and seventeenth centuries within the Uskoks raiding tribes of the Adriatic coast, see C.W. Bracewell, *The Uskoks of Senj: Piracy, banditry, and holy war in the sixteenth-century Adriatic* (Ithaca: Cornell University Press, 1992) and C.W. Bracewell, 'Women Among the Uskoks: Literary images and reality', in Pennell (ed.), *Bandits at Sea*, pp. 321–34.

6. Mainwaring, 'A Discourse in Four Fragments', *Cottonian MSS* Otho E/VIII, ff. 329–344r (TNA London, State Papers Online, Gale Document No. MC4318895326); H. Mainwaring, 'Discourse – Of the Beginnings, Practices and Suppression of Pirates', p. 11.

7. Examinations taken at Youghall by Edward Morris and Henry Gosnold, esquires and chief second justice of the Province of Munster, the 19 February 1610, HCA Examinations 13/226, f. 96; Appleby, *A Calendar of Material*, pp. 284–99.

8. Edwards (ed.), 'Letter-Book of Sir Arthur Chichester', pp. 61–2.

9. Lords of the Council to Sir Arthur Chichester, 18 November 1612, *Cal. S.P. Ire. 1611–1614*, p. 301.

10. Deposition of Richard Bushoppe of Scull in Ireland, gent., 20 August 1614, HCA Examinations 13/98, f. 213v.

11. Examination of Jo. West, 5 May 1610, HCA Examination 13/226, ff. 99r–100v; Appleby, *A Calendar of Material*, p. 298.

12. Examination of John Lambert, 5 May 1610, HCA Examinations 13/266, ff. 98–99.

13. He is variously referred to as Richard Roberts and Richard Robinson.

14. Senior, 'An Investigation of the Activities and Importance of English Pirates, 1603–40', pp. 427–8.

15. Examination of George Darsely, 14 May 1610, HCA Examinations 13/266, ff. 106r–107v.

16. Examination of Roger Salter, 14 May 1610, HCA Examinations 13/266, ff. 106–106v.

17. Deposition of John Baker, 5 May 1610, HCA Examinations 13/226, f. 101v.

18. Deposition of Simon Hudson, of Newhaven in the county of Surrey, mariner, 17 August 1614, HCA Examinations, 13/98, ff. 212v–213r.

19. Examination of John Lambert, 5 May 1610.

20. Senior, 'An Investigation of the Activities and Importance of English Pirates, 1603–40', p. 410.

21. Examination of Edward Higgins, 5 May 1610, HCA Examinations 13/266, ff. 98v–99r.

22. Ibid.

23. Examination of John Lee, 5 May 1610, HCA Examinations 13/266, f 99v–100.

24. Examination of Roger Salter, 14 May 1610.

25. Examination of John Walker, 7 May 1610, HCA Examinations 13/266, ff. 104r–104v.

26. Senior, 'An Investigation of the Activities and Importance of English Pirates, 1603–40', pp. 392, 437–8; Examination of John Walker, 7 May 1610.

27. Examination of William Sares, 5 May 1610, HCA Examinations 13/266, f 105r.

28. Examination of Nicholas Thompson of Ratcliffe, Sailor, HCA Examinations 1/48, ff. 64r–65r.

29. Examination of John Sares, 7 May 1610, HCA Examinations 13/266, f 103v–104r.

30. Senior, 'An Investigation of the Activities and Importance of English Pirates, 1603–40', p. 227.

31. Examination of Robert Dunne, 5 May 1610, HCA Examinations 13/266, f. 101r.

32. Examination of Thomas Champion, 7 May 1610, HCA Examinations 13/266, ff. 103r–103v.

33. Examination of Simon Ashdon, 5 May 1610, HCA Examinations 13/266, ff. 105–106.

34. Examination of Samuel Man, 14 May 1610, HCA Examinations 13/266, ff. 106–107.

35. Whitbourne, *A Discourse and Discovery of Newfoundland*, pp. 13–14.

36. 1641 Depositions MS 824, ff. 253r–259v: Deposition of Sir William Hull knight & one of his Maiesties Councell of Mounster, 22 October 1642 (Trinity College Dublin 1641 Depositions Project); Appleby, 'Settlers and Pirates', p. 94.

37. Nunan, 'The Planting of Munster', pp. 67–72.

38. D. Dickson, *Old World Colony*, p. 20; Examination of John Lee, 5 May 1610, HCA Examinations 12/266, ff. 99v–100.

39. Senior, 'An Investigation of the Activities and Importance of English Pirates, 1603–40', pp. 383, 400.

40. M.B. Donovan, 'Dún na Séad: The history of Baltimore castle', master's thesis, University College Cork, 2008, pp. 70–5; McCarthy, *Dún na Séad*, pp. 18–31; C. Smith, *Ancient and Present State of the County and City of Cork*, vol. 1, 1750 (Cork: John Connor, 1815), p. 276.

41. V. Treadwell, 'The Irish Customs Administration in the Sixteenth Century', *Irish Historical Studies*, vol. 20, no. 80, 1977, p. 390; Treadwell, 'The Establishment of the Farm of the Irish Customs', p. 588.

42. WWM/Str P 20/100 Map of Baltimore: Wentworth Woodhouse (Sheffield City Library Archives, UK).

43. Earl of Cork to Lord Viscount Dorchester, 19 February 1631, from Cork, Letter-Book of the Great Earl of Cork; see Rev. J. Coombes, 'The Sack of Baltimore: A forewarning', *Journal of the Cork Historical and Archaeological Society*, vol. 77, no. 225, 1972, pp. 60–1.

44. Priestley, 'An Early 17th Century Map of Baltimore', pp. 55–7; Kelleher, 'In a Harbour Long Ago'.

45. Cotter, 'Dún na Séad Castle', pp. 43–7.

46. Agreement between Thomas Wilson, Dudley Norton, and Thomas Crooke, 22 November 1608, SP 63/225, ff 224 (TNA, London, State Papers Online, Gale Document No. MC4347580165); *Cal. S.P. Ire. 1608–1610*, p. 101; it is signed by Thomas Crooke and part signed by Norton.

47. Ohlmeyer, *Making Ireland English*, p. 375 and see also n. 70.

48. E. McCracken, 'The Woodlands of Ireland circa 1600', *Irish Historical Studies*, vol. 11, no. 44, 1959, p. 219; 'Desmond Country' refers to south Munster, and generally Kerry but could equally refer to the borderlands between west Cork and Kerry.

49. Examination of Simon Ashdon, 5 May 1610, HCA Examinations 13/266, ff. 105–106.

50. Examination of Richard Robinson, 19 February 1610, HCA Examinations 13/226 ff. 96v–97r.

51. Roger Myddleton to Salisbury, 23 August 1611, SP 63/231, ff. 182–182v (TNA, London, State Papers Online, Gale Document No. MC4347680227).

52. Senior, 'An Investigation of the Activities and Importance of English Pirates, 1603–40', p. 247.

53. Ibid., pp. 246–7.

54. Geanacopoulos, *The Pirate Next Door*, pp. 93–4.

55. Senior, 'An Investigation of the Activities and Importance of English Pirates, 1603–40', pp. 246–7.

56. Examination of Richard Jobson, 21 April 1610, HCA Examinations, 1/47, ff. 109r–109v; Examination of Rich. Kerry, 27 January 1610, HCA Examinations, 1/47, ff. 79v–80r; Senior, 'An Investigation of the Activities and Importance of English Pirates, 1603–40', pp. 290, 418.

57. Examination of Richard Jobson, 21 April 1610, HCA Examinations 1/47, f. 107v; Senior, 'An Investigation of the Activities and Importance of English Pirates, 1603–40', pp. 103–4.

58. 'On Account' – see Glossary.

59. Examination of Henry Duffield, 19 February 1610, HCA Examinations 13/266, ff. 96r–96v.

60. Examination of John Pharoe, 19 February 1610, HCA Examinations 13/266, f. 97v. The examinate was re-examined on 19 May 1610; the examination is signed 'John Farrowe', but whether this is by the examinate or by a clerk is not clear as the examination does not appear to show a 'pirate's mark', suggesting John Pharoe may have been able to write.

61. Examination of William Thompson, 4 May 1610, HCA Examinations, 1/47, ff. 116v–117r.

62. Ibid.

63. Senior, 'An Investigation of the Activities and Importance of English Pirates, 1603–40', p. 432.

64. Sir Richard Moryson to Salisbury, 22 August 1609, *Cal. S.P. Ire. 1608–1611*, p. 277.

65. R.L. Stevenson, *Treasure Island* (London: The Thames Publishing Co., 1948), pp. 11–17.

66. Pope, *Fish into Wine*, pp. 393–6.

67. Treadwell, *Buckingham and Ireland*, p. 83.

68. Horning, 'The Cultural Role of the Alehouse in the Ulster Plantation', pp. 113–31.

69. Ibid., p. 120; Beer and rum became the drink of preference from the latter part of the sixteenth century, at least among the general coastal populace and seafaring communities; see F.H. Smith, *Caribbean Rum: A social and economic history* (Gainesville: University Press of Florida, 2005), in particular pp. 6–30.

70. Horning, 'The Cultural Role of the Alehouse in the Ulster Plantation', p. 118.

71. Treadwell, *Buckingham and Ireland*, pp. 82–3.

72. Horning, 'The Cultural Role of the Alehouse in the Ulster Plantation', p. 118; Treadwell, *Buckingham and Ireland*, pp. 81–92; 'By the Lord President of Munster: Instruccions sent to the Maiors, Soveraignses, Provosts and other Chiefe officers of the Citties, Townes and borroughes throughout the Province of Mounster to be observed within the seuerall Liberties 25 February 1621', in Clayton (ed.), *Council Book for the Province of Munster*, p. 229, see Instruction 4, where the opening times of taverns and drinking places are to be regulated.

73. Letter of Henry Skipwith, 2 October 1611 *Carew MSS* 629, f. 178 (National Library of Ireland).

74. Deposition of Edmunde Flinte, 3 September 1613, HCA Examinations 13/42, ff. 223v–224r.

75. Senior, 'An Investigation of the Activities and Importance of English Pirates, 1603–40', p. 417.

76. Examination of Thomas Williams, no date, HCA Examinations 13/226, f. 105v.

77. Senior, 'An Investigation of the Activities and Importance of English Pirates, 1603–40', p. 253.

78. Deposition of Edmunde Flinte, 224r; Appleby, *A Calendar of Material*, p. 138; Senior, 'An Investigation of the Activities and Importance of English Pirates, 1603–40', p. 417.

79. Edwards (ed.), 'Letter-book of Sir Arthur Chichester', p. 62.

80. Mainwaring, 'Discourse – Of the Beginnings, Practices and Suppression of Pirates', p. 40.

81. Report of Richard Kerry, 29 January 1609, HCA Examinations 1/47, ff. 81–81v.

82. Deposition of Emanuell Butta, mariner, 16 January 1616, HCA Examinations 1//48, f. 68r; Examination of Nicholas Thompson of Ratcliffe, Sailor, 1/48, ff. 64r–65r.

83. W.R. Lusardi, 'The Beaufort Inlet Shipwreck Artifact Assemblage', in Skowronek and Ewen (eds), *X Marks the Spot*, pp. 196–218, at 207–9; F. Tucker, 'Kill or Cure? The osteological evidence of the mercury treatment of syphilis in 17th- to 19th-century London', *London Archaeologist*, vol. 11, no. 8, 2007, pp. 220–4; M.U. Wilde-Ramsing and L.F. Carnes-McNaughton, *Blackbeard's Sunken Prize: The 300-year voyage of Queen Anne's Revenge* (Chapel Hill: University of North Carolina Press, 2018), pp. 122–4.

84. Arber, 'The Travels and Observations of Captaine Smith', p. 915.

85. Senior, 'An Investigation of the Activities and Importance of English Pirates, 1603–40', pp. 245–6.

86. Examination of Hugh Baker, of Youghal, Sailor, taken before mee [Lawrence Parsons] on 22 May 1623: Caulfield, *The Council Book of the Corporation of Youghal*, pp. xlviii–xlix.

87. Appleby, *Women and English Piracy*, pp. 195–6.

88. Ibid.; *The Lives, Apprehensions, Arraignments and Executions of the 19 Late Pyrates, namely Capt. Harris, Jennings, Longcastle, Downes, Haulsey, and their companions, as they were severally indited on St Margret's Hill, in Southwark, on the 22 of December last and executed the Friday following, 1609* (London: E. Allde, printed for John Busby the Elder, 1609).

89. Maria Luddy had produced an excellent study of prostitution in Ireland during the later period; see Luddy, *Prostitution and Irish Society, 1800–1940* (Cambridge: Cambridge University Press, 2007). She similarly points out that 'It is very difficult to know what women who worked as prostitutes thought of their lives. They did not leave records of their own … Nevertheless, it is through a critical examination of … sources that we can begin to answer some of these questions' (p. 17). For a study of the role of women in this early modern period see M. MacCurtain and M. O'Dowd, *Women in Early Modern Ireland* (Edinburgh: Edinburgh University Press, 1991) and in particular Chapter 4; Appleby, 'Women and Piracy in Ireland: From Gráinne O'Malley to Anne Bonny', in Appleby, *Women and English Piracy*, pp. 53–68. For an insight into the legal rights of women for the period covered in this book, see M. O'Dowd, 'Women and the Irish Chancery Court in the Late Sixteenth and Early Seventeenth Centuries', *Irish Historical Studies*, vol. 31, no. 124, 1999, pp. 470–87. What is of interest from O'Dowd's work on the Chancery Court is it shows that only women who had some standing, or whose family had some standing, are primarily represented, with litigants from the poorest levels of society seldom appearing in the records (pp. 474–5).

90. Examination of Lordinge Barrye of the Cittye of London, Gent. Aged 30 yeares or thereaboute, 2 July 1616, HCA Examinations 1/48, f. 104r.

91. Senior, 'An Investigation of the Activities and Importance of English Pirates, 1603–40', pp. 375 and 388; Lorimer, *English and Irish Settlement on the River Amazon*, and for Duppa's involvement in particular, pp. 98–9, 101–3, 116–17, 353, 439–45.

92. Lo. Barry, *Ram-Alley or Merry Tricks, 1611*, J.S. Farmer (ed.) (London: The Tudor Facsimile Texts, 1913); D. Kathman, 'Barry, Lording (*bap*. 1580, *d*. 1629)', *Dictionary of National Biography*.

93. P. Somerville-Large, *The Coast of West Cork* (London: Victor Gollancz Ltd., 1974), p. 126. I am grateful to my late friend, archaeologist Lee Snodgrass, for relaying the tale of the slave girl; no background to the story is known but Ms Snodgrass, who at one point lived in Leamcon House, recounted that it was a story told of old and generally accepted as fact by the local populace.

94. C. Kelleher, 'Jilts, Cracks, Night-walkers and Others of the Linnen-lifting Tribe', in M. Davies, U. MacConville and G. Cooney (eds), *A Grand Gallimaufry: Collected*

in honour of Nick Maxwell (Wicklow: Wordwell Ltd., 2010), pp. 122–6; Hanna, *Pirate Nests and the Rise of the British Empire*, p. 245.

95. Appleby, *Women and English Piracy*, pp. 53–4; Appleby's study, pp. 60–6, importantly points out that as most of the surviving evidence is from a male perspective, the majority of women involved remain as nameless and faceless characters but nevertheless, piracy at the time clearly influenced the lives of women in the local communities ashore; it is suggested that they too influenced the lives and actions of the men they encountered. K. Martin, *Have Ye No Homes to Go To? The history of the Irish pub* (Cork: The Collins Press, 2016), pp. 23–4.

96. Senior, 'An Investigation of the Activities and Importance of English Pirates, 1603–40', p. 177 and n. 4.

97. Examination of Henry Duffield, 19 February 1609, HCA Examinations 13/226, ff. 96–96v. A Thomas Barloe, mariner, examined in December 1610 by Richard Moryson, lived in Baltimore and it is plausible that Mrs Barloe was related, perhaps wife or mother: Thomas Barloe's Deposition, 14 December 1610, *Cal. S.P. Ire. 1603–1625* (TNA London, State Papers Online, Gale Document No. MC4345500934). The deposition is signed 'Thomas Barlow'; the original source for this is in the *Carew MSS Papers*, 691, p. 145 (National Library of Ireland).

98. Senior, 'An Investigation of the Activities and Importance of English Pirates, 1603–40', p. 156.

99. Two examinations concerning pirates, taken before the E. of Northampton, no date (document damaged); *Cottonian* MSS Otho E/VIII f. 368, full citation (British Library, London, Gale Document No. MC4318895334).

100. Earl of Northampton to Sir Thom. Lake, 7 December 1609, SP 14/50 ff. 38–39 (TNA London, State Papers Online, Gale Document No. MC4323588271).

101. M. Porter, '"She was Skipper of the Shore-Crew": Notes on the history of the sexual division of labour in Newfoundland', *Labour/Le Travail*, vol. 15, 1985, pp. 109–20.

102. APUD Corck, 6 August 1610, Rich: Morysen, Dom: Sarsfeld, Edw: Harris, in Clayton (ed.), *Council Book of Munster*, pp. 71–2; Lord Deputy to the Lords of the Council, 31 October 1612, Edwards, 'Letter-Book', p. 62; Horning, *Ireland in the Virginian Sea*, pp. 294–5.

103. By the Lord President and Councell of Mounster, 21 September 1605, Hen. Brouncker, Donogh Thomond, Dom: Sarsfield, fra: Barkeley, Ro: Marshall, J. Walley, in Clayton (ed.), *Council Book of Munster*, pp. 425–6.

104. J. Brown, 'The Landscape of Drink: Inns, taverns and alehouses in early modern Southampton', PhD thesis, University of Warwick, 2007; S.N. Duensing, 'Taverns, Inns and Alehouses? An archaeology of consumption practices in the city of London, 1666–1780', PhD thesis, University of Manchester, 2014.

105. A. Horning, 'The Root of all Vice and Bestiality: Exploring the cultural role of the alehouse in the Ulster plantation', in Lyttleton and Rynne (eds), *Plantation Ireland*, pp. 113–31, 126–7.

106. G.L. Good, 'The Excavation of Two Docks at Narrow Quay, Bristol, 1978–9', *Post-Medieval Archaeology*, vol. 21, 1987, pp. 125–6.

107. Horning, 'The Root of all Vice and Bestiality'.

108. Cotter, 'Dún na Séad Castle', pp. 49–52; E. Cotter, 'Kilcoe Castle: Excavations of a late medieval coastal stronghold in County Cork', *Journal of the Cork Historical and Archaeological Society*, vol. 117, 2012, pp. 1–23; A. Lynch, 'The Franciscan Friary on Sherkin Island, Co. Cork. Excavations 1987–1990', *Journal of the Cork Historical and Archaeological Society*, vol. 123, 2019, pp. 55–127. I am indebted to Dr Lynch for supplying me with this information in advance of her publication.

109. D. Killock and F. Meddens, 'Pottery as Plunder: A 17th-century maritime site in Limehouse, London', *Post-Medieval Archaeology*, vol. 39, no. 1, 2005, pp. 1, 34–82.

110. H. Trotter, 'Dockside Prostitution in South African Ports', *History Compass*, vol. 6, no. 3, 2008, pp. 673–90. This is an interesting study into dockside prostitution, providing a good argument as to why such women were and still are invisible in the records and supporting the need for further studies into the coastal sex trade.

111. By the Vice-President and Council of Mounster, 26 August 1610, signed Edw: Harris, in Clayton (ed.), *The Council Book of Munster*, p. 72.

CHAPTER 7
The Beginning of the End: Suppression, commission and execution

1. Skipwyth to the Lord Deputy, 25 July 1611, *Cal. S.P. Ire. 1611–1614*, p. 91.

2. Lords of the Privy Council to Sir Arthur Chichester, 27 Sept. 1612, *Cal. S.P. Ireland*, p. 287.

3. Moryson to Salisbury, 22 August 1609, *Cal. S.P. Ire. 1608–1610*, pp. 277–8; Sir Arthur Chichester to the Privy Council, 5 February 1609, 7 April 1609, *Cal. S.P. Ire. 1608–1610*, pp. 141–3, 186–7.

4. Rodger, '*The Safeguard of the Sea*, pp. 349–52.

5. Murdoch, *The Terror of the Seas?* p. 129.

6. A. Clarke, 'Pacification, Plantation, and the Catholic Question, 1603–23', in Moody et al., *New History of Ireland*, pp. 210–19; Moody, 'The Irish Parliament under Elizabeth and James I', pp. 41–81; Treadwell, 'House of Lords in the Irish Parliament 1613–1615', pp. 92–107.

7. 1612, Heads or titles of the Acts concerning the Common Weal, no. 7: An Act against pirates, *Cal. S.P. Ire. 1611–1614*, p. 250; Sir John Davys to the Earl of Somerset, 31 October 1614, passing of the Act against pirates, ibid., p. 516; Piracy Act 1613: 11, 12, and 13 Jas, 1, c. 2, www.irishstatutebook.ie

8. Piracy continued albeit in a different form, and the king continued his actions against pirates from 1616 onwards; see Hebb, *Piracy and the English Government*, pp. 8–20. This aspect of piracy is discussed further in Chapter 8.

9. M. Bulut, 'The Role of the Ottomans and Dutch in the Commercial Integration between the Levant and Atlantic in the Seventeenth Century', *Journal of the Economic and Social History of the Orient*, vol. 45, no. 2, 2002, pp. 197, 201; see also Andrews, *Trade, Plunder and Settlement*, pp. 87–100, and Rodger, *The Safeguard of the Sea*, pp. 347–52.

10. Hebb, *Piracy and the English Government*, pp. 8–20; V. Barbour, 'Privateers and Pirates of the West Indies', *The American Historical Review*, vol. 16, no. 3, 1911, pp. 553–66; Senning, 'Piracy, Politics and Plunder under James 1', pp. 187–222; Murdoch, *The Terror of the Seas?*, pp. 134–56.

11. Lord Deputy to Salisbury and Nottingham, 21 September 1610, SP 63/229, f. 124 (TNA London, State Papers Online, Gale Document No. MC4347580875).

12. Lord Danvers to the Lords of the Privy Council or Lord Salisbury, 19 January 1609, *Cal. S.P. Ire. 1608–1610*, p. 130.

13. Report on England presented to the Government of Venice in the year 1607, by the illustrious Gentleman Nicolo Molin, Ambassador there, May 1607, *Cal. S.P. Ven. 1603–1607*; https://www-british-history-ac-uk.elib.tcd.ie/cal-state-papers/venice/vol10/pp501-524; Penn, *The Navy Under the Early Stuarts*, p. 11.

14. Penn, *The Navy Under the Early Stuarts*, p. 12.

15. Andrews, *Elizabethan Privateering*, p. 261; Senior, *A Nation of Pirates*, p. 25; Senior, 'An Investigation of the Activities and Importance of English Pirates, 1603–40', pp. 389, 406.

16. J. Corbett, *England in the Mediterranean: A study of the rise and influence of British power within the Straits, 1603–1713*, vol. I (London, New York and Bombay: Longmans, Green & Co., 1904), pp. 68–9; Kenny, *Elizabeth's Admiral*, pp. 268–73; Sir Thomas Lake to Salisbury, 17 December 1609, *Cal. S.P. Dom. Jas. I, 1603–1610*, p. 573; Lake argues that Nottingham should not need to 'compound' with pirates in order to reach an agreement with them; Senior, 'An Investigation of the Activities and Importance of English Pirates, 1603–40', pp. 272–85.

17. Kenny, *Elizabeth's Admiral*, pp. 302–31; Senior, 'An Investigation of the Activities and Importance of English Pirates, 1603–40', p. 283.

18. Examination of John Jennings, a pirate, before the court of admiralty, undated, *Cottonian* MSS Otho E/VIII, ff. 360–364 (TNA London, State Papers Online, Gale, Document No. MC4318895332).

19. Examination of James Harris from Two Examinations taken before the E. of Northampton, undated, *Cottonian MSS* Otho E/VIII, ff. 367–369.

20. Examination of James Harris, 17 August 1609 and 8 December 1609, HCA Examinations 1/47, ff. 32r–32v and HCA 1/47, ff. 62v–62r.

21. Appleby, 'Settlers and Pirates', p. 83.

22. Senior, ' An Investigation', p. 309, n. 2.

23. Earl of Northampton to Sir Thom. Lake, 7 December 1609, SP 14/50 ff. 38–39 (TNA London, State Papers Online, Gale Document No. MC4323588271). The traditional saying 'dead men tell no tales' has a number of proclaimed origins including spiritual connotations, referring to those who have passed on and can no longer tell secrets, as well as Arabic, Middle Eastern and European usage in varied formats; it is perhaps most familiarly associated with piracy, enhanced by the media. An eighteenth-century English pirate, Hiram Beakes, on the island of Saba in the Caribbean, is credited with coining the phrase there, https://stmaartennews.com/columns/hiram-beakes-saba/

24. Sir Thomas Lake to Salisbury, 8 December 1609, *Cal. S.P. Dom. Jas. I, 1603–1610*, p. 568 states the king ordered the reprieve of Jennings and Harris, pirates; Senior, 'An Investigation of the Activities and Importance of English Pirates, 1603–40', p. 399.

25. Sir Arthur Chichester to the Earls of Salisbury, Northampton, and Nottingham, 16 April 1611, SP 63/231, f. 80r (TNA London, State Papers Online, Gale Document No. MC4347680067) refers to 'John Jennings, lately executed in England'.

26. Clayton (ed.), *The Council Book of Munster*, p. 73.

27. R. Caulfield, Appendix A, 6 August 1610, *The Council Book of the Corporation of Kinsale from 1652 to 1800* (Guildford: J. Billing & Sons, 1878), p. 313; Clayton (ed.), *The Council Book of Munster*, p. 71.

28. Lords of the Council to Sir Arthur Chichester, 9 September 1611, *Cal. S.P. Ire. 1611–1614*, p. 101; The earl of Salisbury to Sir Ralph Winwood, 17 July 1611, *Memorials of Affairs of State in the Reigns of Q. Elizabeth and K. James I collected from the original papers of the Right Honourable Sir Ralph Winwood Kt.*, vol. III (London: W.B. for T. Ward, 1725), pp. 285–6; Winwood, at that point, was the English ambassador to Holland.

29. The earl of Salisbury to Sir Ralph Winwood, 17 July 1611, p. 286; The Privy Council to Lord [unknown], 1611, *Cal. of MSS of the most Hon. Marquis of Salisbury, 21, 1609–1612*, p. 319 (TNA London, State Papers Online, MC4332100858).

30. Examination of Richard Trosse of Dartmouth, mariner, 2 November 1611, HCA Examinations, 1/47, f. 246r; Capt. Skipwith to the Lord Deputy, 25 July 1611, *Cal. S.P. Ire. 1611–1614*, pp. 89–90.

31. Roger Myddleton to Salisbury, 23 August 1611, *Cal. S.P. Ire. 1611–1614*, p. 99.

32. Captain Henry Skipwith to Sir Arthur Chichester, 2 October 1611, *Cal. S.P. Ire. 1611–1614*, p. 138; Sir Arthur Chichester to Salisbury, 10 December 1611, ibid., p. 178.

33. Examination of James Bell of Ratcliff, 12 March 1611, HCA Examinations, 1/47, ff. 177r–177v, Senior, 'An Investigation of the Activities and Importance of English Pirates, 1603–40', p. 149.

34. The Privy Council to Lord [unknown], 1611, *Cal. of MSS of the most Hon. Marquis of Salisbury, 21, 1609–1612*, p. 319 (TNA London, State Papers Online, MC4332100858).

35. Antonio Foscarini, Venetian Ambassador in England, to the Doge and Senate, 14 July 1611, *Cal. S.P. Ven. 1610–1613*, www.british-history.ac.uk

36. Lords of the Council to Sir Arthur Chichester, 9 September 1611, *Cal. S.P. Ire. 1611–1614*, p. 101.

37. SUB Göttingen, 4 H BRIT P III, 6 RARA: Hessel Gerritszoon, *Beschrijvinghe van de Zeecusten ende Havenen van Yerlandt/Description of the Seacoasts and Ports of Ireland*.

38. The career of Captain Moy Lambert is discussed in detail in Lunsford, *Piracy and Privateering in the Golden Age Netherlands*.

39. Hessel Gerritszoon, 'To the noble, honourable, wise and prudent Lord, Sir Guillaume de Soete, called Houthain, lieutenant-admiral of Zeeland', f. 2, Gerritszoon to Houthain, ibid., p. 3.

40. Ibid., f. 3, p. 5

41. Senior, 'An Investigation of the Activities and Importance of English Pirates, 1603–40', pp. 311–13.

42. A letter to the Lord Chichester, Lord Deputie of the Realme of Ireland, 4 May 1613, *Acts of the Privy Council, 1613–1614*, pp. 14–15.

43. Edward Davenant of the island of Whiddy, county Cork, merchant, aged about 45, 1 October 1614, HCA Examinations, 13/226, f. 338.

44. Examination of Nighton Filpes, [3 August] 1614, HCA Examinations 13/98, ff. 209–211r.

45. Edward Davenant of the island of Whiddy, county Cork, merchant, aged about 45, 1 October 1614; Appleby (ed.), *A Calendar of Material*, pp. 285–7.

46. Edward Davenant of the island of Whiddy, county Cork, merchant, aged about 45, 1 October 1614.

47. Appleby (ed.), *A Calendar of Material*, pp. 285–7.

48. A letter to Sir Dudley Carleton, knight, Ambassador for his Majestie with the States of the United Provinces, 30 April 1616, *APC 1615–1616*, pp. 513–14.

49. Acts of the Privy Council, 8 October 1617, p. 341.

50. Appleby (ed.), A *Calendar of Material*, pp. 287–8.

51. Deposition of John Hoskins of Plymouth, mariner, 19 August 1613, HCA Examinations 13/42, ff. 210v–212r.

52. Hawke, 'Canty's Cove', p. 294.

53. J. Bonsall and M. Dowd, 'Emerging from the Waves: A late Bronze Age intertidal saltwater fulacht fia at Coney Island, Co. Clare', *Journal of Irish Archaeology*, vol. 24, 2015, pp. 79–85.

54. F. Moore, Excavation of a possible fulacht fiadh at Lippa, Spiddal, Co. Galway, 2014, unpublished report, National Monuments Service, Department of Culture, Heritage and the Gaeltacht; J. O'Donoghue, Fornaght Strand fulacht fiadh, Creadan, Waterford, Database of Irish Excavation Reports, 2016; www.excavations.ie

55. C. O'Driscoll, 'Churchtown, Hook Head, Human Skeletal Remains', in I. Bennett, *Excavations Bulletin: Summary of archaeological excavations in Ireland* (Wicklow: Wordwell Ltd., 2005), pp. 397–9; K. Brady and C. Kelleher, 'Churchtown, Human Remains: 00E0872', in Bennett, *Excavations Bulletin*, p. 353; O'Driscoll, 'Archaeological Excavation of a Nineteenth Century Shipwreck Victim at Hook Head, Co. Wexford', *Journal of the Wexford Historical Society*, vol. 21, 2006–7, pp. 171–7.

56. Recorded monument number CO:147:05801: *Graveyard*, CO:147:05802: *Church* and CO:147:05803: *Possible earlier church*; D. Power, *Archaeological Inventory of County Cork. Vol. 1: West Cork* (Dublin: Government Stationery Office, 1992), p. 354.

57. W. Maziere Brady, *Clerical and Parochial Records of Cork, Cloyne and Ross*, vol. I (London: Alexander Thom, 1863), p. 172; Samuel Lewis, *A Topographical Dictionary of Ireland*, vol. I (London: S. Lewis & Co., 1837), p. 435.

58. https://www.telegraph.co.uk/news/2018/03/28/americas-largest-mass-pirate-burial-uncovered-300-years

59. C. Manning, P. Gosling and J. Waddell, *New Survey of Clare Island: Volume 4: Abbey* (Dublin: Royal Irish Academy, 2005).

60. Death notice of Richard Roberts [Robinson], 27 April 1611, Parish Register of St James Church, Garlickhithe, City of London, England (Metropolitan Archives, London; Ref. no. P69/JS2/001/MS09138); Senior, 'An Investigation of the Activities and Importance of English Pirates, 1603–40', p. 423.

61. Acts of the Privy Council, 8 October 1617, p. 341.

62. See Lunsford, *Piracy and Privateering in the Golden Age Netherlands*, p. 129.

63. 1612, Heads or titles of the Acts concerning the Common Weal, no. 7: An Act against pirates, *Cal. S.P. Ire. 1611–1614*, p. 250; Sir John Davys to the Earl of Somerset, 31 October 1614, passing of the Act against pirates, ibid., p. 516; Treadwell,

'House of Lords in the Irish Parliament 1613–1615', p. 101; Moody, 'The Irish Parliament under Elizabeth and James I', pp. 52, 60.

64. Yale, 'A Historical Note on the Jurisdiction of the Admiralty in Ireland', p. 149; Senior, 'An Investigation of the Activities and Importance of English Pirates, 1603–40', p. 114.

65. HCA 13/226; see Appleby, *A Calendar of Material*, pp. 284–99.

66. Account of execution of 'certain lusty companions', [non-specific] 1614, *Desiderata Curiosa Hibernia: or A Select Collection of State Papers consisting of Royal Instructions, Directions, Dispatches and Letters to which are added some Historical Tracts*, J. Lodge (ed.), vol. I (Dublin: David Hay, 1772), pp. 313–14.

67. Murdoch, *The Terror of the Seas?*, p. 139; History of Leith, Edinburgh, http://www.leithhistory.co.uk/2011/10/26/the-sands-of-leith/

68. R. Pitcairn, *Ancient Criminal Trials of Scotland: from the Original Records and MSS, with Historical Illustrations, &c.*, vol. III (Edinburgh: Bannatyne Club, 1833), pp. 102–8; Senior, 'An Investigation of the Activities and Importance of English Pirates, 1603–40', pp. 130–1.

69. J.W. Hammond, 'George's Quay and Rogerson's Quay in the Eighteenth Century', *Dublin Historical Record*, vol. 5, no. 2, 1942–3, p. 44.

70. A. Edwards, *Cork Remembrancer, or Tablet of Memory. Enumerating every remarkable circumstance that has happened in the City and County of Cork, and in the kingdom at large. Including all the memorable events in Great Britain with an account of all the Battles by Sea and Land in the present century. Also, the remarkable earthquakes, famines, inundations, storms, frosts, fires and all other accidents of moment, in Every Quarter of the Globe, from the earliest period, to the year 1792* (Cork: Tower Books, 1792); contains a record of four pirates executed in 1766 at a location near St Stephen's Green, Dublin, p. 214.

71. Hammond, 'George's Quay and Rogerson's Quay', p. 44.

72. J. de Courcy Ireland, *The Liffey in Dublin* (Dublin: Gill & Macmillan, 1996), p. 171.

73. Edwards, *Cork Remembrancer*, provides several accounts of executions at Gallows Green in Cork during the eighteenth century, with the form of death varying from straightforward hanging, to burning, to being shot (which seems to have been reserved for soldiers), to being hanged and quartered, to being hanged, quartered and beheaded; see pp. 133, 137, 141, 180, 222. An interesting account is of a tailor named Dennis Sheehan who was hanged at Gallows Green on 9 July 1755 for the murder of his aunt near Macroom, but who 'later came back to life and made his escape', p. 179.

74. Sir John Finet to the earl of Salisbury, 27–9 October 1619, *Cal. of MSS of the Most Hon. Marquis of Salisbury, 1612–1668* (TNA London, State Papers Online, Gale Document No. MC4332200202), p. 96.

75. Oppenheim, *The Naval Tracts of Sir William Monson in Six Books*, pp. 64–5.

76. Hammond, 'George's Quay and Rogerson's Quay', p. 44.

77. Woodward, 'Sir Thomas Button', p. 344.

78. Hanna, *Pirate Nests and the Rise of the British Empire*, p. 19.

79. Pitcairn, *Ancient Criminal Trials of Scotland*; Ritchie, *Captain Kidd and the War Against the Pirates*, pp. 205–29; R. Zacks, *The Pirate Hunter: The true story of Captain Kidd* (London: Review/Headline Book Publishing, 2002), pp. 373–89.

80. It is noted on the 1840s six-inch (1st edition) Ordnance Survey maps of Ireland, though there is confusion between the 1st edition OS map and 2nd edition OS 1880s and 1940s Cassini maps as to where Pregane Point (Hangman's Point) is located; www.osi.ie

81. The author is indebted to Dr Elaine Murphy for this reference.

82. J.B. Jones and C.M. Dowling, 'Capital Punishment in Colonial Virginia: Phase III Data Recovery for Mitigation of Adverse Effects to Site 44WB66 (The Colonial Gallows)', Technical Report Series 18, *William and Mary Centre for Archaeological Research* (Williamsburg: College of William and Mary, 1993), pp. 1–78; M. Andina, 'Bern's Gallows: Archaeologists uncover evidence of past punishments', 26 September 2009, http://www.swissinfo.ch/eng/multimedia/video/Berns_gallows.html?cid=18194; P. Sokol, 'The Gallows near Primda: Archaeological research into a feature of special symbolic and social importance', *Archaeologia Historica*, vol. 41, no. 2, 2015, pp. 501–23.

83. MPF/1/94: *c.* 1558 map of Bantry and Beara (London: The National Archives Map Collection).

84. Lord Danvers to Salisbury, 4 August 1608, *Cal, S.P. Ire. 1608–1610*, p. 14; Earl of Thomond to Salisbury, 10 March 1609, *Cal. S.P. Ire. 1608–1610*, p. 162; Examination of John Jennings, pirate, before the court of admiralty, no date, *Cottonian* MSS Otho E/VIII ff. 360–364 (British Library, State Papers Online, Gale Document No. MC4318815332); Sir Arthur Chichester to the Privy Council, 5 February 1609, *State Papers for Ireland*, 63/226, ff. 62r–63v (TNA, State Papers Online; Gale Document No. MC4347580260); Sir Arthur Chichester to the Privy Council, 5 February 1609, *Cal. S.P. Ire. 1608–1610*, p. 142.

85. Jennings, the Pirate, to the Earl of Thomond, 23 January 1609, *Cal. S.P. Ire. 1608–1610*, p. 145, 'prays his Lordship to be a mediator for their pardon. Offers to deliver up the ship and stores'; Earl of Northampton to Sir Thos. Lake, 7 December 1609, *Cal. St. P. Dom. Jas. I, 1603–1610*, p. 568; Earl of Northampton to Sir Thom. Lake, 7 December 1609, SP 14/50 ff. 38–39 (TNA London, State papers Online, Gale Document No. MC4323588271); Examination of John Jennings, a pirate, before the court of admiralty, no date, *Cottonian* MSS Otho E/VIII, ff. 360–365; Two examinations concerning pirates, taken before the E. of Northampton, no date, *Cottonian* MSS Otho E/VIII, ff. 367–369 (TNA London, State Papers Online, Gale Document No. MC4318815332 and MC4318815334).

86. Two examinations concerning pirates, ibid.

87. Sir Arthur Chichester to the Earls of Salisbury, Northampton, and Nottingham, 16 April 1611, refers to 'John Jennings, lately executed in England', *Cal. S.P. Ire. 1611–1614*, p. 29.

88. Sir Arthur Chichester to the Earl of Salisbury, 14 June 1608, *Cal. S.P. Ire. 1616–1608*, p. 559, reports that pirate Richard Robinson had lately come into Baltimore and delivered his ship to the President of Munster.

89. J.C. Appleby, 'A Nursery of Pirates: The English pirate community in Ireland in the early seventeenth century', *International Journal of Maritime History*, vol. II, no. 1, 1990, p. 16.

90. Sir Arthur Chichester to Salisbury, 19 July 1610, *Cal. S.P. Ire. 1608–1610*, p. 480.

91. Lords of the Council to Sir Arthur Chichester, 27 April 1609, *Cal. S.P. Ire. 1608–1610*, p. 200.

92. Charles Earl of Nottingham to the Earl of Salisbury, 2 September 1609, *Cal. S.P. Dom. James I, 1603–1610*, p. 541.

93. Sir Arthur Chichester to Salisbury, 23 October 1609, *Cal. S.P. Ire. 1608–1610*, p. 301; Earl of Nottingham to Salisbury, 3 July 1609, *Cal. S.P. Dom. Jas. I 1603–1610*, p. 525; John Hopkins to Lord Admiral Nottingham, 6 February 1610, ibid., p. 586.

94. Appleby, 'The Affairs of Pirates', pp. 72–4; Appleby, *A Calendar of Material*, pp. 124–38.

95. Sir Arthur Chichester to the Privy Council, 7 April 1609, *Cal. S.P. Ire. 1608–1610*, pp. 186–8; Senior, 'An Investigation of the Activities and Importance of English Pirates, 1603–40', p. 314.

96. Capt. Henry Skipwith to the Lord Deputy, 2 October 1611, Kinsale, *Cal. Carew MSS. 1603–1623*, pp. 120–1.

97. Capt. Skipwyth to the Lord Deputy, 25 July 1611, SP 63/231 f. 166r (TNA London, State Papers Online, Gale Document No. MC4347600208).

98. Ibid., f. 167r.

99. Ibid.

100. Sir Richard Moryson to Salisbury, 22 August 1609, Youghall, *Cal. S.P. Ire. 1608–1610*, p. 278.

101. Senior, 'An Investigation of the Activities and Importance of English Pirates, 1603–40', p. 314.

102. Examination of Stephen Davis of Bristol, merchant, 28 June 1613, HCA Examinations, 13/42, ff 186–187; Appleby, *A Calendar of Material*, p. 132.

103. Senior, 'An Investigation of the Activities and Importance of English Pirates, 1603–40', p. 314.

104. Ibid., p. 317; Senior refers here to HCA 30/858, bundle E. 1612–1620, that contain various reports detailing how the pirates were forced to return to the High Court of Admiralty in London to claim their booty.

105. At the Court of Whitehall, 20 March 1613, Lord Archbishop of Canterbury, Duke of Lennox, Lord Chamberlen, Earl of Shrewsbury, Earl of Worcester, Earl of Pembroke, Lord Zouche, Lord Knollis, Lord Wotton, Sir Julius Caesar, *APC 1613–1614*, pp. 384–7.

106. Capt. Skipwyth to the Lord Deputy, 25 July 1611, SP 63/231, f. 167v (TNA London, State Papers Online, Gale Document No. MC4347680208).

107. Vincenzo Gussoni, Venetian Ambassador in Savoy, to the Doge and Senate, 30 March 1613, *Cal. S.P. Ven. 1610–1613*, entries 804 and 824; the *Cal. S.P. Ven.* contain numerous entries concerned with Easton's eventual settlement in Savoy.

108. Dr David Heffernan, pers. comm., 24 May 2017 with sources quoted *NLI, MS. 6,139*, p. 85 and *NLI, MS. 6,142*, p. 3; the author is very grateful to Dr Heffernan for providing this information.

109. Examination of William Jackson of Ratcliffe, mariner, 9 August 1614, HCA Examinations 13/98, ff. 211r–211v; Senior, 'An Investigation of the Activities and Importance of English Pirates, 1603–40', pp. 150–1.

110. D. Goodman, *Spanish Naval Power, 1589–1665: Reconstruction and defeat* (Cambridge: Cambridge University Press, 1997), p. 16; Hebb, *Piracy and the English Government*, p. 13; Carr, *Blood & Faith*.

111. Piero Priuli, Venetian Ambassador in Spain, to the Doge & Senate, 30 July and 17 August 1611, *Cal S.P. Ven. 1610–1613*, entries no. 290 and 305.

112. Antonio Foscarini, Venetian Ambassador in England, to the Doge and Senate, 25 August 1611, entry no. 310.

113. C.R. Pennell, *Morocco: From empire to independence* (Oxford: Oneworld Publications, 2003), p. 94.

114. Examination of William Jackson of Ratcliffe, mariner, 9 August 1614, HCA Examinations 13/98, ff. 211–212v; Senior, 'An Investigation of the Activities and Importance of English Pirates, 1603–40', p. 151.

115. Mainwaring, 'Discourse – Of the Beginnings, Practices and Suppression of Pirates', pp. 3–52.

116. Andrade, 'The Company's Chinese Pirates', p. 415.

117. C.S. Schen, 'Breaching "Community" in Britain: Captives, renegades, and the redeemed', in M.J. Halvorson and K.E. Spierling (eds), *Defining Community in Early Modern Europe* (Hampshire, UK and Vermont, USA: Ashgate Publishing Co., 2008), pp. 230–1.

118. Mainwaring, 'Discourse – Of the Beginnings, Practices and Suppression of Pirates', p. 11.

119. Schen, 'Breaching "Community" in Britain'.

120. Oppenheim, *The Naval Tracts of Sir William Monson in Six Books*, pp. 70–1; Schen, 'Breaching "Community" in Britain'.

121. Senior, 'An Investigation of the Activities and Importance of English Pirates, 1603–40', p. 439.

122. Mainwaring, 'Discourse – Of the Beginnings, Practices and Suppression of Pirates', p. 40.

123. Sir Oliver St John [Lord Deputy of Ireland] to Winwood, 4 April 1617, *Report on the Manuscripts of the Duke of Buccleuch and Queensberry, preserved at Montagu House, Whitehall, 1483–1778*, vol. I (Canada: Historical Manuscripts Commission, 2009), pp. 193–4.

124. Mainwaring, 'Discourse – Of the Beginnings, Practices and Suppression of Pirates', p. 46, n. 4: 'By merely ceasing to exist'.

125. Senior, 'An Investigation of the Activities and Importance of English Pirates, 1603–40', pp. 13–15; Brotton, *This Orient Isle*, p. 298.

126. Bulut, 'The Role of the Ottomans and Dutch', p. 201.

127. Matar, *Turks, Moors and Englishmen*, pp. 57–8.

CHAPTER 8
Decline and Transformations

1. The Lord Justices and the Council to the English Privy Council, 10 July 1631, SP 63/252, f. 183 (TNA London, State Papers Online, Gale Document No. MC4347801966).

2. Examination of Richard Millington, 21 August 1613, HCA Examinations 13/42, f. 214r.

3. Sir Oliver St John [Lord Deputy of Ireland] to Winwood, 4 April 1617, pp. 193–4.

4. Senior, 'An Investigation of the Activities and Importance of English Pirates, 1603–40', p. 165.

5. STC/725.15: A. Barker, *A True and Certaine Report of the Beginning, Proceedings, Overthrowes, and now present Estate of Captaine Ward and Danseker, the two late famous Pirates: from their first setting foorth to this present time* (1609), p. 25 (Early English Books Online – EEBO); Senior, 'An Investigation of the Activities and Importance of English Pirates, 1603–40', pp. 117, 379.

6. Senior, 'An Investigation of the Activities and Importance of English Pirates, 1603–40', p. 427.

7. Sir Arthur Chichester to the Earls of Salisbury, Northampton and Nottingham, 16 April 1611, SP 63/231, f. 80r (TNA London, State Papers Online, Gale Document No. MC4347680067).

8. Woodward, 'Sir Thomas Button', p. 344.

9. Sir Oliver St John [Lord Deputy of Ireland] to Winwood, 4 April 1617, p. 194.

10. Lord Admiral Nottingham to Salisbury, 8 August 1609, SP 14/47, f. 118 (TNA London, State Papers Online, Gale Document No. MC4323587796); Deposition of Wm. Young, 17 April 1610, taken prisoner by Capt. Thomas Salkeld, a pirate, 17 April 1610, SP 14/53, f. 148 (TNA London, State Papers Online, Gale Document No. MC4323508772); Senior, 'An Investigation of the Activities and Importance of English Pirates, 1603–40', pp. 428–9.

11. Lord Deputy to Salisbury and Nottingham, 21 September 1610, SP 63/229, f. 124 (TNA London, State Papers Online, Gale Document No. MC4347580875).

12. Senior, *A Nation of Pirates*, p. 36.

13. *Cal S.P. Ven. 1610–1613*, 'The Englishman [Easton] has covered himself with glory', entry 824, p. 528; Vincenzo Gussoni, Venetian Ambassador in Savoy, to the Doge and Senate, 30 March 1613, *Cal S.P. Ven. 1610–1613*, entry 784, p. 505.

14. Edward Waterhous to Secretary Wylson, 16 September 1579, SP 63/69, f. 0060 (TNA London, State Papers Online, Gale Document No. MD4309602152).

15. H. Horwood, *Plunder and Pillage: Atlantic Canada's brutal and bloodthirsty pirates and privateers* (Halifax: Formac Publishing Company Ltd., 2011), pp. 20–1.

16. M. Rediker, *Between the Devil and the Deep Blue Sea: Merchant seamen, pirates and the Anglo-American maritime world, 1700–1750* (New York: Cambridge University Press, 1987), pp. 254–87; Rediker provides an excellent overview of life at sea, and the general duration of pirate careers, primarily for the early part of the eighteenth century.

17. Oppenheim, *The Naval Tracts of Sir William Monson in Six Books*, pp. 293–9; see in particular Monson's 'A Story of Two Pirates' where Tucker is specifically named as one of the pirates in Ireland.

18. Senior, 'An Investigation of the Activities and Importance of English Pirates, 1603–40', pp. 92, 435–6.

19. Oppenheim, *The Naval Tracts of Sir William Monson in Six Books*, vol. V, 'A Story of Two Pirates', pp. 293–9; 'An Investigation of the Activities and Importance of English Pirates, 1603–40', pp. 150, 158, 355.

20. Oppenheim, 'Piracy in Ireland', pp. 59–63; Mainwaring, 'A Discourse in Four Fragments', *Cottonian* MSS Otho E/VIII, ff. 330r–331v; Henry Mainwaring, 'Discourse – Of the Beginnings, Practices and Suppression of Pirates', pp. 16–17.

21. For a full account of Mainwaring's life and exploits, see Mainwaring and Perrin, *The Life and Works of Sir Henry Mainwaring*.

22. Examination of William Jackson, 9 August 1614, HCA Examinations 13/98, ff. 211r–211v.

23. C. Senior, 'Robert Walsingham: A Jacobean pirate', *Mariners' Mirror*, vol. 60, no. 2, 1974, pp. 141–2.

24. Ibid.

25. A. Grosart (ed.), *The Lismore Letters (First Series) of Sir Richard Boyle, First and 'Great' Earl of Cork*, vol II (London: Chiswick Press, 1886), pp. 158–9; Letter of Lord Cork, Sir Richard Aldworth, and Sir Lawrence Parsons to Lord Falkland, 13 June 1625, SP 63/241, ff. 111r–111v (TNA London, State Papers Online, Gale Document No. MC4347800069); Letter of Lord Cork, Sir Richard Aldworth, and Sir Lawrence Parsons to Lord Falkland, 13 June 1625, *Cal. S.P. Ire. 1625–1632*, p. 18.

26. Letter of Lord Cork, Sir Richard Aldworth, and Sir Lawrence Parsons to Lord Falkland, 13 June 1625, p. 18.

27. Deposition of Hugh Sampson of Plymouth, 5 September 1625, in Appleby (ed.), *A Calendar of Material*, p. 304.

28. Letter of Lord Cork, Sir Richard Aldworth, and Sir Lawrence Parsons to Lord Falkland, 13 June 1625, p. 18.

29. For the right honorable the earle of Thomond Lord President of Mounster [no date], *Harlaein MSS*, f. 199v, signed by Oliver St John; from Clayton (ed.), *Council Book for the Province of Munster*, p. 46.

30. Appleby, 'Settlers and Pirates', pp. 87–8.

31. Inquiries to be made relative to certain Rewards for Connivance taken by Sir Laurence Parsons, Vice-Admiral of Minister [Munster] and Sir William Hull, without making any account to the Lord High Admiral Buckingham [undated], 1627, SP 63/268, ff. 118r–119r (TNA London, State Papers Online, Gale Document No. MC4348080227); G.E. Cokayne, *The Complete Peerage of England, Scotland, Ireland, Great Britain, and the United Kingdom* (London: The St Catherine Press Ltd., 1910), pp. 397–8.

32. Treadwell, *Buckingham and Ireland*, pp. 81–91; Horning, 'The Cultural Role of the Alehouse in the Ulster Plantation', pp. 124–5; Horning, *Ireland in the Virginian Sea*, pp. 236–7.

33. Appleby, 'Settlers and Pirates', pp. 88–104; Deposition of Sir William Hull knight & one of his Maiesties Councell of Mounster, 22 October 1642, MS 824, ff. 253r–259v (Dublin: 1641 Depositions, Trinity College).

34. Appleby, 'Settlers and Pirates', pp. 96–7.

35. K.R. Andrews, *Ships, Money and Politics: Seafaring and naval enterprise in the reign of Charles I* (Cambridge: Cambridge University Press, 1991), pp. 4–12.

36. Penn, *The Navy Under the Early Stuarts*, pp. 240–1.

37. Senior, 'An Investigation of the Activities and Importance of English Pirates, 1603–40', p. 366.

38. Senior, 'Robert Walsingham', pp. 141–2.

39. Rodger, 'The Law and Language of Private Naval Warfare', pp. 11–13.

40. Ibid.

41. Lunsford, *Piracy and Privateering in the Golden Age Netherlands*, pp. 9–10, 131–4, 161–8.

42. The Names of those who bought Goods of the Pirate Campane at Lymecon, in the West of Ireland [?], 1625, *Cal S.P. Ire. 1603–1625* (TNA London, State Papers Online, Gale Document No. MC4347701417).

43. Relation of the wrongs done by the great pirat Campaan, aswel upon Inglish shipps as other [undated, 1625?], SP 16/522, ff. 190r–191r (TNA London, State Papers Online, Gale Document No. MC4326080368).

44. The Names of those who bought Goods of the Pirate Campane at Lymecon, in the West of Ireland [?], 1625.

45. Relation of the wrongs done by the great pirat Campaan, f. 190r.

46. Sir Francis Cottington, to the Duke, 1 October 1616, Madrid, *Cabala: Sive SCRINIA SACRA, Mysteries of State and Government in Letters of Illustrious Persons and Great Ministers of State As well Forreign as Domestick, In the Reigns of King Henry the Eighth, Q: Elizabeth, K: James, and K: Charles* (London: G. Bedell & T. Collins Printers, 1663), pp. 217–18; Hebb, *Piracy and the English Government*, pp. 2, 12.

47. Sir Francis Cottington, to the Duke, 1 October 1616, Madrid, *Cabala*, p. 217; Hebb, *Piracy and the English Government*, pp. 14–15; P. Earle, *Corsairs of Malta and Barbary* (London: Sidgwick & Jackson, 1970), pp. 23–71, provides a very comprehensive overview of the regencies' and Corsairs' operations during the sixteenth and seventeenth centuries.

48. K. Smári Hreinsson and A. Nichols, *The Travels of Reverend Ólafur Egilsson: Captured by pirates in 1627* (Reykjavik: Fjölvi Publishers, 2008), p. 20; this is a translation of the original account, the *Reisubók* (the *Travels*) and the quoted reference above is based on the translation, not the original documentary account; see also N. Annandale, *The Faroes and Iceland: Studies in island life* (Oxford: Clarendon Press, 1905), particularly Chapter 3 'The Algerians in Iceland', pp. 67–92.

49. John de Courcy Ireland, 'The Algerine Raid on Baltimore', *The Irish Sword*, vol. 10, 1970–1, p. 69; de Courcy Ireland argues that Algerine Turks were frequent visitors to northern shores before they began raiding coastal areas.

50. Björn Jónsson of Skardsá, *The Turkish Raid Saga*, 1643 (Reykjavik: Einar Thórdarson, 1866 translation), published online by Tina Türkiye Sualti Arkeolojisi Vakfi (İstanbul: Koç Üniversitesi, Sariyer, 2018), www.tinaturk.org

51. The Mayor of Limerick to Lord Falkland, 25 October 1626, *Cal. SP. Ire. 1625–1632*, p. 170.

52. The Earl of Cork to [Lord Dorchester], 24 January 1631, *Cal. S.P. Ire. 1625–1632*, p. 598.

53. Coombes, 'The Sack of Baltimore', pp. 60–1.

54. Lunsford, *Piracy and Privateering in the Golden Age Netherlands*, pp. 142–6.

55. Joseph Carter (sovereign of Baltimore) to Sir William Hull, 26 June 1631, SP 63/252, f. 161 (TNA London, State Papers Online, Gale Document No. MC4347881980).

56. Barnby, 'Sack of Baltimore', pp. 115–16.

57. Sir William Hull to the Earl of Cork, 21 June 1631, SP 63/252, ff. 149v–150r (TNA London, State Papers Online, Gale Document No. MC4347881975).

58. Joseph Carter (sovereign of Baltimore) to Sir William Hull, 26 June 1631, SP 63/252, f. 161.

59. The second relation of the insolency of the Turks done at Baltymore which is more true and punctuall than the former, this being attested by the Soveragn, the burgesses, and Sir Samuell Crooke Barronnet, c. 25 June 1631, SP 63/252, ff. 159r–160r (TNA London, State Papers Online, Gale Document No. MC4347881979).

60. The Lords Justices and Council to the English Privy Council, 10 July 1631, SP/252, ff. 183–185v (TNA London, State Papers Online, Gale Document No. MC4347881996).

61. A corresponding note of interest from 1592, though perhaps unconnected, another Mathew Gunter is recorded as executed for piracy by the Admiralty in Scotland; see S. Murdoch, *The Terror of the Seas? Scottish maritime warfare, 1513–1713* (Leiden and Boston: Brill Publications, 2010), p. 126.

62. Barnby, 'The Sack of Baltimore', pp. 117–18; D. Ekin, *The Stolen Village* (Dublin: The O'Brien Press, 2006), pp. 108–10; D. Murray, 'From Baltimore to Barbary: The 1631 Sack of Baltimore', *History Ireland*, vol. 14, no. 4, 2006, p. 16; B. McCarthy, 'Algerine Pirates: The Sack of Baltimore', in *Pirates of Baltimore*, pp. 40–62. Barnby refers to the houses as 'thatched with straw' and 'built of wood and plaster' and as 'cabins'. Ekin's account is more or less a retelling of Barnby's, including referring to thatch and cabins; Murray suggests that the 'cottages' were 'along the shoreline' at the Cove, when the settlement was more practically located on the hill overlooking the strand at the Cove, as confirmed by elder locals in the area, who remember houses there. This is borne out by both archaeological and cartographic evidence (www.osi.ie); The distance from the Cove to what would have been Crooke's settlement in Baltimore, and the present village, is no more than half a kilometre.

63. C. Kelleher, 'The Insolency of the Turks Done at Baltimore', *Archaeology Ireland*, vol. 27, no. 4, 2013, pp. 26–9; Bernie McCarthy, while not ruling out that some of the pirates may have landed at the Cove, also includes the possibility that they could have landed elsewhere (p. 46). McCarthy's publication is a welcome update on the raid, which uses original sources and is supported by knowledge of the area; it discusses the raid, its wider impacts and long-term repercussions. See also Kelleher, 'The Confederacy of Pirates in Southwest Cork in the Early Seventeenth Century', Appendix 5, pp. 513–22, for a more extended argument on the raid and possible landing place for the Algerine pirates.

64. Recorded monument CO150-049 *fish palace*, Baltimore (National Monuments Service; www.archaeology.ie; C. Kelleher, New coastal sites at Tramadroum, Coney Island, Baltimore, Co. Cork (again see the National Monuments Service's Historic Environment Viewer at www.archaeology.ie). The author is grateful to Dr Brian Marten for first drawing attention to these sites at Tramadroum, for his help with surveying and for his local knowledge.

65. The Lords Justices and Council to the English Privy Council, 10 July 1631, SP/252, ff. 184r–185v; McCarthy addresses this point too in her published account, p. 49.

66. 1612 Dutch chart by John Hunt; SUB Göttingen, 4 H BRIT P III, 6 RARA: Hessel Gerritszoon, *Beschrijvinghe van de Zeecusten ende Havenen van Yerlandt/ Description of the Seacoasts and Ports of Ireland* (Amsterdam, 1612 and housed in Universitätsbibliothek, Göttingen); Wentworth Woodhouse Muniments WWM/Str P 20/100; Priestley, in his publication on the map, suggests that the ships shown are anchored at the Cove; Priestley, 'An Early 17th Century Map of Baltimore', pp. 55–7.

67. The Lords Justices and Council to the English Privy Council, 10 July 1631, SP/252, ff. 183–185v.

68. Barnby, 'The Sack of Baltimore', p. 118.

69. Senior, 'An Investigation of the Activities and Importance of English Pirates, 1603–40', p. 416; as indicated by Senior, there were two pirates named Nutt, and he provides information on both of them. C. Kelleher, 'Early 17th-century Piracy along the South-West Coast: The Kerry connections', *The Kerry Magazine*, Kerry Archaeological and Historical Society, vol. 27, 2017, pp. 29–31.

70. M.B. Fuller, 'Sir John Eliot and John Nutt, the Pirate', *Smith College Studies in History*, vol. 6, no. 2, 1919, pp. 71–94.

71. John Nutt from Devon is recorded as married with three children; Senior, 'An Investigation of the Activities and Importance of English Pirates, 1603–40', pp. 166 and 416. There is a strong chance that both John and Robert Nutt have been mixed up over the decades in the historical accounts and thus caution is advised when reviewing any information pertaining to both individuals. See also Earle, *Corsairs of Malta and Barbary*, for John Nutt, pp. 92–3 and for Robert Nutt, p. 108; Tinniswood, *Pirates of Barbary*, in particular for John Nutt, see pp. 72–4, though this does not add much to current knowledge. Raymond White's book *Their Bones Are Scattered:*

A history of the Old Head of Kinsale and surrounding areas (Kinsale: Kilmore Enterprises, 2003), pp. 172–3, refers to a 'Pieter Nutt', a Dutch pirate who infested the areas around Kinsale from about 1627 to 1632.

72. Capt. William Thomas to Nicholas, 6 April 1632, SP 16/215, f. 20 (TNA London, State Papers Online, Gale Document No. MC4324282483).

73. The Lords Justices and Council to the Lords of the Admiralty, 27 October 1632, SP 63/235, f. 230r (TNA London, State Papers Online, Gale Document No. MC4347882176); Sir Thomas Harris to Lord Falkland, 26 November 1632, SP 63/253 f. 245 (TNA London, State Papers Online, MC4347882186): Nutt is at this point in Ballinskelligs, County Kerry.

74. Appleby (ed.), *A Calendar of Material*, pp. 205, 212, 215–16; Kelleher, 'Early 17th-century Piracy along the South-West Coast', pp. 29–31.

75. Examination of Hugh Baker, of Youghal, Sailor, taken before mee [Lawrence Parsons] on 22 May 1623: Caulfield, *The Council Book of the Corporation of Youghal*, pp. xlviii–xlix.

76. G. Bennett, *A History of Bandon and the Principal Towns in the West Riding of the County Cork* (Cork: Francis Guy Printers & Publishers, 1869), pp. 80–2, 90–2. Bennett does not provide a source for his reference to the wreck, and he draws on both fact and fiction within his publication. There is a high probability that the wreck Bennett described is the remains of a later ship, that of the Royal African Company's slave ship the *Amity*, lost in the bay in 1700; for a fuller discussion on this see Kelleher, 'The Dunworley Bay Shipwreck', pp. 138–45; Kelleher, 'The 17th-century Dunworley Bay Shipwreck', pp. 130–9.

77. Kelleher, 'The Dunworley Bay Shipwreck', pp. 138–45.

78. Dr R. Brown, Specialist Report on the iron guns from the Dunworley Bay shipwreck site, unpublished report for the National Monuments Service, Department of Culture, Heritage and the Gaeltacht, 2009.

79. Ibid.; National Museum of Ireland cannon identifier number: 09E0494:C6: Dunworley Bay Shipwreck.

80. Brown, Specialist Report; R. Schalk, 'Financing the Dutch Golden Age: The credit market of Enkhuizen, 1580–1700', unpublished master's thesis, Utrecht University, The Netherlands, 2010; R. Schalk, O. Gelderblom and J. Jonker, 'Schipperen op de Aziatische vaart', *BMGN-Low Countries Historical Review*, vol. 127, no. 4, 2012, pp. 3–27.

81. Senior, 'An Investigation of the Activities and Importance of English Pirates, 1603–40', pp. 14–15.

82. Christopher Harding, '*Hostis Humani Generis* – The Pirate as Outlaw in the Early Modern Law of the Sea', in Jowitt (ed.), *Pirates?*, pp. 20–38. For an interesting discussion on this definition with respect to its direct meaning – that of violation of

human rights – and comparing piracy with terrorism and how this 300-year-old legal mechanism generally applied to piracy was used in 2005 in the United States, see J. Greene, 'Hostis Humani Generis', *Critical Inquiry*, vol. 34, no. 4, 2008, pp. 683–705.

83. Rodger, 'The Law and Language of Private Naval Warfare', p. 7.

84. Mainwaring, 'Discourse – Of the Beginnings, Practices and Suppression of Pirates', p. 46, n. 4, 'By merely ceasing to exist'.

85. Appleby, *Under the Bloody Flag*, pp. 211–46.

EPILOGUE

1. Mainwaring, 'A Discourse in Four Fragments', *Cottonian* MSS Otho E/VIII, f. 341v.

2. For a more in-depth look at particular characters in the history of the corsairs, see E. Bradford, *The Sultan's Admiral: Barbarossa – pirate and empire builder* (New York: Tauris Parke Printing, 2009).

3. Lunsford, *Piracy and Privateering in the Golden Age Netherlands*, pp. 161–2.

4. Hanna, *Pirate Nests and the Rise of the British Empire*, p. 417.

5. Ibid., p. 418.

6. Appleby (ed.), *A Calendar of Material*, pp. 141–2.

7. Appleby, 'A Nursery of Pirates', pp. 1–27; MacCarthy-Morrogh, *The Munster Plantation*.

8. Exquemelin, *The Buccaneers of America*, pp. 70–85; Captain C. Johnson, *A General History of the Robberies and Murders of the Most Notorious Pirates* (London: Routledge & Kegan Paul, 1955, first published 1724), pp. 182–6; Geanacopoulos, *The Pirate Next Door*, pp. 31–4, 910; E. Moisan, *Master of the Sweet Trade: A story of the pirate Samuel Bellamy, Mariah Hallett and the Whydah* (New York: iUniverse, Inc. Publishers, 2009), pp. 304–5.

9. Senior, 'An Investigation of the Activities and Importance of English Pirates, 1603–40', pp. 246–7.

10. 'A note of the Pirates', undated but possibly May 1610, HCA Examinations 1/47, f. 105; Report from Richard Kerry, 27 January 1610, HCA Examinations 1/47, ff. 78–79r.

11. H.B. Wheatley, *The Story of London* (London: J.M. Dent & Co., Publishers, 1909), pp. 319–21; Heal, *The London Goldsmiths*.

12. https://www.thegoldsmiths.co.uk/company/history/history-of-the-company/

13. H. Forsyth, *The Cheapside Hoard: London's lost jewels* (London: Museum of London and Philip Wilson Publishers, 2013); K.E. Lane, *Colour of Paradise: The*

emerald in the age of gunpowder empires (New Haven and London: Yale University Press, 2010).

14. Lane, *Colour of Paradise*.

15. Deposition of Edmunde Flinte, 3 September 1613, HCA Examinations 13/42, ff. 223v–224r; Senior, 'An Investigation of the Activities and Importance of English Pirates, 1603–40', p. 253; Appleby (ed.), *A Calendar of Material*, p. 138.

16. Semple, 'Pirate Coasts of the Mediterranean Sea', pp. 134–51; Galvin, *Patterns of Pillage*.

17. 'South coast exposed as drug smugglers' gateway', *Irish Independent*, 7 September 1998, ttp://www.independent.ie/national-news/south-coast-exposed-as-drug-smugglers-gateway-431873.html

18. Mainwaring, 'A Discourse in Four Fragments', *Cottonian* MSS Otho E VIII, f. 330r; Mainwaring, 'Discourse – Of the Beginnings, Practices and Suppression of Pirates', p. 17.

19. Killock and Meddens, 'Pottery as Plunder', pp. 1–9; C. Ewen, 'Introduction', in Skowronek and Ewen (eds), *X Marks the Spot*, p. 7; D. Finamore, 'A Mariner's Utopia: Pirates and logwood in the Bay of Honduras', in Skowronek and Ewen (eds), *X Marks the Spot*, pp. 64–78; Marangou, 'Carved Rocks', pp. 95–7; H. Hatch, 'Material Culture and Maritime Identity: Identifying maritime subcultures through artifacts', in B. Ford (ed.), *The Archaeology of Maritime Landscapes: When the land meets the sea* (New York: Springer Publications, 2011), pp. 217–31.

20. Deposition of Edward Davenant of Whiddy Island, 1 October 1614, HCA Examinations 13/226 f. 338: loss of captain Patrick Myagh's ship in Crookhaven; Examination of Rich. Kerry, 29 January 1610, HCA Examinations 1/47 ff. 82v–83r: loss of pirate captain Sammes' ship in Berehaven harbour.

21. O'Donoghue, 'The Coconut Wreck', pp. 1–65; Kelleher, 'The Dunworley Bay Shipwreck', pp. 138–45; Kelleher, 'The 17th-century Dunworley Bay Shipwreck', pp. 130–9; P. Lizé, 'The Wreck of the Pirate Ship *Speaker* on Mauritius in 1702', *International Journal of Nautical Archaeology and Underwater Exploration*, vol. 13, no. 2, 1984, pp. 121–32; B. Clifford, *The Pirate Prince: Discovering the priceless treasures of the sunken ship Whydah* (New York: Simon & Schuster, 1993); B. Clifford, *Expedition Whydah* (New York: Harper Collins, 1999); Charles R. Ewen and R.K. Skowronek (eds), *Pieces of Eight: More archaeology of piracy* (Tampa: Florida University Press, 2016); J. de Bry, 'Christopher Condent's *Fiery Dragon*: Investigating an early eighteenth-century pirate shipwreck off the coast of Madagascar', in Skowronek and Ewen (eds), *X Marks the Spot*, pp. 100–30; W.R. Lusardi, 'The Beaufort Inlet Shipwreck Artifact Assemblage', in Skowronek and Ewen (eds), *X Marks the Spot*, pp. 207–9, 196–218; M.U. Ramsing and C.R. Ewen, 'Beyond Reasonable Doubt: A case for "Queen Anne's Revenge"', *Historical Archaeology*, vol. 46, no. 2, 2012, pp. 110–33; F.H. Hanselmann, *Captain Kidd's Lost Ship: The Wreck of the Quedagh Merchant* (Gainesville: University of Florida Press, 2019).

22. Midheach, https://www.libraryireland.com/names/mai/midheach.php; A. O'Driscoll and B. Hodkinson, *Who Was Who in Early Modern Limerick*, https://www.limerick.ie/sites/default/files/atoms/files/who_was_who_in_early_modern_limerick_1.pdf

23. E. Bolster, 'A Landgable Roll of Cork City', *Collectanea Hibernica*, vol. 13, 1970, p. 11.

24. *Calendar of Vanderplas Cork Deeds*, 1598, 1610–77, 1694 (Cork: Ref. IE CCCA/U675, Cork City and County Archives, 2010), pp. 1–32.

25. Clayton (ed.), *Council Book for the Province of Munster*, pp. 16–17, 30–1, 88, 123, 125, 129, 132, 288.

26. K. Costello, *The Court of Admiralty of Ireland, 1575–1893* (Dublin: Four Courts Press, 2011), p. 65; R. Caulfield (ed), 'Annals of Kinsale' from *The Council Book of the Corporation of Kinsale from 1652 to 1800* (Guildford, Surrey: J. Billing & Sons, 1879), pp. lxxxii–lxxxiii.

27. Lunsford, *Piracy and Privateering*, pp. 128–30.

28. D. Moore, 'A General History of Blackbeard the Pirate, the *Queen Anne's Revenge* and the *Adventure*', *Tributaries*, vol. VII, 1997, pp. 31–5; D. Leigh, 'Ghost of the Gallows: The historical record of Black Caesar', *Creating Knowledge: The LAS student research journal* (DePaul University), vol. 5, 2012, pp. 28–32.

29. Senior, 'An Investigation of the Activities and Importance of English Pirates, 1603–40', p. 94.

30. A. Bialuschewski, 'Black People under the Black Flag: Piracy and the slave trade on the west coast of Africa, 1718–1723', *Slavery and Abolition: A journal of slavery and post-slave studies*, vol. 29, no. 4, 2004, pp. 461–75.

31. Horning, *Ireland in the Virginian Sea*, pp. 305–6.

32. Examination of Roger Salter, 14 May 1610, HCA Examinations 13/266, ff. 106–106v.

33. A. Margey, 'Representing Plantation Landscapes: The mapping of Ulster, c. 1560–1640', in Lyttleton and Rynne (eds), *Plantation Ireland*, pp. 159–60; P. Hanks, R. Coates and P. McClure (eds), *The Oxford Dictionary of Family Names of Britain and Ireland* (Oxford: Oxford University Press, 2016), p. 3559.

34. B. Kümin, 'The Devil's Altar? Crime and the early modern public house', *History Compass*, vol. 2, 2004, pp. 1–3; Brown, 'The Landscape of Drink', pp. 244–5.

35. Appleby, *Women and English Piracy*, p. 85.

36. Ibid., pp. 225–30.

BIBLIOGRAPHY

MANUSCRIPT SOURCES, IRELAND

National Library of Ireland

Carew MSS (microfilm)

MSS 619, f. 138	Richard Grice, Deputy-Vice-Admiral, 2 December 1610
MSS 629, f. 178	Captain Henry Skipwith to Sir Arthur Chichester, October 1611
Westport Estate Papers	1540–1993, Collection List No. 78, in reference to Michael Cormick of Inver, County Mayo

Trinity College Dublin

1641 Depositions

MS 824, ff. 253r–259v	Deposition of Sir William Hull knight & one of his Maiesties Councell of Mounster, 22 October 1642

Down Survey Parish Maps

The Barony of Carbury and Ibaune, in the County of Corke, dc. 1908. Ordnance Survey (Southampton, original housed as MSS Anglais 1–2, Bibliotheque National de France)

Royal Society of Antiquaries of Ireland

John Windele Papers

RIA Ms 12m 15 (169)	Sketch of Dunasead Castle, Baltimore, April 1835

MANUSCRIPT SOURCES, ENGLAND

British Library, London

Lansdowne MSS 142

f. 236	'Names of pirates of the companies of the Captains Ward and Hull, 15 November 1604'

Cottonian MSS Otho E/VIII

f. 170	A petition of Rich. Bishop and Wil. Wollman, in behalf of themselves and others living in piracy, no date
f. 188	A project concerning a force to be employed against pirates (two fragments), no date

ff. 329–345	'A Discourse in Four Fragments Concerning Proceedings Against Pirates', no date (but *c.* 1616–18)
ff. 360–364	Examination of John Jennings, pirate, before the court of admiralty, no date (but probably 1609 or 1610)
ff. 367–369	Examination of James Harris, before the E. of Northampton, no date
ff. 367–369	Two examinations concerning pirates, taken before the E. of Northampton, no date

Guildhall Library, London Metropolitan Archives

DL/C//B/05/MS9172/039	Last Will and Testament of Sir Thomas Crooke, proved in the Commissary Court of London, 27 May 1613; Will no. 208A

Chatsworth House, Derbyshire

Hardwick MSS 78	Letter book of Richard Boyle, first earl of Cork

National Archives: Public Records Office (Kew, London)

High Court of Admiralty	
HCA 1 (various)	Includes Books of Indictments, 1603–40
HCA 1/46–48	Examinations Books, 1543–1776
HCA 13/40	Examinations, 1608–10
HCA 13/41	Examinations, 1610–11
HCA 13/42	Examinations, 1601–14
HCA 13/46	Examinations, 1627–8
HCA 13/49	Examinations, 1630–2
HCA 13/97	Criminal Examination, 1607–9 (in conservation, not consulted)
HCA 13/98	Criminal Examinations, 1612–14
HCA 13/226	Examinations on Commission, 1606–14
HCA 13/227	Examinations on Commission, 1615–23
HCA 13/228	Examinations on Commissions, 1624–5
HCA 30/858	Bundle E. 1612–20 (not consulted but relevant to piracy for that period as it contains details of representations by pirates for return of all or part of their pirated goods)
State Papers	
SP 14	Domestic Series, James I (1603–40)
SP 15	Domestic Series, Elizabeth I (1547–1625)
SP 63	Papers relating to Ireland (1558–1782)

Maps
MPF/1/94 — *c*. 1558 map of Bantry and Beara; extracted from SP 64/1 (item 27)

Sheffield City Library Archives

WWM/Str P 20/100 — Map of Baltimore: Wentworth Woodhouse Muniments Strafford Folio Map (courtesy of the Director of Sheffield City Libraries and the Trustees of the Fitzwilliam Estates; HM Revenue; The Wentworth Woodhouse Muniments have been accepted in lieu of Inheritance Tax by HM Government and allocated to Sheffield City Council)

Lambeth Palace Library, London

Carew MSS
MSS 634 — Thomas Raven, 'A Plot of the lands of the worshipful company of Mercers' at Movanagher, 1622, from 'A True survey of the present estate of the County of Londonderry

Bodleian Library, Oxford

Carte MSS
Carte Papers, 61 — Sir Finie O'Driscoll's Petition, 22 Oct. 1606, p. 225

Admiralty Office, Taunton

Chart 833 — 'Crookhaven' by Capt. Martin White, 1817

MANUSCRIPT SOURCES, FOREIGN

Universitätsbibliothek, Göttingen. Germany

SUB Göttingen, 4 H — BRIT P III, 6 RARA: Hessel Gerritszoon, *Beschrijvinghe van de Zeecusten ende Havenen van Yerlandt/Description of the Seacoasts and Ports of Ireland* (Amsterdam, 1612 and courtesy of Universitätsbibliothek, Göttingen, Germany)

National Archives, Simancas, Spain

MPyD58/051 — Simancus: Guerra y Ma Leg. 3145: Sketch map of Baltimore, 1600?

PROCLAMATIONS, PAMPHLETS AND BROADSHEETS

Accessed via Early English Books Online (EEBO) and published in London unless otherwise stated.

STC/455:82	*A Proclamation against the maintenaunce of Pirates*, 1569 (Bodleian Library, Oxford)
STC/1875:25	*By the King, a proclamation for the search and apprehension of certaine pirats*, 1604 (Society of Antiquaries), 1 sheet
STC/725.15	Barker, A. *A True and Certaine Report of the Beginning, Proceedings, Overthrowes, and now present Estate of Captaine Ward and Danseker, the two late famous Pirates: from their first setting foorth to this present time* (1609), pp. 1–25
Th/74:E.462[29]	Nixon, A. *Newes from Sea of two notorious Pyrats Ward the Englishman and Danseker the Dutchman. With a true relation of all or the most piracies by them committed unto the sixt of Aprill 1609* (printed in London by Edward Allde for N. Butter, and sold at his shop, at the signe of the pide Bull, 1609)
Greg I:292(b)	*Ram-Alley: or Merrie-Trickes. A comedy divers times here-to-fore acted. By the Children of the Kings Reuels*, by Lo. Barrey 1611
STC/851.14	Squire, W. *Newes from Mamora or Summary Relation sent to the King of Spaine of the good success of a voyage, which it hath pleased God to giue in taking, and surprising, of Mamora, a Port in Barbary. By the Armado and Hoast Royall, of the Ocean sea, whereof ws Captaine Generall Don Luis Faxardo: assisted with three Galleis of Portinfall, vnder the command of the Conde de Elda, and fiue Gallies of Spaine, vnder the Duke of Fermandina*, 1614
STC/945:05	Whitbourne, R. *A Discourse and Discovery of Nevv-found-land with many reasons to proove how worthy and beneficiall a plantation may there be made. After a far better manner than now it is. Together with the laying open of certaine enormities and abuses commited by some that trade to that countrey, and the meanes laide downe for reformation thereof*, 1620

STC/11857:20	*To the most honourable assembly of knights, ctizens, and burgesses of the House of Parliament, the humble petition of the adventures in the ship called the Pearle*, 1621

Accessed via Henry E. Huntington Library and Art Gallery online: https://openlibrary.org/authors/OL575762A/Henry_E._Huntington_Library_and_Art_Gallery

STC/725:21	The Lives, Apprehensions, Arraignments and Executions of the 19 Late Pyrates, namely Capt. Harris, Jennings, Longcastle, Downes, Haulsey, and their companions, as they were severally indited on St Margret's Hill, in Southwark, on the 22 of December last and executed the Friday following, 1609 (London: E. Allde, printed for John Busby the Elder, 1609)

PRINTED SOURCES

Acts of the Privy Council of England (accessed via British History Online)

1571–5 (London: John Dasent, Editor, Her Majesty's Stationery Office, 1894)

1615–16 (London: E.G. Atkinson, Editor, Her Majesty's Stationer Office, 1925)

Annandale, N., *The Faroes and Iceland: Studies in island life* (Oxford: Clarendon Press, 1905)

Appleby, J.C. (ed.), *A Calendar of Material Relating to Ireland from the High Court of Admiralty Examinations, 1536–1641* (Dublin: Irish Manuscripts Commission, 1992)

Arber, E., 'The Travels and Observations of Captaine Smith', *Capt. John Smith, of Willoughby by Alford, Lincolnshire; President of Virginia, and Admiral of New England. Works. 1608-1631*, vol. II (Birmingham: John Connor Publisher, 1884)

Ball, F.E., *The Judges in Ireland, 1221–1921*, book III, 1603–90 (London: John Murray Publishers, 1926)

Barry, L., *Ram-Alley or Merry Tricks, 1611*, J.S. Farmer (ed.) (London: The Tudor Facsimile Texts, 1913)

Blaeu, J., 'Fezzae et Marocchi Regna Africae Celeberrima, 1662', *Atlas Maior, Sive Cosmographia Blaviana, Qua Solum, Salum, Coelum, Accuratissime Describuntur* (Amsterdam: J. Blaeu, 1662–5)

Boate, G., *Ireland's Naturall History* (London: Imprinted for John Wright, 1652)

Brady, W.M., *Clerical and Parochial Records of Cork, Cloyne and Ross*, vol. I (Dublin: Alexander Thom, 1863)

Cabala: Sive Scrinia Sacra, Mysteries of State and Government in Letters of Illustrious Persons and Great Ministers of State as well Foreign as Donestick, in the Reigns of

KingHenry the Eighth, Q: Elizabeth, K: James and K: Charles (London: Printed for G. Bedell & T. Collins, 1654)

Calendar of Carew Papers, preserved in the archiepiscopal library at Lambeth

1515–1574, J.S. Brewer and W. Bullen (eds) (London: Longmans, Green, Reader & Dyer Publishing, 1867)

1575–1588, J.S. Brewer and W. Bullen (eds) (London: Longmans, Green, Reader & Dyer Publishing, 1868)

1601–1603, J.S. Brewer and W. Bullen (eds) (London: Longmans, Green, Reader & Dyer Publishing, 1870)

1603–1623, J.S. Brewer and W. Bullen (eds) (London: Her Majesty's Stationery Office, 1873; Kraus Reprint, Kraus-Thomson Organisation Ltd.,1974)

Calendar of the Manuscripts of the Most Hon. the Marquis of Salisbury

1612–68 (Hatfield House, Hertfordshire. Accessed via State Papers Online, The National Archives, London)

Calendar of State Papers, domestic series (accessed via British History Online)

1603–1610, Mary Anne Everett Green (ed.) (London: Her Majesty's Stationery Office, 1857)

1611–1618, Mary Anne Everett Green (ed.) (London: Her Majesty's Stationery Office, 1858)

1619–1623, Mary Anne Everett Green (ed.) (London: Her Majesty's Stationery Office, 1858)

Calendar of State Papers, relating to Ireland (accessed via British History Online)

1603–1606, C.W. Russell and J.P. Prendergast (eds) (London: Longman & Co., 1872)

1606–1608, C.W. Russell and J.P. Prendergast (eds) (London: Longman & Co., 1874)

1608–1610, C.W. Russell and J.P. Prendergast (eds) (London: Longman & Co., 1874)

1611–1614, C.W. Russell and J.P. Prendergast (eds) (London: Longman & Co., 1877)

1615–1625, C.W. Russell and J.P. Prendergast (eds) (London: Longman & Co., 1880)

1611–1618, C.W. Russell and J.P. Prendergast (eds) (London: Longman & Co., 1858)

Calendar of State, Venetian (accessed via British History Online)

1603–1607, H.F. Brown (ed.) (London: Her Majesty's Stationery Office, 1900)

1607–1610, H.F. Brown (ed.) (London: Her Majesty's Stationery Office, 1904)

1610–1613, H.F. Brown (ed.) (London: Her Majesty's Stationery Office, 1905)

1613–1615, Allen B. Hinds (ed.) (London: Her Majesty's Stationery Office, 1907)

1621–1623, Allen B. Hinds (ed.) (London: His Majesty's Stationery Office, 1911) *Calendar of State Papers Colonial, America and West Indies* (accessed via British History Online)*1720–1721*, Cecil Headlam (ed.) (London: His Majesty's Stationery Office, 1933)

Calendar of Vanderplas Cork Deeds, 1598, 1610–77, 1694 (Cork: Ref. IE CCCA/U675, Cork City and County Archives, 2010)

Coke, Sir Edward, Certain Select Cases in Law, reported: knight, late Lord Chief Justice of England And one of His Majesties Council of State. Part XIII: XXI Trinity Term, anno 7 Jacobi Regis. The Case of the Admiralty (London: R. & E. Arkins Esq., 1677) *Desiderata Curiosa Hibernica: or A select collection of State Papers consisting of Royal instructions, directions, dispatches and letters to which are added some historical tracts*, ed. J. Lodge, 2 vols (Dublin: David Hay, 1772)

Caulfield, R., *The Council Book of the Corporation of Youghal* (Guildford: J. Billing & Sons, 1878)

— *Annals of Kinsale: Council Book of the Corporation of Kinsale* (Guildford: J. Billing & Sons, 1879)

Chevalier, J., 'Sketch of Sir Henry Mainwaring, *c*. 1646–47', in G.E. Mainwaring and W.G. Perrin, *The Life and Works of Sir Henry Mainwaring*, 4 vols (London: The Navy Records Society, 1922), pp. 276–7

Cokayne, G.E., *The Complete Peerage of England, Scotland, Ireland, Great Britain and the United Kingdom* (London: The St Catherine Press, 1887 and 1912)

Devon, F., *Issues of the Exchequer: Being payments made out of His Majesty's Revenue during the reign of James I* (London: William Clowes & Sons, 1836)

Dineen, Rev. P.S., *Foclóir Gaedhilge agus Béarla* (Dublin: M.H. Gill & Sons, 1904)

Dunlop, R. and O'Brien, G., 'An Unpublished Survey of the Plantation of Munster in 1622', *Journal of the Royal Society of Antiquaries of Ireland*, vol. 14, no. 2, 1924, pp. 128–46

Edwards, A., *Cork Remembrancer, or Tablet of Memory. Enumerating every remarkable circumstance that has happened in the City and County of Cork, and in the kingdom at large. Including all the memorable events in Great Britain with an account of all the Battles by Sea and Land in the present century. Also, the remarkable earthquakes, famines, inundations, storms, frosts, fires and all other accidents of moment, in Every Quarter of the Globe, from the earliest period, to the year 1792* (Cork: Tower Books, 1792)

Edwards, R.D. (ed.), 'Letter-Book of Sir Arthur Chichester, 1612–14', *Analecta Hibernica*, vol. 62, no. 8, 1938, pp. 3–178

Exquemelin, A.O., *The Buccaneers of America*, translated by Alexis Brown (New York: Dover Publications Inc., 1893 and 1996)

Gilbert, J.T. (ed.), *Calendar of the Ancient Records of Dublin in the Possession of the Municipal Corporation*, vol. I (Dublin: Joseph Dollard Publishers, 1889–95)

Grosart, Rev. A.B., *The Lismore Papers: The private and public (or State) correspondence of Sir Richard Boyle, first and 'Great' earl of Cork* (London: Chiswick Press, 1886–8)

Hardinge, W.H., 'On Manuscript Mapped Townland Surveys in Ireland of a Public Character, from Their Introduction to 23rd October 1641', *Proceedings of the Royal Irish Academy*, vol. VIII, 1861–4, pp. 39–55

Heal, Sir A., *The London Goldsmiths, 1200–1800: A record of the names and addresses of the craftsman, their shop-signs and trade-cards* (Newton Abbot: David & Charles, 1972)

Heard before the King: Register of petitions to James I, 1603–16, vol. 2 (London: Anthony Roe Ltd., 2006)

Historical Manuscripts Commission: Report on the manuscripts of the Duke of Buccleuch and Queensberry, preserved at Montagu House, Whitehall, vol. 1, 1483–1778. The Strafford Inquisition of County Mayo R.I.A. MS. 24 E 15, ed. William O'Sullivan (Dublin: Irish Manuscripts Commission, 1958)

Lewis, S., A *Topographical Dictionary of Ireland*, vol. II (London: S. Lewis & Co., 1837)

Jamestown Society, *Qualifying Ancestors: Stockholders in the Virginia Company* (Ancestor Register, 2007), pp. 1–9, http://www.jamestowne.org

Johnson, Captain C. / D. Defoe, *A General History of the Robberies and Murders of the Most Notorious Pirates* (London: Routledge & Kegan Paul, 1724 and 1955)

Mainwaring, Henry, 'Discourse – Of the Beginnings, Practices and Suppression of Pirates', in Mainwaring and Perrin, *The Life and Works of Sir Henry Mainwaring*, pp. 3–52

— 'The Seaman's Dictionary', in Mainwaring and Perrin, *The Life and Works of Sir Henry Mainwaring*, pp. 69–262.

Mainwaring, G.E. and Perrin, W.G. (eds), *The Life and Works of Sir Henry Mainwaring*, 2 vols (London: Navy Records Society, 1920–2)

Marsden, R.G., *Documents Relating to Law and Custom of the Sea*, 1205–1767 (London: Navy Records Society, 1915–16)

Pender S., A *Census of Ireland, circa 1659* (Dublin: Irish Manuscripts Commission, The Stationery Office, 1939)

Pitcairn, R., *Ancient Criminal Trials of Scotland: From the original records and MSS, with historical illustrations, &c.*, vol. III (Edinburgh: Bannatyne Club, 1833)

Purchas, S., *Hakluytus Posthumus; or Purchas his Pilgrims: contayning a history of the world in sea voyages and lande travells by Englishmen and others in 1626*, vol. XIX (Reprinted as *Purchas his Pilgrims*, Glasgow: James MacLehose & Sons, 1907)

Smith, C., *The Ancient and Present State of the City and County of Cork* (Cork: John Connor, 1815)

Stafford, T., *Pacata Hibernia or a History of the Wars in Ireland during the Reign of Queen Elizabeth 1602*, ed. S. O'Grady, vol. II (London: Downey & Co. Ltd., 1896)

Steele, R., *Tudor and Stuart Proclamations, 1485–1714* (Oxford: Clarendon Press, 1910)

Went, A.E.J., 'Sir William Hull's Losses in 1641', *Journal of the Cork Historical and Archaeological Society*, vol. 52, 1947, pp. 55–68

Wheatley, H.B., *The Story of London* (London: J.M. Dent & Co., 1909)

Whitburn, T., *Westward Hoe for Avalon: In the New-found-land, as described by Captain Richard Whitbourne, of Exmouth, Devon, 1622* (London: Sampson Low, Son, & Marston, 1870)

Winwood, Sir R., *Memorials of Affairs of State in the Reigns of Q. Elizabeth and K. James I collected from the original papers of the Right Honourable Sir Ralph Winwood Kt.*, vol. III (London: W.B. for T. Ward, 1725)

SECONDARY SOURCES

Abeyratne, R., 'The Responsibility of Somalia for the Acts of the Somali Pirates', *Journal of Transportation Security*, vol. 2, 2009, pp. 63–76

Al-Olaqi, F.M.T., 'The Fear of Conversion to Islam in Daborne's *A Christian Turn'd Turk* (1609)', *Studies in Literature and Language*, vol. 14, no. 3, 2017, pp. 1–12

Anderson, J.L., 'Piracy and World History: An economic perspective on maritime predation', *Journal of World History*, vol. 6, no. 2, 1995, pp. 175–99

Andina, M., 'Bern's Gallows: Archaeologists uncover evidence of past punishments', 26 September 2009; https://www.swissinfo.ch/eng/bern-s-gallows_archaeologists-uncover-evidence-of-past-punishment/18194

Andrade, T., 'The Company's Chinese Pirates: How the Dutch East India Company tried to lead a coalition of pirates to war against China, 1621–1662', *Journal of World History*, vol. 15, no. 4, 2005, pp. 415–44

Andrews, K.R., '*Elizabethan Privateering: English privateering during the Spanish War, 1585–1603* (Cambridge: Cambridge University Press, 1964)

— *Drake's Voyages: A reassessment of their place in Elizabethan maritime expansion* (Cambridge: Cambridge University Press, 1967)

— 'Sir Robert Cecil and Mediterranean Plunder', *English Historical Review*, vol. 87, no. 344, 1972, pp. 513–32

— *Trade, Plunder and Settlement: Maritime enterprise and the genesis of the British Empire, 1480–1630* (Cambridge: Cambridge University Press, 1984)

— *Ships, Money and Politics: Seafaring and naval enterprise in the reign of Charles I* (Cambridge: Cambridge University Press, 1991)

Andrews, K.R., Canny, N.P. and Hair, P.E.H. (eds), *The Westward Enterprise: English activities in Ireland, the Atlantic and America, 1480–1650* (Detroit: Wayne State University Press, 1979)

Appleby, J.C., 'An Irish Letter of Marque', *Irish Sword*, vol. 15, no. 61, 1983, pp. 218–21

— 'The 'Affairs of Pirates': The surrender and submission of Captain William Baugh at Kinsale, 1611–1612', *Journal of the Cork Historical and Archaeological Society*, vol. 91, 1986, pp. 68–84

— 'Merchants and Mariners, Pirates and Privateers: An introductory survey of the records of the High Court of Admiralty as a source for regional maritime history, c. 1500–1800', in M. McCaughan and J. Appleby (eds), *The Irish Sea: Aspects of maritime history* (Belfast: Institute of Irish Studies, 1989), pp. 47–58

— 'A Nursery of Pirates: The English pirate community in Ireland in the early seventeenth century', *International Journal of Maritime History*, vol. II, no. 1, 1990, pp. 1–27

— 'Settlers and Pirates in Early Seventeenth-century Ireland: A profile of Sir William Hull', *Studia Hibernica*, vol. 25, 1990, pp. 76–104

— 'Women and Piracy in Ireland: From Gráinne O'Malley to Anne Bonny', in M. MacCurtain and M. O'Dowd (eds), *Women in Early Modern Ireland* (Edinburgh: Edinburgh University Press, 1991), pp. 55–68

— *A Calendar of Material Relating to Ireland from the High Court of Admiralty, 1536–1641* (Dublin: Irish Manuscripts Commission, 1992)

— 'The Defence of Ireland: A naval journal of 1627', *Analecta Hibernica*, vol. 37, 1998, pp. 237–48

— 'War, Politics and Colonization, 1558–1625', in N. Canny (ed.), *The Origins of Empire* (Oxford and New York: Oxford University Press, 1998), pp. 55–78

— 'Women and Piracy in Ireland: From Gráinne O'Malley to Anne Bonny', in C.R. Pennell (ed.), *Bandits at Sea* (New York: New York University Press, 2001), pp. 283–98

— 'The Problem with Piracy in Ireland, 1570–1630', in C. Jowitt (ed.), *Pirates? The Politics of Plunder, 1550–1650* (New York: Palgrave Macmillan, 2007), pp. 41–55

— 'Pirates and Communities: Scenes from Elizabethan England and Wales', in J.C. Appleby and P. Dalton (eds), *Outlaws in Medieval and Early Modern England*, vol. 5 (Surrey: Ashgate Publishing Company, 2009), pp. 149–77

— *Under the Bloody Flag: Pirates of the Tudor age* (Stroud: The History Press, 2009)

— *Women and English Piracy, 1540–1720* (Woodbridge: The Boydell Press, 2013)

Appleby, J.C. and O'Dowd, M., The Irish Admiralty: Its organization and Development, *c.* 1570–1640', *Irish Historical Studies*, vol. 24, no. 9, 1985, pp. 299–326

Bagwell, R., *Ireland under the Stuarts and during the Interregnum, 1603–1642*, vol. I (London: Longmans, Green, & Co., 1909)

Bak, G., *Barbary Pirate: The life and times of John Ward, the most infamous privateer of his time* (Gloucester: Sutton Publishing, 2006)

Barbour, V., 'Privateers and Pirates of the West Indies', *The American Historical Review*, vol. 16, no. 3, 1911, pp. 553–66

— 'Dutch and English Shipping in the Seventeenth Century', *Economic History Review*, vol. 2, 1930, pp. 261–90

Barker, R., 'Careening: Art and anecdote', *Mare Liberum*, vol. 2, 1991, pp. 177–207

Barnby, H., 'The Sack of Baltimore', *Journal of the Cork Historical and Archaeological Society*, vol. 74, 1969, pp. 101–29

— 'The Algerine Attack on Baltimore, 1631', *The Mariner's Mirror*, vol. 56, no. 1, 1970, pp. 27–31

Bennett, G., *The History of Bandon and the Principal Towns in the West* (Cork: Francis Guy Printers & Publishers, 1869)

Benton, L., 'Legal Spaces of Empire: Piracy and the origins of ocean regionalism', *Journal of Comparative Study of Society and History*, vol. 47, no. 4, 2005, pp. 700–24

— 'Oceans of Law: The legal geography of the seventeenth-century seas', *Proceedings of the Seascapes, Littoral Cultures, and Trans-Oceanic Exchanges Conference, 2003* (Washington DC: Library of Congress, 2003)

Berckmanm, E., *Victims of Piracy in the Admiralty Court, 1575–1678* (London: Hamish Hamilton, 1979)

Bialuschewski, A., 'Black People under the Black Flag: Piracy and the slave trade on the west coast of Africa, 1718–1723', *Slavery and Abolition: A journal of slavery and post-slave studies*, vol. 29, no. 4, 2004, pp. 461–75

Bolster, E., 'A Landgable Roll of Cork City', *Collectanea Hibernica*, vol. 13, 1970, pp. 7–20

Bonsall, J. and Dowd, M., 'Emerging from the Waves: A late Bronze Age intertidal saltwater fulacht fia at Coney Island, Co. Clare', *Journal of Irish Archaeology*, vol. 24, 2015, pp. 79–85

Bookin-Weiner, J., 'The "Salé Rovers": Morocco and its corsairs in the seventeenth century', in R.S. Simon and J.C. Hurewitz (eds), *The Middle East and North Africa: Essays in honor of J.C. Hurewitz* (New York: Columbia University Press, 1990), pp. 151–98

— 'The Moroccan Corsairs of Rabat-Salé', in A. Bencherifa and K. Zemrag (eds), *Le Maroc et l'Atlantique* (Rabat: Publications de la Faculté des Lettres et des Sciences Humaines, 1992), pp. 163–91

Bourke, E., Hayden, A. and Lynch, A., *Skellig Michael, Co. Kerry: Archaeological stratigraphic report: excavations 1986–2010* (Dublin: Government of Ireland, 2011)

Boxer, C.R., *The Dutch Seaborne Empire, 1600–1800* (New York: Harmondsworth Penguin Books, 1965)

— *The Portuguese Seaborne Empire, 1415–1825* (London: Hutchinson & Co., 1969)

Bracewell, C.W., *The Uskoks of Senj: Piracy, banditry, and holy war in the sixteenth-century Adriatic* (Ithaca: Cornell University Press, 1992)

— 'Women Among the Uskoks: Literary images and reality', in Pennell (ed.), *Bandits at Sea*, pp. 321–34

Bradford, G., *The Mariner's Dictionary* (New York: Weathervane Books, 1952)

Bradford, E., *The Sultan's Admiral: Barbarossa – pirate and empire builder* (London: Tauris Parke Publishers, 2009)

Brady, C. and Gillespie, R., *Natives and Newcomers: The making of Irish colonial society, 1534–1641* (Suffolk: Irish Academic Press, 1986)

Brady, K. and Kelleher, C., 'Churchtown, Human Remains: 00E0872', in I. Bennett (ed.), *Excavations Bulletin: Summary of archaeological excavations in Ireland, 2000* (Wicklow: Wordwell Ltd., 2000), p. 353

Brady, K., *Shipwreck Inventory of Ireland: Louth, Meath, Dublin and Wicklow*, vol. I (Dublin: Government Stationery Office, 2008)

Breen, C., 'The Maritime Cultural Landscape in Medieval Gaelic Ireland', in P.J. Duffy, D. Edwards and E. Fitzpatrick (eds), *Gaelic Ireland: Land, lordship and settlement c. 1250–1650* (Dublin: Four Courts Press, 2001), pp. 418–35

— 'The Gaelic Maritime Lordship of O'Sullivan Beara', *Journal of the Cork Historical and Archaeological Society*, vol. 106, 2001, pp. 21–36

— *The Gaelic Lordship of the O'Sullivan Beare: A landscape cultural history* (Dublin: Four Courts Press, 2005)

— *An Archaeology of Southwest Ireland, 1570–1670* (Dublin: Four Courts Press, 2007)

— 'The Post-Medieval Coastal Landscape of Bantry and Beara', in Horning et al. (eds), *The Post-Medieval Archaeology of Ireland*, pp. 206–9

— 'Famine and Displacement in Plantation-Period Munster', in C. Rynne and J. Lyttleton (eds), *Plantation Ireland: Settlement and material culture, 1550–1700* (Dublin: Four Courts Press, 2009), pp. 132–9

— 'Galley-Castles in Gaelic Medieval Ireland?', in P. Martin (ed.), *Castles and Galleys: A reassessment of the historic galley-castles of the Norse-Gaelic seaways* (Barra: Islands Book Trust, 2017), pp. 208–16

Brickley, M., Miles, A. and Stainer, H., *The Cross Bones Burial Ground, Redcross Way, Southwark, London* (London: Museum of London Archaeology Service, 1999)

Brotton, J., *This Orient Isle: Elizabethan England and the Islamic world* (London: Penguin Random House Books, 2016)

Bulut, M., 'The Role of the Ottomans and Dutch in the Commercial Integration between the Levant and Atlantic in the Seventeenth Century', *Journal of the Economic and Social History of the Orient*, vol. 45, no. 2, 2002, pp. 197–230

Butlin, R.A., 'Land and People, *c.* 1600', in T.W. Moody, F.X. Martin and F.J. Byrne (eds), *A New History of Ireland. Vol III: Modern Ireland, 1534–1691* (Oxford: Oxford University Press, 1976, 2003 reprint), pp. 142–67

Caball, M., 'Culture, Continuity and Change in Early Seventeenth-Century South-West Munster', *Studia Hibernica*, vol. 38, 2012, pp. 37–56

Canny, N., 'The Permissive Frontier: The problem of social control in English settlement in Ireland and Virginia, 1550–1650', in K.R. Andrews, N.P. Canny and P.E.H. Hair (eds), *The Westward Enterprise: English activities in Ireland, the Atlantic and America, 1480–1650* (Detroit: Wayne State University Press, 1979), pp. 17–44

— *The Upstart Earl: A study of the social and mental world of Richard Boyle, first earl of Cork, 1566–1643* (New York: Cambridge University Press, 1982)

— *The Origins of Empire*, The Oxford History of the British Empire (Oxford: Oxford University Press, 1998)

— 'War, Politics and Colonisation', in *The Origins of Empire*, pp. 55–78

— *Making Ireland British, 1580–1650* (Oxford: Oxford University Press, 2001), pp. 311–13

Carr, M., *Blood & Faith: The purging of Muslim Spain, 1492–1614* (London: Hurst & Co., 2017)

Carter, J., 'Spanish Olive Jars from Fermeuse Harbour, Newfoundland', *Material History Bulletin: Ceramics in Canada*, vol. 16, 1982, pp. 99–108

Cell, G., 'The Newfoundland Company: A study of subscribers to a colonizing venture', *The William and Mary Quarterly*, vol. 22, no. 4, 1965, pp. 611–25

— *Newfoundland Discovered: English attempts at colonisation, 1610–1630* (London: The Hakluyt Society, 1982)

Chambers, A., *Granuaile: The life and times of Grace O'Malley* (Dublin: Wolfhound Press, 1979 and 1983)

Chavasse, T., *Past Speech of the Sea: A maritime history of Castlehaven* (Cork: Galley Head Press, 2003)

Clarke, A., 'The Irish Economy, 1600–60', in Moody et al. (eds), *A New History of Ireland*, pp. 168–86

Clarke, A. and Dudley Edwards, R., 'Pacification, Plantation and the Catholic Question, 1603–23', in Moody et al. (eds), *A New History of Ireland*, pp. 187–232

Clark, G.N., 'The Barbary Corsairs in the Seventeenth Century', *Cambridge Historical Journal*, vol. 8, no. 1, 1944, pp. 22–35

Clifford, B., *The Pirate Prince: Discovering the priceless treasures of the sunken ship Whydah* (New York: Simon & Schuster, 1993)

— *Expedition Whydah* (New York: Harper Collins, 1999)

Cokayne, G.E., *The Complete Peerage of England, Scotland, Ireland, Great Britain, and the United Kingdom* (London: The St Catherine Press Ltd., 1910)

Coleman, R., 'The Old Castles of South-West Cork', *Journal of the Cork Historical and Archaeological Society*, vol. 30, 1924–6, pp. 26–35

Colfer, B., *The Hook Peninsula* (Cork: Cork University Press, 2004)

Collins English Dictionary (Glasgow: Harper Collins, 1992)

Cook, J., *Pirate Queen: The life of Grace O'Malley, 1530–1603* (Cork: Mercier Press, 2004)

Coombes, Rev. J., 'The Sack of Baltimore: A forewarning', *Journal of the Cork Historical and Archaeological Society*, vol. 63, 1958, pp. 60–1

Coombes, Rev. J. and Ware, N.J., 'The Letter Book of General de Zubiaur: A calendar of the "Irish" letters', *Journal of the Cork Historical and Archaeological Society*, vol. 83, 1978, pp. 50–8

Corbett, J., *England in the Mediterranean: A study of the rise and influence of British power within the Straits, 1603–1713*, vol. I (London, New York and Bombay: Longmans, Green & Co., 1904)

Cordingly, D., *Life Among the Pirates: The romance and the reality* (London: Little, Brown & Co., 1995)

— *Women Sailors and Sailors' Women* (New York: Random House, 2001 and 2007)

Corn, C., *The Scents of Eden: A history of the spice trade* (New York: Kodansha International, 1998)

Costello, K., *The Court of Admiralty of Ireland, 1575–1893* (Dublin: Four Courts Press, 2011)

Cotter, E., 'Dún na Séad Castle: An early 17th-century house in Baltimore, Co. Cork', *Journal of the Cork Historical and Archaeological Society*, vol. 115, 2010, pp. 31–54

— 'Kilcoe Castle: Excavations of a late medieval coastal stronghold in County Cork', *Journal of the Cork Historical and Archaeological Society*, vol. 117, 2012, pp. 1–23

Craven, W.F., 'The Earl of Warwick: A speculator in piracy', *Hispanic American Historical Review*, vol. 30, 1930, pp. 457–97

Curtis Clayton, M. (ed.), *Council Book for the Province of Munster c. 1599–1649* (Dublin: Irish Manuscripts Commission, 2008)

Dalby, A., *Dangerous Tastes: The story of spices* (Berkeley: University of California Press, 2000)

Davies, R.C., *Christian Slaves, Muslim Masters: White slavery in the Mediterranean, the Barbary coast and Italy, 1500–1800* (New York: Palgrave Macmillan, 2004)

Deagan, K., 'Eliciting Contraband through Archaeology: Illicit trade in eighteenth-century St Augustine', *Historical Archaeology*, vol. 41, no. 4, 2007, pp. 98–116

de Castro, F.V., *The Pepper Wreck: A Portuguese Indiaman at the mouth of the Tagus River* (College Station, TX: A&M University Press, 2005)

de Courcy Ireland, J., 'The Algerine Raid on Baltimore', *The Irish Sword*, vol. 10, 1970–1, p. 69

— 'Algerine Raid on Baltimore', *The Mariner's Mirror*, vol. 56, no. 3, 1970, p. 298

— *Ireland and the Irish in Maritime History* (Dublin: Glendale Press, 1986)

— *The Liffey in Dublin* (Dublin: Gill & Macmillan, 1996)

de Bry, J., 'Christopher Condent's *Fiery Dragon*: Investigating an early eighteenth-century pirate shipwreck off the coast of Madagascar', in R.K. Skowronek and C.R. Ewen (eds), *X Marks the Spot: The archaeology of piracy* (Gainesville: University Press of Florida, 2006), pp. 100–30

de Lisle, L., *After Elizabeth: The death of Elizabeth and the coming of King James* (London: Harper Perennial, 2005)

Dickson, D., *Old World Colony: Cork and south Munster, 1630–1830* (Cork: Cork University Press, 2005)

Dictionary of National Biography (Oxford: Oxford University Press, 2004–7), http://www.oxforddnb.com

Dictionary of Canadian Biography (Toronto: University of Toronto Press, 2000), http://www.biographi.ca

Dictionary of Irish Biography (Dublin and Cambridge: Cambridge University Press, 2010), http://dib.cambridge.org.elib.tcd.ie/

Donnelly, C., 'The Archaeology of the Ulster Plantation', in Horning et al. (eds), *The Post-Medieval Archaeology of Ireland*, pp. 37–50

Donovan, D., *Sketches in Carbery, Co. Cork: Its antiquities, history, legends and topography* (Dublin: McGlashan & Gill, 1876)

Earle, P., *The Pirate Wars* (London: Methuen Press, 2004)

— *Corsairs of Malta and Barbary* (London: Sidgwick & Jackson, 1970)

Eddington, B., 'The Gentleman Pirate: When Peter Easton arrived in Newfoundland in 1602', *The Beaver: Exploring Canada's history*, vol. 83, no. 4, 2003, pp. 42–3

Ekin, D., *The Stolen Village: Baltimore and the Barbary pirates* (Dublin: O'Brien Press, 2006)

Erbati, E. and Trakadas, A., *The Moroccan Maritime Survey: An archaeological contribution to the history of the Tangier peninsula*, BAR International Series 1890 (Oxford: Archaeopress Publications, 2008)

Evans, A., 'Defining Jamaica Sloops: A preliminary model for identifying an abstract concept', *Journal of Maritime Archaeology*, vol. 2, 2007, pp. 83–92

Ewen, C., 'Introduction', in Skowronek and Ewen (eds), *X Marks the Spot*, pp. 1–10

Ewen C. and Skowronek, R. (eds), *Pieces of Eight: More archaeology of piracy* (Gainesville: Florida University Press, 2016)

Ewen, C.L, *Lording Barry, poet and pirate* (privately printed, 1938)

— Organised Piracy round England in the Sixteenth Century', *The Mariner's Mirror*, vol. 35, no. 1, 1949, pp. 29–42

Eysturlid, L.W., 'Where Everything Is Weighed in the Scales of Material Interest: Anglo-Turkish trade, piracy and diplomacy in the Mediterranean during the Jacobean period', *Journal of European Economic History*, vol. 22, no. 3, 1993, pp. 613–22

Fanning, T. and Hurst, J.G., 'A Mid-Seventeenth-century Pottery Group and Other Objects from Ballyhack Castle, Co. Wexford', *Proceedings of the Royal Irish Academy*, vol. 75, Sect. C, 1975, pp. 103–18

Fawcett, J.A., 'Challenges to Apprehension and Prosecution of East African Maritime Pirates', *Journal of Maritime Policy and Management*, vol. 37, no. 7, 2010, pp. 753–65

Finamore, D., 'A Mariner's Utopia: Pirates and logwood in the Bay of Honduras', in Skowronek and Ewen (eds), *X Marks the Spot*, pp. 64–78

Fisher, G., *Barbary Legend: War, trade and piracy in North Africa, 1415–1830* (Oxford: Clarendon Press, 1957)

Flavin, S. and Jones, E.T., *Bristol's Trade with Ireland and the Continent, 1503–1601* (Dublin: Four Courts Press, 2009)

Ford, B. (ed.), *The Archaeology of Maritime Landscapes: When the land meets the sea* (New York: Springer Publications, 2011)

Forsyth, H., *The Cheapside Hoard: London's lost jewels* (London: Museum of London and Philip Wilson Publishers, 2013)

Frankopan, P. *The Silk Roads: A new history of the world* (London: Bloomsbury, 2015)

Friedman, E., 'North African Piracy on the Coasts of Spain in the Seventeenth Century: A new perspective on the expulsion of the Moriscos', *The International History Review*, vol. 1, 1979, pp. 1–16

Fuchs, B., 'Faithless Empires: Pirates, renegades, and the English nation', *English Literary History*, vol. 67, no. 1, 2000, pp. 45–69

— 'Spanish Lessons: Spenser and the Irish Moriscos', *Studies in English Literature, 1500–1700*, vol. 42, no. 1, 2002, pp. 43–62

Fuller, M.B., 'Sir John Eliot and John Nutt, the Pirate', *Smith College Studies in History*, vol. 6, no. 2, 1919, pp. 71–94

Fuller, B. and Leslie-Melville, R., *Pirate Harbours and Their Secrets* (London: Stanley Paul & Co. Ltd., 1935)

Galvin, Peter R., *Patterns of Pillage: A geography of Caribbean-based piracy in Spanish America, 1536–1718* (New York: Peter Lang Publishing, 1999)

Gaulton, B. and Tuck, J.A., 'The Archaeology of Ferryland, Newfoundland until 1696', *Avalon Chronicles: The English in America, 1497–1696*, vol. 8, 2003, pp. 187–224

Geanacopoulos, D.P., *The Pirate Next Door: The untold story of eighteenth-century pirates' wives, families and communities* (Durham, NC: Carolina Academic Press, 2017)

Gibson, Rev. C.B., *The History of the County and City of Cork*, vol. II (London: Thomas C. Newby Publishers, 1861)

Good, G.L., 'The Excavation of Two Docks at Narrow Quay, Bristol, 1978–9', *Post-Medieval Archaeology*, vol. 21, 1987, pp. 25–126

Goodman, D., *Spanish Naval Power, 1589–1665: Reconstruction and defeat* (Cambridge: Cambridge University Press, 1997)

Gosse, P., *The History of Piracy* (Santa Fe: Rio Grande Press Inc., 1932 and 1990 reprint)

Greene, J., 'Hostis Humani Generis', *Critical Inquiry*, vol. 34, no. 4, 2008, pp. 683–705

Gregory, D., 'Shipworm Invading the Baltic?', *International Journal of Nautical Archaeology*, vol. 39, no. 2, 2010, p. 431

Gwynn, A., 'Early Irish Emigration to the West Indies, 1612–1643', *Studies: An Irish quarterly review*, vol. 18, no. 71, 1929, pp. 377–93

Hamilton, C.E., 'The Pirate Ship *Whydah*', in Skowronek and Ewen (eds), *X Marks the Spot*, pp. 131–59

Hamilton, D.L., 'Pirates and Merchants: Port Royal, Jamaica', in Skowronek and Ewen (eds), *X Marks the Spot*, pp. 13–30

Hammond, J.W., 'George's Quay and Rogerson's Quay in the Eighteenth Century', *Dublin Historical Record*, vol. 5, no. 2, 1942–3, pp. 41–54

Hancock, D., 'Combining Success and Failure: Scottish networks in the Atlantic wine trade', in D. Dickson, J. Parmentier and J. Ohlmeyer (eds), *Irish and Scottish Mercantile Networks in Europe and Overseas in the Seventeenth and Eighteenth Centuries* (Ghent: Academic Press, 2006), pp. 5–38

Hanks, P., Coates, R. and McClure, P. (eds), *The Oxford Dictionary of Family Names of Britain and* Ireland (Oxford: Oxford University Press, 2016)

Hanna, M.G., *Pirate Nests and the Rise of the British Empire, 1570–1740* (Williamsburg: University of North Carolina Press, 2015)

Hanselmann, F.H. *Captain Kidd's Lost Ship: The Wreck of the Quedagh Merchant* (Gainesville: University of Florida Press, 2019)

Hardiman, J., *History of the Town and County of Galway*, Appendix III, Charter of Elizabeth to the Town of Galway (Dublin: W. Folds & Sons, 1820)

Harding, C., '*Hostis Humani Generis* – The Pirate as Outlaw in the Early Modern Law of the Sea', in Jowitt (ed.), *Pirates?*, pp. 20–38

Harris, F.W., 'The Commission of 1609: Legal aspects', *Studia Hibernica*, vol. 20, 1980, pp. 31–55

Hatch, H., 'Material Culture and Maritime Identity: Identifying maritime subcultures through artifacts', in Ford (ed.), *The Archaeology of Maritime Landscapes*, pp. 217–31

Hausner, S.L., *The Spirits of Crossbones Graveyard: Time, ritual, and sexual commerce in London* (Bloomington, IN: Indiana University Press, 2016)

Hawke, J., 'Canty's Cove – Legend and History', *The Mizen Journal*, vol. 5, Selections from *The Mizen Journal*, 1993–2004 (Skibbereen: Inspire Design and Print, 2004), pp. 292–302

Healy, J.N., *The Castles of County Cork* (Cork: Mercier Press, 1988)

Hebb, D.D., *Piracy and the English Government, 1616–1642* (London: Scolar Press, 1994)

Hill, L.M., 'The Admiralty Circuit of 1591: Some comments on the relations between central government and local interests', *The Historical Journal*, vol. xiv, no. 1, 1971, pp. 3–14

Hobsbawm, E., *Bandits* (London: Abacus History Press, 2000)

Hoppe, K.N., 'Teredo Navalis – The Cryptogenic Shipworm', in E. Leppäkoski, S. Gollasch and S. Olenin (eds), *Invasive Aquatic Species of Europe: Distribution, impact and management* (Dordrecht: Springer Science & Media, BV, 2002), pp. 116–19

Horning, A., 'The Archaeology of British Expansion: Ireland and North America in the seventeenth century', in Horning et al. (eds), *The Post-medieval Archaeology of Ireland*, pp. 51–70

— 'The Root of all Vice and Bestiality': Exploring the cultural role of the alehouse in the Ulster plantation', in J. Lyttleton and C. Rynne (eds), *Plantation Ireland: Settlement and material culture, c. 1550 – c. 1700* (Dublin: Four Courts Press, 2009), pp. 113–31

— *Ireland in the Virginian Sea: Colonialism in the British Atlantic* (Williamsburg: University of North Carolina Press, 2013)

Horning, A., Ó Baoill, R, Donnelly, C. and Logue, P. (eds), *The Post-Medieval Archaeology of Ireland, 1550–1850* (Wicklow: Wordwell Ltd., 2007)

Horwood, H. and Butts, E., *Pirates & Outlaws of Canada, 1610–1932* (Toronto: Doubleday Press Ltd., 1984)

Horwood, H., *Plunder and Pillage: Atlantic Canada's brutal and bloodthirsty pirates and privateers* (Halifax: Formac Publishing Company Ltd., 2011)

Jameson, J.G., *Privateering and Piracy in the Colonial Period: Illustrative documents* (New York: The Macmillan Company, 1923)

Jónsson, B. of Skardsá, *The Turkish Raid Saga*, 1643 (Reykjavik: Einar Thórdarson, 1866 translation), published online by Tina Türkiye Sualti Arkeolojisi Vakfi (stanbul: Ko Üniversitesi, Sariyer, 2018)

Jones, E.T., 'Illicit Business: Accounting for smuggling in mid sixteenth-century Bristol', *Economic History Review*, vol. 54, no. 1, 2001, pp. 17–38

Jones, J.B. and Dowling, C.M., 'Capital Punishment in Colonial Virginia, Phase III: Data recovery for mitigation of adverse effects to Site 44WB66 (The Colonial Gallows)', Technical Report Series 18, William and Mary Centre for Archaeological Research (Williamsburg: College of William and Mary, 1993), pp. 1–78

Jones, E.T. and Flavin, S., 'Ireland–Bristol Trade in the Sixteenth Century', ESRC Research Report, Bristol Port Accounts Project (Swindon: RES-000-23-1461; Department of History, University of Bristol, 2009), pp. 13–21

Jowitt, C. (ed.), *Pirates? The politics of plunder, 1550–1650* (New York: Palgrave Macmillan, 2007)

— *The Culture of Piracy, 1580–1630: English literature and seaborne crime* (Farnham, Surrey: Ashgate Publishing Company, 2010)

— 'Parrots and Pieces of Eight: Recent trends in pirate studies', *Literature Compass*, vol. 1, 2003, pp. 1–23

Kathman, D., 'Barry, Lording (*bap.* 1580, *d.* 1629)', *Oxford Dictionary of National Biography* (Oxford: Oxford University Press, 2004)

Keay, J., *The Honourable Company: A history of the English East India Company* (London: Harper Collins Publishers, 1993)

Kearney, H.F., 'Richard Boyle, Ironmaster', *Journal of the Royal Society of Antiquaries of Ireland*, vol. 83, no. 2, 1953, pp. 156–62

Kelleher, C., 'In a Harbour Long Ago', in J. Fenwick (ed.), *Lost and Found: Discovering Ireland's past* (Wicklow: Wordwell Ltd., 2003), pp. 273–86

— 'The Fort of the Ships', in C. Manning (ed.), *From Ringforts to Fortified Houses: Studies of Irish monuments in honour of David Sweetman* (Wicklow: Wordwell Ltd., 2007), pp. 195–208

— 'The Gaelic O'Driscoll Lords of Baltimore, Co. Cork: Settlement, economy and conflict in a "maritime" cultural landscape', in L. Doran and J. Lyttleton (eds), *Gaelic Ireland: Lordship in medieval and early modern Ireland* (Dublin: Four Courts Press, 2007), pp. 130–59

— 'Connections and Conflict by Sea', in Horning et al. (eds), *The Post-medieval Archaeology of Ireland*, pp. 53–82

— 'The Dunworley Bay Shipwreck: 17th-century evidence for piracy and slavery in Ireland?', in C. Horrell and M. Damour (eds), *ACUA Archaeology Conference Proceedings, 2010* (USA: Advisory Council on Underwater Archaeology, 2010), pp. 138–45

— 'Depicting a Pirate Landscape: The anti-pirate chart from 1612 and archaeological footprints on the ground', *Journal of Irish Archaeology*, vol. 23, 2013, pp. 77–92

— 'Pirate Ports and Harbours of West Cork in the Early Seventeenth Century', *Journal of Maritime Archaeology, Special Edition: The social archaeology of ports and harbours*, vol. 8, no. 2, 2013, pp. 347–66

— 'The 17th-Century Dunworley Bay Shipwreck: Illegal activity, archaeological investigations and possible identity', *Skibbereen and District Historical Society Journal*, vol. 10, 2014, pp. 130–9

— '*Santa Ana Maria*: 1628 wreck of the Capitana of La Flota de la Nueva Espaňa', in J. Henderson (ed.), *Beyond Boundaries: Proceedings of the 3rd International Congress on Underwater Archaeology* (London: IKUWA3, 2008), pp. 175–82

— 'Jilts, Cracks, Night-walkers and others of the Linnen-lifting Tribe', in M. Davies, U. MacConville and G. Cooney (eds), *A Grand Gallimaufry: Collected in honour of Nick Maxwell* (Wicklow: Wordwell Ltd., 2010), pp. 122–6

— 'The Insolency of the Turks Done at Baltimore', *Archaeology Ireland*, vol. 27, no. 4, 2013, pp. 26–9

— 'Ireland's Golden Age of Piracy: History, cartography and emerging archaeology', in C. Ewen and R. Skowronek (eds), *Pieces of Eight: More archaeology of piracy* (Gainesville: Florida University Press, 2016), pp. 165–92

— 'Early 17th-Century Piracy along the South-West Coast: The Kerry connections', *The Kerry Magazine*, Kerry Archaeological and Historical Society, vol. 27, 2017, pp. 29–31

— 'Death by Disgrace: Juan de Benevides y Bazán, the 1628 capture of the Spanish treasure fleet and the wreck of *Santa Ana Maria*', in D.M. Downey and I. Pérez Tostado (eds), *Commerce, Culture, Politics and Warfare: Studies in Spanish–Irish connections* (Valencia: Albatross Press, 2019), Chapter 23

Kenny, R.W., *Elizabeth's Admiral: The political career of Charles Howard, earl of Nottingham, 1536–1624* (Baltimore and London: Johns Hopkins University Press, 1970)

Kerrigan, P.M., *Castles and Fortifications in Ireland, 1485–1945* (Cork: The Collins Press, 1995)

Keuning, J., 'Hessel Gerritsz', *Imago Mundi*, vol. 6, 1949, pp. 48–66

Killock, D. and Meddens, F., 'Pottery as Plunder: A 17th-century maritime site in Limehouse, London', *Post-Medieval Archaeology*, vol. 39, no. 1, 2005, pp. 1–91

Kinkor, K., 'Black Men under a Black Flag', in C.R. Pennell (ed.), *Bandits at Sea: A pirates reader* (New York: New York University Press, 2001), pp. 195–210

Kümin, B., 'The Devil's Altar? Crime and the early modern public house', *History Compass*, vol. 2, 2004, pp. 1–3

Laing L.H., 'Historic Origins of Admiralty Jurisdiction in England', *Michigan Law Review*, vol. 45, no. 2, 1946, pp. 163–82

Lane, K., *Pillaging the Empire: Piracy in the Americas, 1500–1750* (New York: M.E. Sharpe Inc., 1998)

— *Colour of Paradise: The emerald in the age of gunpowder empires* (New Haven & London: Yale University Press, 2010)

Lane-Poole, S., *The Story of the Barbary Corsairs* (New York: G.P. Putnam's Sons, 1890)

— *The Story of the Nations: The Barbary corsairs*, with collaboration of Lieut. J.D. Jerrold Kelley, US Navy (Westport, CT: Negro University Press, 1901)

Lehr, P., *Pirates: A new history, from the Vikings to Somali raiders* (New Haven: Yale University Press, 2019)

Leigh, D., 'Ghost of the Gallows: The historical record of Black Caesar', *Creating Knowledge: The LAS student research journal* (DePaul University), vol. 5, 2012, pp. 28–32

Lavery, B., *The Arming and Fitting of English Ships of War, 1600–1815* (London: Conway Maritime Press, 1987)

Leeson, P., *The Invisible Hook: The hidden economics of pirates* (Princeton, NJ: Princeton University Press, 2009)

Lizé, P., 'The Wreck of the Pirate Ship *Speaker* on Mauritius in 1702', *International Journal of Nautical Archaeology*, vol. 13, no. 2, 1984, pp. 121–32

— 'Piracy in the Indian Ocean: Mauritius and the pirate ship *Speaker*', in Skowronek and Ewen (eds), *X Marks the Spot*, pp. 81–99

Longfield, A.K., 'Anglo-Irish Trade in the Sixteenth Century as Illustrated by the English Customs Accounts and Port Books', *Proceedings of the Royal Irish Academy, Section C: Archaeology, Celtic Studies, History, Linguistics, Literature*, vol. 36, 1921–4, pp. 326–7

— *Anglo-Irish Trade in the Sixteenth Century* (London: Routledge, 1929)

Lorimer, J., *English and Irish Settlement on the River Amazon, 1550–1646* (London: The Hakluyt Society, 1989)

Luddy, M., *Prostitution and Irish Society, 1800–1940* (Cambridge: Cambridge University Press, 2007)

Lunsford, V.W., *Piracy and Privateering in the Golden Age Netherlands* (New York: Palgrave Macmillan, 2005)

Lusardi, W.R., 'The Beaufort Inlet Shipwreck Artifact Assemblage', in Skowronek and Ewen (eds), *X Marks the Spot*, pp. 196–218

Lynch, A., 'Sherkin Island Friary, Farranacoush', in I. Bennett (ed.), *Excavations Bulletin: Summary accounts of archaeological excavations in Ireland, 1990* (Wicklow: Wordwell Ltd., 1991), pp. 52–3

— 'The Franciscan Friary on Sherkin Island, Co. Cork: Excavations, 1987–1990', *Journal of the Cork Historical and Archaeological Society*, vol. 123, 2019, pp. 55–127

Lyttleton, J. and Rynne, C., *Plantation Ireland: Settlement and material culture, c. 1550 – c. 1700* (Dublin: Four Courts Press, 2009)

MacCurtain, M. and O'Dowd, M., *Women in Early Modern Ireland* (Edinburgh: Edinburgh University Press, 1991)

MacMillan, K., 'Discourse on History, Geography, and the Law: John Dee and the limits of the British Empire, 1576–80', *Canadian Journal of History*, vol. 36, no. 1, 2001, pp. 1–26

— 'John Dee's "Brytanici Imperii Limites"', *Huntington Library Quarterly*, vol. 64, nos. 1 & 2, 2001, pp. 151–9

McCarthy, B., *Dún na Séad: The history of Baltimore castle* (Skibbereen: Baltimore Castle Publications, 2012)

— *Pirates of Baltimore: From the Middle Ages to the seventeenth century* (Skibbereen: Baltimore Castle Publications, 2012)

McCarthy, P. and Hawkes, R., *Northside of the Mizen* (Cork: Mizen Productions, 1999)

MacCarthy-Morrogh, M., *The Munster Plantation: English migration to southern Ireland, 1583–1641* (Oxford: Clarendon Press, 1986)

— 'English Presence in Munster', in C. Brady and R. Gillespie (eds), *Native and Newcomers: The making of Irish colonial society, 1534–1614* (Suffolk: Irish Academic Press, 1986), pp. 170–1

— 'Credit and Remittance: Monetary problems in early seventeenth-century Munster', *Irish Economic and Social History*, vol. XlV, 1987, pp. 17–18

McCracken, E., 'Charcoal-Burning Ironworks in Seventeenth- and Eighteenth-Century Ireland', *Ulster Journal of Archaeology*, vol. 20, 1957, pp. 123–38

— 'The Woodlands of Ireland Circa 1600', *Irish Historical Studies*, vol. 11, no. 44, 1959, pp. 271–96

Malcomson, A.K.W., *Calendar of the Rosse Papers* (Dublin: Irish Manuscripts Commission, 2008)

Marangou, C., 'Carved Rocks, Functional and Symbolic (Lemnos Island, Greece)', in L. Oosterbeek, M. Otte, L. Remacle and D. Seglie (eds), *Prehistoric Art: Signs, symbols, myth, ideology*, XV UISPP World Congress (Lisbon: BAR S2029, 2006 & 2009), pp. 93–101

Margey, A., 'Representing Plantation Landscapes: The mapping of Ulster, *c.* 1560–1640', in J. Lyttleton and C. Rynne (eds), *Plantation Ireland: Settlement and material culture, c. 1550 – c. 1700* (Dublin: Four Courts Press, 2009), pp. 140–64

Marken, M.W., *Pottery from Spanish Shipwrecks, 1500–1800* (Gainesville, University of Florida Press, 1994)

Manning, C., Gosling P. and Waddell, J., *New Survey of Clare Island, Volume 4: Abbey* (Dublin: Royal Irish Academy, 2005)

Marsden, R.G., 'The High Court of Admiralty in Relation to National History, Commerce and the Colonisation of America, AD 1550–1650', *Transactions of the Royal Historical Society*, new series, vol. 16, 1902, pp. 76–8

— 'English Ships under the Reign of James I', *Transactions of the Royal Historical Society*, new series, vol. 19, 1905, pp. 309–42

— 'The Vice-Admirals of the Coast', *English Historical Review*, vol. 22, 1907, pp. 468–774

— 'Early Prize Jurisdiction and Prize Law in England', *English Historical Review*, vol. 24, 1909, pp. 675–97

— 'Early Prize Jurisdiction and Prize Law in England', *The English Historical Review*, vol. 25, 1910, pp. 243–63

Martin, K., *Have Ye No Homes to Go To? The history of the Irish pub* (Cork: The Collins Press, 2016)

Matar, N., 'The Renegade in English Seventeenth-Century Imagination', *Studies in English Literature, 1500–1900, Restoration and Eighteenth Century*, vol. 33, no. 3, 1993, pp. 489–505

— *Turks, Moors and Englishmen in the Age of Discovery* (New York: Columbia University Press, 1999)

— 'The Barbary Corsairs, Charles I and the Civil War', in M. Birchwood and M. Dinnock, *Cultural Encounters Between East and West, 1453–1699* (Newcastle-upon-Tyne: Cambridge Scholars Press, 2005), pp. 239–58

Mathew, D., 'The Cornish and Welsh Pirates in the Reign of Elizabeth', *English Historical Review*, vol. 34, 1924, pp. 337–48

Meehan, R., 'The Pottery', in A. Lynch, 'The Franciscan Friary on Sherkin Island, Co. Cork. Excavations 1987–1990', *Journal of the Cork Historical and Archaeological Society*, vol. 123, 2019, pp. 86–101.

Moisan, E., *Master of the Sweet Trade: A story of the pirate Samuel Bellamy, Mariah Hallett and the Whydah* (New York: iUniverse, Inc. Publishers, 2009)

Moody, T., 'The Irish Parliament under Elizabeth and James I: A general survey', *Proceedings of the Royal Irish Academy, Section C: Archaeology, Celtic Studies, History, Linguistics, Literature*, vol. 45, 1939/1940, pp. 41–81

Moore, D., 'A General History of Blackbeard the Pirate, the *Queen Anne's Revenge* and the *Adventure*', *Tributaries*, vol. VII, 1997, pp. 31–5

Moore, F., 'Excavation of a possible fulacht fiadh at Lippa, Spiddal, Co. Galway', 2014, National Monuments Service, Department of Culture, Heritage and the Gaeltacht.

Morales, Ó.R., 'Identity and Loyalty: Irish traders in seventeenth-century Iberia', in D. Dickson, J. Parmentier and J. Ohlmeyer (eds), *Irish and Scottish Mercantile Networks in Europe and Overseas in the Seventeenth and Eighteenth Centuries* (Gent: Academia Publishing, 2006), pp. 197–210

— *Ireland and the Spanish Empire, 1600–1826* (Dublin: Four Courts Press, 2010)

Murdoch, S., *The Terror of the Seas? Scottish maritime warfare, 1513–1713* (Leiden and Boston: Brill Publications, 2010)

Murphy, E., *Ireland and the War at Sea, 1641–1653* (Suffolk: Royal Historical Society and Boydell Press, 2012)

Murphy, M.M., *Somalia: The new Barbary? Piracy and Islam in the Horn of Africa* (New York and West Sussex: Columbia University Press, 2011)

Murray, T.D., 'From Baltimore to Barbary: The 1631 Sack of Baltimore', *History Ireland*, vol. 14, no. 4, 2006, pp. 14–18

Naessens, P., 'Gaelic Lords of the Sea: The coastal tower houses of south Connemara', in L. Doran and J. Lyttleton (eds), *Gaelic Ireland: Lordship in medieval and early modern Ireland* (Dublin: Four Courts Press, 2007), pp. 217–35

Neufeld, J., 'The Evolution of the Legal Concept of Piracy in Early Modern England', *Journal of World History*, 2011, pp. 1–13

Newitt, M., *A History of Portuguese Overseas Expansion, 1400–1668* (London and New York: Routledge, 2005)

Nicholls, K., *Gaelic and Gaelicized Ireland in the Middle Ages* (Dublin: The Lilliput Press, 2003)

Ní Loingsigh, M., 'An Assessment of Castles and Landownership in Late Medieval North Donegal', *Ulster Journal of Archaeology*, vol. 57, 1994, pp. 145–58

North, C.M., 'Not Just Guidelines: Pirate codes and the emergence of property rights in *The Invisible Hook*', *Review of Austrian Economics*, vol. 23, 2010, pp. 307–13

Nunan, J., 'The Fortified House: A review', http://www.jpnunan.com/fortifiedhouse_review.html

Ohlmeyer, J., 'Civilizing of Those Rude Partes: Colonization within Britain and Ireland, 1580s–1640s', in Canny (ed.), *The Origins of Empire*, pp. 124–47

— 'A Laboratory for Empire? Early Modern Ireland and English Imperialism', in K. Kenny (ed.), *Ireland and the British Empire* (Oxford: Oxford University Press, 2004), pp. 26–60

— *Making Ireland English: The Irish aristocracy in the seventeenth century* (New Haven and London: Yale University Press, 2012)

Oppenheim, M., *A History of the Administration of the Royal Navy from 1509 to 1660* (London: Gower Publishing Co., 1896 and 1988)

— *The Naval Tracts of Sir William Monson in Six Books*, vol. III (London: Navy Records Society, 1913)

— 'The Royal Navy under James I', *The English Historical Review*, vol. 7, no. 27, July 1892, pp. 471–96

Oresko, R., 'Bastards as Clients: The House of Savoy and its illegitimate children', in R. Mettam and C. Giry-Deloison (eds), *Patronages et Clientélismes, 1550–1750 (France, Angleterre, Espagne, Italie)* (Lille: Institut de Recherches Historiques due Septentrion, 1995), pp. 36–67

O'Brien, A.F., 'The Royal Boroughs, the Seaport Towns and Royal Revenue in Medieval Ireland', *Journal of the Royal Society of Antiquaries of Ireland*, vol. 118, 1988, pp. 13–26

O'Donnell, M., 'Excavations at James Fort, Kinsale, 1974–1998', *Journal of the Cork Historical and Archaeological Society*, vol. 107, 2002, pp. 1–70

O'Donoghue, B., *Parish Histories and Placenames of West Cork* (Privately published, 1986)

O'Donoghue, J., Fornaght Strand fulacht fiadh, Creadan, Waterford, Database of Irish Excavation Reports, 2016, www.excavations.ie

O'Donovan, J., *Miscellany of the Celtic Society* (Dublin: The Celtic Society, 1849)

O'Dowd, M., 'Gaelic Economy and Society', in C. Brady and R. Gillespie (eds), *Natives and Newcomers: The making of Irish colonial society, 1534–1641* (Suffolk: Irish Academic Press, 1986), pp. 120–47

— 'Women and the Irish Chancery Court in the Late Sixteenth and Early Seventeenth Centuries', *Irish Historical Studies*, vol. 31, no. 12, 1999, pp. 470–87

O'Driscoll, C., 'Churchtown, Hook Head, Human Skeletal Remains', in I. Bennett, *Excavations Bulletin: Summary of archaeological excavations in Ireland* (Wicklow: Wordwell Ltd., 2005), pp. 397–9

— 'Archaeological Excavation of a Nineteenth Century Shipwreck Victim at Hook Head, Co. Wexford', *Journal of the Wexford Historical Society*, vol. 21, 2006–7, pp. 171–7.

O'Mahony, E., 'The Sack of Baltimore', *The Irish Sword*, vol. 21, no. 84, 1998, pp. 138–54

— 'Baltimore, the O'Driscolls and the End of Gaelic Civilization, 1538–1615', *Mizen Journal*, vol. 8, 2000, pp. 110–27

— 'The O'Driscolls and Their Revenues from Fishing – the 1609 Inquisition', *Mizen Journal*, vol. 8, 2004, pp. 190–3

O'Mahony, J., 'A History of the O'Mahony Septs of Kinelmeky and Ivagha', *Journal of the Cork Historical and Archaeological Society*, vol. 15, no. 84, 1909, pp. 184–96

— 'A History of the O'Mahony Septs of Kinelmeky and Ivagha', *Journal of the Cork Historical and Archaeological Society*, vol. 16, no. 85, 1910, pp. 9–24

O'Neill, T., *Merchants and Mariners in Medieval Ireland* (Dublin: Irish Academic Press, 1987)

O'Sullivan, A. and Breen, C., *Maritime Ireland: An archaeology of coastal communities* (Stroud, Gloucestershire: Tempus Publishing Ltd., 2007)

Paasch's *Illustrated Marine Dictionary* (London: Conway Classics, 1997)

Parker, K., 'Reading "Barbary" in Early Modern England, 1550–1685', in M. Birchwood and M. Dimmock (eds), *Cultural Encounters between East and West, 1453–1699* (Newcastle-Upon-Tyne: Cambridge Scholars Press, 2005), pp. 87–115

Penn, C.P., *The Navy Under the Early Stuarts and Its Influence on English History* (Portsmouth: Gieves Publishing Co., 1920)

Pennell, C.R. (ed.), *Bandits at Sea: A pirates reader* (New York: New York University Press, 2001)

— *Morocco: From empire to independence* (Oxford: Oneworld Publications, 2003)

— 'Who Needs Pirate Heroes?', *The Northern Mariner*, vol. 8, no. 2, 1998, pp. 61–79

— 'The Geography of Piracy: Northern Morocco in the mid-nineteenth century', *Journal of Historical Geography*, vol. 20, no. 3, 1994, pp. 272–82

Percy, S. and Shortland, A., 'The Business of Piracy in Somalia', *Journal of Strategic Studies*, vol. 36, no. 4, 2013, pp. 541–78

Perrin, W.G., 'The Lord High Admiral and the Board of Admiralty', *The Mariner's Mirror*, vol. 12, no. 2, 1926, pp. 117–44

Phillips, A. and Sharman, J.C., *International Order in Diversity: War, trade and rule in the Indian Ocean* (Cambridge: Cambridge University Press, 2015)

Piracy and Privateering: Catalogue 4, National Maritime Museum Library, Greenwich, London (London: Her Majesty's Stationery Office, 1972)

Pochin Mould, D., *Discovering Cork* (Kerry: Brandon Press, 1991)

Ponasik, D.S., 'The System of Administered Trade as a Defense Mechanism in Pre-Protectorate Morocco', *International Journal of Middle East Studies*, vol. 8, no. 2, 1977, pp. 195–207

Pope, P., *Fish into Wine: The Newfoundland plantation in the seventeenth century* (Chapel Hill and London: University of North Carolina Press, 2004)

Porter, M., '"She was Skipper of the Shore-Crew": Notes on the history of the sexual division of labour in Newfoundland', *Labour/Le Travail*, vol. 15, 1985, pp. 105–23

Powell, J.W.D., 'The Explorations of John Guy in Newfoundland, *The Geographical Journal*, vol. 86, no. 6, 1935, pp. 512–18

Power, D. (ed.), *Archaeological Inventory of County Cork, Volume 1: West Cork* (Dublin: Government Stationery Office, 1992)

— 'The Archaeology of the Munster Plantation', in Horning et al. (eds), *The Post-medieval Archaeology of Ireland*, pp. 23–36

Price, L., 'Armed Forces of the Irish Chiefs in the Early 16th Century', *Journal of the Royal Society of Antiquaries*, vol. 62, 1932, pp. 201–7

Priestley, E.J., 'An Early 17th-Century Map of Baltimore', *Journal of the Cork Historical and Archaeological Society*, vol. 89, 1984, pp. 55–7

Prowse, D.W., *A History of Newfoundland from the English, Colonial and Foreign Records* (London: Eyre & Spottiswoode, 1896)

Quinn, D.B., 'Advice for Investors in Virginia, Bermuda, and Newfoundland, 1611', *The William and Mary Quarterly*, vol. 23, no. 1, 1966, pp. 136–45

— 'The Voyage of the *Triall*, 1606–7', in D.B. Quinn, *Explorers and Colonies: America, 1500–1625* (London: Bloomsbury Publishers, 1990), pp. 363–81

Quinn D.B. and Nicholls, K., 'Ireland in 1534', in Moody et al. (eds), *A New History of Ireland*, pp. 9–12

Rabb, T., 'Investment in English Overseas Enterprise, 1575–1630', *The Economic History Review*, vol. 19, no. 1, 1966, pp. 70–81

Reddaway, T.F., 'Elizabethan London – Goldsmiths' Row in Cheapside, 1558–1645', *Guildhall Miscellany*, vol. 2, 1963, pp. 181–206

Rediker, M., *Between the Devil and the Deep Blue Sea: Merchant seamen, pirates and the Anglo-American maritime world, 1700–1750* (New York: Cambridge University Press, 1987)

— *Villains of All Nations: Atlantic pirates in the Golden Age* (London and New York: Verso Publications, 2004)

— 'Life under the Jolly Roger', *The Wilson Quarterly*, vol. 12, no. 3, 1988, pp. 154–66

Ritchie, R.C., *Captain Kidd and the War Against the Pirates* (New York: Barnes & Noble, 2006)

Roche, R. and Merne, O., *Saltees: Islands of birds and legends* (Dublin: The O'Brien Press, 1977)

Rodger, N.A.M., '*The Safeguard of the Sea: A naval history of Great Britain, Vol. 1: AD 660–1649* (London: Harper Collins, 1997)

— 'The Law and Language of Private Naval Warfare', *The Mariner's Mirror*, vol. 100, no. 1, 2014, pp. 5–16

Rogers, J.D., *A Historical Geography of the British Colonies: Newfoundland*, vol. 5, part IV (Oxford: Oxford Clarendon Press, 1861)

Schalk, R., Gelderblom O. and Jonker, J., 'Schipperen op de Aziatische Vaart', *BMGN-Low Countries Historical Review*, vol. 127, no. 4, 2012, pp. 3–27

Schen, C.S., 'Breaching "Community" in Britain: Captives, renegades, and the redeemed', in M.J. Halvorson and K.E. Spierling (eds), *Defining Community in Early Modern Europe* (Hampshire, UK and Vermont, USA: Ashgate Publishing Co., 2008), pp. 229–46

Semple, E.C., 'Pirate Coasts of the Mediterranean Sea', *Geographical Review*, vol. 2, no. 2, 1916, pp. 134–51

Senior, C., *A Nation of Pirates: English piracy in its heyday* (London, Vancouver and New York: David & Charles Publishers, 1976)

— 'Robert Walsingham: A Jacobean pirate', *The Mariner's Mirror*, vol. 60, 1974, pp. 141–2

Senning, C.F., 'Piracy, Politics and Plunder under James I: The voyage of the "Pearl" and its aftermath', *The Huntington Library Quarterly*, vol. 46, no. 3, 1983, pp. 187–222

Shuval, T., 'The Ottoman Algerian Élite and Its Ideology', *International Journal of Middle Eastern Studies*, vol. 32, 2000, pp. 323–44

Skellig Michael World Heritage Site Management Plan 2008–2018 (Dublin: Department of Culture, Heritage and the Gaeltacht and the Office of Public Works Publications Report, 2008)

Skowronek, R.K. and Ewen, C.R. (eds), *X Marks the Spot: The archaeology of piracy* (Gainesville: University Press of Florida, 2006)

Smári Hreinsson, K. and Nichols, A. (eds), *The Travels of Reverend Ólafur Egilsson: Captured by pirates in 1627* (Reykjavik: Fjölvi Publishers, 2008)

Smith, J., '"More Rude and Antique Than E'er Was Sodom": Piracy and the tavern community in Port Royal, Jamaica, 1680–1692', distinction paper, Minnesota, 2010, pp. 1–44

Smith, F.H., *Caribbean Rum: A social and economic history* (Gainesville: University Press of Florida, 2005)

Sokol, P. 'The Gallows near Primda: Archaeological research into a feature of special symbolic and social importance', *Archaeologia Historica*, vol. 41, no. 2, 2015, pp. 501–23.

Somerville-Large, P., *The Coast of West Cork* (London: Victor Gollancz Ltd., 1974)

Spate, O.H.K., *The Spanish Lake* (Canberra: Australia National University Press, 2004)

Starkey, D.J., 'Pirates and Markets', in Pennell (ed.), *Bandits at Sea*, pp. 107–24

Steckley, G.F., 'Merchants and the Admiralty Court During the English Revolution', *The American Journal of Legal History*, vol. 22, no. 2, 1978, pp. 137–75

Stevens Curl, J., 'The City of London and the Plantation of Ulster' (London: British Broadcasting Corporation, British History Online, 2001), pp. 1–11

Stevenson, R.L., *Treasure Island* (London: The Thames Publishing Co., 1948)

Stone, J.R., *The Routledge Dictionary of Latin Quotations: The illiterati's guide to Latin maxims, mottos, proverbs and sayings* (New York and London: Routledge Publishing Ltd., 2005)

Tenenti, A., *Piracy and the Decline of Venice, 1580–1615* (London: Longmans, 1967)

Tinniswood, A., *Pirates of Barbary: Corsairs, conquests and captivity in the 17th-century Mediterranean* (London: Jonathan Cape Publishers, 2010)

Treadwell, V., 'House of Lords in the Irish Parliament, 1613–1615', *English Historical Review*, vol. 80, no. 314, 1965, pp. 92–107

— 'The Establishment of the Farm of the Irish Customs, 1603–1613', *English Historical Review*, vol. 93, no. 368, 1978, pp. 580–602

— *Buckingham and Ireland, 1616–1628: A study in Anglo-Irish politics* (Dublin: Four Courts Press, 1998)

Trotter, H., 'Dockside Prostitution in South African Ports', *History Compass*, vol. 6, no. 3, 2008, pp. 673–90

Tucker F., 'Kill or Cure? The osteological evidence of the mercury treatment of syphilis in 17th- to 19th-century London', *London Archaeologist*, vol. 11, no. 8, 2007, pp. 220–4

Vitkus, D., 'Turning Turk in Othello: The conversion and damnation of the Moor', *Shakespeare Quarterly*, vol. 48, no. 2, 1997, pp. 145–76.

— *Three Turk Plays from Early Modern England* (New York: Columbia University Press, 2000)

von Archenholz, J.W., *The History of Pirates, Freebooters and Buccaneers of America* (London: W. Calvert Publishers, 1807)

Voorbeijtel Cannenburg, W., 'An Unknown "Pilot" by Hessel Gerritsz, Dating from 1612', *Imago Mundi*, vol. I, 1935, pp. 49–51

Weiss, E.A., *Spice Crops* (Wallingford and New York: CABI Publishing, 2002)

White, Capt. M.R.N., *Sailing Directions for the English Channel, including a general description of the south coasts of England and Ireland, and a detailed account of the Channel Islands* (London: William Clowes & Sons, 1835)

White, R., *Their Bones Are Scattered: A history of the Old Head of Kinsale and the surrounding area* (Kinsale: Kilmore Enterprises, 2003)

Whittlesey, D., *The Earth and the State* (New York: Henry Holt & Company, 1939, reprinted with maps 1944)

Wilde-Ramsing, M.U. and Ewen, C.R., 'Beyond Reasonable Doubt: A case for "Queen Anne's Revenge"', *Historical Archaeology*, vol. 46, no. 2, 2012, pp. 110–33

Wilde-Ramsing, M.U. and Carnes-McNaughton, L.F., *Blackbeard's Sunken Prize: The 300-year voyage of Queen Anne's Revenge* (Chapel Hill, NC: University of North Carolina Press, 2018)

Williams, A.F., *John Guy of Bristol and Newfoundland* (St John's, NL: Flankers Press Ltd., 2010)

Williams, N., *Captains Outrageous: Seven centuries of piracy* (London: Barrie & Rockliff, 1961)

— *The Sea Dogs: Privateers, plunder & piracy in the Elizabethan age* (New York: Macmillan Publishing Company Inc., 1975)

Willis, S., 'The Archaeology of Smuggling and the Falmouth King's Pipe', *Journal of Maritime Archaeology*, vol. 4, 2009, pp. 51–65

Woodward, D., 'Sir Thomas Button, the *Phoenix* and the Defence of the Irish Coast, 1614–1622', *The Mariner's Mirror*, vol. 59, no. 3, 1973, pp. 343–4

Yale, D.E.C., 'A Historical Note on the Jurisdiction of the Admiralty in Ireland', *The Irish Jurist*, vol. III, 1968, pp. 146–9

Zacks, R., *The Pirate Hunter: The true story of Captain Kidd* (London: Review/Headline Book Publishing, 2002)

THESES CONSULTED

Acosta, J., 'Piracy's Influence in the Atlantic World', master's thesis, University of Florida, 2005

Brown, J.A., 'The Landscape of Drink: Inns, taverns and alehouses in early modern Southampton', PhD thesis, University of Warwick, 2007

Costello, K., 'The Court of Admiralty of Ireland, 1580–1877', PhD thesis, University College Dublin, 2005

Donovan, M.B., 'Dún na Séad: The history of Baltimore castle', master's thesis, University College Cork, 2008

Duensing, S.N., 'Taverns, Inns and Alehouses? An archaeology of consumption practices in the city of London, 1666–1780', PhD thesis, University of Manchester, 2014

Duncan, B.G., 'The Maritime Archaeology and Maritime Cultural Landscape of Queenscliffe: A nineteenth-century Australian coastal community', PhD thesis, James Cook University, 2006

Fox, E.T., '"Piratical Schemes and Contracts": Pirate articles and their society, 1660–1730', PhD thesis, University of Exeter, 2013

Goelet, M.P., 'The Careening and Bottom Maintenance of Wooden Sailing Vessels', master's thesis, Texas A&M University, 1986

Hebb, D.D., 'The English Government and the Problem of Piracy, 1616–1642', PhD thesis, Bedford College, 1985

Hughes, C.E., 'Wales and Piracy: A study in Tudor administration, 1540–1640', master's thesis, University College of Swansea, 1937

Hurd, D.G.E., 'Some Aspects of the Attempts of the Government to Suppress Piracy During the Reign of Elizabeth I', master's thesis, London University, 1961

Kelleher, C.E., 'The Maritime Archaeological Landscape of Baltimore, Co. Cork', master's thesis, University College Cork, 1998

— 'The Confederacy of Pirates in Southwest Cork in the Early Seventeenth Century: Trade, plunder and settlement. A historical and archaeological study', PhD thesis, Trinity College Dublin, 2013

Kelleher, H., 'The Archaeology of Fish Palaces in West Cork', master's thesis, University College Cork, 1995

MacCarthy-Morrogh, M., 'The Munster Plantation, 1583–1641', PhD thesis, London University, 1983

Marten, M.G., 'Spatial and Temporal Analyses of the Harbor at Antiochia ad Cragum', master's thesis, Florida State University, 2005

Moore, R.O., 'Some Aspects of the Origin and Nature of English Piracy, 1603–40', PhD thesis, Virginia University, 1960

Murphy, E., 'War at Sea in Ireland, 1641–53', PhD thesis, Trinity College Dublin, 2007

Senior, C.M., 'An Investigation of the Activities and Importance of English Pirates, 1603–40', PhD thesis, Bristol University, 1972

Schalk, R., 'Financing the Dutch Golden Age: The credit market of Enkhuizen, 1580– 1700', master's thesis, Utrecht University, 2010

Taylor, W.J.H., 'Investigation of the Evolving Relationship of Pirate, Buccaneer and Privateer Between the English State, and the Ways in Which They Contributed to Laying the Foundations of the British Empire in the Caribbean During the Period 1650–1725', Bachelor of Arts degree thesis, University of Wales, 2010

Thomas, E., 'Towards an Archaeology of Piracy', PhD thesis, Queen's University Belfast, 2001

ARCHAEOLOGICAL REPORTS

Brown, Dr R.R., Specialist report on the iron guns from the Dunworley Bay shipwreck site (National Monuments Service, Department of Culture, Heritage and the Gaeltacht, 2009)

Cotter, E., 'An Archaeological Study of Dunasead Castle, Baltimore, Co. Cork' (Cork, 1997)

Kelleher, C., 'The Dunworley Bay Shipwreck: Report on the ongoing survey and investigation of the early seventeenth-century wreck in Cork, 2004–2007' (National Monuments Service, Department of Culture, Heritage and the Gaeltacht, 2007)

O'Donoghue, J., 'The Coconut Wreck: Rapid archaeological assessment report' (Mizen Archaeology Ltd., 2012), pp. 1–19

Wreck Inventory of Ireland Database (WIID): Wrecks of West Cork (Department of Culture, Heritage and the Gaeltacht)

INDEX

Illustrations are indicated by page numbers in **bold**.